NORTH AFRICA
AND THE
MIDDLE EAST
1942–1944

DESPATCHES FROM THE FRONT
*The Commanding Officers' Reports from
the Field and at Sea*

NORTH AFRICA AND THE MIDDLE EAST 1942–1944

El Alamein, Tunisia, Algeria and Operation Torch

Introduced and compiled by
John Grehan and Martin Mace
with additional research by
Sara Mitchell

Pen & Sword
MILITARY

First published in Great Britain in 2015 by
PEN & SWORD MILITARY
An imprint of
Pen & Sword Books Ltd
47 Church Street
Barnsley
South Yorkshire
S70 2AS

ISBN 978-1-78346-194-3

Typeset by Concept, Huddersfield, West Yorkshire HD4 5JL.
Printed and bound in England by CPI Group (UK) Ltd, Croydon CR0 4YY.

Pen & Sword Books Ltd incorporates the imprints of Pen & Sword Archaeology, Atlas, Aviation, Battleground, Discovery, Family History, History, Maritime, Military, Naval, Politics, Railways, Select, Social History, Transport, True Crime, and Claymore Press, Frontline Books, Leo Cooper, Praetorian Press, Remember When, Seaforth Publishing and Wharncliffe.

For a complete list of Pen & Sword titles please contact
PEN & SWORD BOOKS LIMITED
47 Church Street, Barnsley, South Yorkshire, S70 2AS, England
E-mail: enquiries@pen-and-sword.co.uk
Website: www.pen-and-sword.co.uk

Contents

List of Plates

Field Marshal Viscount Alexander.

Admiral Sir Andrew Cunningham.

Lieutenant General B.L. Montgomery, General Officer Commanding Eighth Army, watches the beginning of the German retreat from El Alamein from the turret of his Grant tank, 5 November 1942.

A large convoy of British vehicles is queued up during the Allied advance east.

'Australians storm a strongpoint'.

A stylised drawing which, depicting British gunners in action in North Africa, was commissioned by the Ministry of Information during the Second World War.

Troops of the US Army's 1st Infantry Division, known as "The Big Red One", go ashore at Oran, Algeria, on 8 November 1942 during Operation *Torch*.

The severe damage to the stern of the anti-aircraft cruiser HMS *Delhi* seen here was caused during operations off North Africa in late 1942.

Bombs fall away from a Boeing B-17 of the USAAF's Twelfth Air Force during an attack on the important Axis airfield at El Aouina near Tunis, on 14 February 1943.

British transport passes a knocked-out Italian field gun in its emplacement.

Two German SC 1000 (1,000kg) bombs in front of a wrecked Heinkel He 111H bomber at Benghazi airfield in early 1943.

Three *Afrika Korps* prisoners of war are searched by Allied troops as the tide of the fighting in North Africa turns against the Axis forces.

The remains of a number of wrecked *Luftwaffe* Messerschmitt Bf 109 fighters pictured in late 1942.

An Eighth Army officer inspects a German 88mm gun which had been put out of action by British artillery during the fighting in North Africa.

Allied vehicles pictured travelling along a road heading in to Tripoli after the Allied victory in May 1943.

A batch of PoWs in a prisoner of war cage waiting to be processed.

Introduction

General Harold Alexander took over Middle East Command from General Claude Auchinleck in August 1942. His area of responsibility extended throughout Egypt, Palestine, Sudan, Cyprus, Kenya and British Somaliland and North Africa. However, when he took up his command, Alexander was informed that his 'prime and main duty' was 'to take or destroy at the earliest opportunity the German-Italian Army commanded by Field-Marshal Rommel together with all its supplies and establishments in Egypt and Libya.' Under him he had Lieutenant General Bernard Montgomery who was nominated for the command of the Eighth Army following the death of General Gott en route to Cairo.

Rommel's Axis forces were drawn up in front of El Alamein. It was expected that once Rommel had built up his strength once again, he would attack the British defences in the hope of pushing onto Cairo. What Alexander needed was time – time to build up his own forces before Rommel attacked.

In his despatch, which is over 50,000 words long, Alexander details his arrangements for holding Rommel and his plans to move onto the offensive. His main concern was regarding the German armoured divisions which were equipped with Mark III and Mark IV tanks, a few of which were of the newer type with the high velocity 75mm gun, and with the anti-tanks guns which both the German and Italian divisions were armed. 'Though all desert warfare is not armoured warfare, it is always conditioned by the presence of armour,' Alexander wrote, 'since the desert allows infinite mobility and flanks are nearly always open, every formation and unit down to the smallest must be capable at any moment of all-round defence and prepared to meet an armoured attack.' For this reason anti-tank guns were decentralized down to infantry companies each of which had a total of at least three and, where possible, six guns. These were the greatest danger facing the British tank battalions.

Alexander, interestingly, felt the need to comment on his adversary, Rommel, who had achieved such notoriety. 'A considerable body of legends had grown up around him,' Alexander explained, '... but this interest had led to an exaggeration of his undoubted qualities which tended to have a depressing effect on our own troops, however much it may have appealed to the newspaper reader at home. I have always considered it vital to obtain all the information possible about my principal opponents and I took steps shortly after my arrival to sort out the truth from the legends about Rommel.'

Alexander then delves into the background of Rommel, before analysing his operations in North Africa: 'As I studied the records of his African campaigns it was soon clear to me that he was a tactician of the greatest ability with a firm grasp of every detail of the employment of armour in action and very quick to seize the fleeting opportunity and the critical turning points of a mobile battle. I felt certain doubts, however, about his strategical ability, in particular as to whether he fully understood the importance of a sound administrative plan. Happiest when controlling a mobile force directly under his own eyes he was liable to over-exploit immediate success without sufficient thought for the future.'

This over-exploitation, in Alexander's view, had led Rommel to advance to the point where he had become over-stretched, which was why the Axis forces had been unable to complete their advance into Egypt. Rommel, though, was hampered by the difficulty of supplying his forces from across the Mediterranean. This meant that Alexander was able to reinforce the Eighth Army quicker than Rommel was able to strengthen the *Afrika Korps*. The result of this was that it was Montgomery, not Rommel, who undertook the next great offensive in North Africa.

That offensive began with the Second Battle of El Alamein and continued until the capture of Tripoli. Alexander clearly had a gift for language and his despatch reads more like a history of the campaign in the desert during the period he was at Middle East Command.

In February 1943 General Maitland Wilson took over Middle East Command, and at the beginning of his despatch, Wilson spelt out the extent of his responsibilities: 'My main tasks, in order of priority, were to maintain Eighth Army and support its present operations to the utmost, to plan for future operations in conformity with the requirements of General Eisenhower, to prepare to support Turkey, and to conduct amphibious operations. In addition I was to make plans, when required, for land operations in the Balkan States, Crete, and the islands in the Aegean; I was to plan possible operations in Arabia and to be ready to assume command of the land forces in Aden should major land operations develop in or beyond the borders of that Protectorate.' No other British command was so extensive or so varied. Helpfully, he provided an order of battle for the Middle East Command which gives a clear view of the extent of his responsibilities. The total number of troops under his command amounted to approximately 31,000 officers and 494,000 men.

What is revealed in this despatch is the scale of the preparations for the offensive into Tunisia. This included the construction of petrol storage depots for tens of thousands of gallons of fuel, medical facilities with more than 5,000 beds and even a complete tin factory was despatched to Tripoli and erected there. To reduce flying time from Egypt twenty-two all-weather runways were completed in Cyrenaica and Tripolitania for the RAF, in addition to about fifty fair-weather landing grounds and the numerous fighter strips made for Eighth Army.

As well as the Tunisian campaign, Wilson relates the operations his command undertook in the Aegean and the difficulties with social unrest in Palestine and Syria. As Allied forces gathered in preparation for the invasion of Italy, following the defeat of the Axis army in North Africa, discussions were held concerning a change in Wilson's responsibilities. The Middle East Command's forces were reduced to a minimum and all possible help was given to Mediterranean Command and to General Eisenhower's Allied Force Headquarters.

The transfer of troops and resources to Mediterranean Command and other theatres saw the end of major operations for Middle East Command. In January 1944, Wilson became Supreme Allied Commander in the Mediterranean.

Whilst the Eighth Army was battling westwards, Anglo-American forces landed in French North Africa as part of Operation *Torch*. The two commands converged in Tunisia and were brought together under Alexander as the 18th Army Group.

The naval element of Operation *Torch* was organised and led by Admiral Andrew Cunningham all the way from the UK to North Africa. The operation was relatively trouble-free both on the passage to North Africa and the amphibious assaults at Oran, the landings at Algiers, however, were a different story. Cunningham states that the analysis of the problems that occurred at Algiers were not 'lessons learnt' but were 'recognised and foreseen disadvantages which had reluctantly to be accepted owing to the speed with which the operation was staged and the consequent short time available for training.' However, the fact that Operation *Torch* was the forerunner of two much larger and more hazardous amphibious operations – the invasion of Italy and the invasion of Normandy – made its successes and failures of considerable interest to those who had to plan those future enterprises. If mistakes could occur when the landings were relatively unopposed, a repetition of those errors in the face of a determined enemy might prove disastrous.

The majority of losses were incurred as the troops were disembarking, with numbers of landing craft being wrecked. This was due, Cunningham believed, to a lack of training and bad seamanship primarily amongst the American crews.

This prompted a suggestion from the US Army, that landing craft should be manned and operated by the Army instead of the Navy in the belief that it would improve co-ordination. Cunningham's response to that was that 'it matters little what uniform the crews wear provided that they are disciplined, trained and practised *seamen* and provided that they are organised and operated by officers competent in their jobs and in close touch with the requirements of the troops they are required to land and maintain.'

The despatch on Operation *Torch* was written by General Kenneth Anderson who commanded the First Army. Anderson experienced considerable difficulty co-ordinating the British, French and US armies and this was not solved until Alexander incorporated the US 2nd Corps into his 18th Army Group, leaving Anderson with just the British and French troops. The Axis forces were unable to resist the combined strength of Anderson's and Alexander's forces and in May 1943 they surrendered.

The reason why the Germans and Italian forces, some 220,000 strong, surrendered was because they had been unable to evacuate across the straits to Sicily. This was because of the naval forces under the command of Admiral

Cunningham, effectively sealed off the Tunisian coast with US and Royal Navy destroyers, submarines and motor gun boats. With the surrender of the Axis forces in North Africa the stage had been set for the next operation – the invasion of Scilly and the Italian mainland.

*   *   *

The objective of this book is to reproduce the despatches of the likes of Auchinleck, Alexander and Cunningham as they first appeared to the general public some seventy years ago. They have not been modified or edited in any way and are therefore the original and unique words of the commanding officers as they saw things at the time. The only change is the manner in which the footnotes are presented, in that they are shown at the end of each despatch rather than at the bottom of the relevant page as they appear in the original despatch. Any grammatical or spelling errors have been left uncorrected to retain the authenticity of the documents.

Abbreviations

A/C	Aircraft
A/S	Anti-Submarine
A/T	Anti-Tank
AA	Anti-Aircraft
ADC	*Aide-de-Camp*
AFC	Air Force Cross
AFV	Armoured Fighting Vehicle
AIF	Australian Imperial Force
AMES	Air Ministry Experimental Station
AMLO	Assistant Military Landing Officer
AOC-in-C	Air Officer Commanding-in-Chief
Armd Div	Armoured Division
ATK	Anti-Tank
Bde	Brigade
Bde GP	Brigade Group
BGGS	Brigadier-General General Staff
BGRA	Brigadier-General Royal Artillery
BGS	Brigadier, General Staff
BM	Brigade Major
Bn	Battalion
Bty	Battery
BST	British Summer Time
B.T.E.	British Troops in Egypt
C. in C. *or* C-in-C	Commander-in-Chief
CB	Companion of The Most Honourable Order of the Bath
CBE	Commander of the Order of the British Empire
CD unit	Civil Defence unit
CENTF	Commander Eastern Naval Task Force
CIE	Companion of The Most Eminent Order of the Indian Empire
CIGS	Chief of the Imperial General Staff
CMG	Companion of The Most Distinguished Order of Saint Michael and Saint George
CSI	Companion of the Order of the Star of India
Div	Division

DME	Director of Medical Services
DOS	Director of Ordnance Services
DQMG	Deputy Quartermaster General
DSC	Distinguished Service Cross
DSO	Distinguished Service Order
DST	Director of Supply and Transport
E Boats	*See S-Boot*
FOO	Forward Observation Officer
GCB	Knight Grand Cross of The Most Honourable Order of the Bath
GCIE	Knight Grand Commander of The Most Eminent Order of the Indian Empire
GCSI	Knight Grand Commander of The Most Exalted Order of the Star of India
GCVO	Knight Grand Cross of The Royal Victorian Order
Gds	Guards
GHQ	General Headquarters
GMT	Greenwich Mean Time
GOC	General Officer Commanding
GOC in C	General Officer Commanding-in-Chief
GSO(I)	General Staff Officer (I)
HM	His Majesty
HMS	His Majesty's Ship
HQ	Headquarters
Hrs	Hours
Ind	Indian
KBE	Knight Commander of the Most Excellent Order of the British Empire
KCB	Knight Commander of the Most Honourable Order of the Bath
KCIE	Knight Commander of The Most Eminent Order of the Indian Empire
KCMG	Knight Commander of The Most Distinguished Order of Saint Michael and Saint George
KCSI	Knight Commander of The Most Exalted Order of the Star of India
KCVO	Knight Commander of The Royal Victorian Order
KG	Knight of the Most Noble Order of the Garter
KMF	UK to North Africa Fast (a convoy designation)
KMS	UK to North Africa Slow (a convoy designation)
KT	Knight Companion of The Most Ancient and Most Noble Order of the Thistle
L of C	Line(s) of Communication

LCM	Landing Craft (Mechanised)
LCP	Landing Craft (Personnel)
LCT	Landing Craft (Tank)
Lieut	Lieutenant
LSI	Landing Ship, Infantry
LST	Landing Ship Tank
Lt-Gen	Lieutenant Colonel
Maj-Gen	Major General
MC	Military Cross
ME	Middle East
MEF	Middle East Forces
MESB	Middle East Supply Board
MG	Machine-Gun
ML	Motor Launch
MLO	Military Landing Officer
MMG	Medium Machine-Gun
MNBDO	Mobile Naval Base Defence Organisation
MT *or* M/T	Motor Transport
MVO	Member of the Royal Victorian Order
NCO	Non Commissioned Officer
NZ	New Zealand
OBE	Most Excellent *Order of the British Empire*
OM	Order of Merit
ORP	*Okręt Rzeczypospolitej Polskiej* (Ship of the Republic of Poland)
PBM	Principal Beach Master
RA	Royal Artillery
RAA	Rear-Admiral Air
RAF	Royal Air Force
RAOC	Royal Army Ordnance Corps
RASC	Royal Army Service Corps
RCT	Regimental Combat Team
RM	Royal Marine
RN	Royal Navy
RTR	Royal Tank Regiment
S-Boot	*Schnellboot* (meaning 'fast boat')
SA	South Africa(n)
SAAF	South African Air Force
SNOL	Senior Naval Officer Landing
SNOL(C)	Senior Naval Officer Landing (C Sector)
SNO(T)	Senior Naval Officer (Transport)
SS	Steam Ship
T/B	Torpedo Bomber
TK	Tank

US	United States
USN	United States Navy
VACNA	Vice-Admiral Commanding, North Atlantic
VC	Victoria Cross
W/T	Wireless Telegraphy/Wireless Telephony
WDF	Western Desert Force(s)

1

FIELD MARSHAL VISCOUNT ALEXANDER OF TUNIS' DESPATCH ON THE AFRICAN CAMPAIGN FROM EL ALAMEIN TO TUNIS, 10 AUGUST 1942 TO 13 MAY 1943

The following Despatch was submitted to the Secretary of State for War on the 23rd May, 1947, by HIS EXCELLENCY FIELD-MARSHAL THE VISCOUNT ALEXANDER OF TUNIS, K.G., G.C.B., G.C.M.G., C.S.I., D.S.O., M.C., former Commander-in-Chief the Middle East Forces and Eighteenth Army Group.

PART I. THE CONQUEST OF LIBYA

Situation in August 1942

The summer months of 1942 formed the most critical period in the history of the war on all fronts. They witnessed the greatest exertion of strength, both on the part of the European Axis powers and of the Japanese, of which our enemies were ever capable and when these great efforts were nullified by the Allied victories of that winter, although it was clear that the struggle would be hard and long before complete victory could be attained, we could feel confident that the possibility of an Allied defeat had now been excluded. It was a tremendous change in the whole climate of the war from the days when the Japanese were hammering at the eastern gates of India, the German armies in Russia were lapping round the northern bulwarks of the Caucasus and a tired and battered British army turned at bay among the sandhills of El Alamein, only sixty miles from Alexandria.

At the centre of these three thrusts stood the British Middle East Forces. For over two years this small but battle-hardened army had stood on guard at the centre of communications of the three great continents of Europe, Africa and Asia. It was originally intended as part only of a larger Anglo-French force, under command of General Weygand; but with the defeat of France and the entry of Italy into the war the defence of the Middle East had become a purely British responsibility and the forces commanded by General Wavell[1] and, later, by General Auchinleck,[2] were in the nature of a beleaguered garrison, connected with the mother country by a perilous sea route of twelve thousand miles. During those two years the garrison, though always outnumbered, had made many sorties; northwards to clear up their defensive flank in Syria, Iraq and Persia, southwards to overrun the Italian Empire in East Africa and safeguard the vital life-line through the Red Sea and, above all, westwards to destroy the closest enemy threat to their positions and to lay the first foundations for the reopening of the Mediterranean. Twice these westward sorties had cleared Cyrenaica and twice the call of other theatres, the Balkans in 1941, and the Far East in early 1942, had robbed us of the strength to exploit further or to retain our conquests. On the second occasion the simultaneous reduction in our strength and increase in the enemy's had been too great and before the necessary reinforcements in men and, above all, in tanks could arrive the enemy had taken the offensive, defeated the Eighth Army at Gazala and Tobruk and driven it back to El Alamein. There it stood and, on the critical day of 2nd July, defeated the enemy's most desperate efforts to break through. By this stand the survivors of the old Desert Army gained the vital time necessary for the arrival of the fresh divisions and improved tanks which were to turn the scale of battle.

I arrived in Cairo by air on 8th August, 1942 and on the morning of the same day I had a private interview with the Prime Minister, Mr. Winston Churchill, and General Sir Alan Brooke,[3] Chief of the Imperial General Staff who had arrived there from Moscow some days previously. At this interview I was notified that I was to assume command of the Middle East Forces. Shortly afterwards I was informed that my commitments were to be reduced by the creation of a separate command, to be known as Persia and Iraq Force, which would assume responsibility for defending the northern frontier of the Middle East block against the threat from the German armies in the Caucasus. I remained responsible for the defence of Syria, Palestine, Trans-Jordan and Cyprus but the threat of a German advance through Anatolia was now considered remote and it was reasonably certain, at the worst, that Germany would not present an ultimatum to Turkey before the spring of 1943. I was free, therefore, to concentrate all my attention on the threat to Egypt from the west and my task is best described in the words of the Directive, written in his own hand, which the Prime Minister handed to me at a subsequent interview on 10th August:

> "1. Your prime and main duty will be to take or destroy at the earliest opportunity the German-Italian Army commanded by Field-Marshal Rommel together with all its supplies and establishments in Egypt and Libya.
> 2. You will discharge or cause to be discharged such other duties as pertain to your Command without prejudice to the task described in paragraph 1, which must be considered paramount in His Majesty's interests."

I assumed command of the Middle East Forces from General Auchinleck on 15th August. I selected as my Chief of General Staff Lieut.-General McCreery who had been my GSO 1 when I commanded 1 Division at Aldershot and in France in 1939 and 1940. His scientific grasp of the whole sphere of military matters made him of the greatest assistance to me throughout my period of command in Africa. My General Headquarters continued to be located in Cairo, but I established an advanced Tactical Headquarters at Burg el Arab,[4] adjoining the Headquarters of the Eighth Army. My predecessor had, as a temporary measure, assumed personal command of Eighth Army but it was intended that he should be succeeded in that capacity by Lieut.-General Gott, previously General Officer

Commanding 13 Corps. Before he could assume command the aircraft in which he was flying to Cairo was shot down by enemy fighters over its airfield and he was killed by machine-gun fire on the ground while assisting the rescue of the other occupants. General Gott had been in every battle in the desert since the beginning; he had commanded 7 Support Group in the first campaign, 7 Armoured Division in 1941 and 13 Corps since February, 1942. It was particularly tragic that, having survived the early days of triumph and disaster when skill and endurance alone could be thrown into the balance against the inadequacy of our resources he should now be robbed of the chance of the high command he had so well deserved at a moment when the balance of power had at last swung favourably to our side. I was fortunate in being able to replace him at once by Lieut.-General Montgomery,[5] who arrived in Egypt on 12th August from the United Kingdom. General Montgomery was an old comrade in arms from the French campaign and, had served under me in Southern Command in 1941; I well knew his capacities as an inspiring leader and an outstanding trainer of men. He soon won the confidence and the affection of the men of the Eighth Army, many of whom, in particular the newly arrived formations, had already served under him in England. He rapidly made himself familiar with the situation in the desert, and by his frequent visits to the various units disposed along the battle front he brought to all ranks the inspiration of his cheerfulness, enthusiasm and confidence.

The Alamein position had been constructed in 1941 though it had been recognized long before that as offering the best defensive line in the Western Desert. Its strength lay in the fact that its southern flank could be covered by the Qattara Depression. This is the dried-up bed of a former inland sea which stretches from the neighbourhood of Siwa oasis, on the Egyptian frontier, to end at a point about a hundred and sixty miles northwest of Cairo and ninety miles south-west of Alexandria; the bed of the depression consists of quicksands and salt marshes, almost everywhere impassable even for a loaded camel, and on the northern side it is surrounded by steep cliffs which descend precipitously from an average height of over six hundred feet above to more than two hundred feet below sea level. At its eastern end the depression approaches to within about forty miles of the coast of the Mediterranean which here has a southerly trend in the large bight known as Arabs Gulf.

This was, for the desert, a very short line and it had the enormous advantage that it could not be outflanked to the south which was true of no other position we had ever held.[6] The prepared defences, which had been constructed by 2 South African Division, were based on four defended localities: at El Alamein itself on the coast road, Deir el Shein, Qaret el Abd and the Taqa Plateau on the edge of the Depression.[7] These four strong positions, thickly surrounded by minefields and wire entanglements, with prepared gun positions and cleared fields of fire, extended right across the belt of good going from the Mediterranean to the Depression; but when I arrived in Egypt only one was still in our possession, the so called Alamein "box". The last success of the German drive into Egypt, on

1st July, had been the capture of the Deir el Shein position. The loss of this position had opened a great gap in the line as planned. It seriously isolated the much stronger fortress of Qaret el Abd, held by the New Zealand Division, and the latter had therefore to be abandoned; as a result the position on the Taqa plateau had also to be evacuated, largely owing to the fact that there was no source of water within the position and even a temporary isolation would have meant inevitable surrender from thirst.

The line, therefore, on which the enemy was finally halted was not the Alamein line as it originally existed; only in the extreme north did we occupy the prepared defences. More serious to all appearance was the fact that our left flank no longer rested on the Depression; instead it had been taken back to a point just north-west of Qaret el Himeimat, a conspicuous peak from the neighbourhood of which a track, known as the "Barrel Track", led direct to Cairo. This track had been reconnoitred before the outbreak of hostilities in the desert and, before the construction of the desert road from Cairo to Alexandria, it had been the principal route from Cairo to the Western Desert. Fortunately its surface proved worse than had been expected and it was badly cut up by the large numbers of supply vehicles which had used it during the operation so that our left flank though not so impressively protected as had been intended, proved firmly based. Between the sea and the Barrel Track the country over which our defended line ran was a bewildering mixture of ridges and depressions with many patches of soft sand providing some of the worst going our forces ever encountered in the desert. The shore line was fringed with saltmarshes inland from which, in a narrow strip of less than two miles, the road and railway from Alexandria to Mersa Matruh ran parallel to each other.

Just south of the railway we had extended our front in July beyond the original line by a westward thrust which had captured the two small ridges of Tell el Eisa and Tell el Makhkhad. From this salient the line bent back south-easterly to the perimeter of the Alamein position. Twelve miles south of the shore line rise the slopes of the Ruweisat ridge, a long, narrow elevation about two hundred feet above sea level; at its western end it runs almost due east and west but as it extends eastwards it increases in height and alters its course slightly to north-east, pointing towards El Imayid station, fifteen miles east of El Alamein. It offers an avenue of reasonably firm going, outflanking the Alamein position, and it was here that the decisive battle of 2nd July had been fought; as a memento of that battle the enemy still held the western end. From here to the south our line trended roughly south by west over ground mainly flat but interrupted here and there by steep-sided depressions of which the Deir el Munassib was the most important. In rear of this part of the front, south-east of the Ruweisat ridge, was a second and higher ridge trending in a north-easterly direction called, from the cairn on its highest point (four hundred and thirty feet), the Alam el Halfa ridge. A strong position for a brigade had been built on the ridge in July defended by wire and minefields. From this position we could command the country to the south, if the enemy, however, succeeded in occupying it, it offered him another corridor of good going by which he could outflank all our positions to the north and drive direct on Alexandria.

In July the initiative had passed to Eighth Army and three attacks on various parts of the line had caused the enemy to disperse his forces and gained us time to improve our own defences. This was the more vital since when these attacks failed it became obvious that the enemy would take the offensive once more. He was quick to recover from the disorganization caused by the rapid advance from Gazala and the scrambling and incoherent battles of July and for the moment his build-up, particularly in tanks, was faster than ours, the construction of defences was therefore our main preoccupation. The front was covered by a triple mine-field from the coast almost to the Taqa plateau. A number of positions were built behind this but their weakness was that, except in the north where we still retained part of the old line, they had been hastily prepared and were not dug deeply enough. More serious was the fact that our mobile reserve was small. In the desert a string of positions, however strong, can be rendered useless unless the defence possesses a mobile reserve strong in armour which can manoeuvre round these fixed positions and engage any enemy who may penetrate between or round them; when I arrived in Egypt, our armour had been so reduced that there was only 7 Armoured Division available with one medium armoured brigade, below strength in tanks, a light armoured brigade of "Stuart" tanks and armoured cars, and a motor brigade.

The plan was to hold as strongly as possible the area between the sea and Ruweisat ridge and to threaten from the flank any enemy advance south of the ridge from a strongly defended prepared position on the Alam el Halfa ridge. General Montgomery, now in command of Eighth Army, accepted this plan in principle, to which I agreed, and hoped that if the enemy should give us enough time, he would be able to improve our positions by strengthening the left or southern flank. At the moment the northern area, down to and including Ruweisat ridge, was held by 30 Corps with under command from north to south 9 Australian, 1 South African and 5 Indian Divisions, reinforced by 23 Armoured Brigade in an infantry support role. These forces I judged to be adequate, the more so as our defences in this sector were stronger than elsewhere. 13 Corps, in the southern sector, consisted of 2 New Zealand and 7 Armoured Divisions, the former of only two brigades. In the prepared positions on Alam el Halfa ridge there was one infantry brigade, and a second brigade occupied the reserve positions on Ruweisat ridge.

In my visits to the front to inspect our positions and prepare for the coming battle I paid particular attention to the morale and bearing of the troops. I found Eighth Army, in Mr. Churchill's phrase, "brave but baffled." A retreat is always a disheartening manoeuvre and the feeling of frustration which it naturally engenders was made the stronger by the fact that many of the troops, particularly in the infantry divisions, could not fully understand the reasons why they had been forced to withdraw from positions which they had stoutly and successfully defended; in many cases the reason had been a battle lost by our armour many miles from those positions. A more serious cause of discouragement was the knowledge that our defeat had been due in part to inferiority of equipment; there is nothing so sure to cause lack of confidence. The soldier who has been forced to retreat through no fault of his own loses confidence in the higher command and the effect of a retreat is cumulative; because he has withdrawn already from several positions in succession he tends to look upon retreat as an undesirable but natural outcome of a battle. It was in any case fairly generally known that, in the last resort, the Army would retreat again, in accordance with the theory that it must be kept in being. My first step in restoring morale, therefore, was to lay down the firm principle, to be made known to all ranks, that no further withdrawal was contemplated and that we would fight the coming battle on the ground on which we stood. General Montgomery, on his arrival, fully concurred in this policy and expressed his confidence in being able to fight a successful defensive battle in our present positions.

At the moment the five divisions which I have already enumerated were the only battle-worthy formations available and with the exception of 9 Australian and 2 New Zealand Divisions they had all been engaged since the battle of Gazala opened at the end of May. We were, however, potentially stronger now than then and in a few weeks I should be able to increase my strength to more than twice that number of formations. I had in reserve four divisions which had not as yet seen action: 8 and 10 Armoured and 44 and 51 Infantry, and two veteran divisions refitting, 1 Armoured and 50 Infantry. These were in the meantime disposed for the defence of the Delta together with other non-divisional forces, including strong elements of the Sudan Defence Force.

When I took over, the plan for the defence of the Delta had been to hold the western edge of cultivation. Along this line the Rosetta Branch of the Nile and the Nubariya Canal, which takes off from it midway between Cairo and Alexandria, form in combination a continuous tank obstacle extending from Cairo almost to Lake Maryut, which covers Alexandria on the south. The defence consisted of denying the three principal crossings at Alexandria, Khatatba and Cairo with infantry and employing armour in the gaps. The Cairo defences were complete and held by the equivalent of six infantry brigades, while another infantry brigade guarded the open southern flank with patrols operating from Bahariya Oasis to give warning of enemy approach to the south of the Qattara Depression. An extensive position was being prepared round the Wadi Natrun to deny the water sources there to the enemy and to act as an advanced position covering the Khatatba crossing. This position had been intended for the infantry of Eighth Army in the event of a withdrawal, 1 and 10 Armoured Divisions were lying at Khatatba itself, engaged in re-equipping, together with 44 Infantry Division, now almost ready for action. The Inner defences of Alexandria were complete but the outer defences, consisting of extensive field works, were still unfinished. The equivalent of six infantry brigades were deployed in this area. Two more infantry brigades were held in reserve.

The original intention, based mainly as I have mentioned, on the necessity of preserving our forces to meet a possible threat from the north, had been to withdraw in the last resort in two directions: eastwards into Palestine with the greater part of the forces and southwards up the Nile valley with the remainder. Command had accordingly been divided between 10 Corps, which was responsible for Alexandria and the Delta, and Headquarters, British Troops in Egypt, which was responsible for Cairo and the Nile valley. Since I had now been relieved of responsibility for the north-eastern front and was in any case determined to stand on the Alamein position I altered this arrangement on 20th August to the extent of making Lieut.-General Stone, commanding British Troops in Egypt, responsible for the defence of the whole of the Delta, and made 10 Corps Headquarters available for Eighth Army. I cancelled the construction of defences at the Wadi Natrun but instructed General Stone to continue working on the outer defences of Alexandria and improving communications between the Nile valley and the Red Sea; I also gave instructions for certain areas round Alexandria, on the banks of the Rosetta Branch and north of Cairo to be flooded. Cairo, Khatatba and Alexandria were to be defended by 51, 1 Armoured and 50 Divisions respectively. These troops would serve to protect vital installations against raids which might penetrate the Alamein position, or against airborne attack, for which the enemy had available both German and Italian parachute formations. They could not have been employed in a more active role at that time: 51 Division had only recently disembarked and was mobilizing and carrying out preliminary desert training and the other two, both of whom had already served over six months in the desert, were engaged in vitally urgent re-equipping. 50 Division had had very heavy losses both at Gazala and Matruh.

I had therefore available, but not all immediately available, four armoured and seven infantry divisions. As against this the Axis forces in Egypt amounted to four armoured and eight infantry divisions, plus five independent regiments or regiment-sized groups. Command was exercised nominally by Mussolini who acted through an Italian Headquarters known as Superlibia, an advanced detachment of the Commando Supremo, under Marshal Bastico. Actual command, however, was exercised by Field-Marshal Rommel. His headquarters bore the name of "German-Italian Armoured Army of Africa,"[8] and under it came all German and Italian troops in the forward area, organized under four Corps Headquarters, the German Africa Corps and the Italian X, XX and XXI Corps. The former consisted of 15 and 21 Panzer Divisions, veterans of the later desert battles. The second of these divisions had come to Africa first, under the name of 5 Light Division, in February, 1941, and 15 Panzer Division followed in the spring of the same year. The reconnaissance battalions of these two divisions were usually brigaded together as a "Reconnaissance Group" under Corps command. 90 Light Division, of motorized infantry, which attained its final form in Africa in January, 1942, was usually employed directly under Army command. 164 Infantry Division had been flown over from Crete at the end of June, 1942; it was always employed to stiffen the Italian infantry nominally under operational command of the Italian XXI Corps but administered direct by Panzer Armee. The same role was given to the Ramcke Parachute Brigade of four battalions. This force was apparently organised in the first place to co-operate with the Italians in an assault on Malta in the summer of 1942 which was cancelled when Rommel's success in the desert seemed to render the operation unnecessary. It fought throughout in a ground role and showed high qualities of training and courage. Finally there was a motorized, heavily armed group known as 288 Special Force, a miniature motorized division, originally organised to take part in the Syrian campaign of 1941 and sent to Africa in April, 1942.

The Italians provided two of the armoured and six of the infantry divisions in the Panzer Armee. The two former, 132 Ariete and 133 Littorio Divisions comprised, together with 101 Trieste Division, XX Corps, usually qualified as XX (Mobile) Corps. The northern end of the line, from the sea to south of Ruweisat ridge, was held by XXI Corps with, from north to south, the German 164 Division, 102 Trento Division[9] and 25 Bologna Division; two battalions of the Ramcke Parachute Brigade were also under command in the sector of the two Italian divisions. The shorter southern sector was held by X Corps with 27 Brescia and 185 Folgore Divisions.[10] The latter was originally a parachute division, the first which Italy had formed. It was rushed across hastily in August to strengthen the infantry of the Panzer Armee and was always used in that role. Unlike the other Italian Divisions, which were recruited on a territorial basis, this division was formed of men of outstanding physique picked from the whole country and, although quite unaccustomed to African conditions and hampered by shortage of equipment and lack of administrative services, it gave a very good account of itself. Besides the formations I have enumerated there were three independent Bersaglieri regiments, of motorized infantry, employed as Corps troops. In rear of the defended line was 17 Pavia Division which was resting at Mersa Matruh under Army command. 16 Pistoia Division, a recent arrival in Libya, was in reserve in the Bardia area and the "Young Fascists" Division at Siwa oasis.

The organization and armament of these troops reflected the prevailing conditions of the desert. All the German formations, except for the newly arrived 164 Division, were motorized; the Italian divisions were not, except for the three in XX (Mobile) Corps. The German armoured divisions were equipped with the Mark III and Mark IV tank; a few of the latter were of the newer type with the high velocity 75 millimetre gun. Italian armoured divisions were equipped with the M13 tank, of thirteen tons and mounting a 47 millimetre gun; it was mechanically unreliable and poorly armoured. In both German and Italian infantry divisions the most striking feature was the very great strength in anti-tank guns. It is fair to say that, though all desert warfare is not armoured warfare, it is always conditioned by the presence of armour; since the desert allows infinite mobility and flanks are nearly always open, every formation and unit down to the smallest must be capable at any moment of all-round defence and prepared to meet an armoured attack. For this reason anti-tank guns were decentralized down to infantry companies which had a total of three apiece and, where possible, six.

They were usually of 50 millimetre calibre though 90 Light Division was equipped with captured Russian 3 inch pieces (7.62 millimetre).[11] The Italians in 1942 had carried out a reorganization of their infantry on similar lines.[12] In both armies, therefore, the unit for infantry was the company, organized on homogeneous lines throughout and heavily armed with anti-tank guns. A characteristic feature was the formation of "Kampfgruppen" or "Raggruppamenti" which we should call "columns of all arms" or "task forces," created for a special mission.

The Axis Commander-in-Chief, Field-Marshal Erwin Rommel, had commanded the German forces in Africa since their first arrival in February, 1941, and a considerable body of legends had grown up around him. It was natural that the British Press should pay particular attention to the German commander whose forces were engaging the only British army in the field at that time, but this interest had led to an exaggeration of his undoubted qualities which tended to have a depressing effect on our own troops, however much it may have appealed to the newspaper reader at home. I have always considered it vital to obtain all the information possible about my principal opponents and I took steps shortly after my arrival to sort out the truth from the legends about Rommel. He was a Wurtemberger of a middle-class professional family who was commissioned in an infantry regiment shortly before the first world war; he served with distinction on the western, Italian and Rumanian fronts, winning among other decorations the order "Pour le Mérite," the highest Prussian award for gallantry. Between the two wars he was chiefly known as the author of works on infantry tactics. A Colonel in 1939 he commanded 7 Panzer Division in France in 1940 as a Major-General. Since arriving in Africa he had been rapidly promoted from Lieutenant-General to Field-Marshal and had been awarded the senior grade of the Ritterkreuz, the highest Nazi decoration. As I studied the records of his African campaigns it was soon clear to me that he was a tactician of the greatest ability with a firm grasp of every detail of the employment of armour in action and very quick to seize the fleeting opportunity and the critical turning points of a mobile battle. I felt certain doubts, however, about his strategical ability, in particular as to whether he fully understood the importance of a sound administrative plan. Happiest when controlling a mobile force directly under his own eyes he was liable to over-exploit immediate success without sufficient thought for the future. An example was the battle of November, 1941, when, after winning a great tactical success at Sidi Rezegh, he had rejected the advice of his two divisional commanders and dashed off on a raid to the Egyptian frontier which, in face of the stubborn British maintenance of the objective, led directly to the loss of his positions round Tobruk and his retreat to Agheila at the cost of sixty per cent. of his forces. His present position in front of Alamein I hoped would turn out to be another example of this tendency. Whether it was on his own initiative or by order of Hitler that he held the whole of his forces forward at Alamein it is impossible to say; but if he had organized a firm defensive position further back, at Matruh or Sollum, with a light covering force to detain us at Alamein, he would have been much more difficult to deal with.

Rommel's superior in the Mediterranean theatre was Field-Marshal Albert Kesselring. Also a regular officer of the old Imperial Army, of Bavarian origin, Kesselring had served as an artillery officer and on the staff until the creation of the Luftwaffe, when he transferred to the new arm in which he rose rapidly. After commanding the 2nd Air Fleet (Luftflotte) in the Battle of Britain and on the Russian front in 1941 he brought it to Italy in October of that year. In April 1942 he assumed the title of Commander-in-Chief South. His authority extended to all the shores of the Mediterranean and by contrast with Rommel, who was an Army commander only, he was now supreme commander of all three services. This superior position reflected his superior strategical abilities but he was naturally obliged to leave the actual conduct of operations in Africa to his more impetuous subordinate. Rommel had a tendency to blame, in certain circumstances, his lack of success on the inadequate logistical support he received from Kesselring – unjustly, for in these matters the latter was obliged to work through the Italians. I was later to be more directly opposed to Kesselring in the Italian campaign and in my judgment he was greatly superior in all elements of generalship to Rommel.

Preparations for a Defensive Battle.

It was obvious that if the enemy were to retain any hopes of success they must attack us before we could develop our full strength and there were not wanting indications that this was their intention. I had decided already that we must meet this attack on our present positions without any thought of withdrawal. As rapidly as possible thereafter we should prepare to concentrate our strength and assume the offensive. On 19th August, therefore, I issued a written Directive to General Montgomery in the following terms, confirming previous verbal instructions:

> "1. Your prime and immediate task is to prepare for offensive action against the German-Italian forces with a view to destroying them at the earliest possible moment.
> 2. Whilst preparing this attack you must hold your present positions and on no account allow the enemy to penetrate east of them."

I ordered that this decision should be made known to all troops.

It was now becoming possible to reinforce the troops in the desert and Eighth Army decided to strengthen 13 Corps on the southern flank, since the northern part of the front was held strongly enough and it was likely that the enemy attack would take the form of an outflanking move to the south. 44 Division, which had arrived in Egypt at the end of June, had just completed its concentration and training and on 15th August I gave orders for it to join Eighth Army. The divisional headquarters, with 131 and 133 Brigades, was sent to relieve 21 Indian Brigade on Alam el Halfa ridge with orders to develop the positions there in the greatest possible strength. The remaining brigade, the 132nd, with one regiment of artillery, was placed under command of 2 New Zealand Division. 10 Armoured Division (8 and 9 Armoured Brigades) had been training for some time but it had never fought as a division, since its tanks had been taken to make up for battle losses in I and 7 Armoured Divisions. 8 Armoured Brigade, however, had just been re-equipped and I ordered the division, less 9 Armoured Brigade, to proceed to the forward area. On arrival it took command of 22 Armoured Brigade, of 7 Armoured Division, and took up positions at the western end of Alam el Halfa ridge, between 44 and 2 New Zealand Divisions. 23 Armoured Brigade, which had been dispersed in support of the infantry of 30 Corps, was concentrated on the Corps left flank where it would be available also as a reserve for 13 Corps. With the arrival of these reinforcements there were ranged on Alam el Halfa ridge, threatening the flank of an enemy advance in the southern sector, some sixteen medium, two hundred and forty field and two hundred anti-tank guns, all under Corps command, besides the guns of nearly four hundred tanks and over a hundred anti-tank guns manned by the infantry. The minefields and wire entanglements had been largely extended and the position was a very strong one.

While these preparations were going on in the desert I paid particular attention to the campaign which was being conducted by the Air Force against the enemy's lines of communication. Never had the Axis supply lines in Africa been so stretched as they were when they stood at El Alamein and the strain was felt, above all, in fuel. In dumps or in motor convoys fuel was relatively immune from air attack but to reach Africa from Italy it had to come in tankers and these had been given the first priority as objects for air attack. Working to a plan drawn up in consultation with my staff, the Royal Air Force, assisted by bombers of the 9th United States Air Force[13] had been waging a most successful war against Axis tankers during which more had been sunk than had arrived. The resulting shortage had a vital effect on the development of the subsequent battle.[14]

The Battle of Alam el Halfa

I had expected the enemy to attack on or immediately after 25th August, the night of the full moon, and this was indeed his original intention, but the fuel situation caused a delay. In the meantime the concentration of forces on the southern flank made obvious the imminence of an attack and the direction it would take. Rommel's plan was to break through our lightly held line of observation on our southern flank and then, turning north, drive to the sea behind 30 Corps and encircle our centre and right. It was the same plan as he had used at Gazala in May and he proposed to use the same force as then, with the addition of one extra Italian armoured division. On the left flank of his marching wing, at the hinge of the encircling movement, was 90 Light Division, under Army command; south of it was the Italian XX (Mobile) Corps with Ariete and Littorio Armoured Divisions, Trieste Motorized Division and a regiment of the Folgore Division; on the extreme right, the outside of the wheel, was the main striking force consisting of the German Africa Corps with 15 and 21 Panzer Divisions.

On the remainder of the front XXI and X Corps held their positions and carried out diversionary attacks. This intention was no surprise to me and, as has been seen, our dispositions had been made to meet just such an attack, facing west and south with a strong armoured force disposed centrally. 13 Corps was to meet the enemy striking force of six divisions with four divisions: 7 and 10 Armoured, 2 New Zealand and 44 Infantry. In armour and artillery the two forces were evenly matched. Both had about three hundred field and medium and four hundred anti-tank guns; the enemy had five hundred medium and light tanks, equally divided between German and Italian; 13 Corps had three hundred medium and eighty light tanks and two hundred and thirty armoured cars. A further hundred tanks with 23 Armoured Brigade constituted a reserve. We had the advantages of ground and prepared defensive positions while the enemy's advantage of the initiative had been diminished by the loss of surprise.

The enemy offensive opened on the night of 30th August with two diversionary attacks on 30 Corps. A German parachute battalion secured temporary posses-sion of one of our positions on Ruweisat ridge but 5 Indian Division won back the position by dawn. An attack in the coastal sector against 9 Australian Division was completely unsuccessful. At 0100 hours on 31st August, shortly after moonrise, the main striking force began to lift the minefields on the southern flank, in the area from Deir el Munassib to Himeimat. During this operation they were enfiladed by the artillery fire of the New Zealand Division and harassed both frontally and from the south by 7 Armoured Division who had excellent shooting in the bright moonlight. In face of the opposition of two artillery regiments and a motor battalion of 4 Light Armoured Brigade it took six hours to clear two gaps for the two German Panzer divisions and it was not until 0930 hours that the Africa Corps was concentrated east of the minefield. Even after overrunning this obstacle they did not advance with their customary speed, largely because the Italians on their left and the 90th Light still further north were encountering even greater difficulties in breaking through the minefields there which were heavily enfiladed by the New Zealand artillery and under direct fire from 7 Motor Brigade. The two Italian armoured divisions, indeed, hardly came into action at all in this battle. For nearly four hours the two Panzer Divisions were known to be gathering in and about the Ragil Depression, where they presented an admirable target. Unfortunately a dust storm which rose about 1100 hours greatly curtailed our air effort, which in favourable weather might have disrupted the enemy's plan at the outset.

When, at about 1530 hours, the German armoured divisions began to move from Deir er Ragil the crucial stage of the battle was reached. The danger was that they should try a wide encircling movement round Alam el Halfa ridge, moving north-east to cut our communications with Alexandria. We had taken steps to discourage such a move in the mind of the enemy[15] and it soon became clear that these had borne fruit. The two divisions headed north and north-north-east, across the very soft going of the Deir el Agram, and launched a heavy attack on the area where 22 Armoured Brigade was stationed, around Point 102, a small feature just off the western end of the Alam el Halfa ridge. This area had mean-while been reinforced by 23 Armoured Brigade which had been placed under 13 Corps as soon as the situation on Ruweisat ridge had been re-established. Our positions were prepared and 13 Corps artillery brought concentrated fire to bear with the result that, when the Germans finally retired at dusk, over a quarter of their tanks were believed to have been disabled. They did achieve a minor success, however, in that a score of tanks settled hull-down well forward in a depression from which they could not be dislodged until the following night.

7 Armoured Division had withdrawn in face of the enemy advance south-east and north-east, either side of the Ragil Depression, and had continued to harass the rear of the armoured column. This drew a reaction just before dusk when part of the enemy armour turned on 4 Light Armoured Brigade at Samaket Gaballa. After a brief engagement the brigade fell back, in accordance with previous instructions, to avoid becoming too closely involved in their isolated position. When night fell the task of harassing the enemy leaguers was taken up by the Royal Air Force who flew over the area continuously, assisted by flare-dropping aircraft of the Fleet Air Arm. 13 Corps artillery joined in also and kept one leaguer, estimated as made up of about a hundred tanks, under fire all night. At the same time the New Zealanders, at the hinge of our positions, sent out parties to prevent 90 Light Division from digging themselves in. In the northern sector the Australians attacked and made a gap through which a raiding force was to pass after daylight. The enemy counter-attacked before dawn, however, and closed the gap, inflicting heavy casualties on the Australians.

Now that it was clear that the enemy was making a short hook rather than a wide sweeping encirclement it was possible to strengthen the southern flank still more. Accordingly on 1st September General Montgomery concentrated the three armoured brigades in the area between 44 Division and the New Zealand Division, 1 South African Infantry Brigade was moved from 30 Corps area to the east end of Ruweisat ridge. Early on that morning the enemy resumed the attempt to batter his way on to the west end of Alam el Halfa ridge and again suffered heavily. His tanks first tried another frontal assault on 22 Armoured Brigade; when that failed they attempted to work round either flank of the brigade. After two hours the enemy drew off to the south. He refuelled and reorganised during the middle of the day and returned to the attack in the late afternoon, when he began to probe for soft spots, tapping 23 and 22 Armoured Brigades in turn. This gave him no encouragement and he drew off again without staging a heavy attack.

The first two days of the battle had ended without any decisive success for the enemy and this was already a decisive success for us. On 2nd September, Rommel changed his tactics. Instead of continuing the attack he decided to put himself in a posture of defence and await the counter-attack which he felt confident that we should shortly deliver; he therefore massed the bulk of his armour south of Alam el Halfa and threw out a screen of anti-tank guns in front of them. On the left of the armour 90 Light and Trieste Divisions consolidated their positions to keep open the corridor through the minefield. It was not our intention, however, to gratify him by a frontal attack on the Africa Corps but rather to operate against the two infantry divisions further west in order to close the gap in the minefield behind the main armoured force. Orders for this operation had been issued the previous day and 5 Indian Infantry Brigade and 7 Medium and 49 Anti-tank Regiments Royal Artillery, from 30 Corps were moving south to reinforce 13 Corps. At the same time 2 South African Brigade was drawn into reserve. On request of Eighth Army I sent up 151 Brigade from 50 Division at Amiriya to strengthen the south-western end of Alam el Halfa ridge. Should the plan prove successful the enemy would be so weakened that an immediate advance might be possible; General Montgomery ordered forward H.Q. 10 Corps in case he should need it to command a pursuit force. It was instructed to be prepared to push through to Daba with all reserves available and possibly the Australian Division. Meanwhile the enemy concentrations provided an excellent target to our aircraft and artillery which gave them no respite. Armoured car patrols to the south and east observed the enemy closely and 7 Armoured Division continued to attack his unarmoured vehicles with great success.

Under these various forms of attack, but without provoking our armour to descend from the ridge and give battle, the enemy lay all day of 2nd September. A new and serious crisis in his fuel situation had arisen, for we had been once more successful in our attacks on his tankers, sinking three in two days. As the day wore on it was evident to him that the last hope had failed and, since it was impossible to remain in this advanced position, he would have to withdraw. It was the nearest the Germans ever got to the Delta. At first light on 3rd September it was reported that they were withdrawing slightly to south and south-west. It was still not clear whether this was the start of a real retreat or another feint to entice our armour into battle; in any case 13 Corps followed up with armoured cars only. By the afternoon there was every indication that the westward movement was developing into a withdrawal. 7 Armoured Division moved westwards to the area, between Gaballa and Himeimat to operate against the southern flank of the retiring columns and heavy air action was organised against the concentrations east of the minefield.

At 2230 hours on 3rd September the New Zealand Division, with 132 Brigade of 44 Division under command, began to attack southwards as the first stage in closing the gap. They were opposed by 90 Light Division to the west and Trieste to the east; both fought well and the attack was only partially successful. 5 New Zealand Brigade on the east gained their objective, 28 (Maori) Battalion fighting a particularly gallant action. 132 Brigade were unsuccessful and had heavy losses and to the west 6 New Zealand Brigade also failed to reach their objective. At dawn and again on the evening of 4th September the enemy put in heavy counter-attacks against the three brigades. All were repulsed but during the night the infantry were withdrawn from their exposed positions, leaving mobile troops to operate southwards. Throughout 4th and 5th September the retreating enemy was assailed from the north, east and south by our mobile troops and heavily bombed by our aircraft. It was unfortunate that on 4th September another dust-storm made observation difficult and flying impossible during the afternoon. By the evening of 5th September the enemy's slow and stubborn withdrawal had brought him back to the area of our minefields. Here he turned to stand and it was clear that he intended to make a strong effort to retain this much at least of his gains. Accordingly at 0700 hours on 7th September the battle was called off and Rommel was left in possession of a thin strip of ground which had advanced his positions on the southern flank to a line running from the eastern end of Deir el Munassib to include the peak of Himeimat. The latter was valuable for the excellent observation which it gave as far north as Ruweisat ridge.

This meagre gain of some four or five miles of desert could in no way be set off against the material losses. Forty-two German tanks and eleven Italian, and nearly seven hundred motor vehicles, were abandoned on the field, together with thirty field and forty anti-tank guns. Casualties were more difficult to assess but we estimated that the enemy had lost two thousand Italians and two thousand five hundred Germans in killed and wounded; three hundred were taken prisoner. Our own losses were sixty-eight tanks, one anti-aircraft and eighteen anti-tank guns; killed, wounded and missing numbered sixteen hundred and forty. But the battle of Alam el Halfa was far more important than would appear from any statistics of gains and losses or the numbers involved. It was the last throw of the German forces in Africa, their last chance of a victory before, as they calculated, our increasing strength would make victory for them impossible. It was hard to realise it at the time, but the moment when the Africa Corps began to retreat, slowly and stubbornly, from the sandy scrub of the Deir el Agram, marked the first westward ebb of the tide which had carried the Axis arms so far to the east, an ebb which was about to begin to the north as well in a few months from then on the Volga Steppe and in the Caucasus. To me at the time the great features of the battle were the immediate improvement in the morale of our own troops, and the confidence I felt in General Montgomery, who had handled his first battle in the desert with great ability. The valuable part played by the R.A.F. during the battle was a good omen for future air support. I now felt sure that we should be able to defeat the enemy when we were ready to take the offensive.

Preparations for the Offensive.
After the victory of Alam el Halfa the enemy went at once on to the defensive. Our own preparations for assuming the offensive were not yet, however, complete. My intention for the coming battle was to destroy the enemy in his present position where he was furthest from his bases and nearest to ours; this was the best opportunity we should have of developing our full strength and it was vital to ensure that we forced a decision there at El Alamein. Eighth Army proposed to use all three Corps Headquarters in the battle, 13 and 30 as Infantry Corps (with some armour) and 10 Corps as an armoured *Corps de Chasse*. It was to this that particular attention was given at the start of the training period; 10 Corps was intended to include 1, 8 and 10 Armoured Divisions and possibly the New Zealand Division to provide the necessary motorized infantry. This powerful force would need a good deal of training before it could be fit for the decisive test of battle. First of all the tank crews had to get used to their new equipment. Three hundred "Sherman" tanks arrived at Suez on 3rd September from the United

States and I proposed to equip three of my six armoured brigades with them. I must express at this point my profound appreciation of the statesmanlike vision shown by President Roosevelt when, on his personal initiative, he ordered these new tanks to be taken from the American armoured division for which they were intended and shipped round the Cape to us in the Middle East. At last we had for the first time a tank which was equal in armour, armament and performance to the best tank in the Africa Corps.

Eighth Army assembled 10 Corps some fifty miles in rear of the line, where their training and re-equipment could proceed uninterruptedly, 1 and 8 Armoured Divisions were already there and on 14th September 10 Armoured Division was withdrawn from the forward area. The New Zealand Division was also withdrawn and reorganized into a "new model" division by the addition of 9 Armoured Brigade in place of a third infantry brigade. 44 Division relieved it in the line. It was not possible to carry out Eighth Army's original intention to include three Armoured Divisions in 10 Corps as there was a shortage of Infantry Brigades to make them up to strength. I was, therefore, obliged to obtain War Office approval to disband 8 Armoured Division, which had no Infantry Brigade on its establishment. I had enough tanks, however, to maintain the planned number of armoured brigades and I placed 24 Armoured Brigade under command of 10 Armoured Division.

The troops previously deployed in the Delta could now be brought forward to acclimatize them, such as were new to the desert, to the conditions in which they were to fight. On 8th September 51 Division moved from Cairo into reserve on Alam el Halfa ridge to continue its training. On the 10th I sent the Headquarters of 4 Indian Infantry Division with 7 Indian Infantry Brigade to Ruweisat ridge to relieve the Headquarters of 5 Indian Division and 9 Indian Brigade, which had been continuously engaged since the end of May. A few days later 50 Division with 69 Brigade left Alexandria to join 151 Brigade in Eighth Army reserve; it was brought up to strength by the addition of 1 Greek Brigade. After a short interval for further training 50 Division relieved 44 Division in 13 Corps sector at the beginning of October. 1 Fighting French Brigade came forward about the same time on the left of 13 Corps where it was placed under command of 7 Armoured Division. The latter had given up its 7 Motor Brigade to 1 Armoured Division but retained 4 Light Armoured and 22 Armoured Brigades.

My infantry strength was the greatest we had yet put in the field, but a high proportion had had no previous battle experience and would require a great deal of training. I could not make a start on this programme until 6th September but thereafter all formations, whether they were withdrawn into rear areas or kept in the line, underwent intensive training in which the features of terrain and the conditions of fighting they were likely to encounter were as far as possible reproduced. Groups of all arms who were to fight together were trained together. Special attention was given to physical fitness, the maintenance of direction by night, the control of movement, minelifting and the use of wireless. We had also been strongly reinforced in artillery, on which I intended to rely heavily for the positional battle which lay ahead. Apart from seven extra field regiments which constituted the divisional artillery of 8 Armoured and 44 and 51 Infantry Divisions, two medium regiments and six additional field regiments also arrived from the United Kingdom and were placed under command of the Eighth Army during September and early October. I also received replacements for losses which enabled me to bring existing units up to strength.

During this necessary interval while our training programme got into full swing I proposed to employ small detachments of the special raiding forces in attacks on the enemy's communications. The Royal Navy and the Allied Air Forces were already, as I have described, operating with success against his shipping bound for Tobruk and Benghazi (Tripoli was being used only to a very minor extent) but with the air forces at our disposal and the great distances to be covered it was impossible to close either of them completely. Ever since the withdrawal from Cyrenaica plans had been under discussion for raids by sea and land on Tobruk and Benghazi. If the oil installations could be destroyed and the port facilities damaged so as to interrupt working even for as little as a week, either before or after a major engagement on the Alamein line, the result might prove fatal to the enemy. It had been found impossible to carry out these operations in July and August and they had consequently been postponed to the favourable moon period of September.

As the operations were sure to prove most hazardous the possible advantages to be gained had to be carefully balanced against the chances of success and the cost of failure. Accordingly I reviewed the project again on 3rd September with the Commander-in-Chief, Mediterranean, Admiral Harwood[16], and the Air Officer Commanding-in-Chief, Air Chief Marshal Tedder.[17] The fighting at El Alamein was then in full swing. Two weeks' reserve of supplies on operational scales were all that the enemy had been able to accumulate for his offensive and, although there was little hope of doing irreparable damage to the ports, a temporary dislocation of supplies following the failure of the offensive (which was now obvious), might well prove disastrous to Rommel's Army. Even if the operations were unsuccessful they would undoubtedly have an effect on enemy morale and probably lead him to take precautions against a future repetition which would diminish the strength available for the defence of his positions in Egypt. Air Chief Marshal Tedder pointed out that no air support whatever could be provided except an attack by bombers to help in covering the approach. Fighter cover was impossible throughout owing to the distance. Admiral Harwood realized that the whole seaborne force, including the two destroyers he proposed to use, might well be lost, but he accepted the risk. It was finally decided that the effects of success would be great enough to justify the risks involved; orders were accordingly given for the operations to be carried out as planned.

The raids were launched on the night of 13th September. At Tobruk the plan was to capture the port by a combined operation from two sides, by sea and overland, and hold it long enough to allow the destruction of the stored fuel and hasty demolition of the port. The small overland force successfully carried out its part of the operation but very few members of the two seaborne forces managed to land and the attack was a failure. The attack on Benghazi was to be carried out by a small motorized column from Kufra, over five hundred miles to the south. It reached its destination successfully but a last-minute alteration in its plans, based on unreliable information, caused an abandonment of the operation after an attack had been made on a part of the defences which was on the alert. A third force attacked Gialo on the night of 14th September, mainly in order to cover the retirement of the column raiding Benghazi but also in the hope of holding it for a short while as a base for future operations. The oasis was strongly held and it was impossible to capture it but the operation served its purpose in that the Benghazi force was able to retire unmolested by the Gialo garrison. A diversionary raid on Barce was completely successful. From the material point of view the raids had been a failure and our losses had been heavy but it is possible that they had had the psychological effects we had hoped for. They probably helped to keep the Pistoia Division at Bardia and assisted in diverting Rommel's attention to the possibility of seaborne raids on his long open flank. 90 Light Division, after the conclusion of the Alam el Halfa battle, was moved back to Daba and employed for defence against a landing and for some weeks the Pavia Division was retained at Matruh in a similar role. The failure of these subsidiary operations had no effect on the plans and preparations for the great offensive which was shortly to be launched against the enemy's main forces.

No further attempt was made to raid the enemy's supply lines by land except for some successful sabotage of the desert railway by the Long Range Desert Group. This standard gauge line, which had been extended to Matruh in 1940, was pushed forward in the summer of 1941 towards the Libyan frontier and just before the Gazala battles had reached Belhamed on the Tobruk perimeter. The enemy had now extended it down to the port and, having repaired the breaks we had made during the retreat, had brought it into use. Our air force, however, continued to attack the railway and intensified their bombardment of enemy ports. Tobruk was raided almost nightly to such an extent that a large proportion of enemy shipping was diverted to Benghazi, thus increasing the road haul. Benghazi too was heavily attacked and all convoys en route to these ports had to run the gauntlet of our naval and air forces. I must also mention the valuable services of the air forces in securing information about the enemy's dispositions and denying him observation of our own. Eighth Army was kept supplied with regular air photographs of the enemy's dispositions on the basis of which most detailed maps were constructed and widely distributed. On the defensive side the Royal Air Force established such complete air superiority that enemy aircraft were unable to interfere with our preparations.

My administrative position was very satisfactory. I found on arrival in Middle East a highly developed administrative machine already in existence and staffs well acquainted with the problems of desert warfare. Repaired and reconditioned tanks, lorries and guns were pouring out of workshops; new equipment was arriving from overseas and being assembled and modified in Egypt. Men from

Great Britain and from hospitals in the Middle East were passing in a steady stream to the front, far exceeding battle casualties. The reinforcement and repair organisations had been working at high pressure for many months, but it needed only the knowledge of the forthcoming offensive as a spur to intensify their efforts. Forty-one thousand men joined units at the front between 1st August and 23rd October, besides those arriving with the new formations. In the same period over a thousand tanks, three hundred and sixty carriers and eight thousand seven hundred vehicles were sent to the Eighth Army. Forty-nine pioneer companies were assembled and equipped to undertake the many manual tasks that would otherwise have fallen on the fighting troops.

Full preparations were made for the enormous extension of the supply services which would be necessary when the enemy had been defeated and we turned to the pursuit. There was no difficulty in accumulating large reserves in the initial stage, since distances were short and we had both rail and road transport available to as great an extent as we could require. But it must be remembered that any advance would be into a desert, completely barren of any kind of resources beyond some rather indifferent water, and all supplies would have to come still from the same base. This would mean that very large quantities of motor transport would be needed. In previous campaigns there had never been sufficient third-line transport to support a strong advance over a long distance. We were better off now and by 23rd August Eighth Army was provided with the equivalent of forty-six General Transport companies to carry stores, ammunition, petrol and water, and six tank transporter companies: seven more General Transport companies were held in reserve.[18] I shall deal with the particular problems of administration as they arose in the course of our advance but I will say at once that, in spite of all difficulties of geography and enemy demolitions, the provisions made were so ample and the problems so well appreciated that the rate of development of ports, roads, railways and pipeline nearly always exceeded estimates and we were never obliged to pause longer than had been calculated for lack of supplies, equipment or reinforcements.

My administrative staff was headed by Lieut.-General (now Sir Wilfred) Lindsell who had an enormous task in the organisation of the Middle East base. At that time the ports of the Middle East were handling four hundred and sixty-six thousand tons of military stores per month; three hundred thousand troops and half a million civilians were employed in all rear services and contracted labour represented about a million and a half more. The vastness of the task was increased by the fact that the great majority of the working force on which we relied for the maintenance of our military effort was not only civilian but oriental, and in large part unskilled, that the countries where our base was formed were not industrialised and that the most important was neutral. In this connection I must express my appreciation of the assistance I received from Mr. Casey, the Resident Minister, and from the British Ambassador in Cairo, Sir Miles Lampson.[19] On my first arrival, when I stayed at the Embassy, the latter assured me that he regarded it as his principal duty to see that the base on which I relied for my operations should be kept politically tranquil. His skill and understanding were crowned with full and deserved success and I never had any anxieties on this score so long as I was in Egypt. Through Mr. Casey I kept in touch with His Majesty's Government and made sure that there was complete reciprocal comprehension on the military situation. I owe him a great debt for the smoothness and friendliness which he imparted to these relations.

Perhaps the most difficult decision I had to face was the timing of the offensive. Obviously the sooner we could attack the better, for the enemy was strenuously perfecting his defences. When I went down to the desert with the Prime Minister he asked me when I thought I should be ready; I replied, as a most tentative estimate, for at that time I had only been in Middle East a few days and had not had time to study an offensive operation in detail, that I thought the end of September a possible date. He asked General Montgomery the same question when we arrived at Eighth Army Headquarters and the latter replied to the same effect, saying "Not before the first week in October" This estimate now needed revision. We had in any case lost a week as a result of the batle of Alam el Halfa and our losses, though comparatively slight, and the redisposition of troops which that battle had caused had set us back perhaps another week. I was determined that Eighth Army should have all the time necessary for training and the assimilation of its new reinforcements. Above all I wanted the armoured divisions of 10 Corps to have ample time to settle down into a well-drilled and confident whole; we were bringing against the enemy almost double his strength in tanks, it was vital to ensure that we were able to make full use of this superiority. On these grounds, therefore, I decided to wait until as late as possible in October. The actual date was determined by the phases of the moon. The plan must involve a series of infantry attacks against strong defences to gain possession of the enemy's minefields and make gaps, in them to pass the armour through. For this a night assault was obviously demanded and if the infantry were to be able to lift the mines quickly and accurately they would need good moonlight. Full moon was on 24th October and in agreement with General Montgomery I therefore decided on 23rd October as D-day.

There was another consideration besides those I have mentioned which affected our timing: the battle of Egypt had to be fitted into the grand strategy of the war, for the Allies were about to assume the strategic offensive. I had been informed before I left England of the decision of the Combined Chiefs of Staff to invade North Africa from the west and clear the whole north shore of the Mediterranean; I had in fact been appointed to command the British First Army which was to be the spearhead of this operation under General Eisenhower. It was a nicely calculated operation, designed to employ our growing resources in a task just within their capabilities, which would, on the firm basis of our command of the sea, extend that command in a tighter ring round the fortress of Europe. It involved political calculations as well, for it was appreciated that if the French Army resisted we might be involved in a long guerilla in the mountains of Algeria and Morocco, which would allow the Germans to get a firm hold on Tunisia.

Certain steps were being taken to assure if possible a friendly reception: the landing was to be under United States command and, although the main forces in Tunisia were to be provided by the British First Army and in the Mediterranean by the Royal Navy, the operation was at the outset to be represented as almost entirely American in character. Obviously, however, the most important effect on opinion in French North Africa would be attained if, just before the landings we could win a decisive victory over the Axis forces at Alamein. It was important, also, to impress General Franco, whose attitude was dubious; had he admitted German forces into Spain, and Spanish Morocco the operation would have been seriously hazarded.

From this point of view it would be an advantage to win our victory as soon as possible and the Prime Minister expressed disappointment that I had put back the date of my offensive a fortnight beyond my first very tentative estimate. I called a Commanders-in-Chief meeting to discuss the problem, with Admiral Harwood, Air Chief Marshal Tedder and Mr. Casey, the Resident Minister in the Middle East. At this meeting I explained the situation fully, pointing out that if the battle was to have its desired effect, both in the military and political fields, it must be crushing and decisive beyond any doubt, and to ensure that I must have an adequate time for full preparations. I laid particular stress also on the importance of having a good moon. TORCH[20] was scheduled for 8th November. My offensive was planned to precede it by just over a fortnight and I was convinced that this was the best interval that could be looked for in the circumstances. It would be long enough to destroy the greater part of the Axis army facing us, but on the other hand it would be too short for the enemy to start reinforcing Africa on any significant scale. Both these facts would be likely to have a strong effect on the French attitude. The decisive factor was that I was certain that to attack before I was ready would be to risk failure if not to court disaster. My colleagues agreed with this exposition of the situation and I sent a telegram explaining in full the decisions of the meeting. On this basis the date of 23rd October was definitely accepted.

Before giving the final plan it will be as well to consider the enemy dispositions as they faced us on D-day. The two preceding months had seen him energetically engaged in strengthening his field works. The most important element in these, as always in the desert, was the minefield, both anti-tank and anti-personnel. In the north a second line of defended localities had been prepared behind the main forward minefields. The two lines were connected with each other by transverse minefields and the idea was to lead our attacking forces by prepared channels into deceptively attractive clear areas entirely surrounded by mines where they could be taken under fire from all sides. The effect was of a belt, between five and eight thousand yards deep, thickly covered with mines and defended posts, stretching from the sea to the Deir el Mreir, a deep depression lying south-west of the end of the Ruweisat ridge. North of El Mreir there was a peculiar minefield in the shape of a shallow S-bend running roughly east to west at right angles to the main positions and extending for some distance behind them; this was presumably intended as a cover for the right flank of the northern sector of the front should we be able to penetrate the southern sector. Behind the main defences in the north a third line of positions, starting just east of Sidi Abd el Rahman, eight miles from Tell el Eisa, and running south for about seven and a half miles, was still in course of preparation but already well advanced. The defences had been less systematically developed to the south of El Mreir, but since the capture of our minefields in September that part of the line also presented a formidable obstacle. There were two lines of defences, based on our old minefield and the original enemy mine-field, with a gap between them. The going on the southern flank was bad and from Qaret el Himeimat the enemy had excellent observation.

Enemy attempts at reinforcement were less successful. Many vessels bringing tanks, guns, stores and supplies were sunk or forced to turn back. The unloading of those which did succeed in making port was a slow process on account of the havoc wrought by our bombers at Tobruk and Benghazi and it must be remem-bered that even Tobruk was three hundred and fifty miles from the front, over an indifferent road. Reinforcements in men arrived by destroyers and aircraft and, except for occasional interception, most of these reached Africa safely. These arrivals, however, which averaged about five thousand men a week, were unable to keep pace with the very heavy sick rate. Possibly owing to the congestion of troops on the ground, greater than ever known before in the desert, and to an inadequate medical and sanitary organization, especially among the Italians, diseases such as dysentery and infective jaundice were extraordinarily prevalent among the Axis troops. Some units suffered up to as much as twenty-five per cent. of their strength. Thanks to the efficiency of our own medical services our sick-ness rate did not rise above the normal for the time of year and to nothing like the extent on the enemy side of the line. The most prominent Axis casualty was the Army Commander. Rommel had been in poor health since August and in September he left for Germany, technically on leave. It appears, however, that he was not intended to return and he was replaced by General Stumme, who had previously commanded an armoured corps on the Russian front.[21] Rommel took advantage of the ceremony at which he was presented with his Field-Marshal's baton in Berlin on 3rd October to declare: "We hold the Gateway to Egypt with the full intention to act. We did not go there with any intention of being flung back sooner or later. You can rely on our holding fast to what we have got".

There had been little change in the general order of battle of the two Corps holding the fixed defences. XXI Corps in the northern sector had received a slight reinforcement in German infantry in addition to its two parachute battalions; otherwise the German 164th and the Italian Trento and Bologna Divisions held the same sectors. In X Corps sector the Pavia Division had been brought forward from Matruh and added to Brescia and Folgore, on the extreme south; the other two parachute battalions of Ramcke's brigade were on this front. The main line of defences was therefore held by rather more than six divisions. In reserve were four armoured and two mobile divisions, equally divided between German and Italian. This reserve had been treated as a single combined force for the purpose of the battle and not divided by nationalities. The armoured divisions were organised in two main groups, a northern one consisting of 15 Panzer Division and Littorio and a southern consisting of 21 Panzer Division and Ariete; these groups were again subdivided each into three mixed battle groups and disposed at intervals all along the rear of the battle front. This was in accordance with the principles for the use of armour in a defensive battle as practiced on the Russian front: dispersion rather than concentration in order to ensure that no part of the threatened area was unsupported by armour. I imagine that these dispositions were adopted on General Stumme's initiative as they differed widely from Rommel's practice of concentrating his armour. Further to the rear still was 90 Light Division, watching the coast in the area of El Ghazal, halfway between Sidi Abd el Rahman and Daba, and the Trieste Division round Daba itself. The system of command of the reserve, as between Headquarters German Africa Corps and the Italian XX Corps, is obscure but the latter probably had little real responsibility beyond administration. It will be noted that throughout these dispositions German and Italian units were closely mingled in order to stiffen the latters' morale.

It is worth while refuting here a legend which has grown up about the enemy dispositions at Alamein, as it has appeared in almost all accounts of the battle, including some semi-official accounts.[22] Briefly this story supposes that Rommel had planned a trap for us: he had deliberately weakened his centre, while keeping his left and right strong, in order to lure us into attacking that point; in rear he had concentrated his armour in two blocks north and south of his centre so that when we emerged between them we would be crushed by simultaneous attacks on both flanks. This is completely contrary to the facts. The centre was not weakened, on the contrary it was specially strengthened by the reinforcement of three German parachute battalions. In general the troops available were fairly evenly divided over the whole front, though the northern sector was stronger than the southern as one of the three divisions there was German; on the other hand Folgore, in the southern sector, was the best of the Italian divisions. The field defences were strongest in the north, as that was the vital sector, and diminished gradually in strength towards the south. Finally the armoured force was not disposed in two concentrated groups but split up into battle groups evenly stationed along the whole front. I do not know the origin of this legend – possibly an imaginative journalist with a vague recollection of Miltiades' alleged stratagem at Marathon – but it was of extraordinary rapid growth since it appeared for the first time immediately after the battle.

In face of these enemy dispositions one fact was quite clear about the coming battle; that in its early stages at least it would be primarily an infantry battle. It would be impossible for Eighth Army to use its armour in a broad outflanking movement because neither of the enemy's flanks was open, nor could the armour break through the thickly developed enemy defences frontally except at a prohibitive cost. The infantry would have to make the gap to pass the armour through and the strength of the defences was such that the operation of making the gap would involve a battle on the grandest scale. The operation would begin, therefore, like a battle of the 1914–1918 war, with the assault of an entrenched position in depth and it would not be until that battle had been fought and won that we should be able to proceed to the more swift-moving clash of armoured forces which had distinguished the decisive campaigns of this war. Fortunately our infantry was superior both in numbers and, above all, in fighting ability to the Italo-German infantry and with the advantage of the initiative it could be concentrated against any chosen portion of the enemy line in very great superiority. In the attack it could be supported by a massed artillery backed by lavish resources in ammunition. Strong though the enemy defences were I felt confident of our ability to pierce them.

I had carried out a thorough reconnaissance of the whole front in my car and had discussed the plan of attack in all possible aspects with General Montgomery. There were two main lines of approach to the problem: an attack in the south, where the enemy defences were rather weaker, which would develop into one more variation on the classic desert theme of an envelopment of the inland flank, or a straight blow at the north where the defences were stronger but the results of success would be more important. The plan which General Montgomery submitted to me was to make the main thrust in the north, with a secondary attack in the south as a feint to pin down the enemy forces there. This plan was in my judgment much the most promising. It was the easiest for us, since our communications would be shorter and on better ground. More important still was the fact that a penetration here, along the line of the coast road, would force the enemy away from his communications, putting all the forces to the south of the breach in imminent danger of isolation, and would produce an immediate threat to his landing grounds and supply centre at El Daba. The hostile front might be compared to a door, hinged at its northern end; to push at the free end might cause it to swing back some way before any serious damage was done but a successful blow at the hinge would dislocate the whole front and throw the doorway wide open. One of the main features of the plan was the concentration of the greatest possible number of guns of all calibres, under centralised control, against the principal point of attack. The key to the enemy's position in the northern sector was the Miteiriya ridge. This is a long, narrow ridge, called after the cistern of Sanyet el Miteiriya, rising to about a hundred feet above sea level and running parallel to the Tell el Eisa ridge about four miles further south of it. If we could break through between these two ridges and wrest the southern one from the enemy – the northern we already held – we should have a corridor through the enemy's defences protected on either flank by slightly higher ground and the enemy minefield on the other side of the Miteiriya ridge would give us additional protection from an enemy counter-attack in that sector. General Montgomery carried out a long reconnaissance of the Miteiriya ridge from our forward outposts and confirmed this plan from inspection of the ground.

The plan for the battle was given the codename LIGHTFOOT. The attack was to be made by 30 Corps using, from north to south, 9 Australian,

51 Highland, 2 New Zealand and 1 South African Divisions. The first two were to drive due west on a line roughly parallel to and below the Tell el Eisa ridge to form the northern corridor and the latter two were to attack south-westerly to secure the Miteiriya ridge and to establish the southern corridor through the defences. 4 Indian Division, which was also under command, was to carry out a diversionary raid along Ruweisat ridge. When 30 Corps had formed these two corridors through the full depth of the enemy defences 10 Corps, with, from north to south, 1 and 10 Armoured Divisions, was to pass through and position itself on ground of its own choosing at the far end of the corridors. It was likely enough that the enemy would counter-attack immediately with his armour in order to close the breach. Whether he did or not the infantry of 30 Corps would proceed at once with the methodical destruction of the enemy infantry first between the two corridors and then on either of its flanks, working northwards from Tell el Eisa and southwards from Miteiriya ridge. 10 Corps would prevent the enemy armour from interfering with these operations. This stage of the battle would be quite certain to provoke a strong reaction from the enemy armour which could hardly sit and watch its infantry being destroyed piecemeal. This would be to our advantage, for we would be forcing the enemy to attack us on ground which we had chosen.

Simultaneously with the main attack 13 Corps, with under command 7 Armoured, 44 and 50 Divisions, was to attack in the southern sector. Two thrusts were to be made, one round the southern flank by 1 Fighting French Brigade, directed against Qaret el Himeimat, and the other north of Himeimat by 44 Division supported by 7 Armoured Division. The intention was, if possible, to make a breach in the enemy positions there as well, through which we might be able to exploit; if the Himeimat operation went well, 4 Light Armoured Brigade would be passed round the southern flank and launched in a raid on El Daba, to destroy the supply installations there and seize the landing grounds. But the main value which I expected from the 13 Corps operation was to distract the enemy attention from the vital thrust in the north and, in particular, to contain opposite it the two armoured divisions already on that flank. In order to ensure that the process of containment and attrition worked in our favour rather than the enemy's it was firmly laid down that 7 Armoured Division must be kept in being and should not incur such casualties as would make it ineffective. 4 Light Armoured Brigade was not to be launched on Daba without specific orders.

I attached very great importance to the deceptive measures to be taken to conceal our intentions from the enemy. It was obviously impossible to conceal from him the fact that we intended to attack; the most we could hope for was to deceive him as to the exact date and place of our attack. We could do this by showing him concentrations of troops and administrative preparations in the southern sector which should be large enough to suggest a full-scale attack there but incomplete, so as to suggest a later date than the actual. Above all it was important to conceal the preparations being made in the north. I decided that we must go to all lengths to make this deception plan a success and no effort was spared to that end which ingenuity could suggest. We were fortunate in that our plans had been decided on over a month in advance of the operation; consequently we could ensure that the appropriate deception measures were taken from the start. The main problems which faced us were to conceal the concentration in 13 Corps' forward area of two extra divisions, two hundred and forty additional guns and a hundred and fifty additional tanks, and in the rear areas of seven thousand five hundred tons of petrol, stores and ammunition, and the construction of six additional tracks leading from assembly areas twenty-five miles in rear up to the actual sector on which the break in was to be made. In 13 Corps we had to conceal the forward movement of artillery to cover the points selected for attack. Most important of all was to conceal the move forward of 10 Corps from their training areas to their assembly areas in the northern sector.

To conceal the reinforcement of 30 Corps careful calculations were made to determine what the area would look like from the air immediately before the battle; the same picture was then reproduced by 1st October by disposing transport in the areas which would be occupied on 23rd October. Dummy lorries were erected in the areas which would be occupied by the artillery regiments so that the guns and limbers could be moved in by night and concealed under the dummies. The additional dumps were elaborately camouflaged, for which purpose the hummocky area near El Imayid station was well adapted. The new tracks could not be concealed, and they were the most revealing indications of our purpose. The only solution which offered itself was to delay until the last the completion of those parts of them which would be most significant to the enemy. In the 13 Corps sector the intended concentrations of artillery were first represented by dummy guns which were later replaced by real guns. Most elaborate measures were taken to conceal the movement of 10 Corps. The two assembly areas were filled by about 6th October with approximately two thousand vehicles in each with over seven hundred dummy vehicles to be placed over the tanks of the three armoured brigades. The Corps moved from its training area to two staging areas on 19th October; these moves were carried out openly as training moves. From the staging areas to the assembly areas the moves were made largely by night and all tanks and guns moved entirely by night. As units moved out of the staging areas they were replaced by dummy tanks, some mobile and some static, dummy guns and transport and by over two thousand real motor vehicles.

Besides these negative measures of concealment positive measures of deception were taken. A dummy pipeline was built stretching from the real pipeline down towards 13 Corps' sector. This was a most realistic production made of old petrol tins, with dummy pumping stations and reservoirs; it was started on 27th September and progress was timed to suggest 5th November as the date of completion. A large mock dump was started in the southern sector on 7th October and this too increased at a rate to suggest completion on 5th November. 10 Armoured Division used as an intermediate staging area a position right down on the southern flank from where it might be expected to move forward to 13 Corps sector. The westward move to this area was made openly in daylight and when the division moved due north after dusk it was represented in the staging area by the measures I have already described. A wireless network of 10 Corps, with all its brigades, was represented as operating in the southern sector up to D-day and from D minus I onwards occasional false messages were sent suggesting a move forward into 13 Corps' area.

To carry out so comprehensive a scheme of deception required a minute attention to detail and planning, the employment of large quantities of labour, transport and materials, mass production of dummies and careful control of the movements of many hundreds of vehicles. Carelessness in any area might have revealed the whole plan. In the event the deception was entirely successful; the main direction of our thrust and the location of our armour were unknown to the enemy at the time the attack began and for some time afterwards. It was not until D plus 3 that he finally concentrated all his resources against our real attack.

When all preparations for the battle had been made I felt that I could regard the coming conflict with a certain confidence but nevertheless with a sober appreciation of the importance of the event. We had the advantage over the enemy in men, tanks and guns and we had a vigorous and enterprising field commander who knew well how to employ these advantages. The Eighth Army was certainly the finest and best equipped that England had put in the field so far but for that very reason the test it faced was a crucial one. One thing gave us particular encouragement: the high standard of morale. From the moment that the troops had learned that retreat was no longer in question morale had begun to improve; it was raised to still greater heights by the successful defensive action of September and maintained at that level and even increased by the sight of the careful preparations, the heavy reinforcement and the arrival of powerful new weapons which had marked the subsequent period. The troops well knew that the battle would be long and costly but they were confident of the outcome and aware of the great change that victory would bring to the whole pattern of the war.

The Battle of El Alamein.

The night of 23rd October was calm and clear and brilliantly illuminated by an almost full moon. At 2140 hours the whole of Eighth Army artillery, almost a thousand field and medium guns, opened up simultaneously for fifteen minutes against located enemy batteries; it was an extraordinary sight, reminiscent of the previous world war, and the intensity of the fire had the effect of silencing almost all the hostile guns. After a five minute pause fire recommenced at 2200 hours against the enemy forward positions and simultaneously the infantry of 13 and 30 Corps advanced to the attack.

In the north the enemy's forward defences were captured in two hours without serious opposition. After an hour's halt for reorganization the attack on the main positions began at about 0100 hours. Much sterner opposition was encountered and progress became slow. By 0530 hours 9 Australian Division on the right had secured most of its final objective, nine thousand yards from the start line; the New Zealand Division had also captured its final objective, the western end of the

Miteiriya ridge. In the centre, however, the left brigade of the Australian Division and the Highland Division were held up about fifteen hundred yards short of their objective by enemy strongpoints in the middle of what should have been the northern corridor and on the left the South African Division fell short of the Miteiriya ridge by about five hundred yards. 10 Corps crossed their start line according to plan at 0200 hours and began to follow 30 Corps. The work of the engineers, advancing behind the infantry to clear the minefields for 10 Corps, was greatly delayed; in fact the whole area was one vast minefield. However, the southern corridor, leading to Miteiriya ridge, was opened by 0630 hours and an hour later 9 Armoured Brigade (New Zealand Division), closely followed by 10 Armoured Division, was on the eastern slopes of the ridge. This was an uncomfortable position, for as day broke the ridge came under heavy fire from artillery to the south-west so that the tanks were unable to cross it without incurring heavy casualties. Meanwhile the deployment of 1 Armoured Division was even more seriously held up, because the northern lane was still blocked by minefields under fire from the enemy strongpoints which the Australian and Highland Divisions had been unable to overcome. 20 Australian Brigade and two companies on the extreme right of the Highland Division captured their final objective soon after dawn; but the rest of the enemy strongpoints continued to resist stubbornly and 2 Armoured Brigade was still in the minefield at daybreak.

This was a serious delay. It was essential to General Montgomery's plan that 10 Corps should debouch and gain freedom of manoeuvre, so that we could enjoy the advantage of our great weight of armour. Moreover it was essential that this should be done at once, so that we could benefit by the tactical surprise gained. General Montgomery therefore ordered 10 and 30 Corps to clear the corridor without delay. At 1500 hours 51 Division and 1 Armoured Division, with massed artillery support, launched a combined attack which was completely successful. 51 Division secured the whole of its final objective, although a few enemy strongpoints continued to hold out in rear until the following day. 2 Armoured Brigade was then able to emerge with very light casualties and complete its deployment under cover of a night attack by 7 Motor Brigade.

On the left flank meanwhile the South African Division had succeeded in capturing its final objective on Miteiriya ridge. Owing to the heavy opposition in this sector, however, the attacks designed to gain more room for the armour to deploy had to be carried out by night. The New Zealand Division was also involved in this south-westerly attack in order to extend its bridgehead according to the original plan. The enemy appeared to be ready for this development and the New Zealanders and 10 Armoured Division came under very heavy shellfire; by dawn, however, all three armoured brigades had completed their deployment and joined hands with 2 Armoured Brigade on the right. The first phase of plan LIGHT-FOOT in this sector had thereby been carried out, but twenty-four hours behind the time-table, largely owing to the extraordinary density of the minefields.

13 Corps' operations in the south met with limited success. The frontal attack on the enemy minefields on the night of 23rd October was preceded by thirty

minutes' intense counter-battery fire and supported by timed concentrations on known enemy defensive localities in the same way as the main assault. 7 Armoured Division broke through the first enemy minefield and established 22 Armoured Brigade in a bridgehead to the west of it. The second minefield, however, was covered by heavy defensive fire and when, by 1000 hours, no breach had been made it was decided to postpone the attempt on it to the following night and widen the bridgehead by reducing the infantry positions on either side of it between the two minefields. These operations were very successful and yielded a large number of prisoners. Meanwhile 1 Fighting French Brigade, after a long and difficult night march, had reached the escarpment south of Himeimat when they were attacked by tanks. Their anti-tank guns had been unable to keep up with the advance in the soft sand, and the brigade was forced to withdraw, after suffering a number of casualties.

The failure to take Himeimat had unfortunate consequences the following night, when 13 Corps returned to the attack. 131 Infantry Brigade succeeded in penetrating the second minefield and formed a narrow bridgehead to the west of it; but, as soon as 22 Armoured Brigade started to go through, the gaps were covered by heavy fire not only from anti-tank guns and hull-down tanks to the immediate front but also by artillery from Himeimat in enfilade. After several attempts to overcome this opposition, which only brought further casualties, the two brigades were ordered to retire. It was clear that any further attempt to batter a passage through the minefield would result in heavy casualties, which could not be accepted. It was equally clear that 13 Corps was fulfilling its chief function of containing the southern group of enemy armour, for 21 Panzer Division, as well as Ariete, was identified on its front. General Montgomery therefore instructed 13 Corps to press the attack no further but to go on creating a diversion by limited operations. He laid stress on the vital importance of keeping 7 Armoured Division "in being."

By dawn on 25th October we could consider that the attack had opened well. 30 Corps had made a breach six miles wide which directly threatened the centre of the enemy's communications. 10 Corps had succeeded in deploying in a position from where it could threaten the envelopment of the enemy's line or bring the full weight of its seven hundred tanks and powerful artillery to bear in the event of the enemy counter-attack which it hoped to provoke. The cover plan had been an unqualified success. During the critical hours of 24th October when 10 Corps was still trying to deploy the enemy was still inclined to believe that the weight of our armour lay behind 13 Corps and launched only a few minor counter-attacks in the north. So, although 13 Corps had failed in its secondary mission, its assault was sufficiently successful to convince the enemy that he must keep two armoured divisions in the south not only on 24th but even on 25th October. Moreover a naval operation which successfully simulated a landing at Ras-el-Kenayis 65 miles west of El Alamein made him keep 90 Light Division back at Daba. Undoubtedly the death of the Axis Commander-in-Chief had assisted the confusion which was evident in the enemy camp. General Stumme had gone forward on a reconnaissance on the night of the 23rd with his Chief Signal Officer; as they were standing close together the latter was struck down by a sudden burst of machine-gun fire and Stumme, who had apparently been overworking in a climate to which he was unaccustomed, was seized by a heart attack of which he died on the spot. It was some time before he was missed and his body recovered and this delayed the assumption of command by General von Thoma, Commander of the German Africa Corps.

The enemy began a series of counter-attacks in the north shortly after daybreak on 25th October. These efforts were not made in great strength but by battle groups containing some twenty to forty tanks each. This was a mistake: 10 Corps was well placed to accept counterattack and against our armoured brigades in strong concentrations small battle groups stood no chance of success. 1 Armoured Division, against whom the attacks were at first directed, destroyed a number of enemy tanks without suffering damage. Later 10 Armoured Division was also repeatedly engaged and able to drive off the attackers without difficulty, though at some cost to itself. All this was in accordance with our plan and it was particularly gratifying that the enemy should be employing only the northern group of his armour, and using that up in piecemeal attacks.

General Montgomery was now ready to proceed with the second phase of the attack. Originally, as I have explained, it had been intended to extend 30 Corps' bridgehead through the enemy's positions to both north and south but the very fierce resistance which the New Zealanders had met when attacking the previous night showed that the southwards attack, which was to have been the more important, would prove extremely costly. It was accordingly decided to begin operations on the northern flank instead. The change of plan was likely to take the enemy by surprise and the operation would result in the capture of certain troublesome positions overlooking the Australians. The attack, which was made at midnight on 25th–26th October by 26 Australian Brigade, was completely successful. Many of the German defenders were killed and many captured, and the salient was extended by about two thousand yards to include the whole of the Tell el Eisa ridge. 1 Armoured Division had been ordered to operate in a due westerly direction on the Australian" left but they were unable to gain any ground. The enemy had succeeded in establishing a good defensive screen across the end of our northern corridor and we would not be able to break out there unless we could widen our hold still further.

The same night 13 Corps carried out a limited operation to divert the enemy's attention. A strong locality in the Deir el Munassib was selected as the objective as being both easily accessible and sufficiently important to call for a strong effort to retain it. 4 Light Armoured Brigade demonstrated in the depression to the south of the post in the afternoon and at night 69 Infantry Brigade (50 Division) attacked from the north. The enemy were found to be in strong force and well posted and the attack was not pressed.

At this point the Eighth Army Commander decided to make a pause. The intention was still to gain ground to the north of our salient but it was clear that

30 Corps needed a rest after its exertions. Casualties in infantry had been fairly heavy and in certain formations, in particular the South African and New Zealand Divisions, there were only limited replacements available. Moreover, since all formations were now in close contact with the enemy it would be necessary, in order to create a reserve, to draw forces out of the line. This could be done by moving the inter-Corps boundary further north and ordering 13 Corps on to the defensive. 10 Corps was temporarily relieved of responsibility for breaking out further and ordered to pass to the defensive while 13 and 30 Corps reorganized.[23] It was first necessary, however, to strengthen and round off the front. On the night of the 26th, accordingly, the South African and New Zealand Divisions advanced about a thousand yards so as to gain more depth in front of the Miteiriya ridge while 51 Division also reinforced its forward positions. At the same time 7 Motor Brigade at last succeeded after a stiff fight in advancing down the northern corridor and capturing Kidney ridge, a strongly fortified rise in the ground on the far edge of the enemy minefields. This was the position which had held up 1 Armoured Division the previous night; in our hands it was to be the key to our now defensive front.

The decision to reorganize and regroup had been taken on the afternoon of the 26th and the next two days were occupied by the necessary moves and reliefs. 13 Corps' front was extended to cover the southern half of Miteiriya ridge; in this sector 4 Indian Division relieved the South Africans who in turn side-stepped north and allowed the relief of the New Zealand Division. 51 Division relieved a brigade of the Australian Division to allow the latter to increase the strength of their northward drive. Besides the New Zealanders 1 Armoured Division was also to be drawn into reserve and joined by 7 Armoured Division from 13 Corps. This was to be the striking force for the new breakthrough when the northerly attack should have widened the breach still further. In order to give it power it was necessary to regroup extensively to create a force capable of maintaining its momentum in spite of casualties. 131 Brigade was therefore taken from 44 Division together with some artillery, and placed under command of 7 Armoured Division as a Lorried Infantry Brigade Group. The New Zealand Division was even more strongly reinforced: besides its original one armoured and two infantry brigades, which had all suffered casualties, it took command of 151 Brigade (50 Division) and 152 Brigade (51 Division); later it also commanded for certain specific attacks 4 Light Armoured Brigade (7 Armoured Division), 23 Armoured Brigade and 133 Brigade (44 Division). These formations were placed under command of 30 Corps but concentrated for the present in reserve. 13 Corps was ordered to carry out no major operations but to keep the enemy on the alert with raids and artillery fire. The Corps was restricted to forty rounds per gun for twenty-five pounders.

While this reorganization proceeded an appreciable change had come over the enemy's conduct of the battle, due without doubt to the return of Field-Marshal Rommel, who had been hastily sent back to Africa as soon as Stumme's death was known. After arriving on the 26th he immediately set to work to retrieve his predecessor's errors by concentrating his armour and mobile reserves, ordering forward the Trieste and 90 Light Divisions and bringing up 21 Panzer Division by forced marches from the south, followed by the Ariete Division. Trieste he put in to plug the gap made in his defences and grouped the remainder for a counter-offensive against our salient. The policy of dispersion had already seriously reduced the strength available for such a policy; 15 Panzer Division had been practically destroyed already and the Littorio Division was heavily depleted. Our defensive position was strong, with its flanks firmly based on the two ridges, our artillery well posted and the air force alert. On the 26th Rommel endeavoured to play once more the card which had so often won him victory in the past, a mass tank attack in the afternoon out of the sun; but the concentrations were broken up by continuous air bombardment and heavy shellfire before he could get to grips. On the 27th when, in spite of sustained bombing, he managed to launch heavy armoured attacks against Kidney ridge and the northern shoulder of the salient, all were driven off with heavy loss to the enemy by the stubborn resistance of 2 Rifle Brigade and of 26 Australian Brigade. The following day large concentrations were again seen to be gathering and it seemed likely that the attacks would be repeated. But the preparations were again disrupted by intensive bombing and such tanks as did probe our lines were held at a distance by the artillery of 10 and 30 Corps. Threatening though they were at times these attacks did not upset our reorganization, whereas they cost the enemy heavy and, worse still for him, disproportionate losses.

The new Eighth Army plan was given the name SUPERCHARGE. The preparatory northward attack by 9 Australian Division went in at 2200 hours on 28th October but it was only partially successful. 26 Brigade on the left gained its objective, just short of the railway, but 20 Brigade on the right was much delayed by heavily defended minefields. The result was that we had gained a small salient sticking out like a cocked thumb from the north side of our original salient, extending to within about half a mile of the coast road. This formed a corresponding salient in the enemy's line also; it was full of strongly held positions, in particular a very well-defended collection of strongpoints just north of Tel el Eisa known as "Thompson's Post". The intention was now to clear up all this area, break out along the axis of the road and send the New Zealand Division, reinforced and regrouped as I have described, to capture Sidi Abd el Rahman. This would get us right through the enemy's prepared positions and turn his northern flank. Before this plan could be set in motion, however, information was received on the morning of the 29th that caused us to alter completely the direction of the attack.

The enemy had realized the probability, and the danger, of the plan which we had decided to employ. In order to meet it he moved up to the Sidi Abd el Rahman area 90 Light Division, leaving the covering of the original gap, where we were now on the defensive, to the Trieste Division. This made it unlikely that we should be able to obtain a decisive break-through on the line of the road, but I considered that the situation could be turned to our advantage by encouraging the enemy's belief that we intended to force our way through to Sidi Abd el Rahman. We would continue the attack by the Australians, thus diverting his attention to the sector of the main road; when all his reserves were engaged there General Montgomery would employ the reserve he had created in a drive due westwards out of our salient to breach the hastily reorganized defences and pass our armour through well into the enemy's rear. This would finally disrupt his defences and the battle would become mobile.

On the night of 30th October, therefore, 26 Australian Infantry Brigade, supported by a great weight of artillery, struck north-east and then east from the salient won by 20 Brigade two nights before. Again it was not possible to clear the whole area in the face of the enemy's stubborn resistance; this part of the front was particularly strong and the defences were so thick that it might almost be called one continuous minefield. However, the Australians reached and crossed the road and drove towards the sea, reducing the corridor to the now encircled enemy to a very narrow strip along the coast. In the pocket thus formed there were two Italian and two German battalions. They were joined next day by a group of about twenty German tanks from 21 Panzer Division which broke through down the road; this was in many ways a good sign, for it meant that that division was being drawn into the area where we wanted it. Indeed the Germans were now devoting their full efforts to counter-attacks on the Australians. The proposed break-through would place us between this northern group and the remnants of 15 Panzer Division, which was still observing the western end of our original salient, and would therefore split the enemy reserves in two.

I had hoped we should be able to attack westwards the same night, 31st October; but the men were greatly fatigued, time was needed for reconnaissance, and the artillery had to be reorganized after the Australian attack. It was accordingly postponed for twenty-four hours but, to compensate for the delay, the depth of the attack was increased from four to six thousand yards. It was to be an operation very similar to that of 23rd October. Advancing due west on a front of four thousand yards 151 and 152 Infantry Brigades (50 and 51 Divisions), supported by 23 Armoured Brigade, were to drive a lane through the enemy's new positions, clearing the minefields as they went. At the same time 28 (Maori) Battalion and 133 Infantry Brigade (44 Division) were to capture certain important enemy localities on the flanks of the advance. 9 Armoured Brigade, following close behind the infantry, was then to advance a further two thousand yards beyond their objective and penetrate a strong screen of guns known to be in position along the Rahman track. The forces mentioned were under command of 30 Corps and their action was to be co-ordinated by the New Zealand Division. 10 Corps was then to follow up with 1 Armoured Division (2 and 8 Armoured Brigades) leading; it was important that all three armoured brigades should reach the open country before first light and General Montgomery issued firm instructions that should 30 Corps not reach their objectives the armoured divisions of 10 Corps were to fight their way through. When the way was clear 10 Corps was to launch two armoured car regiments from the tip of the salient to raid the enemy's rear. 5 and 6 New Zealand Infantry Brigades were to concentrate in the salient ready to exploit success if called on.

The attack was to be supported by a very strong concentration of artillery fire. As in the opening attack all guns were to be employed beforehand in silencing enemy batteries. Then, while a hundred and ninety-two guns put down a creeping barrage over the four thousand yards of front, a further hundred and sixty-eight were to shell known and likely enemy positions in the path of the advance and on either side of it. All available guns were then to be concentrated in support of 9 Armoured Brigade's attack on the Rahman track. The strength of this artillery support was, however, to some extent offset by an inevitable lack of exact knowledge of enemy dispositions. Timing was also a problem. The moon was now on the wane, and zero hour had therefore to be made three hours later than on the opening night of the battle.

When the attack went in at 0105 hours on 2nd November the enemy were able to offer rather more opposition than had been expected, having regard to the gruelling artillery and air bombardment to which they had been subjected. It was not until 0600 hours that 151 Brigade reached its objective. 152 Brigade on the left reached its objective half an hour earlier, but still two hours later than had been planned. Meanwhile 9 Armoured Brigade had been delayed by mines and still more by artillery fire from the flanks which had caused appreciable casualties. As a result the brigade crossed its start line half an hour behind schedule. The delay proved very costly for at dawn it found itself on the muzzles of the powerful screen of anti-tank guns on the Rahman track, instead of beyond it as had been planned. It was here that occurred what has been called the battle of Tell el Aqqaqir,[24] which was the largest clash of armoured formations in the whole battle. The Tell itself is a small rise in the ground just beyond the Sidi Abd el Rahman track.

All three regiments of 9 Armoured Brigade displayed the greatest gallantry in the two hours fight which followed the dawn encounter. They held their ground tenaciously in spite of very heavy losses and though eighty-seven of their tanks were destroyed they accounted for a large number of the enemy guns. At this price they held open the end of the salient for 1 Armoured Division to emerge. It had great difficulty, for it came under heavy fire at once and in a short time the enemy armour began furiously to engage both flanks of the salient. The armoured brigades turned outwards to meet these converging attacks, which were heaviest on the northern flank where 21 Panzer Division was soon engaged. The situation looked dangerous at times, but the enemy had been tricked into allowing his armoured divisions to become separated again and was once more compelled to pit his tanks in two separate groups against our massed armour and artillery. He fought with the certain knowledge that all was at stake and with all the skill of his long experience in armoured fighting. At one moment 21 Panzer Division broke right into the north flank of the salient; but slowly as the day wore on the enemy was forced back. His losses were crippling and the Africa Corps would fight no more as a Corps on Egyptian soil.

The battle of 2nd November was the decisive action and it must have been that night that the enemy decided to withdraw. Indications of a withdrawal came early on 3rd November and increased as the day wore on. One armoured car regiment, the Royal Dragoons, had managed to pass round the enemy's gun line in the dawn mist on the 2nd and was already raiding his communications and firing his dumps in rear; but the main body of our armour was still penned in to the east of the Rahman track. 7 Motor Brigade had made a night attack on the night of the 2nd in an attempt to cut through the gun screen across the track, due west beyond Tell el Aqqaqir, but the country was completely flat and the positions gained would have been untenable by day. At dawn, therefore, 8 Armoured Brigade tried another tack and moved south-west; here too it struck ground sown with mines and raked with anti-tank fire so that after slow progress it was again held up on reaching the Rahman track. 4/6 South African Armoured Car Regiment, however, managed to slip past and raced to join the Royals at El Daba. Meanwhile the full weight of our air attack was switched to the main road, where slow-moving, close-packed transport already in retreat presented excellent targets from Ghazal to Fuka.

But although the enemy had acknowledged defeat and turned to flight he still hoped to be able to conduct an orderly retreat, and of this he had a reasonable chance as long as he maintained his blocking position on the Rahman track. An infantry assault was essential to break through the anti-tank screen, and the infantry on the spot were exhausted; General Montgomery decided accordingly to employ a detached force from 4 Indian Division which had hitherto not been heavily engaged. 5 Indian Brigade, composed of Essex, Baluch and Rajputana Rifles, was selected. After a night approach march of extreme difficulty the brigade attacked at 0230 hours on 4th November, about five miles south of Tell el Aqqaqir, behind a hastily organized but admirably fired moving barrage. The attack was completely successful; by dawn the southern end of the enemy's gun screen had been forced back and it now faced south-east, covering the coast road. Round the end of it the armoured divisions of 10 Corps now poured. At the same time the area immediately south of Tell el Aqqaqir was cleared up under the direction of 51 Division and the Australians in the north, advancing into the central pocket, found that most of the Germans and Italians enclosed there had slipped away in the night.

10 Corps had been reorganized and regrouped for the pursuit and had now under command all three armoured divisions, 1st, 7th and 10th.[25] The New Zealand Division, with 9 Armoured Brigade, now reduced and reorganized as a composite armoured regiment, and adding 4 Light Armoured Brigade to its command, was held in reserve under 30 Corps. The three armoured divisions crossed the Rahman track soon after first light on 4th November with orders to make for the road at Ghazal and beyond it. They had advanced little more than six miles, however, when they again found themselves confronted by the anti-tank gun screen which had again fallen back to form a wide arc covering Ghazal. It was evidently Rommel's hope to extricate the greater part of his northernmost forces

in an orderly manner behind this screen; but the hope was soon frustrated for shortly after midday the New Zealand Division, with 4 Light Armoured Brigade on its right flank, was sent in a wide sweep to the south with orders to press on and secure the escarpment at Fuka.

As this great mass of motorized and armoured troops was observed pressing westwards to the south of the German rearguards Rommel at first refused to believe that it was the British armour and to General von Thoma's expostulations replied that it could only be the Trieste Division, for the British could not have got so far forward in so short a time. The Commander of the German Africa Corps therefore went forward to make a personal reconnaissance to obtain the evidence to convince his superior and was captured in the process by a British tank. When thus dramatically convinced Rommel saw at once that only by the speediest withdrawal could he hope to extricate any of his German troops. The Italians must be abandoned to their fate; the majority of them were in any case already cut off. The whole of X Corps, being without any transport, and the survivors of XXI Corps in the same plight waited on the battlefield to surrender. Some attempted to march off to the west in long, straggling columns and some individuals undoubtedly perished in the desert while attempting to find their own way back. Formations from 13 Corps were employed to round up these stragglers. The Headquarters of XX Corps withdrew straight down the road without having taken any part in the battle; the remains of the Ariete Division followed their Corps Commander until overtaken by fuel shortage, whereupon they abandoned their remaining tanks at various points along the road. The Littorio Division had been practically destroyed and few of the Trieste escaped.

The action around Ghazal on 4th November ended the battle of El Alamein. Rather less than a third of the original Axis force succeeded in making good its escape. We estimated enemy casualties as ten thousand killed and fifteen thousand wounded; over thirty thousand prisoners were taken, ten thousand of them Germans, and nine Generals were included in the bag. Of six hundred enemy tanks four hundred and fifty were left on the battlefield. Over a thousand pieces of artillery were destroyed or captured. Large quantities of ammunition, stores and equipment of all natures fell into our hands intact in the early stages of the pursuit. The hostile force with which we now had to reckon amounted to little more than one composite division. 90 Light Division, upon whom fell the burden of covering the retreat, had been reduced to about a strong regimental group. The survivors of 164 Division equalled about another regimental group. Of the hundred and fifty tanks remaining about seventy belonged to the Ariete Division and shortly fell out along the road. The remnants of 15 and 21 Panzer Divisions, mustering some eighty tanks between them, formed the armoured component of the force. In reserve there were the Pistoia Division on the frontier and 80 Spezia Division which had recently arrived in Tripolitania, both as yet untried.

Our own casualties were not unduly severe – thirteen thousand five hundred killed, wounded and missing, or just under eight per cent. of the force engaged. A hundred guns had been destroyed and, although more than five hundred tanks were disabled in the battle, only a hundred and fifty were found to be beyond repair. It is fitting at this point to mention that it was very largely the high efficiency of the repair and recovery organization which enabled us to retain our superiority in armour throughout the fighting. In 10 Corps alone, of five hundred and thirty tanks received in workshops, three hundred and thirty seven were put in service again during the eleven days the battle lasted.

Our casualties were a negligible factor as far as the pursuit was concerned; on 4th November the Eighth Army could put into the field very nearly six hundred tanks against eighty German. The main problem was, not to find forces strong enough to defeat the fleeing enemy, but to arrange that the pursuit should not outstrip supplies. Great distances, scarcity of communications and scarcity of water are the principal attributes of the Libyan Desert. Tobruk is three hundred and fifty miles from Alamein, Benghazi three hundred miles further on and El Agheila, which on two previous occasions had proved the turning point of hitherto successful campaigns and which is the strongest defensive position in the desert, a hundred and sixty miles further still. The water sources along the coast as far as the frontier were expected to be, and were, thoroughly oiled[26]; the water pipeline from Alexandria could no longer be relied on. The railway ran as far as Tobruk but it was not reasonable to suppose that it would be of any service in the early stages of the pursuit, though preparations had, of course, been made to repair it as fast as possible. For the leading troops road transport was the only means of supply. Even the road was not entirely reliable, since there were many places, such as the escarpment pass at Sollum, where it could easily be demolished, necessitating a long detour. Motor transport, though a great deal more plentiful than in earlier campaigns, was still inadequate to supply the whole of 10 Corps beyond Matruh and a pause would be necessary before we could advance across the frontier. The overriding consideration of the next phase of the offensive, therefore was to cut off and destroy as much as possible of what remained of the enemy before they could withdraw beyond our reach.

The battle of El Alamein had been a stand-up fight, lasting for eleven days but skilful leadership and the tenacity of the fighting soldiers and airmen won the day and with it the first great victory for the Allies. It proved to be the turning point of the war. This great battle was the fore-runner of a series of victories which never ceased until the enemy were finally cleared from the African continent and it had been decisively won four days before the Anglo-American Expeditionary Force under General Eisenhower landed in French North Africa. The world knew that the Axis had suffered a major disaster and there is no doubt that this knowledge, by its influence on French and Spanish opinion, was of vital importance in assisting General Eisenhower's mission.

The Pursuit to Agheila.
The enemy withdrew from his delaying positions south of Ghazal during the night of 4th November and on the 5th the pursuit proper began. 10 Corps

commanded the pursuit force with I and 10 Armoured Divisions directed on Daba and 7 Armoured Division directed on Fuka. The New Zealand Division, which had some difficulty in extricating itself from the confusion of the battlefield, also moved off at dawn on its way to Fuka, passing from 30 to 10 Corps; it had 4 Light Armoured Brigade under command. The importance of Fuka lay in the fact that the road here passes up a three hundred foot escarpment which is almost impassable except on the axis of the road and railway. If we could get there across the desert quicker than the enemy could along the road we should be able to cut off a good deal of his rearguard. 30 Corps, with 51 and 9 Australian Divisions, was held in reserve and ordered to clear up the coastal area; the task of clearing the main battlefield was entrusted to 13 Corps.

The first stage of the pursuit went well. By midday on 5th November 1 Armoured Division had taken Daba and was ordered to strike across the desert to cut the road west of Mersa Matruh. At the same time 10 Armoured Division fought a sharp but short engagement with a German armoured rearguard at Galal, between Daba and Fuka, in which it destroyed or captured forty-four of the enemy's remaining eighty tanks. After this success the division was ordered to press down the main road to Fuka. The enemy rearguard attempted to hold the Fuka escarpment and the New Zealand Division was momentarily held up there south of the road; but 4 Light Armoured Brigade forced its way past late in the evening and by midday on 6th November had reached Baqqush, about thirty miles from Mersa Matruh. There they were joined later by the rest of the division and by 8 Armoured Brigade which had broken through the enemy rearguard on the road and captured over a thousand more prisoners, including the headquarters of the Folgore Division. Meanwhile 7 Armoured Division struck across the desert to the south of the Fuka escarpment and attacked another party of the enemy near Sidi Haneish, on the main road just west of Baqqush. In this action we destroyed fifteen tanks and seven heavy guns and took two thousand prisoners. The enemy's tank strength was now down to about thirty.

By the evening of 6th November we had cleared the road up to a point less than thirty miles east of Matruh with our main forces, and 4/6 South African Armoured Car Regiment was operating with great success on the road west of Matruh where it had taken two thousand prisoners and captured or destroyed numerous vehicles. 1 Armoured Division, advancing through the desert, had drawn level with Matruh to the south and was well on the way to cutting the road beyond it. At this point, however, the pursuit was brought abruptly to a standstill. Light rain had begun to fall during the afternoon of the 6th and during the night it turned into a downpour. The desert became a morass in which tanks could move only very slowly and wheeled transport was completely bogged. This at once stultified the whole conception of the pursuit which consisted in continuously outflanking through the desert the enemy retreating up the road. The New Zealand Division, being lorry-borne, was stuck for thirty-six hours and the motor brigades and the supply echelons of 1 and 7 Armoured Divisions were in a similar predicament. Only the South African armoured cars and the elements of

4 Light Armoured Brigade that were within easy reach of the road were able to move: the latter were too weak to overcome the strong rearguard covering the evacuation of Matruh and a single armoured car regiment was powerless to prevent the escape of the main body of the enemy.

As soon as this state of affairs became known 10 Armoured Division, which had been halted at Fuka for administrative reasons, was ordered to push on to Matruh by the road. This turned the pursuit into a direct following up of the enemy and gave the enemy rearguards every advantage. The armour did not reach the outskirts of the town until shortly before dusk on the 7th and, having launched one unsuccessful attack, could do no more until daylight. Next morning, after a brief engagement, we entered the town to find it evacuated. At the same moment, two thousand miles further west, the first assault waves were coming ashore on the beaches of French North Africa.

Although we had inflicted very heavy damage on the remnants of the enemy during the first two days of the pursuit they had been saved by the rain from complete encirclement at Matruh. The opportunity was unlikely to occur again until Agheila, and our prospects of being able to fight a decisive battle there depended upon our ability to assemble and maintain a sufficiently powerful force to take the offensive before the enemy had organized the position thoroughly and received reinforcements. The principal object of the next phase of the pursuit was therefore to capture the two ports of Tobruk and Benghazi and develop them to their full capacity in as short a time as possible. This was the task of the pursuit force, which had to be reduced in strength as the advance went on, owing to the increasing difficulties of supply. The pursuit force seized any opportunity of rounding up the enemy that occurred, but the task of striking at the enemy's retreat was entrusted mainly to the air forces, operating from landing grounds well forward – often, in fact, in advance of the main body and protected only by armoured cars.

The pursuit force, consisting of 7 Armoured Division and the New Zealand Division (5 New Zealand Infantry Brigade, 9 Armoured Brigade composite regiment and 4 Light Armoured Brigade), under command of 10 Corps, set out at dawn on 8th November with the frontier as the first objective and Tobruk as the next. The pace of the advance was hot. On the coast road the New Zealand Division was opposed east of Sidi Barrani and on the line of our old minefield at Buq Buq. This opposition, however, was swiftly overcome and, after a company of infantry had captured Halfaya Pass, and six hundred prisoners from the Pistoia Division, in a surprise night attack, the division climbed the escarpment on the 11th and occupied Capuzzo, Sollum and Bardia. Meanwhile 7 Armoured Division crossed the frontier on the 10th, after a march across the desert of a hundred and sixty miles by the classic route on top of the escarpment, and swung northwest to join the New Zealanders at Capuzzo. On 12th November , 4 Light Armoured Brigade pressed on and captured Gambut and El Adem and at 0900 hours on the 13th 131 Lorried Infantry Brigade, followed by the main body of 7 Armoured Division, entered Tobruk without opposition.

The main body could proceed no farther until the port of Tobruk was open, but it was essential to secure the landing grounds at Tmimi, Martuba, Derna and Mechili, so as to bring our fighter aircraft within range of the Gebel Akhdar and Benghazi. There was an even more pressing reason for capturing the coastal group of landing grounds. No convoys had sailed to Malta since the previous April owing to the impossibility of providing air protection and the garrison and people of the island were now on the verge of starvation. The situation would be beyond control unless a convoy putting out from Alexandria on 16th November arrived safely and of that there was little hope without strong fighter protection from the coast of Cyrenaica. It might very well have proved impossible to supply any further advance, seeing that 10 Corps had advanced two hundred and twenty miles in six days and that heavy demolitions had been carried out both on the road and the railway. But the administrative arrangements stood the strain, stores were landed at Sollum and the harbours of Matruh and Bardia were opened within two days of their capture so that enough supplies were available to allow 4 Light Armoured Brigade to continue. While the main body hastened down the road and secured Tmimi on 14th November another column moved across the desert via Bir Hacheim and Rotonda Segnali, so as to outflank any possible opposition on the road, and occupied Martuba on the following day. Derna was reported clear on 16th November. On that day the Gazala landing grounds were brought into use and on the 18th our fighters were able to cover the passage of the Malta convoy. Its safe arrival marked the end of the siege and the beginning of the delivery of the brave garrison and people of Malta from the greatest continuous ordeal of the war.

The enemy was withdrawing through the Gebel and it was a great temptation to imitate our previous strategy by pushing a force across the desert to cut him off at or near Agedabia. General Montgomery was determined, however, not to take any chances, especially in view of the difficulties of the maintenance situation, and 10 Corps was instructed to despatch only armoured cars by this route. Later, however, when it appeared that the enemy's retreat had actually been brought to a temporary standstill by lack of fuel, 10 Corps, was ordered to strengthen, if possible, the outflanking force; this proved impracticable in the then existing circumstances. By very careful organisation of reserves 4 Light Armoured Brigade had found it possible to advance to Maraua on 18th November, in spite of demolitions and mines on the road. The main body of 10 Corps was halted around Tmimi.

In the meantime two mobile columns, consisting of 11 Hussars and the Royals, with supporting arms, under command of 7 Armoured Division, were directed on Msus across the desert. By the evening of 16th November they had reported Mechili clear and were operating within forty miles of Msus. Rain now began to fall again and it took the two columns twenty-four hours to struggle through sixty miles of waterlogged ground to the escarpment which the enemy rearguard was holding to cover the evacuation of Benghazi. On 18th November they engaged the rearguard at Sceleidima and Antelat, the two main passes in the escarpment, but were unable to force their way past. During the night the enemy withdrew and the advance of the two columns was again delayed by bad going. On the 20th 11 Hussars entered Benghazi[27] and found the town and neighbourhood clear of enemy, and it was not until midday of the 21st that the Royals made touch with the enemy rearguard again at Agedabia. The administrative position was now becoming easier and the vanguard of 22 Armoured Brigade, having raced across two hundred and sixty miles of desert, at once began to turn the enemy's flank. Thus threatened he lost no time in abandoning Agedabia. The road southwards was heavily mined and the advance was much impeded; but by 25th November patrols were in contact with the next enemy position at Agheila. The whole of Cyrenaica was now in our hands.

During this phase of the pursuit, when 10 Corps was unable to come to grips with the enemy, the work of the Royal Air Force was particularly valuable. All the way from Daba to the frontier, and particularly at Sollum where the congestion was greatest, retreating enemy transport was relentlessly attacked. On 11th November, while the New Zealand Division was occupying the frontier area, our fighters caught up with the enemy air force and had a specially successful day, shooting down enemy aircraft not only over the frontier but also on the enemy's own landing grounds at Gambut and El Adem. By the 13th our own aircraft were based on these same two airfields, bombing and machine-gunning enemy transport in the Gebel Akhdar. On the same day two squadrons of fighters made a bold move, completely by air transport, to a landing ground only a hundred and eighty miles east of Agedabia; well ahead and to the south of our forward troops, and inflicted considerable damage on the enemy's columns retreating round the bend of the Gulf of Sirte. By 16th November the main fighter force was operating from Gazala and destroyed thirty-seven enemy transport aircraft by the use of which the enemy was desperately trying to relieve his fuel shortage. After this the air force, like the main body of the Army, was temporarily chained to the Tobruk area until the supply situation improved and for a few days enemy aircraft were able to attack our light columns in the desert on a scale to which we had long been unused. By 26th November, however, two wings of fighters were established at Msus and our air superiority over the forward area was restored.

The Conquest of Tripolitania.

At Agheila Eighth Army was facing the strongest position in Libya. An army advancing from the east comes first upon a large area of salt marsh, running roughly north to south, known as the Sebkha es Seghira; there is then a gap of about fifteen miles between this and another salt marsh to the south, Sebkhet Gheizel. This gap is filled with soft sand and difficult going, including large areas of wind-blown crescent-shaped dunes. The south side of the position is protected by a partly impassible escarpment, more sand dunes and more salt marshes and the rear is entirely covered by the Sebkha el Kebira. These salt marshes would be at their most difficult in this comparatively rainy season. Remoteness was another great strength of the position; to build up sufficient reserves for a proper attack at a distance of a hundred and fifty miles from Benghazi and three hundred from Tobruk was a matter of some time. This had in the past been one of the reasons why Agheila had twice marked the high-water-mark of a British advance into Libya.

On this occasion, however, the enemy was in no position to reinforce his troops at Agheila. The Anglo-American invasion forces in French North Africa had established themselves firmly in Morocco and Algeria and by the time Eighth Army made contact with the Agheila position the vanguards of First Army were within twenty-five miles of Tunis. All available Axis reinforcements had to be rushed to Tunisia, whose retention was judged by the enemy much more valuable than that of Tripolitania, and there were none available for Rommel. He had picked up three divisions on the way back from Alamein; of these the Pistoia and Young Fascists Divisions were inexperienced and 80 Spezia Division had lost a large part of its artillery on its way across the Mediterranean. With these and the relics of the other Italian divisions he had little more than twenty-five thousand Italians to eke out his ten thousand German survivors. Tank strength was calculated at between sixty and seventy. In spite of the strength of the position these forces were not enough to defend it; the enemy decided therefore to hold Agheila only long enough to force us to deploy in front of it and then to retire, before we could attack, to a position at Buerat, covering Tripoli.

On our side the problem was almost entirely one of maintenance. The enemy had carried out heavy demolitions of certain sectors of the desert railway and of the pipeline from Alexandria; the main road had been blown up at Sollum pass and many places in the Gebel; the water supplies at Bardia, Tobruk and Benghazi had been destroyed; very great damage had been caused at Benghazi and Tobruk by our own bombing and by enemy demolitions. Nevertheless we had allowed for all this; our assessment of probable damage had been conservative and the arrangements for repair proved entirely satisfactory. Railhead was opened at Capuzzo on 21st November and at Tobruk on 1st December. By the latter date three thousand tons of Nile water were being delivered daily twenty-five miles west of Matruh and the water sources at Tobruk and Bardia were rapidly put into commission. The Sollum road was repaired within forty-eight hours, and in the Gebel deviations were constructed fast enough to avoid delay to supply columns. The first ships entered Tobruk and Benghazi four days after capture, in two weeks Tobruk was operating to its full capacity of a thousand tons daily and in three weeks twice that amount was being discharged at Benghazi. Within a very short time sufficient supplies were pouring into Cyrenaica to enable the air forces to continue uninterrupted their heavy attacks on enemy ports and shipping, to allow troops and reserves to be gathered in readiness for a further advance, and strong forces to be maintained in the forward area to ensure an impenetrable screen of observation. The exceptionally long road haul to the forward area and the availability of motor transport, however, were the limiting factors and

General Montgomery calculated that it would be the middle of December before we would be able to resume the advance.

The two weeks which elapsed were fully occupied with preparations and reconnaissance for the attack and with reorganisation. Headquarters 30 Corps assumed command of the forward area from 10 Corps on 26th November. On 3rd December the Corps moved forward to gain close contact with the enemy; 51 Division took over the northern sector with orders to carry out active patrolling and to maintain pressure on the enemy while 7 Armoured Division, stationed farther to the rear, was given the task of observing and harassing the southern flank. At the same time 8 Armoured Brigade relieved 22 Armoured Brigade, which badly needed an opportunity to refit after a continuous advance of over eight hundred miles. By the 9th the New Zealand Division was concentrated round El Haseiat. This is a track junction down in the desert south-east of Agedabia and well back from the enemy positions; the intention was to pass the New Zealanders round the enemy's inland flank, well to the south in the hope of avoiding observation, and strike north to the main road well west of Agheila. By 12th December 30 Corps was ready to advance. In the north the direct blow was to be given by 51 Division both along the road and south of the Sebkha es Seghira; 7 Armoured Division was to follow up the latter blow and the only reserve was 23 Armoured Brigade south of Agedabia.

It had been General Montgomery's intention to launch the attack on 16th December but by the beginning of the month we were already getting clear indications that the enemy was not going to hold.[28] The Italian infantry was the first to go; they had no transport and if their evacuation were delayed they might share the fate of X Corps at El Alamein. The defence of the position was thus left to the German mobile forces, who could delay their departure without undue risk until our attack appeared imminent. There was still a chance, however, that the outflanking movement of the New Zealand Division might be able to catch some of his rearguards and the greater the losses we could inflict on his German troops the less chance there was of his being able to stand on his next position. Accordingly the date of the attack was advanced as much as possible; the New Zealanders started off from El Haseiat on 12th December, 51 Division starting active raiding against the positions north and south of the Sebkha on the 11th to distract attention from the move, and the frontal attack was planned for the 14th.

During the night of 12th December the enemy began to withdraw. He relied principally on mines, booby-traps and demolitions to cover the road, a most effective policy for it was not until the evening of the 15th that 152 Brigade had covered the thirty miles from Mersa Brega to Agheila fort. In view of this slow advance 7 Armoured Division, with 8 Armoured Brigade in the lead, was passed through 153 Brigade round the south end of the Sebkha. Having fought a successful engagement with the enemy rearguard on the Marada road to the south of Agheila the armoured brigade followed hard on the heels of the rearguard until it was held up by an anti-tank ditch running across the main road about twenty miles west of Agheila. This obstacle could not be crossed until the morning of the

16th when the enemy retired and 7 Armoured Division pressed on to chase him, it was hoped, on to the guns of the New Zealand Division which had taken up its position to the west.

The New Zealanders had fetched a wide circuit round the main position. Their objective was the Wadi Matratin, some sixty miles west of Agheila, and they reached it after a most difficult march just as night was falling on 15th December. A large part of the enemy rearguard was still to the east and, as the wadi, though not a complete obstacle, is crossed easily only in the neighbourhood of the road, it seemed that the manoeuvre had succeeded. The division, however, had some difficulty in deploying in unknown country by moonlight and in registering its guns. Next morning, therefore, the enemy, fully aware of his desperate predicament, was able to break up into small parties and race for safety through the gaps in our deployment, losing a number of tanks and guns but succeeding in getting the main body away. As soon as it was seen that by these tactics the enemy was escaping 4 Light Armoured Brigade was sent on to harass the fugitives. But almost every one of the bridges and culverts over the numerous wadis had been blown up, and the wadis sown with mines; in addition the country on either side of the road was exceedingly rough, so that the armoured cars were unable to close with the enemy. In spite of these difficulties the advance guard covered the forty miles to Nofilia by the evening of 16th December. For the next two days the Light Armoured Brigade engaged round Nofilia in skirmishes with the enemy rearguard, which began to retire on the 19th by stages to Sirte. By 22nd December 90 Light and 21 Panzer Divisions had joined the main body, which was hastily preparing a fresh defensive position at Buerat, leaving 15 Panzer Division to cover Sirte.

Beyond Nofilia an advance in force was for the moment impossible for administrative reasons: Nofilia itself is two hundred and sixty miles from Benghazi, the advanced base, and Sirte eighty miles further still. An advance was essential, however, for the sake of the Royal Air Force, since there were very few landing grounds in the area in which we were operating and it was vital to secure those at Sirte, in order to give close support to the attack on the Buerat line. An armoured car regiment was therefore sent to work round to the south of the village. Fearful for the loss of half of his remaining tanks the enemy at once withdrew and shortly after noon on Christmas Day the village was entered without opposition. As the enemy had proved so sensitive to an outflanking movement the manoeuvre was continued until finally, by 30th December, he had fallen back before our armoured car patrols to the main position.

The Buerat position was not particularly strong and could easily be outflanked. East of the village was the broad and difficult Wadi Bey el Kebir and west of it the Wadi Zem Zem; it was on the latter that the enemy established his main position, which was less than twenty-five miles in length. It was a subject of considerable conjecture at the time why Rommel should have decided on standing where he did rather than further back, in particular on the naturally very strong line from

Tarhuna to Homs. The reason, as it now appears, was that the Axis had decided to evacuate the whole of Tripolitania and concentrate all their resources on the defence of Tunisia. The decision had been made by 31st December. Strategically the intention was sound; the German High Command believed that it would be possible to hold a permanent bridgehead in Tunisia which could tie down our forces there and continue to maintain the barrier in the Mediterranean communications at the Sicilian narrows. Naturally the more time that could be obtained for the purpose of evacuation the better and the mobile rearguard would therefore await our attack as far forward as was safe. The Italian infantry divisions began to move back in the first week in January and shortly afterwards the Trieste Division, including the remains of all the Italian divisions destroyed at Alamein, and 21 Panzer Division were detached from the Army and sent to southern Tunisia. The rearguard therefore consisted mainly of 90 Light and 15 Panzer Divisions.

We were naturally unaware of the enemy intention to withdraw right into Tunisia and to all appearance the problem now facing us was a most difficult one. It would be comparatively simple to turn the Buerat line but before we attempted that it was essential to be in a position to advance direct on Tripoli without a pause and seize the port. Just before we reached it we should be six hundred miles from our nearest base, at Benghazi, and to maintain any appreciable force over that distance would present insuperable difficulties. There was no suitable port on the Gulf of Sirte and everything had to come up by the one road; it would require at least two weeks to build up the reserves, especially the petrol, which would be needed for the dash to Tripoli. In the meantime there was a good deal of reconnaissance to be done. This country was quite unknown to us, except from the not very reliable Italian maps, and General Montgomery employed the Long Range Desert Group, which I had put under his command, for an extensive programme of reconnoitring routes forward and landing grounds. I cannot speak too highly of the work of this very specialized organization both now and on previous occasions; its members, all picked volunteers, had reduced the problem of moving across the desert to something between an exact science and a fine art.

General Montgomery's plan was to attack up the main road with 50 and 51 Divisions and make a wide outflanking movement through the desert to the left with 7 Armoured and 2 New Zealand Divisions, all under 30 Corps. He was very anxious, however, not to scare the enemy off his present line prematurely, for a withdrawal would multiply our problems. Accordingly the main bodies of this force were left right back and the enemy observed only with an armoured car screen from 4 Light Armoured Brigade. 7 Armoured Division was forty-five miles further east, the New Zealand Division a hundred miles and 51 Division, except for 154 Brigade on the Wadi Bey el Kebir, two hundred miles behind the front. This, of course, had the additional advantage of easing the problem of maintenance. Advance parties were brought forward to reconnoitre the proposed routes of attack and some artillery registration was carried out. The intention was to attack on 15th January if the enemy showed signs of withdrawing and on the 19th if he was prepared to stand. It was soon clear that the former was the more likely; the infantry began moving off, Pistoia and Spezia on the 3rd and 4th and the Young Fascists shortly afterwards. At this point, however, an unexpected difficulty arose. On 4th and 5th January very heavy gales at Benghazi caused severe damage; the outer mole was breached, four ships, one containing over two thousand tons of ammunition, were sunk and the capacity of the port was reduced by two-thirds. The intake of stores had to be supplemented by road from Tobruk. In order to make up for this while still sticking to the proposed date General Montgomery decided to drop 50 Division from the attack and leave it and the rest of 10 Corps, which he had intended to bring forward to the Agheila area, back in Cyrenaica between Tobruk and Benghazi. Here they would be grounded and all their vehicles used to supplement the transport needed for the extra road-haul, an additional three hundred miles.

The main bodies of the divisions of 30 Corps which had been left in rear moved forward on 14th January and went straight into action from the approach march at 0715 hours on the 15th – a rare example of the "encounter battle". On the right 51 Division met its first opposition beyond Buerat on the Wadi Kfef where it was held up all day. On the left the New Zealanders and 7 Armoured Division felt with some caution round the southern end of the enemy's anti-tank screen. By the evening we had reached the Wadi Zem Zem and seized the main crossing at El Faskia. The battle of the Buerat line was now over in a day and the enemy began to withdraw on his whole front, making for the hilly country covering Tripoli on the south-east. His main anxiety throughout was for his desert flank, since his left, retreating by the road, had to make a fairly wide circuit through Misurata and Zhten. He went back fairly slowly, therefore, on his right, pivoting on Bem Ulid until 90 Light Division on the coast had reached Homs; then he drew his southern forces back to Tarhuna and by the 19th was again facing south-west on the general line Homs – Tarhuna. The two divisions on our left found great difficulty in coming to grips with the enemy for the country was very difficult and, in the early stages, strewn with mines 51 Division, on the coast, met less enemy resistance but was delayed by heavy demolitions and mines all along the road. It was not until the early hours of 18th January that the division entered Misurata and the evening of the 19th when it entered Homs. We were now in close contact with the enemy all along his new position. By this time too our fighter aircraft had been installed on new landing grounds at Bir Dufan, south-west of Misurata, where they could attack the enemy in the hill country all the way to Tripoli.

So far the enemy had not been hustled but we should now be in a position to play on his fear for his right flank. Accordingly 4 Light Armoured Brigade, which had been operating far out on our left, was ordered to edge still more to the west; at the same time 22 Armoured Brigade, which had remained in Army Reserve between the two thrusts and had not yet been engaged, was sent due north to the coast road at Zliten. The intention was that, if the enemy reacted to our threat on the west, 51 Division, now reinforced with a hundred and fifty fresh tanks, should drive hard down the road to Tripoli. The ruse was successful: the enemy armour was kept south-west of Tarhuna to oppose 4 Light Armoured; Brigade and the Ramcke Parachute Brigade was moved across to the same area from Homs. The enemy does not appear to have noticed the arrival of 22 Armoured Brigade at Zliten.

In spite of this success in misleading the enemy, the difficulties of the terrain west of Homs made up for the fewness of the defenders in that sector. For the first thirty-five miles from Homs the road to Tripoli winds through ravines and it had been demolished in many places with great skill and thoroughness. A rapid advance was impossible over such country and in face of opposition. After several sharp actions with the rearguard, notably in the prepared defences west of Homs and again at Corradini, 51 Division emerged into the plain of Tripoli and captured Castelverde on the morning of 22nd January. Here they were only thirty miles from the town and since the country was now more open and suitable for the employment of armour 22 Armoured Brigade was brought into the lead. The rearguard of 90 Light Division made a final stand covering a demolished causeway fifteen miles east of Tripoli and darkness fell as the tanks were struggling in deep, soft sand to work round the flanks. There was only one company of infantry forward to deal with what was essentially an infantry problem. A battalion of 51 Division was therefore ordered forward, riding on "Valentine" tanks, to stage an attack in the full moonlight. The attack was successful and the infantry and tanks pressed on through the night down the main road to Tripoli. 22 Armoured Brigade followed, taking the by-pass road to approach the town from the south.

The advance of the left flanking column proceeded at about the same pace. Having entered Tarhuna on 19th January 7 Armoured Division was held up throughout the next day by enemy holding the hills flanking the defile through which the road descends into the plain of Tripoli. On the 21st the armoured cars of the division worked round the southern flank and entered the plain; at the same time leading elements of the New Zealand Division, which had been ordered to try the descent further west, found another way down the escarpment and came up on their left. But the way was not yet clear; the enemy rearguard was strong and continued to offer stiff resistance at Castel Benito, Azizia and Garian. Moreover it necessarily took some time to deploy our main forces in the plain, as the single road through the Tarhuna defile was demolished in several places and the alternative route which the New Zealanders had discovered traversed rough country. In the late afternoon of the 22nd, however, the enemy began to evacuate Garian, and shortly after Castel Benito also, and the southern approach to Tripoli was open.

11 Hussars entered Tripoli from the south at 0500 hours on 23rd January and at about the same time 1 Gordons of 51 Division came in from the west. At 0900 hours the same day General Montgomery received the formal surrender of the Italian authorities outside the city. The last of the enemy's armed forces had

left some hours before but the entire civilian population remained, in contrast with Benghazi which had been evacuated by the Italians. Eighth Army's entry was accepted peacefully; the Italian municipal and police officials remained at their posts and the British Military Administration assumed the government of the city and province in an atmosphere of calm. A curfew was imposed on military and civilians. Private and civic buildings and establishments were little damaged. The public services were still functioning, but the food supply was restricted. This was remedied as occasion permitted and British soldiers were forbidden to buy civilian food; none of them, except those whose duties made it essential, were quartered in the town. Many of the military establishments and installations had been wrecked and the damage to the port was particularly widespread. Quays and wharves were cratered, the mole breached, and the entrance to the harbour was blocked with sunken ships.

By the end of the month the rest of Tripolitania had been cleared. In this task we were aided by a column of Fighting French from the Chad Territory which, while Eighth Army was advancing along the coast, invaded the country from the south and conquered the Saharan province of the Fezzan. This represented a great feat of endurance and skill, for they started from Fort Lamy, fifteen hundred miles by air line south of Tripoli. The commander was General Leclerc,[29] later famous as the commander of 2 French Armoured Division, which liberated Paris. The Fezzan was held by numerous Italian garrisons, each disposed to cover a water source, so that failure at any one point would have meant the risk of complete lack of water for the force. The first garrison to be overwhelmed was that of Umm el Araneb which surrendered on 4th January. The northern garrisons heeded the warning and began to withdraw before the end of the year. The southern garrisons had greater difficulty in getting away, mainly because of shortage of transport and fuel and the low morale of their native troops. Gatrun, Murzuk and Sciuref surrendered in swift succession. Ghadames, the most westerly, was attacked on 10th January. By the 15th the remnants of the Sahara Command, reduced by desertion and surrender to two thirds of its original strength of about three thousand five hundred, were gathered at Mizda and Garian and it was they who constituted the garrison of the latter place until the 22nd. Next day Mizda surrendered to an attack. With the fall of Ghadames on 29th January the conquest of the Fezzan was completed.

I must mention before concluding this part of the narrative those others under my command in areas where no operations took place but where our forces were employed in the wearisome round of guard duties and the maintenance of law and order. Lieut.-General (now Sir George) Holmes, commanding the Ninth Army in Syria, Palestine and Trans-Jordan, had to deal with a political situation which was always delicate and which might in certain circumstances have become explosive. His forces were very small indeed and of various nationalities but he was entirely successful in the tasks he had been set. With the flight of the enemy from Egypt the task, which had been given the Egyptian army of watching the

Suez Canal for mines dropped by enemy aircraft became superfluous. I visited in the course of the winter our garrisons in Syria, Cyprus, Eritrea and the Sudan to confirm by observation the soundness of our existing arrangements. It was on small detachments such as these that the security of our Middle East base depended and I was glad of the opportunity of assuring them of the value of their unspectacular assignments.

I should like also to express my appreciation of the assistance I received from my colleagues of the Royal Navy and Royal Air Force, Admiral Harwood and Air Chief Marshal Tedder. Admiral Harwood had succeeded to the command of our naval forces in the Eastern Mediterranean at a time when our resources were at their lowest ebb. Our only two battle-ships in the Eastern Mediterranean had been severely damaged in 1941 by a daring assault by Italian swimming saboteurs in Alexandria harbour, leaving only light forces in the area. A large part of Alexandria harbour was occupied by the former French Eastern Mediterranean Squadron to whom we had given refuge and continued maintenance since July 1940; at that time, however, they could not see their way to throwing in their lot with the Allies. Our submarines continued to do most valuable work but perhaps I may be permitted to lay particular stress on the support which the Navy gave to the Army in our westward advance. Their work in reopening demolished ports and the convoying of supplies was of inestimable value and without it we could not have maintained our forces in Libya. Air Chief Marshal Tedder was to be my colleague in many campaigns still lying in the future. He had the most remarkable grasp of air problems of any Royal Air Force officer with whom I have served and a comprehension also of the needs of the Army. He organized, with the invaluable assistance of Air Vice Marshal Coningham, his Air Commander in the Desert throughout the campaign, the most complete measure of air cover for the fighting troops but the services of the Royal Air Force went beyond this purely defensive task, vital though it is; reaching out ahead of our advancing forces and striking the enemy without pause in his retreat he showed how a tactical air force well handled can intervene to effect in the ground battle. These actions are spectacular and obvious, but I would draw attention also to the degree of administrative skill which is required to maintain the forward movement of an air force at such a speed as frequently to outstrip the troops on the ground and seize new bases ever further forward from which to strike the enemy.

The capture of Tripoli, three months to the day from the opening of our offensive, marked a definite phase in the African campaign. Tripoli had always shone as a far distant goal in the eyes of the Desert Army since the time when the first armoured cars crossed the frontier wire into Libya on the morning of 11th June 1940. When Eighth Army advanced further out of Libya into Tunisia it became part of a large machine and a break at this point is therefore appropriate. The desert had been left behind; by comparison Tunisia is almost European. And none could doubt that the end of the long years of fighting in Africa was now near at hand.

PART II. – THE CONQUEST OF TUNISIA.

Formation of Eighteenth Army Group.

On 14th January, 1943, a conference of the Combined Chiefs of Staff opened at Anfa near Casablanca in French Morocco. It was attended by the Prime Minister and the President and by General Eisenhower, Commander-in-Chief, Allied Expeditionary Force. I was also summoned to attend and flew from Cairo with Air Chief Marshal Tedder. Among the other decisions taken at this historic meeting was the decision to reorganize the chain of command in Africa. Eighth Army was to come under General Eisenhower's command when it entered Tunisia from Tripolitania. In order to co-ordinate the action of the large forces, of three different nationalities, which would then be engaged on the same task, the conquest of Tunisia, an Army Group Headquarters was to be set up. I was to assume command of this, which would involve responsibility for the entire conduct of operations in Tunisia; I was also appointed Deputy Commander-in-Chief, Allied Expeditionary Force. My Headquarters was known as Eighteenth Army Group, combining the numbers of First and Eighth Armies; I proposed to make it a very small and mobile Tactical Headquarters to direct the battle from close up. The staff to form this headquarters was flown round by transport aircraft from Cairo; I myself arrived in Algeria on 15th February and assumed command on 19th February. In a directive from General Eisenhower issued on the 17th[30] I was instructed that my mission was the early destruction of all Axis forces in Tunisia.

Situation in February, 1943.

Before proceeding to summarize the dispositions of our own troops and the enemy at the time I assumed command it is essential to recapitulate briefly the course of events in the preceding three months, since the very complicated situation then existing was a natural development of the confused and varied fortunes of the fighting during that period. The original expeditionary force which had come ashore on 8th November, 1942, was divided into three task forces which had landed on the west coast of Morocco, north and south of Casablanca, at Oran, and at Algiers. The former two were American; the landing at Algiers, though under American command, included a British Brigade Group and it was the intention to build up into Algiers as rapidly as possible the advance elements of the British First Army, under Lieut.-General (now Sir Kenneth) Anderson. General Eisenhower's mission was first to secure his base in the three assault areas and establish communications between them, and then to launch First Army eastwards from Algiers into Tunisia to seize the ports of Tunis and Bizerta. In accomplishing the former task he had first to overcome the resistance of the French garrison, numbering over a hundred thousand regular troops in Algeria and Morocco. It was believed that these forces would resist the landings and if that resistance was prolonged, although after the first few days the French would probably have to withdraw to the mountains and conduct a guerrilla campaign, we should probably be faced with at least three months' fighting before our base and communications could be deemed safe. This appreciation, and the danger of venturing without air cover into ports which the German bombers could reach, were the main reasons why the most easterly landing was made at Algiers, instead of nearer to Tunisia, which would have given us a better start in the race for the Tunisian ports. In order to do this it would have been necessary to land all three assault forces inside the Mediterranean, for our limited resources, especially in shipping, could not be stretched to produce a fourth assault force. But this would mean that our lines of communication would run exclusively through the Straits of Gibraltar which could be closed if Spain entered the war on the side of the Axis. For this reason it was essential to employ one of the assault forces on the Atlantic coast of Morocco to secure a possible alternative line of communications.

The French did oppose our landings but on 10th November Admiral Darlan agreed to an armistice and ordered all troops in North Africa to cease resistance. This was a tremendous gain and reduced the unhappy period of hostilities with the French from a possible three months to two days. And not only did they agree to cease resistance but also to throw in their lot with us in the fight against the Axis. The Armistice came in for some criticism on the political side but it seems to me very likely that it may have considerably reduced the duration of the war, for if the Germans had been given time they could probably have built up sufficient strength in their Tunisian bridgehead to hold out all the summer of 1943. As it was General Eisenhower was able to turn all his attention at once to the task of pushing First Army at full speed towards Tunisia. He had the great advantage that he could now rely on the French local authorities to preserve order and the French communications system to facilitate his advance. In spite of this there were still tremendous difficulties to be faced. The distance from Algiers to Tunis is five hundred and sixty miles, by two roads and an indifferent railway. Almost the whole of this stretch of country is very mountainous. Communications were made more difficult by the fact, gratifying in itself, that the French were mobilizing an army of thirty-two battalions and for this had requisitioned almost all available local transport and required the use of the railway. First Army, when it began its eastwards advance, consisted only of one infantry division, the 78th, reinforced later by an armoured regimental group, two commando and two parachute battalions.

The decision to make a dash for Tunis, though bold, was undoubtedly correct. The advance was pressed by land, sea and air; Bougie was occupied by 11th November, Bone on 12th November, by a British parachute battalion, and by 18th November our advanced forces were operating east of Gebel Abiud on the coast road and Béja on the inland road, about sixty miles from Bizerta and Tunis respectively. At both points we were in contact with German troops. These had begun to arrive, in the first place by air, on 10th November, meeting no resistance from the French authorities in Tunisia. On 15th November a United States parachute battalion occupied Youks Les Bains and Tebessa, in south-eastern Algeria, and co-operated with the French detachments at Gafsa in southern

Tunisia. Between 17th November and 25th December two main attempts were made to capture Tunis. The first succeeded in advancing, on 28th November, as far as Djedeida, on the road between Tunis and Bizerta and only twelve miles from the former. At this point the enemy counter-attacked strongly with tanks and dive-bombers; the latter were able to operate from good airfields only a short distance in rear and our own air forces were unable to give cover, since the rain had put all their temporary landing grounds out of action. Our forces on the inland road were therefore obliged to withdraw to Medjez el Bab. This town, as its name "the Ford of the Pass" shows, is of great strategic importance. It lies on the broad Medjerda river which breaks out of the mountains at this point to flow into the plain of Tunis through a defile commanded on the west by the Gebel Ahmera, known to our troops as "Longstop", and on the east by the Gebel Bou Aoukaz. The bridge which has replaced the ford carries the main road from Tunis to the west. On 22nd December, as the first stage of a renewed assault on Tunis, a successful attack was made on Gebel Ahmera. At this point the rain, which had already caused severe difficulties of movement, became torrential for a period of three days. The offensive had to be abandoned and on 25th December the enemy recaptured Gebel Ahmera.

This ended the attempt to take Tunis in a rush and it was clear that we should have to build up forces for a deliberate operation. It was also clear that the enemy would be able to build up faster than we could, for his lines of communication through Italy and Sicily were much more reliable and shorter than ours from the United Kingdom and United States and from his ports of entry to the front they were very short and over good roads in flat country.[31] It was necessary, therefore, to go on to the defensive in the northern sector though General Eisenhower considered the possibilities of mounting an offensive by United States troops against the southern Tunisian port of Sfax in order to cut the lines of supply to Rommel's Panzer Army. This plan was abandoned in January. The next two months were therefore occupied in consolidating the northern sector as far as possible with the limited means available and in beating off enemy attempts to get round our southern flank.

The latter raised difficult problems of command. The area from Pont du Fahs southward along the mountain range of the Eastern Dorsale was held by the French troops of XIX Corps, with some British and United States detachments. Further south the United States II Corps was assembling around Tebessa, with detachments forward co-operating with the French. As a result of General Giraud's refusal to place French troops under the orders of a British commander, XIX Corps had to come under a rather indirect command from Allied Force Headquarters and for this reason II Corps also remained under General Eisenhower. The weakness of this arrangement was show a when a German attack on the French in the Ousseltia valley, at the northern hinge of the two Dorsale ranges, made dangerous progress and had to be halted by the hasty diversion of British and American troops from First Army and II Corps. As a result General Anderson was appointed by General Eisenhower on 21st January to "co-ordinate" the whole front and on 24th January both XIX and II Corps were placed directly under his command. At the same time General Kuter, of the United States Army Air Corps, was appointed to co-ordinate all Allied air support under command of General Spaatz then Deputy Commander-in-Chief Allied Air Forces.

Such, in brief, were the antecedents, of the situation that I found on arriving to assume command in Tunisia. At the actual moment of my arrival I was met by a serious crisis on my southern flank where a battle had been raging since 14th February. I was therefore flung straight into a position where I had to give my main attention to the needs of the tactical situation; but I had already given much thought to the strategy which it would be necessary to pursue and was confident that, when the immediate dangers had been averted, and after a necessary period of complete reorganization, I should be able to work out the strategic answer to the problem of Tunisia on the lines made necessary by the nature of the country and the strength and dispositions of the opposing forces.

Tunisia is bounded politically on the west by a frontier running almost due north and south and therefore parallel to the sea which bounds it on the east. The most important part of this long north-south oblong is the coastal plain, known as the Sahel, which is generally flat and covered with olive groves. In the north, however, the Algerian mountains send down long spurs which run east and west towards the sea at Bizerta. West of Tunis they leave a space for the fertile plain of the Medjerda, after it has burst through the gap at Medjez el Bab, but south of Medjez there is a tangle of mountains to the west of the Goubellat plain which culminate in the three massifs of Gebel Mansour, Fkirine and Zaghouan. These are a nodal point of a new system of relief; from Gebel Zaghouan a series of mountains extends to the Gulf of Tunis in the north and to the sea in the east, reaching, after a gap in the Grombalian plain, up to the peninsula of Cape Bon; from Gebel Fkirine spring two long ridges trending south and south-west and known as the Eastern and Western Dorsales.

The Eastern Dorsale is a long, narrow ridge, rising to between two and three thousand feet, which extends almost due south as far as Maknassy, where it meets an east–west chain stretching from Gafsa. It is pierced by passes at Pichon, Fondouk, Faid and Maknassy, it is only at these four points, therefore, that an army advancing from the west can break into the plain of central and southern Tunisia. Round its southern end it is turned by a road from Gafsa to Gabes but this too runs through a difficult and very long mountain defile. Further to the south lies the region of the "Chotts"; these are very extensive salt marshes which narrow the coastal plain to a gap of only fifteen miles. The town of Gabes lies on the coast at the southern end of this gap. South of the Gabes gap the flat country is split by the north-west to south-east line of the Matmata mountains. To the east is cultivated country, traversed by the main road to Medenine and, eventually Tripoli; to the west is desert, almost entirely waterless and uninhabited. West of the Eastern Dorsale there is another range interposed across the course of an advance from the west. This at its northern end is known as the Western Dorsale, which runs south-west from Gebel Fkirine, and fades out eventually north-west of Gafsa. The range is pierced by passes at Maktar, Sbiba, Kasserine and Feriana; it is not so serious an obstacle as the Eastern Dorsale. In the south the divergence of the two Dorsale ranges leaves a wide plain, in parts semi-desert.

The coastal plain is well roaded and, in general, north–south movement is easy. East–west movement is canalized by the mountains. In the north two roads, from Gebel Abiud and Béja, meet at Mateur and run through Ferryville to Bizerta. In the Medjerda valley the main road leads to Tunis from Medjez el Bab and a secondary road parallels it to the south, starting from Goubellat. The next east–west road, leaving the Medjez road at Le Kef, crosses the Western Dorsale beyond Maktar and the Eastern Dorsale at Pichon, with a by-pass through Fondouk, seventy miles south of Goubellat. Another road from Le Kef runs through Sbiba, Sbeitla and Faid; south of that the roads which cross the Western Dorsale at Kasserine or Feriana have to make a detour through Gafsa, from where a good road runs direct to Gabes and a poor road crosses the Eastern Dorsale at the Maknassy defile. These eight roads offer the only practicable routes for crossing a mountain-defended front of some two hundred and twenty miles; they can all be easily blocked with relatively small forces. One further road leads into Tunisia, the road from Tripoli, and to block this the French had constructed a massive system of permanent defences, the Mareth line.

On 14th February Allied dispositions were as follows. 5 Corps commanded the sector north of a line from Le Kef to south of Bou Arada with under command from north to south 46 and 78 Infantry and 6 Armoured Divisions. One American Regimental Combat Team of 1 Infantry Division was under command of 78 Division, south of Medjez. The line in this sector ran from the coast due north of Jefna south through Sidi Nsir station, then south-east to cover Medjez and then due south through Goubellat and Bou Arada. In the next sector to the south the French XIX Corps held the Eastern Dorsale as far south as Pichon. The northern part of this front was held by the Algerian Division with 1 Guards and 36 Infantry Brigades under command. The southern part of the Corps sector was entrusted to 1 United States Infantry Division, less one Regimental Combat Team, and an Armoured Combat Command of 1 Armoured Division. A British Army Group, Royal Artillery, supported XIX Corps throughout the campaign. From south of a line from Thala to Pichon the United States II Corps commanded the area of the plain between the two Dorsale ranges, supported by the French Constantine Division and part of a British Armoured Car Regiment. The American forces consisted of 1 Armoured Division, less one Combat Command but plus one Regimental Combat Team from I Infantry Division, and a Ranger Battalion. II Corps held in general the line of the Eastern Dorsale with the important exception of the Faid pass. On 30th January the Germans had attacked this pass with a force which included over sixty tanks and overwhelmed the small French garrison before the American armour could come to its assistance. They then dug in firmly and resisted all attempts to dislodge them; an action on 2nd February was costly in American tanks and II Corps decided to pull back to

Sidi Bou Zid and observe the Faid area from there. The Germans thus had a gateway through which, if they chose, they could debouch in considerable strength to attack our tenuously held southern flank.

In the extreme south 30 Corps, after the capture of Tripoli, had followed up the retreating enemy only with light forces. 7 Armoured Division (now 23 Armoured and 131 Lorried Infantry Brigades) maintained pressure along the coast road but were hampered by mines and demolitions. To hasten the enemy's withdrawal 30 Corps used 4 Light Armoured Brigade in a series of outflanking movements south of the main road. By the end of the month the enemy had retired to the edge of the marshes which stretch along the Tunisian frontier from the coast southwards for about forty miles. 4 Light Armoured Brigade patrols pressed on into southern Tunisia but enemy resistance lingered on in the marshes, blocking any further advance down the road. General Montgomery therefore decided to throw more weight into the outflanking movement, using 8 Armoured Brigade, which had been resting near Tripoli and now relieved 23 Armoured Brigade. Moving round by way of El Assa 8 Armoured Brigade secured a bridgehead across the marshes and took up positions astride the track leading to Ben Gardane. The enemy reacted hastily to this move and brought 15 Panzer Division forward from Ben Gardane to support the strongpoint which he had prepared at Taguelmit. At this point, however, heavy rain began to fall again and it was necessary to build a causeway over the marshes before our advance could proceed. As the causeway was nearing completion the enemy withdrew and on 15th February 30 Corps entered Ben Gardane, the first important town in Tunisia, without meeting opposition.

Enemy dispositions, like ours, reflected the effects of circumstances rather than design. At about the same time as the Allies, and for the same reasons, the Axis also created an Army Group Headquarters to control all forces in Tunisia; it was named "Army Group Africa'" and was commanded by Field-Marshal Rommel. Under it were two Army Headquarters, representing the forces which had hurried into the country to oppose First Army and those which had been driven out of Libya by the advance of Eighth Army. The former were known as 5 Panzer Army, commanded by General von Arnim, and the latter, having dropped the title of "German-Italian Panzer Army" when Rommel left with most of his German staff to form the new Army Group Headquarters, were now organized as I (Italian) Army. 1 Army was commanded by General Messe (subsequently promoted to Marshal on the day of his capitulation), one of the younger generation of Italian commanders who had acquired a good reputation in command of an Italian Corps in Russia. It was organized into the same three Corps, German Africa Corps, Italian XX and XXI Corps. 5 Panzer Army had no Corps Headquarters under command except the Italian XXX Corps which had been set up at Sfax in the early days of the campaign but never played any significant part. The Corps organization is of very little importance to an understanding of the course of operations and even the Army organization was liable to sudden modifications in the interests of creating an Army Group reserve; it will be more useful, therefore, to sketch out the divisional dispositions on the ground as they were on 14th February.

In the north the sector from the coast to inclusive Mateur was held by the Broich Division. This was a scratch formation called after the commander (and later, when the commander changed, called the Manteuffel Division) which consisted largely of the assorted units which had been the first to arrive in November. Taken by surprise by our North African landings the German High Command naturally turned first to airborne troops and two regiments and an engineer battalion were hastily flown in,[32] including the Koch Storm Regiment and the Barenthin Regiment, formed from two airborne training establishments. These two regiments, together with various independent battalions and spare tank and artillery units, made up Broich's command. To his south, covering the Medjerda valley, was 334 Infantry Division, a newly raised formation which arrived in the second half of December and first half of January. On its left, covering the Goubellat plain, was 10 Panzer Division, a regular armoured division which had fought in the French campaign; it had arrived by the middle of December. The greater part of the Eastern Dorsale was the responsibility of the Italians, under the command of 1 Superga Division. This was reinforced with two battalions of Italian marines and the German 47 Grenadier Regiment from Crete. Also in this general area was a German heavy tank battalion, the 501st, equipped with the new Mark VI "Tiger" tank, and the advance elements of the Hermann Goering Panzer Division.

In the centre, behind Faid, the enemy had accumulated an Army Group Reserve which was intended to strike out at our southern flank. The main strength of this was provided by 21 Panzer Division, which had been withdrawn from Tripolitania in January ahead of the withdrawal of the other forces there and reinforced in tanks by the absorption of an independent tank battalion which had arrived earlier in Tunisia; also included were half 10 Panzer Division and a detachment of 501 Tank Battalion. Operating on the southern axis from Gabes to Gafsa was the Italian 131 Centauro Armoured Division and a detachment of infantry and armour from the German Africa Corps, mainly from 15 Panzer Division. Facing Eighth Army were XX and XXI Corps with four Italian infantry divisions, Spezia, Young Fascists, Trieste and Pistoia, plus the German 90 and 164 Light Divisions, and the remainder of the German Africa Corps. The Saharan Group, the remains of the Italian Saharan command, was operating in the desert west of the Matmata mountains, reinforced by a German reconnaissance unit. Field-Marshal Rommel's intention, having abandoned Tripolitania and fallen back to the Mareth line, was to deal a swift blow at the Americans in the plain west of Faid in order to make sure that they would not be able to come in on his rear when he was heavily engaged with Eighth Army. He knew he would have time for this, because there must necessarily be a considerable interval before General Montgomery would be able to bring really strong forces into southern Tunisia and begin the assault of the Mareth line. His long term policy was defensive: to retain a bridgehead in Africa, and there is considerable evidence to show that the German High Command expected to be able to retain at least part of Tunisia for a long time to come.

The Axis forces in Tunisia amounted to the equivalent of fourteen divisions, of which about half were Italian, including one Italian and three German armoured divisions. The Allied forces at that date in contact with the enemy amounted to nine divisions, including two-French divisions with obsolete and inadequate equipment; two more divisions in Tripoli would soon become available. I expected to be able to build up to a strength of about twenty divisions by May, if all went well, but at the moment Rommel was being reinforced faster than I was and his normal intake was about a thousand men per day. The reason for this was that he had a short and easy route of entry from Sicily and I determined that my main effort must be directed to cutting this line of communications. In order to do this it would be necessary to gain air superiority over the Sicilian narrows, and for this we should need the airfields in the Tunisian plain, especially those at and around Kairouan. The immediate problem was therefore to get Eighth Army through the Gabes gap into the flat country where their armoured superiority would have full play and could be expected to carry them in one sweep to the beginning of the mountainous area at Enfidaville. With the enemy once back in a comparatively small perimeter round Tunis and Bizerta we should be able to establish a tight blockade by sea and air. This would mean that I had the enemy held in a complete strangle-hold and, with full command of the initiative, could deliver the *coup de grace* at the time and place of my own choosing.

The Battle of Kasserine.

On the morning of 14th February a strong German force, estimated to contain about a hundred tanks, emerged from the Faid pass and attacked the positions held by 1 United States Armoured Division at Sidi Bou Zid. The American division was rather dispersed at the time the attack was made, with detachments at Sidi Bou Zid, on the Gebel Lessouda, an isolated mountain north of the village, at Sbeitla and south of Hadjeb el Aioun on the Sbeitla – Pichon road. The German armour was handled with great dash and supported by a strong force of dive-bombers. Our forward battery positions were overrun and while a tank battle raged in front of Sidi Bou Zid another enemy force had by 1130 hours cut off the infantry holding positions on the Gebel Lessouda. Our tank losses were heavy and the battle became fluid and difficult to control. By evening 1 Armoured Division had concentrated between Sidi Bou Zid and Sbeitla, and next day, the 15th, attempted a counter-attack. This was unsuccessful and the armour drew off towards Sbeitla, leaving the infantry on Gebel Lessouda still isolated; some were able to withdraw but many were taken prisoner. It was now clear that our armour had been too depleted to hold the plain and a withdrawal was ordered back to the Western Dorsale. To conform, the Ranger battalion and the Derbyshire Yeomanry detachment had been already withdrawn from Gafsa which was entered by the enemy on the afternoon of the 15th and the French withdrew in their sector from the Eastern to the Western Dorsale. This movement was carried out in good order and the enemy followed up only slowly. General Anderson began to prepare a reserve to restore the situation. 26 Armoured Brigade had moved back to Siliana in order to hand in their "Crusader" tanks in exchange for the "Shermans" with which they were to be re-equipped; instead they were moved hastily southwards to Maktar, still with their "Crusaders," and two squadrons of "Shermans" from the replacement pool, with scratch British crews, were ordered south to join 1 Armoured Division, 1 Guards Brigade and 39 United States Regimental Combat Team (the advanced unit of 9 Division) were ordered to Sbiba, north of Sbeitla.

American losses now amounted to about eighty-six medium tanks and thirty field guns and 1 Armoured Division was therefore very considerably weakened. At midnight on 16th/17th February the enemy once more attacked at Sbeitla, in bright moonlight, and after fighting all that night and next morning broke into the town. 1 Armoured Division, withdrew westwards and went into reserve south-east of Tebessa to re-form. The enemy followed up and occupied Kasserine; Feriana had already been occupied by the force operating from the south which had been joined by the detachment from the German Africa Corps. II Corps had by this been forced back off the plain into the hills; the loss of the airfield at Thelepte, near Feriana, was a heavy blow but all aircraft and stores there were either evacuated or destroyed. Rommel had now his whole force concentrated and halted his troops during the 18th to allow for the necessary re-grouping and replenishing. He had driven a big salient into our lines and had the choice of three roads on which to exploit to turn our flank still further: through Sbeitla and Sbiba or through Kasserine and Thala, both converging on Le Kef, and through Feriana on Tebessa. His forces, though they had suffered loss, were relatively intact; the Allied dispositions for defence had been hastily taken up and suffered from the inevitable intermingling of units of three different nationalities.

This was the situation with which I was presented when I landed at Algiers from Tripoli on 15th February. After discussions with General Eisenhower I flew on to Telergma, south-west of Constantine. From here I went straight to General Anderson's headquarters and set out on a tour of inspection of the front. On the 16th I visited 5 Corps, on the northern front and on the 17th XIX Corps. I then went on to II Corps sector where I spent the 18th and 19th. I found the position even more critical than I had expected and a visit to the Kasserine area showed that in the inevitable confusion of the retreat American, French and British troops had been inextricably mingled, there was no co-ordinated plan of defence and definite uncertainty as to command. At the first pass I visited, the Dernaia pass, I had to nominate on the spot the senior American officer as the responsible commander of the sector and ordered him to hold his ground to the last. In view of the situation I decided to assume command at once, without waiting for the 20th, the official date,[33] and after completing this tour of the front returned for that night to Constantine, where my headquarters had been temporarily set up. It was clear to me that although Rommel's original intention had been merely to give such a blow to II Corps as would leave his right rear secure while he prepared to meet Eighth Army, he now had much bigger ideas. From previous experience I knew him to be a man who would always exploit success by every possible means to the limit of rashness, and there now glittered before him the prospect of a great tactical victory. If he could break through our weak screening positions on the Western Dorsale, at Kasserine or Sbiba, he would find few natural obstacles to an advance northwards; such an advance would at once take in rear XIX Corps, whose French troops were already shaken by their losses in January and their sudden withdrawal from the Eastern Dorsale, and if it could be successfully pushed to Le Kef he would be in behind 5 Corps as well. This would disrupt the whole front in Tunisia and bring on a withdrawal if not a disaster. In face of this threat I issued orders that there would be no further withdrawal and that the front would be stabilized on the present positions.

On 19th February the enemy carried out exploratory attacks against all three roads I have mentioned, attempting to find out which would prove the easiest for an attack. His main weight was on the right, against Sbiba; the attack on the pass above Kasserine was made by about a battalion of infantry and the force probing the Dernaia pass above Feriana, on the Tebessa road, was only of the nature of a small reconnaissance. South of Sbiba 1 Guards Brigade held firm and repulsed the enemy but the attack in the Kasserine pass was more successful and the enemy began to infiltrate through the American positions. Accordingly on the next day, the 20th, this thrust was strongly reinforced and the other two abandoned; the pass was cleared and 21 Panzer Division, with the infantry and some of the armour of the detachment from the German Africa Corps, pressed on into the basin beyond. Here Rommel found himself faced with two alternatives, for the road, after traversing the pass, diverges to west and north. The former direction would take him to Tebessa, our main southern base and airfield centre, but the road passes through difficult country; the other route runs mainly on the flat and leads via Thala to Le Kef. Accordingly on 21st February he passed 10 Panzer Division battle group[34] through 21 Panzer Division in a northward thrust, leaving the screening left flank to the German Africa Corps detachment.

The 21st was the critical day. Feeling fairly confident that, after piercing the Kasserine pass, Rommel would thrust up the northern road I had already ordered General Anderson to concentrate his armour for the defence of Thala. Accordingly on the 20th he brought across to that area a composite force based on 26 Armoured Brigade Group, reinforced by the 2/5 Leicesters, and on the 21st they were joined by 2 Hampshires and two field artillery battalions of 9 United States Division, which was being brought up by forced marches to the scene of action. The fighting south of Thala was extremely fierce in relatively open country and the fortunes of war changeable. At one moment a few enemy tanks succeeded in forcing their way over the low pass south of the village but they were shot to pieces by our field guns at close range. The situation was exceedingly grave and was only stabilized after periods of extreme danger by the energy and initiative of the handful of gallant troops on the spot. Subsidiary thrusts were also tried, to see whether our concentrations at Thala had weakened us elsewhere at Sbiba the attack was halted by the opportune arrival of a squadron of "Churchills" from 25 Tank Brigade and on the Kasserine – Tebessa road 1 United States Armoured Division managed to hold, at Gebel Hamra, the first of the mountain passes, the attack of the Panzer Grenadier Regiment Africa. By midday on the 22nd Rommel appreciated that his casualties were increasing at a disproportionate rate and that the opportunity for further exploitation had passed; he therefore ordered the attack to be broken off. His withdrawal was, as always, well conducted with a most liberal use of mines and explosive devices to discourage pursuit. He was able to extricate all his tanks with the exception of nine, which were too heavily damaged and had to be abandoned. Some Italian Bersaglieri from the Centauro Division were employed in an infantry attack to cover the withdrawal of the Germans and suffered fairly heavy losses. Otherwise there was little opposition from enemy troops and by the evening of 25th February the Kasserine pass was again in our hands. By the 28th we had reoccupied Sbeitla, Kasserine and Feriana and the enemy had withdrawn his main force to the Eastern Dorsale. He still retained Gafsa, but it was lightly garrisoned by the Centauro Division and a German battle group.

At the crisis of the Kasserine battle, on 21st February, I ordered General Montgomery to create as powerful a threat as possible on the enemy's southern flank. He was not as yet well placed to do this since his administrative position was not yet firm; on the other hand there was no immediate risk in advancing ahead of his main strength since the enemy main forces were fully engaged elsewhere. Medenine, the road junction in front of the Mareth line, had been occupied by us on the 18th and by the next day headquarters and one Brigade of 51 Division were at Ben Gardane, with the other two brigades moving forward from Tripoli. By the 24th Eighth Army had two armoured car regiments in contact with the outposts of the Mareth line and General Leclerc's force, now known as "L" force, had occupied Ksar Rhilane, a desert outpost thirty miles west of the Matmata mountains; 51 Division continued to move up and all three brigades were forward of Medenine, but not in contact with the enemy, by the 25th. In the meanwhile I had informed General Montgomery on 23rd February that the situation at Kasserine was now improved and ordered him, while keeping up a display of force, not to prejudice the future by undue risks. He replied on the 27th that he had been careful to keep well balanced and considered his present position adequately strong.

The Battle of Kasserine had given me many anxious moments. As in his advance to El Alamein, Rommel had over-exploited a considerable initial success to leave himself in a worse position than before; he can hardly be blamed for his attempts to snatch a great victory, for on both occasions he came very near to it, but the result was equally disastrous for him. The United States II Corps had been unfortunate in that their first major battle had been against such experienced troops and so dashing an enemy commander but, as General Eisenhower reported on 26th February, they were resolved to benefit immediately from the battle experience gained by the intensive training of all formations. Their improvement was indeed continuous and outstanding throughout the campaign. Another result of the battle had been that Allied formations of all three nationalities were very mixed up over the whole front and my first intention was to carry out a thorough reorganization. On the day I assumed command, in an order issued on 19th February, I laid down the following principles. Separate British, American and French sectors were to be organized forthwith under their respective commanders. The "bits and pieces" were to be collected, and reorganized into their proper formations. The front was to be held by static troops, and armoured and mobile forces withdrawn and grouped to form a reserve striking force; all troops were to be extensively trained and re-equipped where necessary. Finally, immediate plans were to be prepared to regain the initiative, starting with carefully planned minor operations to force the enemy to react, but, I added, "there must be no failures". I organized at the same time an Anglo-American battle school, attended also when possible by French officers, where with the assistance of some experienced officers from Eighth Army the tactical lessons of recent battles were studied.

My strategic intentions I explained in a signal on the 21st. The object of the whole operation was to destroy the entire enemy force in Tunisia and the key to this was the capture of Tunis. The campaign would be divided into two phases. In the first the main object would be to get Eighth Army north of the Gabes gap, where it would gain contact with First Army and gain freedom of manoeuvre to develop its superiority in mobility and striking power. In this phase the role of the First Army would be to assist Eighth Army in getting through the gap – as soon, that is to say, as the Kasserine situation had been stabilized and First Army had regained the initiative. The method would be to stage carefully prepared, timed and controlled operations aimed at securing dominating localities from which further advances could be made, this would force the enemy to react and draw off reserves which could be used against Eighth Army. These restricted operations, as I have already noted, would have the additional effect of assisting the training of the less experienced troops in First Army and of increasing self-confidence and raising morale. In the second phase of operations the efforts of both Armies would be directed towards securing airfields which would enable us to develop the ever-growing strength of our Anglo-American air forces. When we had achieved that we should be able to co-ordinate to the full the striking power of all three services in drawing a tight net round the enemy's position in Tunisia.

One of the main difficulties of the problem was that I was working within severe limitations of time. The Casablanca conference had decided that after Tunisia had been cleared the operation to open the Mediterranean to our shipping should be completed by the invasion and conquest of Sicily. In making plans for this operation it was appreciated that the campaign in Africa must end by the middle of May in order to give us a chance to bring the Tunisian ports into full use. Otherwise the invasion would have to be postponed until August when the deterioration of weather conditions might make the operation impossible. This was a difficult time-table to observe and it was with great satisfaction that

I found in the event that I had Bizerta and Tunis eight days before the allotted date and that all resistance ceased in Africa with two days yet to spare.

Fifth Army Offensive in the North.

Before these plans could be put into effect or any thorough reorganization undertaken I found myself faced once more by a new enemy initiative. As the rearguards of Rommel's striking force were trailing back to the Eastern Dorsale von Arnim attacked with the full strength of 5 Army all along the British 5 Corps front, from the sea to Gebel Mansour. The four principal thrusts were made towards Jefna, on the northernmost road, Sidi Nsir on the Mateur – Béja road, at Medjez and north of Bou Arada. No doubt the intention was to keep us at full strain at a time when it was known that the Kasserine crisis had forced us to weaken the northern sector and produced a certain disorganization of our forces; it would also distract us from the pursuit of Rommel, who now proposed to use his Army Group reserve in a blow at Eighth Army. It must, however, have also been the German intention to drive us back into the mountains in the north, if possible capturing Medjez, in order to increase their security in this sector and release reserves, especially of armour, for the coming battle in the more open country of southern Tunisia. The attack came at an awkward time for us, for it prevented us from forming that mobile reserve which I had in mind and forced us to delay still further the necessary reorganisation; for instance General Anderson saw himself obliged to create an *ad hoc* divisional organization, given the name of "Y" Division, to control 38 Infantry Brigade and 1 Parachute Brigade in the area of Goubellat and Bou Arada. The fighting was hard, and the enemy gained some important ground but were unable to attain any vital objectives. The most important feature in our favour was that we retained our essential gateway at Medjez el Bab.

The main blows on 26th February were down the Béja road from Mateur and south of Medjez, the former was made by the Barenthin parachutists and part of 334 Division and the latter by the recently arrived Hermann Goering Regiment, both supported by tanks. An attack on Medjez itself, south of the river, was repulsed with heavy losses after small initial success. The attack further south penetrated deeply into our lines but was beaten back north of El Aroussa while our defences round Bou Arada, some ten miles to the west, held firm in spite of being threatened from three sides. The attack down the Béja road was more formidable; our outpost at Sidi Nsir was overwhelmed after a very gallant resistance but the time gained allowed 46 Division to occupy the pass leading to Béja. Very heavy fighting continued here for a week; losses in 46 Division were heavy but the defence held firm. The enemy were able, however, to advance their positions in the mountains over-looking the Béja – Medjez road from the north, and Medjez now represented the extreme point of a dangerous-looking salient. There was some feeling at First Army Headquarters that it would be advisable to evacuate Medjez, on the grounds that its fall was almost inevitable and that a withdrawal into the mountains to the west would place us in a stronger defensive position and enable us to economize in troops. I was determined, however, to retain our gateway into the Tunis plain and ordered the town to be held at all costs.

While these attacks on Béja and Medjez were proceeding with varying success the enemy was finding better fortune in his thrust on the northernmost road. The first attacks on our positions west of Jefna, mainly by Italian troops, were held; but on 2nd March the offensive was renewed in this sector with five German battalions, four of them parachutists, and succeeded in gaining several miles. On the 3rd the enemy captured Sedjenane, some twelve miles west of Jefna. 46 Division was obliged to withdraw to a fresh position at Gebel Tamera, about eight miles further west. The enemy's advance on the northernmost road, which had hitherto been of little importance from the point of view of ground lost by us, was now becoming more serious as it threatened Gebel Abiod and the vital lateral road from there to Béja. 46 Division had been weakened by continuous losses in men and General Anderson therefore reinforced it with I Parachute Brigade and the Corps Franc d'Afrique, a French volunteer unit. In spite of this reinforcement the enemy continued to advance. After a succession of heavy attacks supported by dive-bombers Tamera was captured on the 17th and by the 21st we had been forced back to Gebel Abiod. This was bitter mountain fighting in miserable weather; the country either side of the road is high and covered with scrub, making the deployment of artillery, our main strength, most difficult.

The Battle of Medenine.

While the enemy were thus vigorously and persistently attacking in the north, Eighth Army continued to build up gradually in front of the Mareth line. This famous fortified position was inspired by the same military conceptions as produced the Maginot line in France, though the Tunisian line was later in date and incorporated ideas derived from the earlier and larger fortification. It ran for a total length of about twenty-two miles on a course roughly north-east to south-west just in front of the small town of Mareth from which it took its name; one flank rested on the sea, the other on the steep-sided Matmata mountains. At the north-east end the Wadi Zigzaou runs in front of the line and, artificially scarped, made a first class anti-tank obstacle. The defences themselves consisted of a system of interconnected strong-points, partly underground, reinforced with concrete.[35] The fire plan was well conceived to cover all parts of the front with enfilade fire of all calibres and the minefields and wire obstacles were thick and well sited. The mountains shielding the western flank are almost impassable for wheeled traffic and the one poor road which crosses them was blocked at the pass of Ksar el Hallouf. The desert west of the mountains was considered by the French as completely impassable for any significant force; the going is most difficult and there is very little water. This appreciation had been apparently confirmed by manoeuvres held before the war. The French therefore calculated that any force which wished to invade Tunisia from Tripolitania would have to assemble in the area between Medenine and the line[36] and launch a frontal attack.

When this had been repulsed, as was confidently expected, or while it was still in progress, the defenders would deliver a counter-attack from the area of the Ksar el Hallouf pass on to the left flank and rear of the attackers.

As I have already explained it would be some time before General Montgomery could assemble sufficient troops for an attack on the Mareth line and he was determined not to attack before he was ready. In the meanwhile Field-Marshal Rommel still had his Army Group reserve under his hand, amounting to about two armoured divisions. They would also need a certain amount of time to recuperate from their losses in the Kasserine battle but after that they could obviously be best used in a spoiling attack against Eighth Army. The blow at II Corps had won the enemy a breathing space on that side and he could clearly appreciate that he would be ready to take the offensive again before Eighth Army was. I signalled to General Montgomery on 26th February to say that I thought Rommel would certainly try to attack him as soon as he could, following the original French plan; he replied in a letter on the 27th that it would be a very good thing if Rommel did attack and he only feared that he would not. In any case Eighth Army was well poised and ready for anything; on 26th February two divisions were forward in position, the 51st to the north of the road with all three brigades up and 7 Armoured Division astride and to the south of the road. The front was covered with an armoured car screen and the area round Medenine, juncture of the Mareth and Ksar el Hallouf roads, was being organised as a defensive position.

On 26th February it became apparent that the detachment of 15 Panzer Division which had taken part in the Kasserine battle was rejoining its parent formation, and on the 28th 21 Panzer Division, and that part of 10 Panzer Division which was co-operating with it, also began to move south. I considered, therefore, that my appreciation was confirmed and so informed Eighth Army. Shortly afterwards the enemy began to thin out in Gafsa though he clearly intended to continue to block the Gafsa – Gabes road at El Guettar, a defile which offered a very strong position to the defenders. On 2nd March our aircraft on tactical reconnaissance saw large bodies of enemy transport moving south from Gabes to Matmata, at the northern end of the mountains and, although the enemy simultaneously showed us a concentration on the Mareth – Medenine road, with deceptive intent, it was clear that Rommel was going to follow the French plan and attack out of the mountains on to our left. On the same day the New Zealand Division, which had secretly and swiftly been brought forward from Tripoli, concentrated in the area south of Medenine. On the 3rd a local attack by Italian troops on the Mareth front, which cost them severe casualties, was also probably designed to distract our attention from the west but the signs there were too strong: all that day and the next heavy movement continued in the mountains, at Toujane, Cheguimi and Ksar el Hallouf. The enemy rested all day of 5th March and on the 6th poured down from the mountains to the attack. As the Panzer Grenadiers moved off on the evening of the 5th down the steep, winding road from Ksar el Hallouf they defiled past the Army Group Commander, standing in his open car at the top of the pass. According to an eye witness on the spot Rommel was obviously a sick man, with a dirty bandage round his neck where he was suffering from desert sores; to a party who stopped near him he said that unless they won this battle the last hope in Africa was gone.

Eighth Army was disposed with three divisions forward. On the right 51 Division, with 23 Armoured Brigade under command, covered the area north of the road, opposite the Wadi Zigzaou. To the south was 7 Armoured Division, reinforced by 8 Armoured Brigade and 1 Fighting French Flying Column. The position round Medenine was held by the New Zealand Division with 201 Guards Brigade and 4 Light Armoured Brigade under command. The key position here was the Gebel Tadjera, a hill which rises abruptly from the plain north-west of the town; this was defended by the Guards Brigade. The enemy's intention was clearly the capture of Medenine, which would cut our communications with Tripoli and encircle the greater part of our forces to the north. There had been no time to lay minefields or erect wire and our defences were based on anti-tank guns well dug in to give a short field of fire in enfilade. The enemy attacking forces were 21 and 10 Panzer Divisions from the west, with a detachment from 15 Panzer Division and some additional infantry; the remainder of 15 Panzer Division and 90 Light Division were to hold us by a frontal exploratory attack which could be converted into a genuine offensive if all went well.

The story of the battle can be told very briefly. The enemy appear to have been unaware of the strength of our positions – they expected to find Gebel Tadjera unoccupied – and probably also hoped to have escaped our notice on their long flank march. Their concentrated attacks were beaten off by the infantry with anti-tank guns, without the intervention of any of our tanks except one squadron; our casualties were light and we lost no tanks at all. The enemy made four attacks during the day, the first in the early morning mist, but in none of them was he able to score any success. That evening he drew off with the loss of fifty-two tanks, the greatest total loss he had so far suffered in one day's battle in Africa. It represented probably a third of the total tank strength engaged on the southern front and, perhaps nearer half of the tanks engaged in the actual attack. In many ways this battle resembled the battle of Alam el Halfa, before Alamein: for the second time Rommel had committed the error of throwing his tanks against well-emplaced anti-tank guns. Our defensive success was a good omen for the attack on the Mareth line. Medenine was Rommel's last battle in Africa. Shortly afterwards (before 19th March) he handed over command of the Army Group to von Arnim. The latter was succeeded at 5 Panzer Army Headquarters by General von Vaerst who had commanded, without much distinction, 15 Panzer Division in Africa up to September, 1942. It seems certain that Rommel's return to Germany was genuinely due to sickness, but no doubt also the German High Command wanted to run no risk of the capture of a General with so great a reputation.

In spite of the failure at Medenine the enemy were unwilling to be forced back on the defensive and on 10th March launched a sudden and violent attack against "L" Force at Ksar Rhilane. This outpost in the desert west of the Matmata mountains was assuming greater importance for, as I shall explain, we already had plans for passing an outflanking force through the desert. The attack was made by the reconnaissance units of 15 and 21 Panzer Divisions and some Italian mobile units, assisted by dive-bombers. General Leclerc's force, which included a Greek detachment, stood firm in a style reminiscent of Koenig's defence of Bir Hacheim and, strongly supported by the Western Desert Air Force, beat off the attack with substantial losses to the enemy. I think the main purpose of this attack was to win some offensive success, even a small one, as his persistence in the north showed, the enemy still hoped to keep us at bay as long as possible by reiterated attacks.[37] He showed, however, a certain apprehension about our intentions in the area between Gafsa and Faid, and drew off the greater part of his southern group of armour north of the Gabes gap to watch that flank.

On 14th March I issued a directive on policy to confirm my previous instructions on the way in which I wanted the battle in Tunisia to be fought; it was co-ordinated with a brief statement on Air Force policy by Air Marshal Coningham.[38] I had taken II United States Corps under direct command on 8th March, leaving the French XIX Corps under First Army, so that I was now dealing with three subordinate headquarters. I proposed also to form an Army Group reserve to be commanded by Headquarters 9 Corps which had just arrived in Africa; it was intended to consist of 6 Armoured Division, one British infantry division and specialist troops such as parachutists and commandos whom I was anxious to pull out of the line. I laid particular stress, for the benefit of First Army, on the policy of not attempting to hold a continuous line over all the mountainous areas of the front but of concentrating on the defence of really vital positions and leaving the areas in between to be observed by patrols. This was for the present defensive phase, which I hoped soon to be able to abandon, but even while on the defensive I ordered an offensive spirit to be shown in small actions to improve our positions. It was an advantage that we had now begun to sort out the troops originally under General Anderson into their respective national units and given a definite sector to each nationality.

On 15th March I moved my headquarters to a tented site on a well wooded mountainside south of Ain Beida. This was on the main road from Constantine to Tebessa, well situated between First and Eighth Armies and close to Headquarters II Corps, which was near Tebessa. For the present, operations in the south were the most important.

The Mareth Line Battles.

As a defensive position the Mareth line was almost as strong as the enemy line at El Alamein. The Eighth Army plan, therefore, called for a deliberate and well organized attack with all the forces which we could maintain forward. General Montgomery sent me an advanced copy of his proposed plan on 27th February.

For PUGILIST, as the operation was called, Eighth Army was to be organized for the frontal attack in two Corps, 30 Corps with 50, 51 and 4 Indian Divisions and 201 Guards Brigade, and 10 Corps with 1 and 7 Armoured Divisions. The plan was that 30 Corps should make a very heavy attack on the north-eastern end of the line, near the coast, to break into and roll up the line from the right, 10 Corps, which would be initially in Army reserve, would then be ready to exploit success by passing through and advancing towards Gabes and Sfax. There was a difference, however, between the situation here and at Alamein in that we had now proved, thanks to the Long Range Desert Group, that we could move an outflanking force through the desert west of the Matmata mountains. Provision was accordingly made for this in the plan; the outflanking troops consisted mainly of the New Zealand Division but included also 8 Armoured Brigade and General Leclerc's "L" Force and for this reason were designated New Zealand Corps. The object of this force was defined as to establish itself across the Gabes – Matmata road so as to cut off the enemy and prevent his escape, in order to do this it would have to break through a subsidiary defensive line, mainly consisting of minefields, which the enemy had constructed between the Gebel Tebaga and the Gebel Melab.

In the plan as fixed on 26th February General Montgomery stated that D-day for the attack would be 20th March. This apparently long delay was rendered necessary by his desire to have all the logistical preparations perfect. I sent my Major-General, Administration, Major-General Miller, to Tripoli on 6th March to investigate the administrative situation and his report on his return on 11th March was very satisfactory. The port was discharging over three thousand tons per day, to be shortly raised to four thousand tons, (on 6th March seven thousand tons were discharged, but this was exceptionally good); the ration, petrol and ammunition situation was therefore good and we could already assume as certain that the operation could proceed according to time-table. Eighth Army was anxious to know, however, what logistical support we could give in the case that the enemy, after a prolonged resistance on the Mareth line, broke completely and we should wish to pursue him for a long distance. This would impose a heavy strain a force based on Tripoli, over two hundred miles from Mareth and three hundred miles from the next port at Sfax. I had already discussed this point with General Montgomery. In view of the time available I had decided to employ II United States Corps in a limited operation on the extreme right of my line in Tunisia; the objects of this were to restore confidence after the earlier setbacks by a carefully planned successful operation, to exert pressure on the right rear of the enemy defending the Mareth positions, and to be ready to open an alternative line of supply for Eighth Army after they had broken through the Gabes Gap. I planned, therefore, that II Corps, now commanded by General Patton, who had relieved General Fredendall, should attack Gafsa on or about 15th March with 1 Armoured and 1 Infantry Divisions. They would secure firm possession of Gafsa and build up there a dump of petrol for the use of Eighth Army, subsequently exploiting down the Gabes road, and towards the Maknassy defile in order to draw the enemy's attention and provoke counter-attack. General Patton was to try to capture the El Guettar defile, south-east of Gafsa, but would not operate any strong forces beyond that until further orders. The thrust against the Maknassy defile was in the initial phase to be of a secondary and subsidiary nature.

The American operations against Gafsa were delayed in starting by very heavy rain which bogged down their tracked vehicles, but 1 Armoured Division moved off at first light on the 16th. There was practically no enemy opposition and next day 1 Infantry Division entered the town, which had been evacuated by the Italian garrison; a German reconnaissance unit forming the rearguard consented itself with keeping our troops under observation. A Regimental Combat Team from 1 Infantry Division pushed on through the town and occupied the high ground six miles to the south-east, sending patrols towards El Guettar. These showed that, as we had expected, the enemy intended to hold the defile there, 1 Armoured Division, though again seriously delayed by the state of the ground, moved off down the Maknassy road, and by nightfall had reached a point twenty miles east of Gafsa against opposition from the air and artillery fire only. The weather continued exceptionally bad on the 18th but General Patton was able to establish himself in El Guettar village and make contact with the enemy positions in the defile to the east of it.

On the Eighth Army front preliminary operations to drive in the enemy's out-post positions were carried out on the nights of 16th and 17th March; they were generally successful at small cost, except for an operation by 201 Guards Brigade which suffered fairly heavy casualties on the first night when it became involved in an enemy minefield. On 19th March the New Zealand Corps, with twenty-seven thousand men and two hundred tanks, started on its flanking move from south of Foum Tatahouine and by nightfall on 20th March was only a few miles short of the gap between Gebel Tebaga and Gebel Melab; General Montgomery had decided not to attempt concealment, in the hope of drawing enemy attention from 30 Corps' attack. This was scheduled for the night of the 20th. Enemy dispositions at that time were as follows. The north-eastern end of the Mareth line was held by XX Corps with under command the Young Fascists and Trieste Divisions and the German 90 Light Division. The south-western end, where the Matmata foothills begin, was under XXI Corps with the Spezia, Pistoia and 164 Light Divisions. 15 Panzer Division was held in immediate reserve for this part of the front. 21 Panzer Division was also in reserve, but further back, in order to be available, if necessary, for the defence of the Tebaga – Gebel Melab gap, the infantry holding this position was provided by the Saharan Group under General Mannerim, reinforced by various units from Italian divisions destroyed at El Alamein. 10 Panzer Division, which had withdrawn to central Tunisia after the battle of Medenine, was moving south at this time, but it was not destined for the Mareth front; instead it went to the Gafsa – Gabes road to oppose II Corps.

The main attack by 30 Corps began at 2230 hours on 20th March when 50 Division advanced to the assault under cover of very heavy artillery fire and following an air bombardment. The Wadi Zigzaou, which ran in front of the enemy's positions in this sector, was very deep and steep-sided and the bottom was everywhere muddy and in some places had standing water in it. It resembled, in fact, the fosse of an old-fashioned fortress and our troops advanced to the assault carrying fascines and scaling-ladders as though at the storm of Badajoz. The enemy's fire, both frontal and enfilade, was very heavy and it was only by the greatest dash and courage that our advanced troops succeeded in crossing the wadi and establishing themselves on the far bank. Three of the powerful enemy strongpoints were captured and the infantry were firmly established. Unfortunately it was proving impossible to reinforce them, for the wadi which they had crossed on foot was quite impassable for wheels and almost impassable for tanks. A few of the supporting "Valentines" managed to get across but none of the anti-tank guns could be brought forward. A heavy downfall of rain on the 22nd added to our difficulties. As a result, when the enemy in the afternoon of 22nd March put in a heavy counter-attack, using the whole of 15 Panzer Division and part of 90 Light, our position became untenable. 50 Division bridgehead was dangerously narrowed down and on the night of the 23rd our troops fell back once more, on orders, across the Wadi Zigzaou, under cover of artillery fire.

The original plan for PUGILIST had therefore to be abandoned but General Montgomery was quick to take advantage of the alternative which was open to him. By the evening of the 22nd, when it was obvious that our right hand thrust could make no further progress, General Freyberg's forces were already engaged with the enemy west of the Gebel Melab and had broken through one line of minefields in an attack the previous night. The enemy had already begun to move reinforcements to this area, including 164 Division from the western end of the Mareth line, together with some Italians, and 21 Panzer Division from Army Group reserve. General Montgomery therefore decided to call off his frontal attack and reinforce his outflanking move with 10 Corps Headquarters and 1 Armoured Division. They were to move off after dusk on 23rd March and were expected to join the New Zealanders on 25th March. This would give us a force of over three hundred tanks with which to attack the enemy's rear. At the same time 4 Indian Division, under command of 30 Corps, was to thrust into the mountains to the west of the Mareth line. Its first task was to open the road from Medenine to Bir Soltane via Ksar el Hallouf, as a shorter route of supply for 10 Corps; subsequently it was to advance along the spine of the Matmata mountains and descend from there to cut the Mareth – Gabes road. This plan, with reminiscences of El Alamein, was christened SUPERCHARGE.

In view of the development of Eighth Army's battle I ordered General Patton late on 22nd March to increase his pressure down the Gafsa – Gabes road with 1 Infantry Division and down the Gafsa – Maknassy road with 1 Armoured Division. II Corps was to seize and hold the two defiles on these roads, which it was now facing, and operate raiding columns from them against the enemy's lines of communication, 1 Armoured Division had entered Maknassy itself without opposition at 0700 hours on the 22nd but failed to seize a fleeting opportunity and was forestalled at the vital defile some five miles east of the town; when it advanced eastwards later in the day it found that the enemy had hastily organized a defensive position there from a German and an Italian reconnaissance unit. Subsequently a battalion of infantry from 10 Panzer Division and some Italian tanks arrived between 23rd and 24th March and with these, reinforced by two more infantry battalions and some German tanks, the enemy succeeded in holding the pass. The advance down the Gafsa-Gabes road was also frustrated, for before it could develop the enemy launched a strong attack with the whole of the rest of 10 Panzer Division. This counter-attack had some initial success but 1 Infantry Division held firm and inflicted losses in tanks on the enemy. The attacks were renewed on the 24th and 25th, again without success. It was greatly to the credit of II Corps that they thus kept in play the whole of 10 Panzer Division while the decisive battle was being fought and won by Eighth Army, and although they were denied the pleasure of a spectacular advance into the enemy's rear they made a solid contribution to the success of operations in southern Tunisia.

While 10 Corps was pressing on across the difficult desert terrain to join the New Zealanders 4 Indian Division plunged into the mountains west of Medenine. By the 26th they had cleared the road through the Ksar el Hallouf pass and turned northwards to work towards Cheguimi. In the meantime the advance of 10 Corps was taking rather longer than expected and Eighth Army decided to postpone the proposed attack from the 25th to the 26th. The problem was to burst through a long defile between Gebel Tebaga and Gebel Melab; the defences in this six thousand yards bottleneck had been strengthened with mines and on the 25th General Messe moved 15 Panzer Division north to this area. This practically stripped the Mareth line of German troops and he simultaneously began to thin out his Italians leaving 90 Light Division, as usual, to conduct the rearguard. While these forces were got away it was vital for Messe to hold the flanks of the north-south corridor as firmly as possible and with two German armoured divisions and one infantry division facing us, to say nothing of the Italians, it seemed we might find the task of breaking through difficult. General Montgomery therefore, in consultation with Air Vice Marshal Broadhurst, commanding the Western Desert Air Force, arranged for a very heavy air attack employing every available aircraft to precede the ground attack; as a new feature control was to be exercised from aircraft flying over the battlefield.

Following a favourite enemy plan 10 Corps attacked in the late afternoon of 26th March, with the sun behind them. For two and a half hours previously the Royal Air Force had attacked the enemy's positions with bombs and machine-gun fire, creating great destruction among his guns and transport and having a most serious effect on morale. The New Zealand Division began the attack with 8 Armoured Brigade leading and rapidly overran the enemy's defences. 1 Armoured Division followed through and advanced nearly four miles before being halted by darkness. When the moon rose they pressed on again. It was a daring but successful move; in the bright moonlight they drove straight past the bulk of the enemy's armour and at dawn were within a few miles of El Hamma which is only fifteen miles from Gabes on a good road. A further advance at first light put them within two miles of El Hamma, facing a strong enemy anti-tank gun screen. 164 Light Division was engaged here, with 15 Panzer Division to its south. 21 Panzer Division was still cut off between 1 Armoured Division and the New Zealanders and fought very fiercely to extricate itself. The efforts of the three German divisions were successful, in spite of heavy losses, in holding onto El Hamma and keeping open the corridor through which the troops from the Mareth line were withdrawn to the next defensive position north of Gabes. 30 Corps was hampered in following up by many mines and demolitions. 10 Corps was also hindered in its operations against El Hamma on 28th March and the enemy evacuated the village that night. The New Zealanders entered Gabes at 1300 hours on the 29th and were shortly afterwards joined there by the advance elements of 51 Division. The enemy had lost seven thousand prisoners and many tanks and guns.

First Army resumes the Offensive.
First Army, like II Corps, had been able to start on its programme of reorganization and training after the enemy's defeat at Thala, though it had been to a certain extent upset by the enemy offensive which started on 26th February. With the arrival of fresh formations this programme was now beginning to show results: "Y" Division was dissolved on 16th March when relieved by 3 Infantry Brigade, the first to arrive of 1 Infantry Division; the other two brigades of the division took over sectors of the front on 19th and 23rd March and Divisional Headquarters assumed command in the Medjez area. 78 Division and 1 Guards Brigade were relieved and the latter went to join 6 Armoured Division in reserve. The Germans were also reinforcing simultaneously, though not on the same scale. In the middle of March the second regiment of the Hermann Goering Division began to arrive and shortly afterwards the first troops of a new formation, 999 Africa Division, were identified. This was formed mainly from former residents of concentration camps and included a few genuine criminals. In spite of this peculiar origin it fought as well as the average German formation; it was particularly noticeable that the political offenders who made up the great majority, influenced more by the tradition of discipline and the military virtues of the race than by their political convictions, fought with great skill and stubbornness even in a losing battle.

I had ordered General Anderson to take the earliest opportunity of restoring the situation on the northern road and to relieve the pressure on Medjez by extending our line here to the north of the Béja road. The first task was entrusted to 46 Division, using 138 Brigade, 36 Brigade from 78 Division and 1 Parachute Brigade. It was facilitated by the fact that the enemy had thinned out in this area to reinforce other sectors but even so the dense scrub and the boulder-covered mountains were most serious obstacles. The attack began on 28th March in very heavy rain and made steady progress, assisted by the Corps Franc d'Afrique and a

Tabor of Moroccan Goumiers on the left flank. On 30th March we re-entered Sedjenane, and the capture was completed by next day. The enemy was now reinforcing by recommitting his carefully husbanded reserves but they were unable to halt our progress. On 31st March we recaptured our former positions east of El Aouana; shortly afterwards the enemy withdrew from his positions on Cap Serrat. By this advance of eighteen miles we had won back all the ground which the enemy had taken three weeks to capture; prisoners amounted to over eight hundred and fifty and there is no doubt that his losses in killed and wounded were heavy.

On 5th April 4 Infantry Division assumed command in the sector north-east of Béja and on 7th April 78 Division attacked north of Oued Zarga to carry out the second part of the Army task. It met opposition from the German 334 Division but continued to press forward on a front of about ten miles to a depth, eventually, of ten miles. This is a most desolate and barren area of mountains, with few and scattered villages. The most important success was the capture on 14th April of Gebel el Ang and Gebel Tanngouche, two ridges over three thousand feet high eight miles north of Medjez, the enemy recaptured both next day but in a further attack we recovered Gebel el Ang and part of Tanngouche. The mountain village of Heidous, which the enemy had converted into a strongpoint, remained in his hands but was now threatened from both north and south. The object of our operations had been achieved. Medjez had been freed from enemy threat and we were able to build up there, in security, the stores required for our final offensive.

The Battle of Wadi Akarit.
After his defeat by Eighth Army General Messe withdrew to the northern end of the Gabes gap and endeavoured to make a new stand there, on the very threshold of the Tunisian plain. His position was based on the Wadi Akarit, a steep-sided obstacle which had been extended by an anti-tank ditch to cover the whole of the gap between the sea and the Chott el Fedjadj. This gave him a line of about twelve to fifteen miles in length. On the north side the wadi is dominated by two mountains, Gebel Fatnassa on the west and Gebel er Roumana on the east, extending almost to the sea. The road from Gabes to Gafsa runs round the western end of Fatnassa, in a defile between the mountain and the salt marsh, and the road to Sfax runs along the coast round the eastern end of Er Roumana. There is a low col between the two peaks which is traversed by a few tracks and was thought to be practicable for our use if the high ground commanding it could be cleared. Taken all round it was a very strong position, much stronger by nature than the Mareth line.

10 Corps made contact with the enemy's new line on 30th March with the New Zealand Division on the right and 1 Armoured Division on the left. Having inspected the position the Corps Commander reported that it could not be carried by assault with his present forces and General Montgomery decided to wait until he could bring up stronger forces in infantry. His plan was to assault

with three infantry divisions, 50th, 51st and 4th Indian, attacking through 10 Corps as now disposed; after a breach had been made 10 Corps would pass through, with the New Zealanders leading. It would take about a week for the attack to be prepared. This would give me time to co-ordinate Eighth Army's offensive with two other thrusts which I had planned. I issued a plan of operations on 3rd April. My object was still "to seize and secure airfields and potential airfields from which we can develop the full weight of our great superiority in the air, thereby paralysing the enemy's supply system to an extent which will greatly facilitate the rapid advance of our ground forces." The first phase was to drive the enemy from the Gabes gap by a frontal attack by Eighth Army and flanking pressure by II Corps. When this operation was completed II Corps would be pulled out and transferred to the extreme northern flank. The second phase was to coincide with Eighth Army's advance towards Sousse. I had organized an Army Group reserve under the recently arrived Headquarters 9 Corps, consisting of 6 Armoured Division, a British infantry brigade and 34 United States Division. At a date after 7th April, and dependent on Eighth Army's progress, this force, on orders from me, would secure the Fondouk gap in the Eastern Dorsale and pass the armoured division through towards Kairouan, threatening the rear of Messe's army. Throughout this period 5 Corps and XIX Corps were to tie down the enemy on their front by thrusts aimed at the capture of important features.

On 27th March the preliminary stage of this plan began when 34 United States Division entered the village of Fondouk, at the western end of the defile, and 9 United States Division reinforced 1 Infantry Division at El Guettar. After this I allowed the Fondouk area to remain quiet but tried to press on with II Corps down the Gafsa – Gabes road. In spite of the favourable development of the Mareth battle very strong resistance was met to any progress beyond El Guettar. On 31st March General Patton tried to push an armoured force down the road but it was held up by mines after advancing only a short distance. He then tried a more deliberate advance with 1 Division working along the mountains north of the road and 9 Division doing the same to the south. The former made a little ground on 2nd April but the latter was unable to advance. Nevertheless Messe was now thoroughly alarmed by this threat to has right flank; 10 Panzer Division, which was at that time by far the strongest of the three, had already been kept fully engaged on the El Guettar road and by the 3rd it had been joined by 21 Panzer Division. A strong enemy counter-attack on that day gained some ground from 9 Division. The deadlock continued until Eighth Army attacked and broke through the Wadi Akarit line; even on the first day of that battle, when the position of the enemy's main forces was already desperate, the two Panzer divisions continued to resist the American pressure with great stubbornness. 9 Division suffered heavy casualties that day for no gains and 1 Division only succeeded in advancing two miles. Meanwhile at Maknassy we restricted our operations to feint attacks designed to distract attention from our main effort on the El Guettar road.

The plan for the attack on the Wadi Akarit line provided for an infantry assault by all three divisions of 30 Corps: 4 Indian Division against Gebel Fatnassa, 51 Division against Er Roumana and 50 Division in the centre. The enemy forces were disposed in much the same order of battle as in the Mareth line with XX Corps (Young Fascists and Trieste) at the seaward end and XXI Corps (Pistoia, Spezia and 164 Light) at the inland end. 15 Panzer and 90 Light Divisions were held in reserve behind the centre of the line but 10 and 21 Panzer Divisions were nearly forty miles away to the west, engaged with II Corps, and a strong force, including a "Tiger" tank battalion, was observing 1 Armoured Division at Maknassy. It is peculiar that Messe should have been more anxious about his right flank than his centre, but such seems to have been the case; perhaps she relied on the obvious strength of his positions at Akarit to cause Eighth Army to delay, or else he expected us to wait for the moon to be right. He had already, however, begun to move some of his heavy guns back to the next defence line, at Enfidaville, and can have been under no illusions as to his ability to hold us in the south for much longer.

The battle of the Wadi Akarit lasted only a day but the fighting was described by General Montgomery as "heavier and more savage than any we have had since Alamein". Attack and counter-attack clashed in the hills and both Germans and Italians showed a quite reckless determination and unimpaired morale. 30 Corps attacked at 0400 hours on 6th April, supported by four hundred and fifty guns. It was completely dark at that time and this undoubtedly assisted us in gaining surprise. The major credit for the victory goes to 4 Indian Division, 51 Division gained its original objective but was driven off by a counter-attack and 50 Division in the centre was seriously delayed by resistance on the line of the wadi. The attack on Fatnassa was brilliantly successful against great difficulties of terrain; 7 Indian Brigade, led by the Royal Sussex and 2 Gurkhas, captured all their objectives by dawn and 5 Indian Brigade, which then passed through, completed the mopping up and was in a position to take in rear the defences which were holding up the Corps' centre and right. At 0845 hours the division reported that it had bitten six thousand yards out of the enemy position and at 1200 hours General Montgomery put in 10 Corps. It looked like a complete *débâcle* for the enemy, but 15 Panzer and 90 Light Divisions, fighting perhaps the best battle of their distinguished careers, counter-attacked with great vigour and by their self-sacrifice enabled Messe to stabilize the situation. That night the enemy withdrew and the two Panzer Divisions which had been fighting a hard but irrelevant battle on the El Guettar road also broke contact and drew off to the north-east. At 1600 hours on 7th April an American patrol met a patrol of 4 Indian Division. At last the two Armies, from the east and the west, had made contact after their long and triumphant advances.[39]

The battle had cost the enemy over six thousand prisoners and heavy casualties. There was no chance of making a stand south of the mountain line at Enfidaville and retreat was essential. Messe showed a not unnatural solicitude for his Italian troops, who went straight back to the new line, leaving the Germans to form a rearguard for which they were better suited. The second phase of my plan for interfering with the retreat now came into action. 9 Corps, which had been lying concealed in the forest of Kessera, east of Maktar, moved forward to the Fondouk area and on 7th April launched an attack to secure the pass. The plan was to clear the heights dominating the north side of the defile with 128 Brigade (46 Division) and the heights to the south with 34 Division and then pass 6 Armoured Division through the middle. The former attack went well. We entered Pichon on the 8th and pressed forward to the east against fairly strong resistance. South of the pass 34 United States Division was unable to make any progress on the 7th or 8th. Meanwhile the enemy rearguards in the plain to the east were conducting a very skilful withdrawal in front of Eighth Army. Sfax was entered on 10th April by 30 Corps, which had advanced up the coast, and 10 Corps to the west had kept level. 10 and 21 Panzer Divisions were withdrawing on the western flank of Messe's army and I foresaw that they would soon arrive in the Kairouan area. I therefore ordered 9 Corps to disregard 34 Division's failure to the south and launch 6 Armoured Division straight at the pass. This gallant attack went in on the afternoon of the 9th. The motor battalion of the armoured brigade advanced into the throat of the defile under heavy cross fire to make a gap in the minefield and two armoured regiments then plunged through. Unswept mines and anti-tank guns in enfilade took a toll but our tanks pressed on undeterred and the pass was forced.

On 10th April 6 Armoured Division fought a successful action against enemy tanks south of Kairouan and entered the holy city next morning at 1015 hours. This was an unwelcome acceleration to the enemy's withdrawal timetable and 10 and 21 Panzer Divisions suffered more losses which in their weakened state were serious for them. Eighth Army had on 10th April paused for two days, for administrative reasons, on a line running east and west through Sfax, sending the armoured cars of 4 Light Armoured Brigade to flood the country to the north. On the 12th the advance was resumed again with 10 Corps while 30 Corps halted round Sfax. Sousse fell on 12th April and by next day our leading troops were in contact with the first defences north of Enfidaville. XIX Corps had also joined in the attack, working in close harmony with 9 Corps, and had driven the enemy from the Eastern Dorsale as far as ten miles north of Pichon. 9 Corps made contact with patrols from Eighth Army on 11th April.

Preparations for the Final Assault.
I had now achieved my first object in the capture of the whole of the coastal plain and we were in a position to exploit from there our air superiority. A striking demonstration was given on 18th April when our fighters intercepted off Cape Bon a large flight of German transport aircraft carrying troops and shot down over fifty of them; it was also a significant confirmation of the fact that the enemy, so far from thinking of evacuation, was using every possible means to rush troops into his now much diminished Tunisian bridgehead. My next object was to complete the destruction of the forces still opposing me as quickly as possible, in

order to obtain the use of the ports of Tunis and Bizerta for the invasion of Sicily. The enemy positions presented to us two fronts at right angles, facing west and south, with the salient angle protected by the tangled mountain country of the Gebel Mansour and the Gebel Fkirine. I decided, for topographical reasons, to make my main attack on the western face of this perimeter. My intention was to break through to Tunis from the west and thereby split the enemy forces in two. I would then leave the smaller body of enemy to the north to be mopped up by the Allied troops on the spot and, turning southwards with the greater part of my forces, drive the larger body of enemy on the right flank of the penetration against the line firmly held by Eighth Army. It was particularly important in carrying out this manoeuvre to prevent the enemy establishing himself in the peninsula terminating in Cape Bon, where he might have been able to hold out for some time.

I had rejected the idea of making my main thrust with Eighth Army partly because an advance against the southern face of the perimeter would drive the enemy in on themselves rather than split them and partly because of the difficulty of the terrain. From the sea just north of Enfidaville to the Gebel Fkirine massif the mountains present a continuous wall of abrupt peaks. This wall is pierced by three roads, all starting from Enfidaville: the only good road follows the coast, with salt marshes on its right and mountains on its left; the other two run via Saouaf and Zaghouan through a series of narrow passes. On the First Army front there are also three routes to Tunis, but more widely separated. The southern-most runs from Bou Arada to Pont du Fahs and thence northeast. This could be blocked by the enemy fairly easily at the Pont du Fahs defile and commanded from the mountains on the south side of the Bou Arada plain. The second route starts from the Goubellat plain, which gives good opportunities for deployment. It would then be possible to advance north-eastwards, north of the salt marshes of Sebkret el Kourzia, and enter the plain of Tunis by various minor roads running south-west from the city. The difficulty here was a belt of broken country without roads which interposes to the northeast of the salt marshes. The third route follows the axis of the Medjez-Massicault road, the main road to Tunis from the west. This was the most direct route and gave the best opportunities for the use of tanks; we had fought all winter for our foothold at its gate. For these very reasons, however, the enemy defences were here at their strongest.

In order to develop their full strength for the decisive blow First Army had to be more concentrated and reinforced. For the former purpose I had already decided to relieve 46 and 4 Divisions on its northernmost flank with two divisions from II Corps. On 3rd April I ordered General Patton to be prepared to despatch his 9 Infantry Division to take over from 46 Division as soon as Eighth Army had broken through the Wadi Akarit line and to follow as rapidly as possible with the rest of II Corps. 9 Division, after regrouping and refitting, assumed command of the northernmost sector on 14th April and on 19th April 1 United States Infantry Division began to relieve 4 Division; on the same day II Corps assumed command of the area north of the Oued et Tine. I intended that simultaneously with

First Army's offensive and Eighth Army's holding attack II Corps should also develop operations down the Sedjenane road and the Béja – Mateur road to contain the enemy there and, if possible, to accelerate the capture of Bizerta. I must mention here that the way in which four United States divisions were transferred from one end of the line to the other, crossing at right angles the lines of communication of First Army, was a considerable triumph of staff work. Reinforcements for First Army could only come from Eighth Army. On 11th April I informed General Montgomery that the main effort in the final phase of operations would be by General Anderson and ordered him to make available to join 9 Corps as soon as possible an armoured division and an armoured car regiment, 1 Armoured Division and the King's Dragoon Guards were nominated, being well placed on the Faid – Sbeitla road for such a transfer.

On 12th April I ordered General Anderson to prepare a large-scale offensive to capture Tunis, with a target date of 22nd April. I informed him that I was placing 9 Corps under his command, reinforced by 1 Armoured Division, and that II Corps would simultaneously be attacking in the direction of Bizerta. First Army was to give such assistance as should be possible to II Corps' attack but the latter was remaining under Army Group command. I indicated that the area for the main attack, by 5 and 9 Corps with four infantry and two armoured divisions, would be on the front from Medjez el Bab to north of Bou Arada with 5 Corps attacking north-east on the axis Medjez-Massicault and 9 Corps north of the Sebkret el Kourzia on a parallel axis. XIX Corps would be prepared in the event of success to advance towards the Pont du Fahs defile.

After discussion with the two Army commanders and General Patton, commanding II Corps, the final plan was worked out in the following form as reported by me in a signal of 18th April. Eighth Army was to start its attack on the night of 19th–20th April with 50 Division on the coast, 2 New Zealand Division just west of Enfidaville and 4 Indian Division, with "L" Force under command, west of Takrouna. 7 Armoured Division guarded the western flank, made contact with XIX Corps and was available to exploit success. XIX Corps was to attack three mountain positions commanding Pont du Fahs from the south; no date was set for this attack and it was not to be launched until First Army considered that the enemy in these strong positions had been sufficiently weakened by the attacks on either flank. First Army was to attack on 22nd April. 9 Corps would begin in the early morning with 46 Infantry and I and 6 Armoured Divisions. The infantry were to destroy the enemy positions west of the saltmarshes of Sebkret el Kourzia and the armour was then to follow through as quickly as possible directed on Gebel Mengoub, an eight hundred foot feature fifteen miles from the north end of the marshes and the same distance from Tunis. 5 Corps would attack in the evening of 22nd April with I and 4 Divisions south of the river, directed on Massicault, and 78 Division in the mountains north of the river with Gebel Ahmera ("Longstop") as their first objective. II Corps' attack was timed for the next day, 23rd April, with 1 Division attacking on the Sidi Nsir road with its final objective the pass above Chouigui, and 9 Division on the axis Sedjenane –

Mateur. In order to control the battle I had moved my Headquarters to a wood near Le Kef, after a short period at Haidra, between Tebessa and Thala.

When speaking of the plans for the final battles of the campaign I must take the opportunity of recording my obligations to my Chief of Staff, General McCreery. He had accompanied me from the Middle East where he had filled the same appointment. Both as a personal friend and as a brilliant Staff Officer he was invaluable to me in the whole course of operations in Africa, and was later to show, both as a Corps and an Army Commander that he added to his intellectual qualities the highest gifts of command.

General von Arnim still disposed of over two hundred thousand troops for a front of a hundred and twenty miles. Messe's Army held the southern front with German and Italian infantry in line from the sea to west of Takrouna: 90 Light Division was responsible for the coast road and 164 Light Division was on its inland flank; there were various Italian remnants, organized mainly under command of Headquarters Trieste Division, interspersed with the German troops and continuing the line westwards. The German Africa Corps, which had now taken under command the Superga Division, held the angle between the two fronts. The order of battle of von Vaerst's 5 Panzer Army was relatively un-changed. The Manteuffel Division faced II Corps in the northern most sector, then 334 Division in the mountains on the north bank of the Medjerda and 999 Africa Division, now almost complete, astride the river. In the area of 5 and 9 Corps was the Hermann Goering Division, reinforced with additional infantry and tanks, including part of a very recently arrived heavy tank battalion. As soon as Messe was back on his Enfidaville line von Arnim removed 10 Panzer Division, still his strongest armoured formation, and transferred it to the area between Sebkret el Kourzia and the Medjerda. This was clearly the most threatened point and it was vital to have an armoured reserve to cover the plain of Tunis. It was, however, the only reserve that Army Group Africa had and it is a little surprising that von Arnim made no effort to create a larger one by shortening his line at the less important points. Nor did he attempt to construct any defensive systems in rear of his present line except for some not very impressive perimeter defences round Tunis.

Eighth Army's attack on the Enfidaville position began at 2130 hours on 19th April. 50 Division captured Enfidaville itself and pushed forward patrols beyond it. The New Zealanders advanced to a point three miles north-west of the town. 4 Indian Division, further west, had a very fierce struggle for Gebel Garci; the enemy counter-attacked continuously and, at the cost, of very heavy casualties, succeeded in holding the attack. It was noticed that the Italians fought partic-ularly well, outdoing the Germans in line with them. The New Zealanders next day had an equally bloody struggle for the hill village of Takrouna. In spite of severe losses from our massed artillery fire the enemy kept up his policy of con-tinuous counter-attacks and it became clear that it would cost us heavily to advance further into this tangled mass of mountains. General Montgomery therefore decided late on the 21st to abandon the thrust in the centre and con-centrate on forcing the coastal defile.

This change of plan would involve fairly extensive regrouping and at the same time he wished to send back to the Delta one of the divisions which would be needed for the invasion of Sicily. 50 Division was selected as it had been weak-ened by its losses in the Mareth and Akarit battles. It was to be relieved by 56 Division, which had had no previous operational experience. The plan was to relieve 4 Indian and New Zealand Divisions opposite Gebel Garci and Takrouna with 51 Division brought forward from rest; this division had also had fairly heavy losses and was to be restricted to a holding role. The two former divisions, with the 56th, were to make the assault on the right. The first stage was on the night 24th/25th April when the New Zealanders and 201 Guards Brigade captured Gebel Terhouna, a strongly contested hill feature overlooking the coast about five miles north of Enfidaville. The main attack was planned for 29th April and its object was to establish all three divisions in the area of Hammamet, at the base of the Cape Bon peninsula. On the 29th, however, I received a signal from General Montgomery saying that, as a result of a failure by 56 Division on that day when coming under artillery fire as it was about to take up positions for the attack, he now felt unhappy about the possibilities of success. As this was not going to interfere with the plans I was already forming for finishing off enemy resistance in the Tunis plain I authorized the abandonment of the attack. 1 Fighting French Division was brought forward on 6th May to relieve 51 Division and the Eighth Army front became a holding front except for the western flank where the New Zealanders carried out local operations to assist XIX Corps and attract enemy attention.

The Enfidaville line thus marked the culmination of Eighth Army's great advance across Africa. This holding and diversionary role was not indeed its sole contribution to the final victory, for three and a half divisions were transferred to First Army to give weight to the main attack on Tunis. It is right, however, to take note at this point of the extent of Eighth Army's achievements. In six months they had advanced eighteen hundred miles and fought numerous battles in which they were always successful. This would be an astonishing rate of progress even in a civilized country with all the modern facilities of transport – the equivalent of an advance from London to two hundred miles east of Moscow – but in a desert it was even more remarkable. It reflects in particular the greatest credit on the administrative services. Their problems might have seemed quite insoluble but thanks to the admirable preparations made and the sound basis of experience gained in earlier campaigns administration had kept pace with operations and never failed in its support of the fighting troops.

Before First Army opened its offensive the enemy gave a last demonstration of tactics that had become almost traditional in Tunisia, the spoiling attack. On the night of 20th–21st April he attacked with sudden violence between Medjez and Goubellat, using a force of five battalions and about seventy tanks. The infantry came mainly from the Hermann Goering Division and advanced to the attack with great vigour and determination. We had had little warning of what was imminent and in the early stages of the battle parties of enemy succeeded in infiltrating into our forward positions where the troops were assembling for the offensive, into the gun lines and as far as 4 Division Headquarters. In spite of the darkness and the confusion the attack, given the codename LILACBLOSSOM by the Germans, was a failure; we took over four hundred and fifty prisoners and claimed over thirty tanks destroyed. Nor were our plans for the offensive upset or delayed, except to a minor degree on 9 Corps front, where 46 Division attack had to be postponed four hours.

9 Corps' offensive started on the morning of 22nd April when 46 Division advanced to the attack in the area of the Kourzia salt marshes. On the right, south-west of the marshes, the division was unsuccessful in face of strong defended localities and dense minefields which inflicted casualties on the supporting tanks. The attack on the left, to the north of the marshes, made better progress. Ground was gained steadily and by the late afternoon the Corps commander put in 6 Armoured Division to attack through the infantry. This met opposition from 10 Panzer Division and a tank battle developed. It continued next day when the enemy was reinforced by the tanks of 21 Panzer Division and on the 24th when 15 Panzer Division also arrived. General von Arnim was clearly worried about the danger in this area, and concentrated all his armour here; by the 26th all three armoured divisions were opposing us between Medjez and Bou Arada and the Headquarters of the German Africa Corps had been brought round to take command. With these reinforcements he succeeded in stabilizing his front in the broken ground north-east of the marshes and although 1 Armoured Division was committed on 24th April we were unable to score any significant gains. We had, however, caused the enemy to concentrate almost all his mobile reserves against this sector, and had inflicted heavy losses on him. It was a good preparation for the final blow. On 25th April the enemy withdrew from the salient now protruding south of the Bou Arada – Pont du Fahs road, followed up by XIX Corps. The latter were now within striking distance of the Pont du Fahs defile, having cleared Gebel Fkirine on 26th April. Tank battles continued on 9 Corps front all day of the 26th but that evening 6 Armoured Division was withdrawn into Army reserve.

While the main enemy attention was concentrated on the battle in the Goubellat plain 5 and II Corps had been able to make important advances on the whole front from the Medjerda to the sea. Resistance, indeed, was as strong as ever and all our gains were most stubbornly contested. 78 Division began on 22nd April with an attack on Gebel Ahmera, the left hand bastion of the Medjez gate which had defied us since the previous December. In very heavy fighting they had cleared all but the north-eastern end by midday of the 23rd and mopped up the remaining enemy pockets on Gebel Tanngouche. On the same day 1 and 4 Divisions attacked to the south of the Medjerda; the former captured Grich el Oued and the latter Goubellat. On 25th April 78 Division captured Heidous and next day Gebel Ahmera was finally cleared. We were now firmly based on the left bank of the river and continued to extend our ground on the right bank. On the 26th 1 Division pushed the enemy's positions back as far as Gebel Bou Aoukaz, a dominating feature four miles down stream from Gebel Ahmera on the opposite bank and 4 Division advanced down the main Tunis road to a distance of seven miles beyond Medjez. At this point the enemy began to launch a series of furious counter-attacks. On the 27th he drove back the left flank of 4 Division at Ksar Tyr and for the next three days he continued these attacks with a mixed battle group from 15 Panzer Division. He regained a little ground at the point of juncture of I and 4 Divisions; his losses were heavy but his troops continued to show an excellent spirit.

On the northernmost sector progress by II Corps was steady and continuous throughout this period. The enemy defences were strong and long-established and the terrain, as I have said, was particularly difficult; these advantages outweighed in the early stages their numerical inferiority and the lack of reserves for the defence, but as position after position was wrested away there were increasingly less troops to man the positions in rear. 9 and 1 Infantry Divisions attacked on the morning of 23rd April on the Sedjenane – Mateur and Béja – Mateur axes respectively. On the first day 9 Division gained its objective west of El Aouana. 1 Division made slightly slower progress but by the 25th had reached the high ground a mile to the south-east of Sidi Nsir station. This advance had exposed the left flank of the division and 34 Infantry Division was now brought in between the other two to clear up the area astride the Sidi Nsir – Mateur road. The ridge of hills west of Sidi Nsir was cleared by 28th April after three days of concentrated artillery fire and on the same day the high ground east of the village was captured after close and heavy fighting. Further east 1 Division advanced along the long range overlooking the Oued et Tine valley on the northern side.

On 27th April General Bradley relieved General Patton in command of II Corps and the latter went to take command of the Seventh Army which he was to lead in the invasion of Sicily. General Patton had produced, during his period of command, what I might almost call a transformation in the troops of II Corps. By his influence they had recovered from the natural depression caused by the early setbacks, they had absorbed with great rapidity the benefits of the intensive training to which they had been subjected and were now showing in hard mountain fighting that they had added the skill of the trained soldier to those excellent natural qualities which had been previously in part obscured by inexperience. General Patton was to score other triumphs in the Mediterranean and in North-west Europe but I think this not the least of his achievements. General Bradley had been attached to II Corps Headquarters and General Eisenhower now thought that this would be a good time to give him experience of actual command in operations before commanding a Corps in Sicily.

The attack by 9 Division on the northernmost road progressed rather more slowly. The enemy positions at Jefna were particularly strong and before they could be grappled with there were many outlying positions, on the hills either side of the road, which had to be cleared. Manteuffel's parachutists fought as well as usual and by 2nd May we were still held up at the immediate approaches to Jefna, though to the north we had outflanked it by some three miles. Heavy fighting continued on 1 Infantry Division front both on Gebel Sidi Meftah and to the north of it but in anticipation of its fall II Corps were now bringing up 1 Armoured Division to operate on the extreme right of the Corps in the valley of the Oued et Tine. This valley leads direct to Mateur; no road follows it but it is practicable for armour once the left flank is freed by securing Gebel Sidi Meftah. 78 Division to the east of the Oued had gained ground north of Gebel Ahmera and north-east of Heidous. On 30th April 34 Division scored its most noteworthy success with the capture of Gebel Tahent (Point 609). This commanding dome-shaped hill, east-north-east of Sidi Nsir, was defended by parachutists from the Barenthin Regiment, perhaps the best German troops in Africa.

The Final Offensive.

By 29th April I had decided that it was necessary to reinforce First Army again and change the point of attack further to the north. The heavy pressure which we had been bringing to bear since the 22nd had gained us a foothold at the entrance to the plain of Tunis and had stretched the enemy's powers of resistance almost to breaking point, but if I was to finish the campaign quickly, to fit in with the time-table for Sicily, a sudden powerful stroke was necessary. The events of the past week had shown that Eighth Army was unable to make any vital contribution by attacks on their front; indeed, in spite of the pressure they had kept up, the enemy had found himself able to withdraw all his armour from the southern front. I therefore ordered General Montgomery on 30th April to despatch at once to First Army the best formations he could spare to reinforce the main blow from Medjez. He nominated 7 Armoured Division, 4 Indian Division and 201 Guards Brigade. These were both the freshest and the most experienced formations in Eighth Army. They were, indeed, the nucleus around which Eighth Army had grown up, for in 1940 they made up the whole of the Western Desert Force.[40] It was particularly appropriate that the two divisions which had won our first victory in Africa, at Sidi Barrani, should be chosen for the main role in our last victory, the battle of Tunis.

I informed General Anderson on the same day of these proposed reinforcements and of my plan for their employment. The operations of 9 Corps, though falling short of their original objective, had attracted enemy attention to the southern part of the Goubellat plain. I intended to keep his attention fixed there by retaining there 1 Armoured Division, reinforced with a large concentration of dummy tanks and transport, and to make my main blow straight at Tunis along the Medjez – Massicault road. For this I intended to employ, under command of 9 Corps, two infantry and two armoured divisions. They would be assisted in the initial assault by the greatest weight of artillery that could be made available and by a very heavy air attack in the "blitzkrieg" style. I laid all the emphasis in planning on speed and the maintenance of the objective. The armoured divisions were to move off behind the infantry divisions simultaneously with them so that there would be no delay or hesitation in pushing them through the infantry the moment a break through was achieved. I insisted that none of the divisions of 9 Corps should turn aside to mop up isolated areas of resistance or to attempt to roll up the enemy's exposed flanks but were to continue straight for Tunis, ignoring any enemy to left or right. By this means they would forestall the enemy on his defences round Tunis and split his whole front in half. If these instructions could be strictly followed I felt confident of turning the German "blitzkrieg" technique on its inventors and preventing an African "Dunkirk".

This question of an enemy evacuation of Tunisia naturally occupied a great deal of our thoughts at the time and although our success was in the event so rapid as to prevent any attempt being made it is worth while giving a brief study to the subject. From our point of view it was vital to prevent any substantial evacuation, both because of the psychological value of complete annihilation and because a reinforcement of Sicily by large numbers of German troops would make our next task much more difficult. I was uncertain whether the well-known German reluctance to abandon any position, however untenable, would work against an evacuation; it now seems likely that they would have attempted it had they been given a chance. We were, however, by then in a position to throw a naval and air blockade round the Tunisian coast which, in spite of the extensive minefields at sea, could be relied on to let very little pass. In the worst case, assuming the enemy was able to stabilize a firm bridgehead position, it was calculated that it would be theoretically possible to remove up to a maximum of seventy thousand men; in the event only just over six hundred got away and these were nearly all sailors or dockworkers.

The move of formations from Eighth Army, the redisposition of 9 Corps and the dumping of ammunition and other stores would take some time, and D-day for the attack, which was given the codename VULCAN, was fixed as 6th May. As a preliminary 5 Corps was to capture Gebel Bou Aoukaz on the afternoon of 5th May in order to free the left flank of the attack from threat from this direction. On the morning of the 6th the 9 Corps attack would start before dawn on a front of three thousand yards with 4 British Division right and 4 Indian Division left, supported by artillery concentrations from over four hundred guns, centrally controlled. The infantry were to begin by seizing a line north of the road through the small village of Frendj, about six thousand yards from the start line. 6 Armoured Division was to follow 4 British, and 7 Armoured 4 Indian. Their first bound was to the area of St. Cyprien, twelve miles further on and the same distance from Tunis, before the enemy could recover from the shock and occupy the perimeter defences. 5 Corps, which had 46 Division north of the river and I and 78 Divisions to the south, was to hold the corridor open and be prepared to support 9 Corps. XIX Corps was to launch an attack against Gebel Zaghouan on 4th May; on the same day the New Zealanders on Eighth Army's left would mount local attacks south of Saouaf to assist the French and pin down the enemy on their front. II Corps was to continue its successful advance towards Bizerta.

I summed up these orders in a personal letter to General Anderson on 3rd May which I reproduce here as giving the clearest picture of my conception of the final plan.

"1. The primary object of your attack is to capture Tunis. Every effort must be made to pass the two armoured divisions through on the same day as the infantry attack starts so that the enemy is not allowed time to build up a strong anti-tank screen.

2. 9 Corps must seize a bridgehead through the immediate defences of Tunis as early as possible, before the enemy has time to man these defences.

3. The mopping up of localities which the enemy continues to hold on the fronts of 78 and 1 Divisions must come later. The chief task of 5 Corps after the armour has passed through is to keep open the funnel.

4. Concentration must be maintained and it would not be sound to aim at advancing on too wide a front. For instance, 46 Division may well be required to nourish the threat and to assist 5 Corps to keep the funnel open. An advance north of the river Medjerda would not contribute to the main object. Troops north of the river will be forced to withdraw when you reach Tunis and cut their communications.

5. I consider the best way to prevent the enemy withdrawing a large part of his forces to the Cape Bon peninsula is to reach Tunis as early as possible, thus cutting off all troops north of Tunis. In any case I do not wish your operations for the early capture of Tunis to be prejudiced by preoccupation with preventing the enemy withdrawing to Cape Bon".

During the period before the offensive opened my plans for deceiving the enemy as to our intentions continued and showed evidence of producing good results. The enemy did not reinforce the area which I had selected for my point of main effort but left its defence to 15 Panzer Division, now in a very weak state. By contrast he retained both 10 and 21 Panzer Divisions in the Kourzia area, opposite my 1 Armoured Division. Shortly before the attack began a battalion from 90 Light Division was brought round from Eighth Army front to St. Cyprien but on 4th May, on the other hand, the enemy removed two battalions of heavy anti-tank guns from the Massicault area to the area north-east of the Kourzia marshes. It was gratifying to realise that we had been so successful in obtaining surprise and that the enemy had split his armour, leaving the stronger part of it away to the south of our point of main effort.

The attack on Gebel Bou Aoukaz by 1 Division went in on 5th May at 1700 hours with strong and effective air support. As I have already explained the capture of this mountain was essential to the whole conduct of operations in order to clear the left flank of the attack. The fighting on the mountain was severe and the enemy counter-attacked many times; major credit for the success must go to 1 Irish Guards who finally cleared the crest, at the cost of many casualties, within the time table laid down for the operation. Gebel Bou Aoukaz was in our hands by nightfall and all that night the infantry of 4 British and 4 Indian Divisions were moving forward to their assembly areas. On 6th May, at 0330 hours, they advanced to the attack side by side on a very narrow front. The massed artillery of First Army, backed by the dumps of ammunition which we had been nourishing so long for this event, fired concentrations on known enemy localities. At dawn the air forces went in. It was their greatest effort in the war up to that date, over two thousand sorties of all types. The weight of the attack was too much for the defenders, already weakened physically and morally by the heavy fighting since 22nd April. Most of them did their duty but there were isolated instances of demoralisation. By 1030 hours the first infantry objectives were captured and by 1130 hours the village of Frendj was reported clear. The two armoured divisions, which were close on the heels of the attacking infantry, at once passed into the lead. So deep had been our initial penetration that they found enemy resistance, though gallant and desperate, to be but little organised, they met some groups of enemy tanks, from 15 Panzer Division, and many of the 88 millimetre guns withdrawn from airfield defence, but the impetus of the offensive was so strong that it carried them by nightfall as far as Massicault, half-way to Tunis. 6 Armoured Division leaguered for the night to the south-east and 7 Armoured Division to the north-east of the village. The enemy were endeavouring to form a new defensive position at St. Cyprien.

The first day's fighting in the Medjerda valley had thus ended in a great success. Meanwhile II Corps to the north was about to reap the reward of its steady and well conducted advance. Under this constant and increasing pressure the German front in the mountains broke on the night of 2nd May and next day reconnaissance elements of 1 Armoured Division entered Mateur. The enemy tried to hold a line on the high ground east of the Mateur – Tebourba road and especially the pass leading to Chouigui, which was strongly defended by the Barenthin Regiment. North of Mateur, however, 1 Division to the south and 9 Division to the north of Garaet Achkel continued to make progress. The Moroccan Goums attached to 9 Division were particularly useful in the mountains to the north of the lake. These were strong positions by nature but the German defenders had been too much weakened by their losses round Jefna. On the morning of the 7th May resistance broke, on the edge of the last hills, and the American Corps started the final attack which was to bring them into Bizerta.

At first light on 7th May 6 and 7 Armoured Divisions moved forward once more from Massicault. Despite his best efforts the enemy had been unable to organise a defence in the area of the break through, though he was hastily summoning back the forces cut off to the south of our penetration. 6 Armoured Division fought a stiff action south-east of St. Cyprien while 7 Armoured Division, advancing north of the road, captured the village by 0830 hours and pressed on for the suburb of Le Bardo. There was a sharp skirmish at the junction of the Medjez and Bizerta roads, a little sniping from isolated houses on the outskirts but at 1445 hours 11 Hussars and 1 Derbyshire Yeomanry entered Tunis. The enthusiasm of the population was unrestrained; it was the first of many experiences we were to have of the liberation of a great city. An hour and a half after the British entry into Tunis 47 Regimental Combat Team of 9 United States Division entered Bizerta. It was a happy coincidence that we should have gained our two main objectives simultaneously and that both the major Allies should have won a notable victory on the same day; I had of course planned this division of the spoils but I had not expected so dramatic a climax.

The fall of Tunis and Bizerta clearly came to the German Command, both in Africa and Berlin, as a most severe shock. It was not until the evening of 8th May that the High Command issued a statement that Africa would now be abandoned and "the thirty-one thousand Germans and thirty thousand Italians remaining" would be withdrawn by sea. I commented in a report to General Eisenhower that night that the Navy and Air Forces would interfere with this programme, which in any event depended on the enemy holding a firm bridgehead in Cape Bon, and reminded him of Mr. Churchill's words in August, 1940: "We are waiting, so are the fishes". In fact no effort of this sort was made, for the enemy's plans of defence had been completely disrupted. The divided forces were not given a moment's pause to recover. As soon as the situation in Tunis was under control 9 Corps split its forces according to the pre-arranged plan and proceded to mop up to left and right. On the left 7 Armoured Division was directed northwards up the Bizerta road towards Protville and the Medjerda; simultaneously 1 United States Armoured Division was moving towards the same area, north of the Protville marshes, from Mateur. The troops entrapped in this pocket consisted of the Manteuffel Division, 15 Panzer and 334 Infantry Divisions. They had little hope of resistance and none of evacuation and at noon on 9th May they accepted unconditional surrender. Six Generals were among the prisoners, including von Vaerst, the Commander-in-Chief of 5 Panzer Army.

The forces cut off on the south of our wedge of penetration, between 9 Corps and Eighth Army, were larger than those to the north. In order to deal with these the first essential was to establish ourselves across the base of the Cape Bon peninsula, for should they be able to withdraw into it they might prolong resistance unduly. Provided we followed up our success vigorously, however, there could be no chance for them of withdrawing in time. Accordingly 6 Armoured Division, after passing through Tunis, wheeled right down the road which runs across the base of the peninsula. It was followed by 4 Infantry Division, and 1 Armoured Division came up on its right from the Goubellat area. The first obstacle encountered was the Hammam Lif defile. At the bottom of the Gulf of Tunis Gebel Bou Kournine, the sacred "twin-horned" mountain of the Carthaginians, rises steeply above the road leaving a narrow gap of about three hundred yards between it and the sea shore. The pass was held by some of the remaining troops of the Hermann Goering Division, strongly supported by heavy anti-aircraft guns withdrawn from airfield defence. For two days this exceptionally strong position held 6 Armoured Division at bay but on the morning of 10th May they broke through by sending a body of tanks through the very edge of the surf.

With the forcing of the Hamman Lif defile our advance was rapid and met no further obstacles. 6 Armoured Division poured through the pass down the main road to the south and by nightfall on the 10th had reached Hammamet on the east coast. Next day 4 Division swept rapidly round the peninsula, encountering no opposition and demonstrating that no important forces had withdrawn there. On 12th May 6 Armoured Division attacked southwards from Bou Ficha, 56 Division co-operated with shelling from the south and after a brief resistance the enemy raised the white flag. Our encircling ring had joined up and the only enemy still resisting were in isolated pockets to the northwest of Enfidaville.

Up to this time the enemy facing Eighth Army had held their ground and continued to show resistance; indeed the front had been livelier than ever, for the Germans had greatly increased their artillery fire in order to get rid of as much ammunition as possible.[41] On the 12th, however, mass surrenders occurred. General Graf von Sponeck, commanding 90 Light Division, surrendered to Lieut.-General Sir Bernard Freyberg of the New Zealand Division, old opponents on many hard-fought fields. General von Arnim, the Army Group Commander, surrendered to the Commanding Officer of 2 Gurkhas. He was brought to my Headquarters at Le Kef, where he still seemed surprised by the suddenness of the disaster. The Italians in the more inaccessible hill-country north of Saouaf held out the longest, and General Messe delayed his surrender until the morning of the 13th; shortly before, he had been informed by radio of his promotion to the rank of Marshal. The troops in general surrendered to anyone they could find willing to accept their surrender. It was an astonishing sight to see long lines of Germans driving themselves, in their own transport or in commandeered horse-carts, westwards in search of prisoner of war cages. Men who had, so short a time before, been fighting like tigers now seemed transformed into a cheerful and docile crowd, resigned to the acceptance of their fate.

The campaign which culminated in the battle of Tunis was noteworthy not only for the fact that it was the first wholly successful campaign against the Axis, the "end of the beginning" in Mr. Churchill's phrase, working up through checks and disappointments to the "battle without a tomorrow." It was remarkable also for the manner of its winning. We had produced in Tunisia a new instrument of victory in the form of the close collaboration between the Allies, a principle which was to be not only a battle-winning but a war-winning factor. The importance and the magnitude of this achievement tend now to be obscured by the fact that this spirit of Allied unity came into being so early and grew so rapidly that it seems to have a character of inevitability which reduces the unique value of its creation. The history of previous wars and previous coalitions demonstrates that this is far from being the case. It was not inevitable by any means that British and American troops should show, in the first battle they had fought together since 1918, such a whole hearted spirit of comradeship, nor that British and French, between whom the past three years had thrown many shadows, should recapture once more the same degree of trust and mutual respect which had animated the old alliance. The credit must go to the soldiers of all three nations and in a very large degree to General Eisenhower who by word and example inspired those efforts. My relations with General Eisenhower were of the happiest and I valued them both for personal reasons and from the point of view of the task in hand: he backed me up in every possible way and I knew that I could in all circumstances rely on his complete understanding, sympathy and support.

Besides this co-operation between the three nationalities involved there is also to be noted the degree of co-operation achieved between the three services. The battle of Tunis gave the fullest scope for a demonstration of this, for it was so designed and planned as to enable the Navy and Air Forces to play their full part and produce their full strength simultaneously with the supreme effort of the Army. They held the enemy in the "Tunisian tip" in a stranglehold while the Army finished them off. In this respect also the campaign marked the beginning of a collaboration which was to grow ever stronger until the final victory. The Naval Commander-in-Chief in the Mediterranean was Admiral Cunningham,[42] returning to the scene of his former triumphs. Air Chief Marshal Tedder was the Air Officer Commanding-in-Chief. The Commander of the Tactical Air Force, Air Marshal Coningham, had established a joint headquarters with me. We shared the same mess, worked side by side, and had collaborated from the first days of the campaign until the day of final victory. It was thanks to him that the co-operation between the air and ground forces on the battlefield were so close and automatic.

The final victory in Africa was an unusually complete example of the battle of annihilation. Never before had a great army been so totally destroyed. A quarter of a million men laid down their arms in unconditional surrender; six hundred and sixty three escaped. Immense stocks of arms, ammunition and supplies of all natures were the booty of the victors. Our own casualties in the final battle were less than two thousand men. At 1415 hours on 13th May I sent the following signal to the Prime Minister:

"Sir, it is my duty to report that the Tunisian campaign is over. All enemy resistance has ceased. We are masters of the North African shores."

APPENDIX "A".
Directive to Commander-in-Chief, Middle East Command.
PART I.

Special Responsibilities.

1. Your prime and main duty will be to take or destroy at the earliest opportunity, the German and Italian Armies in Libya and Egypt together with all their supplies and establishments.

2. You will discharge or cause to be discharged, the duties enumerated below, without prejudice to the task given in paragraph 1, which is of paramount importance.

General Responsibilities.

3. You will command and be responsible for the administration of all Imperial Land Forces, and such Allied Forces as may be specifically placed under your command in the following territories:-

Egypt.
Libya.
Malta.
Palestine and Trans-Jordan.
Cyprus.
Syria (west of the Inter-Command boundary).
Iraq (west of the Inter-Command boundary).
Sudan.
Eritrea.

Your Eastern boundary (with Persia and Iraq Command) will be:-

Inclusive Malatya – exclusive Siverek – Ras El Ain – inclusive Hasseche – Garat Motteb – thence Syrian-Iraqi Frontier to inclusive Abu Kemal – exclusive Kasr Muhaiwir thence a line due south to Saudi Arabian Frontier – thence exclusive Riyadh – inclusive Saiala.

4. You will also be responsible for the preparation of plans, when required, for the employment of land forces in the following territories:-

Italian territories in North Africa.
Turkey (in conjunction with C.-in-C., Persia and Iraq Command).
The Balkan States (Yugoslavia, Roumania, Bulgaria and Greece).
Crete.
The Islands in the Aegean.
Arabia (in conjunction with C.-in-C., Persia and Iraq Command).

5. Subject to the direction of the Chiefs of Staff and of the War Office in respect of land forces, you are responsible, in conjunction with the Commanders-in-Chief, Mediterranean and Eastern Fleet, and the Air Officer Commanding-in-Chief, Middle East, and C.in-C., Persia and Iraq, for the co-ordination of the operations of Imperial and Allied Forces under your Command in the territories mentioned in paragraphs 3 and 4 above with those of the Allies of His Majesty's Government.

6. Should you wish to make recommendations regarding the transfer of any formations or units of the land forces between the Middle East and Persia and Iraq Command you will consult the Commander-in-Chief, Persia and Iraq Command, and will, if possible forward an agreed recommendation. No moves between the two Commands will take place without the authority of the War Office.

7. You will be responsible in conjunction with the Air Officer Commanding-in-Chief, Middle East, for the preparation of plans for the employment of land

forces in Aden to meet the eventuality of major land operations in or beyond the borders of this Protectorate. In that eventuality you will assume command of the land forces in Aden. This in no way affects the responsibilities of the Air Officer Commanding, British Forces in Aden, for the conduct of purely local operations of a minor character.

8. You are responsible for advising His Majesty's Government as regards their policy towards the armed forces of Egypt. Questions relating to those forces will be dealt with through the channel of His Majesty's Representative in Egypt except where arrangements to the contrary have been agreed upon by all concerned.

PART II.

Liaison with Service Authorities.

9. In carrying out these tasks, you will, where appropriate, consult and co-operate with the Commanders-in-Chief, Mediterranean and Eastern Fleet, the Commanders-in-Chief, India and Persia and Iraq Command, the General Officers Commanding-in-Chief, East and West Africa and the Air Officer Commanding-in-Chief, Middle East.

Allocation of Air Forces.

10. The allocation of air forces as between Middle East on the one hand and Persia and Iraq on the other will be a matter for the general direction of the Chiefs of Staff.

The temporary reinforcement of one Command at the expense of the other is a matter for the judgment of the Air Officer, Commanding-in-Chief, subject to any directions he may from time to time receive from the Chiefs of Staff or the Air Ministry and to the closest consultation with you, the Minister of State, the Commander-in-Chief, Persia and Iraq, and the Naval Commander-in-Chief, Mediterranean.

Relations with the Air Officer Commanding-in-Chief Middle East during active operations.

11. When you consider that active operations are in prospect, you will, with the approval of the Chiefs of Staff, notify the Air Officer Commanding-in-Chief, Middle East. He will then give you all possible aid.

Liaison with Civil Authorities.

12. You will, either direct through His Majesty's Minister of State or through the General Officers Commanding-in-Chief, as maybe appropriate, maintain touch with His Majesty's Representatives in Egypt, Turkey (in conjunction with the Commander-in-Chief, Persia and Iraq Command), the Governor General of the Sudan, the High Commissioner for Palestine and Trans-Jordan, and the Governors of Aden, Cyprus and Malta. You will also maintain touch with Le Commandant en Chef Délégué Général et Plénipotentiaire de la France Libre au Levant, either direct or through His Majesty's Minister of State.

PART III.
Responsibilities in respect of occupied enemy territories.
13. Political, administrative and legislative authority in occupied enemy territory within your command is vested in you at international law. You should, however, delegate this authority in full to your Chief Political Officer.

PART IV.
Relations with His Majesty's Minister of State.
14. You will refer any question requiring immediate decision by His Majesty's War Cabinet to His Majesty's Minister of State, who has the authority to take such a decision on behalf of His Majesty's War Cabinet should the occasion demand.

It is the responsibility of His Majesty's Minister of State to decide whether, according to the degree of urgency, he will take a decision or refer it to His Majesty's War Cabinet.

15. You will consult His Majesty's Minister of State, where appropriate, on all political questions affecting your command.

(Sgd.) P.J. GRIGG.

The War Office.
13th November, 1942.

APPENDIX "B".
ALLIED FORCE HEADQUARTERS.
17th February, 1943.

OPERATIONS IN TUNISIA.
Directive to Deputy Commander-in-Chief.
To: General the Honourable Sir H.R.L.G. Alexander, G.C.B.
1. In pursuance of the conclusions reached at the 63rd meeting of the Combined Chiefs of Staff, held on 20th January, 1943, you are appointed Deputy Commander-in-Chief of the Allied Forces in French North Africa. Further, you are appointed Commander of the Group of Armies operating in Tunisia.

2. This appointment takes effect on 20th February, 1943, on which date you will take command of all Allied forward forces engaged in operations in Tunisia. These consist of the British First Army, which exercises command over the United States and French forces operating in Tunisia, the British Eighth Army, and such reserve formations as may be placed under your command.

3. Your mission is the early destruction of all Axis forces in Tunisia.

4. You will establish an Army Group Headquarters initially at Constantine, or other suitable point of your selection.

5. A naval officer from the Staff of C.-in-C., Mediterranean, will be located at your Headquarters to furnish you with such naval advice and assistance as you may require.

6. An Air Officer Commanding the Tactical Air Force will share your Headquarters and will direct the Air Forces assigned to him for direct support of your Armies to the best advantage of the land operations prescribed by you.

Army support wings will be attached to First and Eighth Armies. The Wing Commanders will act as air advisors to the Army Commanders and will command such Air Forces as may be assigned to them from time to time by the Air Officer Commanding the Tactical Air Force.

7. Responsibility for supply and maintenance of the forces under your command will remain as follows:-

Allied Force H.Q. for First Army (including all United States and French Forces under command) and for any reserves and Air Forces found from Allied Forces.

G.H.Q., Middle East, for Eighth Army and for Air Forces found from R.A.F., Middle East.

8. The rear (Western) boundary of your command will be the line of all inclusive Zribet El Oued V99 – La Meskiana M90 – Dj Mesloula No3 – Point 1110 No6 – St^on De Nador M89 – Boudarouah G80 – road Munier H31 – Le Tarf H43 – Lac Melah H45.

By Command of General EISENHOWER:
W.B. SMITH,
Major General, G.S.C.,
Chief of Staff.

Copies to:
C.-in-C. Mediterranean.
A.O.C.-in-C. Mediterranean.

APPENDIX "C".

14th March, 1943.

EIGHTEENTH ARMY GROUP.

Policy.

1. *Object.* – To destroy the Axis Forces, in Tunisia as early as possible.

2. *Grouping.* – Eighteenth Army Group will directly control:-

Eighth Army,
2 U.S. Corps,
First Army with the French troops (XIX Corps) under command.

3. *Sectors.* – British, French, and American troops will be allotted separate sectors as far as possible under their own commanders.

4. *Organisation.* – Divisions will live, train, and fight as divisions and will not be split up into small groups or combat teams.

5. *Specialist Troops.* – such as parachute troops and commandos, will be withdrawn for rest, refitting, and training, as early as possible.

6. *Eighteenth Army Group Reserve:*

> 6 Armoured Division   }
> One British Infantry Division } 9 Corps.
> 9 Corps troops   }
> 1 Parachute Brigade.
> 1 and 6 Commandos.

9 Corps will carry out intensive training for offensive operations under Commander 9 Corps.

7. *Local Reserves.* – Corps sectors must aim at having the equivalent of one infantry division or one armoured division in Corps reserve.

8. *Armour.* – Tanks will be withdrawn from the front line and grouped as local reserves for the counter-attack role.

9. *Firm Bases.* – Key positions will be prepared and held strongly as firm bases, and pivots, well supported by artillery and tanks. Areas between these firm bases will be carefully patrolled and watched. Enemy penetration into these gaps in small numbers will be dealt with by local reserves. Enemy penetration in strength will be dealt with by Corps reserves.

10. The front will at present be held defensively but in an offensive spirit with active patrolling and minor operations undertaken to improve positions, train units, and keep the initiative over the enemy.

11. *Training.* – Intensive training in tactics and the use of weapons will be undertaken by all troops, both in and out of the line, with a view to future offensive operations. Attention is called to "Tactical and Training Notes" issued down to Company and equivalent commanders.

12. *Morale.* – Everything possible will be done to raise the morale and fighting spirit of the troops to the highest pitch.

13. *Administrative.* – Everything possible will be done to build up reserves of material and supplies for future offensive operations.

14. *Air Forces.* – The Air Force organisation will be parallel to that of the land forces. The policy is to reorganise the air forces so that the Tactical Air Force H.Q. will control balanced formations linked with the operational Armies and Corps comprising Eighteenth-Army Group.

15. Develop the hitting power of the air forces in Tunisia by the creation of a tactical bomber force for operation in the battle area.

16. Co-ordinate the operations of all formations comprising the Tactical Air Force and ensure maximum flexibility and mutual support of one another.

17. To provide airfield and supply resources, which will enable the maximum air striking force to be used where it is most needed.

18. To ensure co-ordination with external air forces whereby the strategic air commands and Malta units may be brought into the approved plan.

19. Whilst doing everything possible in the Tunisian land battles to prepare the most effective operations to prevent a successful enemy evacuation from Africa.

20. To build up the Tactical Air Forces to the highest possible operational standard for any tasks that may be required after completion of the African fighting.

H.R. ALEXANDER,
GENERAL.
Commander, Eighteenth Army Group.

Notes
 1. Now Field-Marshal The Earl Wavell, P.C., G.C.B., G.C.S.I., G.C.I.E., C.M.G., M.C.
 2. Now Field-Marshal Sir Claude J.E. Auchinleck, G.C.B., G.C.I.E., C.S.I., D.S.O., O.B.E., A.D.C.
 3. Now Field-Marshal The Viscount Alanbrooke of Brookeborough, K.G., G.C.B., O.M., D.S.O.
 4. General Catroux, when he spent the opening night of the Battle of Alamein with me there, suggested we might rename it "La Belle Alliance".
 5. Now Field Marshal The Viscount Montgomery of Alamein, K.G., G.C.B., D.S.O.
 6. It was not practicable to pass a force through the desert south of the Qattara Depression to reach the Nile Valley through the Fayum, the Germans sent a reconnaissance detachment this way, organized by the Hungarian traveller, Baron Almassy, but it was detected and secured by us.
 7. El Alamein, after which the line and the battle were called, is nothing but a halt on the Desert Railway to Mersa Matruh. The name, which is descriptive as are most names in the desert, means "the twin cairns". Deir means a depression, of which there are several small examples between the main depression and the sea, Qaret el Abd means "the hill of the slave".
 8. Deutsch-Italienisch Panzer Armee Afrika or Armata Corazzata Italo-Tedesca, referred to by the Italians as ACIT.
 9. Originally a motorized division but now called "appiedata" or dismounted.
 10. I use the name by which it was later known. At this time the division was called Cacciatori d'Africa or "African Sharpshooters"; it adopted the name Folgore in September.
 11. There was also, of course, the 88 millimetre anti-aircraft gun, beloved of Allied War Correspondents, who appeared to be unaware of the existence of any other calibre in German artillery.
 12. Italian infantry divisions, by contrast with the German, had only two infantry regiments.
 13. Three squadrons of American fighter aircraft of this force at this time formed part of Western Desert Air Force under Air Vice Marshal Coningham; by January, 1943, eight American fighter squadrons were co-operating with Eighth Army.
 14. The shortage was so serious that the Germans were reduced to flying in fuel from Greece, a most wasteful procedure.
 15. Shortly before the battle, Eighth Army allowed to fall into enemy hands, abandoned in a purposely sacrificed armoured car, what purported to be a "going" map of the area. It showed an area of very bad going extending across the route we did not wish the enemy to take and a belt of good going extending up to the crest of the Alam el Halfa ridge and thence along the ridge to the railway. From General von Thoma, whom we subsequently captured, we learned that this ruse had been effective; the enemy had intended to outflank the ridge to the north-east but had altered his plan on the basis of this false information.
 16. Now Admiral Sir Henry Harwood, K.C.B., O.B.E.

17. Now Marshal of the Royal Air Force Lord Tedder, G.C.B.
18. Theoretically one General Transport company can maintain one division fifty miles from railhead or a port i.e. for every fifty miles of an advance you need one extra company per division. This rule of thumb calculation is based on working seven days a week and ten hours a day, over good roads, in the desert it needs modification and on occasions it took six companies to do the work of one.
19. Now The Right Honourable Lord Killearn, P.C., G.C.M.G., C.B., M.V.O.
20. Code name for the North African landings.
21. The Commander of the German Africa Corps was also a recent arrival from the Russian front General von Thoma, who had succeeded General Cruewell, taken prisoner in June.
22. For example the film "Desert Victory" and the War Office pamphlet "The Battle of Egypt".
23. This pause was misinterpreted by the enemy and, among the Italians in particular, it was thought that we had called the battle off for good, accepting defeat.
24. There was a previous battle of Tell el Aqqaqir on 26th February, 1916, in the campaign against the Senussi, but this is another place of the same name, fifteen miles south-east of Sidi Barrani.
25. 1 Armoured Division with 2 Armoured and 7 Motor Brigades, the 7th with 22 Armoured and 131 Lorried Infantry Brigades and the 10th with 8 Armoured and 133 Lorried Infantry Brigades. The two Lorried Infantry Brigades were taken from 44 Division; the association of 131 Brigade with 7 Armoured Division, which began in this purely fortuitous manner, became permanent and 1 Armoured retained 7 Motor Brigade, the original 7 Armoured Division Support Group.
26. The best way of rendering a well unusable, as practised by both sides, was to pour in bone oil. This is not poisonous, but very nauseating.
27. 11 Hussars had been the first British troops to enter Benghazi on its first capture in February, 1941; they were also first into Tripoli in January, 1943, and Tunis in May 1943 (with 1 Derbyshire Yeomanry).
28. From the Ciano Diaries it appears that the decision to evacuate had been taken at least by 8th December.
29. He later added this "nom de guerre" to his family name and is known as Général d'Armée J.P. Leclerc de Hautecloque.
30. Appendix "B".
31. Build-up in First Army was as follows. 78 Division completed 1st December, 6 Armoured Division 15th December, 46 Division first week in February, 1943, 1 Division 22nd March, 4 Division end of second week in April.
32. But, contrary to general popular belief at the time and later, the Germans did not bring in tanks by air.
33. Eighth Army came under command Eighteenth Army Group from 0001 hours, 20th February.
34. About half the divisional infantry and artillery and a battalion of tanks.
35. From the point of view of the Axis, however, there was one disadvantage; the bunkers had been planned for the French 25 and 47 millimetre anti-tank guns and were too small to house, the German 50 and 75 millimetre pieces which had therefore to be emplaced in the open.
36. Where, incidentally, the water, though plentiful, is so full of magnesium salts as to threaten to debilitate any troops who had to drink it for long.
37. In a signal on 12th March, giving my appreciation of the enemy situation, I concluded "For Rommel's general intentions see Revelations XII, 12", ("The devil is come down unto you, having great wrath, because he knoweth that he hath but a short time.").
38. Appendix "C".
39. Various parties, from the Long Range Desert Group and the Raiding Forces, had already made contact with First Army; but these had come the long way round west of the Chotts, an impracticable route for any large body.
40. 201 Guards Brigade was at that time numbered 22.
41. Contrary to reports at the time, they were well provided with supplies of all natures.
42. Now Admiral of the Fleet The Viscount Cunningham of Hyndhope, K.T., G.C.B., O.M., D.S.O.

2

ADMIRAL SIR ANDREW CUNNINGHAM'S DESPATCH ON OPERATION *TORCH*, THE LANDINGS IN NORTH AFRICA 22 OCTOBER TO 17 NOVEMBER 1942

THE LANDINGS IN NORTH AFRICA

The following Despatch was submitted to the Commander-in-Chief, Allied Forces on the 30th March, 1943, by Admiral of the Fleet Sir ANDREW B. CUNNINGHAM, G.C.B., D.S.O., Commander-in-Chief, Mediterranean.

> *Office of the Commander-in-Chief,*
> *Mediterranean,*
> *Algiers.*
> *30th March, 1943.*

OPERATION "TORCH" – REPORT OF PROCEEDINGS.

I have the honour to render the following report on Operation "Torch" covering the period 22nd October to 17th November, 1942, from the sailings of the assault convoy from the United Kingdom until the occupation of Bone. This report deals mainly with the British naval assaults, since the naval operations of the Western Naval Task Force have already been reported in the Commander, Task Force 34's letter of 28th November, 1942 to the Commander-in-Chief, United States Atlantic Fleet.[1]

2. The early stages of the operation prior to D day were remarkable for lack of incident. This was indeed fortunate since, in the course of this vast and complex movement, delays caused by casualties or stress of weather would have rendered the timely delivery of the assaults improbable.

3. The movement of the assault convoys and Force "H"[2] through the Straits of Gibraltar on the 5th/6th November and the continuous entry and departure of all classes of ships for fuelling placed a heavy strain on the resources and organisation of Gibraltar. The manner in which this strain was withstood reflects credit on the Vice-Admiral, Gibraltar and Commodore Superintendent, Gibraltar and their staffs.

4. It is also a tribute to the skill and seamanship of individual Commanding Officers that this continuous flow of movements and berthing in a congested harbour and anchorage in the dark was accomplished with but a single minor collision.

SUPPLEMENT TO THE LONDON GAZETTE, 23 MARCH, 1949   1525

OPERATION "TORCH"
NORTH AFRICA — NOVEMBER, 1942.
LANDING BEACHES

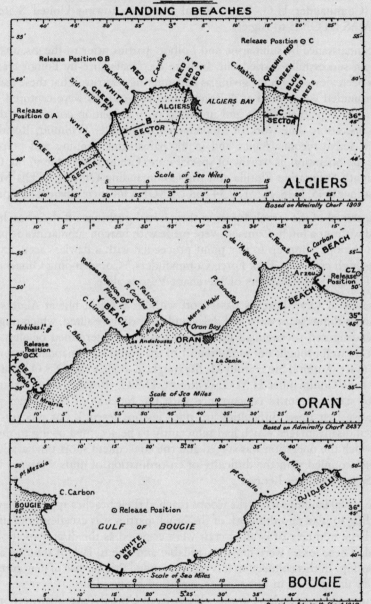

5. The only major incident inside the Mediterranean before the assaults was the torpedoing of United States Ship THOMAS STONE at 0535 on 7th November. A notably courageous decision was taken by Captain O.R. Bennehoff, United States Navy to send on his escort and boats to the assault, leaving his ship defenceless; tenacity and seamanship was displayed by His Majesty's Ship WISH-ART (Commander H.G. Scott, Royal Navy) in towing United States Ship THOMAS STONE to Algiers.

6. Reconnaissance by submarine and Folbot[3] parties prior to the assaults was in the main successfully carried out. Inshore reconnaissance by Folbot teams had always been viewed with misgiving as endangering security. That these fears were well grounded was proved at A Beach when two officers were captured. Fortunately they kept their heads and imparted no information concerning the projected operation. The work of Lieutenant-Commander Willmott, Royal Navy, both in active reconnaissance and in his painstaking training and preparation before the operation, is worthy of special note. Credit is also due to the Captain (S), Eighth Submarine Flotilla and the Commanding Officers of His Majesty's Submarines P.45, P.48, P.221, P.54 and URSULA for their efficient co-operation.

7. The arrival of the assault forces at their initial positions off their beaches proceeded without a hitch. Contacts were made with beacon submarines as planned. In fact the operation up to this point proceeded with a flawless accuracy which reflects high credit on Task Force Commanders,[4] Commanding Officers of His Majesty's Ships and Masters of Merchant Vessels alike.

8. Assaults at Oran beaches passed off without a hitch; but at Algiers B and C Beaches things went awry and delay and confusion resulted, which might well have endangered success had the opposition been determined or alert. These points are well brought out in the report of the Naval Commander Eastern Task Force (Vice-Admiral Sir Harold M. Burrough, K.B.E., C.B., D.S.O.) and that of Lieutenant-Commander H.M.C. Willmott, D.S.O., Royal Navy.[5] I would only wish to state my entire concurrence with the remarks of the former and re-emphasise that these difficulties are not "lessons learnt", but recognised and foreseen disadvantages which had reluctantly to be accepted owing to the speed with which the operation was staged and the consequent short time available for training, coupled with the difficulty of co-ordination of units scattered initially from Scapa to Sierra Leone.

9. The actual landings when the troops reached their beaches appear to have gone according to plan and the work of the beach parties was excellent, but unnecessarily large numbers of landing craft were crippled as the disembarkations proceeded. These losses were mostly avoidable and due to lack of training and bad seamanship. In this connection it is recommended that the use of new entries, not properly disciplined, in this type of operation be avoided.

Various suggestions have arisen, chiefly from United States Army reports, that landing craft should be manned and operated by the Army on the score of improved co-ordination and training. In fact, it is felt that it matters little what uniform the crews wear provided that they are disciplined, trained and practised *seamen* and provided that they are organised and operated by officers competent in their jobs and in close touch with the requirements of the troops they are required to land and maintain. As, however, the ships taking part in an assault are tied to a great degree to their landing craft during the period of unloading, it remains essential that the control of the latter should rest in the hands of those responsible for the safety of the ships.

10. The direct assaults planned against the harbour of Algiers and Oran (Operations "Terminal" and "Reservist") were in no sense planned as imitations of Zeebrugge but were intended to be launched just before the surrender or capture of the ports with the purpose of preventing sabotage of ships and port installations. The choice of the correct moment for entry was a difficult one, depending on the existing situation and the large degree of resistance encountered.

In the event, neither operation was successful in its object but both were remarkable for the determination and gallantry with which all concerned tackled their task, and both were successful in forcing an entry through the booms.

Operation "Terminal".
11. His Majesty's Ship BROKE (Lieutenant-Commander A.F.C. Layard, Royal Navy) succeeded in getting alongside in Algiers and disembarked her troops, but they were pinned by machine-gun fire and did no good. It is considered that the Commanding Officer's decision to retire from a position rapidly becoming untenable was a correct one. It is much to be regretted that an underestimate of damage sustained should have led to the subsequent foundering of this ship when she might by then have been safely berthed in Algiers harbour.

Operation "Reservist".
12. The choice of the ships for this operation had rested on their American appearance, and their chance of a friendly reception lay largely in this appearance and the use of the American Ensign. In the face of serious opposition it could not be expected that they would succeed in their task. In the event, the moment chosen could hardly have been less fortunate, since the French alarm to arms was in its first full flush, whilst darkness prevented any American complexion to the operation being apparent.

The expedition was a failure, redeemed by the gallantry displayed by officers and men of both nations as they strove to achieve their object in the face of hopeless odds. It is much to be regretted that Captain F.T. Peters, V.C., D.S.O., D.S.C., Royal Navy, the leader, having survived this ordeal, lost his life in an aircraft accident on his way to the United Kingdom.

Support Fire.
13. The experience of units detailed to provide supporting fire for soldiers ashore served only to re-emphasise the well known fact that ship gunfire cannot be expected to knock out forts by obtaining direct hits on gun positions. Ships'

gunfire is capable of very considerable moral effect when using heavy calibre guns, and of smothering effect from the rapid volume of medium calibre fire of any calibre gun at close range, but that is the most that should be expected. Cases reported of delays in responding to calls for fire are attributable to two main causes, namely, inability of military authority to appreciate that a ship cannot remain waiting indefinitely in her bombarding position in submarine infested waters, and failure to make proper use of the support wave for rapid communication.

Air Support.
Fighters.
14. Taken as a whole the provision of fighter support over the shipping and beaches left little to be desired. It suffered from all the known limitations of carrier-operated aircraft, but was fully effective within those limitations. In general, it is considered that the operations of carrier-borne fighters reflected great credit on the foresight and planning of the Rear- Admiral Aircraft Carriers, on the spirit and training of the Fleet Air Arm and the efficiency of the carriers alike.

Bombers.
15. The provision of close support bombing by carrier-borne aircraft suffers from similar limitations to those referred to in paragraphs 13 and 14 above. In spite of these drawbacks it proved remarkably effective whenever opportunity was given.

  In particular the dive bombing of La Senia aerodrome was most striking not only for its accuracy and effect, but also for the extremely gallant and determined manner in which it was pressed home.

16. A point which emerged was the ineffectiveness of the means provided for the destruction of the Fleet Air Arm aircraft in the event of landing in hostile territory.

Communications.
17. The complication of the communications inherent in any Combined Operation was enhanced in "Torch" by the fact that a W/T organisation had to be evolved for a new station concurrently with carrying out a major operation therein.

18. Further difficulties were the number of services involved and the manner in which they were inextricably mingled in both the Eastern and Centre Task Forces. The mounting of the Western Task Force in the United States of America added considerably to the troubles of the planning stage.

19. Naval communications were generally satisfactory and stood up well to the heavy load of traffic which was considerably increased by the failure of certain W/T links of the other services.

20. The two Headquarters Ships – His Majesty's Ships BULOLO (Captain R.O. Hamer, D.S.O., Royal Navy) and LARGS (Commander E.A. Divers, R.D., Royal Naval Reserve) – were of inestimable value.[6]

Naval Operations.

21. The complaisant attitude of the Italian fleet, and the inactivity of the French main fleet, unfortunately gave Force "H" no scope for action. This powerful force had in fact to be kept cruising idly in an area where it was subject to sporadic air attack and faced with an increasing concentration of U-Boats. We were perhaps fortunate that torpedo casualties were limited to the two destroyers, His Majesty's Ship MARTIN and Her Netherlands Majesty's Ship ISAAC SWEERS.

22. The value of Force "R" was amply demonstrated. These two oilers, Royal Fleet Auxiliary DINGLEDALE and Royal Fleet Auxiliary BROWN RANGER, did yeoman service. It was not my intention that large cruisers should fuel from this force, nor should I have permitted it except in emergency. It is considered very fortunate that His Majesty's Ship BERMUDA (Captain T.H. Back, Royal Navy) escaped damage in her prolonged fuelling at dead slow speed on a steady course inadequately screened.

23. In this connection it has been observed from numerous reports that many Commanding Officers without Mediterranean experience lacked appreciation of the problem with which they were faced in these narrow submarine and aircraft infested waters. It is clear that advice on this subject should have been promulgated beforehand. This has now been done within the "Torch" area, and will be available for future operations.

24. Such surface actions as did take place were somewhat distasteful and one sided encounters with the French destroyers trying to break out of Oran. His Majesty's Ship BRILLIANT (Lieutenant-Commander A.G. Poe, Royal Navy) fought a satisfactory duel with the French destroyer LA SURPRISE. His Majesty's Ship AURORA (Captain W.G. Agnew, C.B., Royal Navy) polished off her opponents on each occasion with practised ease. The performance of His Majesty's Ship JAMAICA in expending 501 rounds to damage one destroyer was less praiseworthy.

Unloading.

25. The weather only held in our favour long enough to enable the smooth working of the assault and early maintenance. The break of weather on $D+1$ was not sufficient to stop disembarkation, but speedily reduced the flow of supply and served to show up the need for greater robustness in the landing craft and for training in rough water and surf conditions for the crews.

26. The early seizure of Arzeu and the surrender of Algiers were invaluable in assisting unloading of the convoys. Even so, we were left with the great anxiety of vast masses of shipping anchored in open roadsteads for many days. Had the enemy shown more enterprise with his U-Boats or had more torpedo aircraft

been at his call, our losses might well have been uncomfortably high. This had of course been recognised as an unavoidable and acceptable risk.

Shipping Casualties.

27. I was concerned to get shipping away as soon as possible from these crowded anchorages. Orders had been issued on this subject in accordance with which the fast troopships were sailed independently for Gibraltar as soon as empty. We were most unfortunate, I consider, in that two of these ships blundered on to U-Boats and were destroyed. It was an even chance whether they would be safer at sea proceeding at high speed for Gibraltar alone, or anchored in the mass, escorts not being available.

28. This ill fortune with the big troopships persisted with the destruction of ETTRICK and WARWICK CASTLE in convoy M.K.F.1 after they had passed clear of the Mediterranean.

29. Other personnel ship losses, notably NARKUNDA, CATHAY, and His Majesty's Ship KARANJA (Acting Commander D.S. Hore-Lacy, Royal Navy), were part of the price which may be expected to be paid for taking such large and valuable vessels into the forward area in order to ensure the early occupation of a port, in this case, Bougie. These losses and the damage suffered by various ships at Algiers serve to point again to the essential importance of establishing properly directed fighter protection at the earliest moment. This was a lesson well learnt in the Western Desert campaign, and well digested by all concerned; but now in the novel circumstances of amphibious entry to a new theatre of operations new lessons had to be learnt by bitter experience. These lessons all relate to the necessity, in the combined planning stage, of assuring the necessary priority for the establishment of R.A.F. ground control and servicing equipment ashore at an early stage.

Anti-Aircraft Gunfire.

30. A striking feature of the operation at Algiers and to eastward of that port was the number of enemy aircraft shot down by ships' gunfire, warships and merchant vessels alike. This was perhaps the first great undertaking by our seaborne forces in which ships entered the area of operations adequately armed. We suffered loss, but the toll paid by the enemy was high.

31. The presence of the anti-aircraft ships at occupied ports was invaluable.

Administrative Arrangements.

32. The administrative arrangements for this operation worked well, due chiefly to the detailed planning carried out by the Admiralty departments and the administrative staff at Norfolk House.[7]

The efficiency with which the administrative section of the Plans Division at the Admiralty met all my requirements and interpreted them to the Supply Departments, where they were well implemented, fully justified the establishment of this section and, together with the assistance rendered by the Second Sea

Lord's office and the department of the Director of Personal Services, contributed greatly to the success of the operation.

In future operations the planning should ensure an adequate supply of clothing for naval and merchant seamen from D day.

The Naval and Victualling Store Departments at Gibraltar were inadequately manned to achieve their full functions.

Advance to the East.

33. No sooner was Algiers occupied than the Flag Officer, Inshore Squadron[8] in co-operation with the General Officer Commanding 1st Army pressed on energetically with the task of expanding the occupation eastward. The acquiescence of the French enabled the occupation of Bone to be quickly undertaken, and it was not until we were within 16 miles of Tunis that the Axis forces were able to stop the tide of our advance.

34. During the initial planning stage, I advocated a landing at Bizerta, and it is a matter of lasting regret to me that this bolder conception was not implemented. Had we been prepared to throw even a small force into the eastward ports, the Axis would have been forestalled in their first token occupation and success would have been complete. They were surprised and off their balance. We failed to give the final push which would have tipped the scales.

35. To sum up, there were few new lessons learnt, but many old ones received fresh emphasis. Those which require most firmly to be borne in mind are

(*a*) The need for boldness and the value of holding even a small highly mobile reserve to exploit success daringly.

(*b*) The importance of not overestimating the enemy's resources, exemplified in this case by the infra-red equipment bogey, which led us to lie too far offshore at the initial landings.

(*c*) The importance of training in a service which is no longer manned by a majority of prime seamen, and the need for combined training with the soldiers with whom they are to work.

(*d*) The importance of carrying out such beach reconnaissance as is required well in advance, to gain security.

(*e*) The vital necessity for immediate installation of a proper air defence system at occupied ports.

(*f*) The need of co-ordination in the various elements of Naval Port Parties who should be assembled and organised under one command before embarkation.

(*g*) The necessity for promulgating experienced advice about conditions in a theatre of operations to units joining from other stations.

36. That the operation achieved the success it did was due, in so far as general operations are concerned,

(*a*) To the high measure of secrecy achieved, which enabled us to gain surprise.

(*b*) To the sound planning and forethought shown in the Naval sphere by Admiral Sir Bertram H. Ramsay, K.C.B., M.V.O.[9], who made a contribution not easily measured to the smooth running of the seaborne operations.

(*c*) To the excellent co-operation which existed through all ranks of the services of both nations, the foundations of which were laid during the period of combined planning at Norfolk House.

(*d*) To the compact and efficient arrangement of the Combined Headquarters at Gibraltar.

(*e*) To the high standard of seamanship and technical efficiency which is mercifully still maintained in the units of the Fleet. In this connection the value of the Western Approaches training is outstanding.

(*f*) To the courage, determination and adaptability of the Merchant Navy.

37. In conclusion I feel it should be placed on record that in this most difficult of all types of operation with a number of services involved and despite the difficulties inherent in welding together the systems of command and organisation of two nations, there reigned a spirit of comradeship and understanding which provided that vital force which brought success to our undertaking. The embodiment of that spirit was exemplified in our Commander-in-Chief, General Dwight D. Eisenhower; we counted it a privilege to follow in his train.

(Signed) A.B. CUNNINGHAM.
Admiral of the Fleet.
The Commander-in-Chief, Allied Forces.

ENCLOSURE I.

The Office of Flag Officer,
Inshore Squadron,
H.M.S. BULOLO.
8th December, 1942.

The following report on Operation "Torch" is forwarded.

Prior to leaving U.K.

2. In compliance with Admiralty instructions I hoisted my Flag as Flag Officer, Force "E", in H.M.S. BULOLO at Greenock at 0800 on 14th October, 1942.

3. Most ships who were to form the fast and slow convoys, K.M.F.1 and K.M.S.1 respectively, had assembled in the Clyde area by 17th October. I took the opportunity on this and succeeding days of visiting all L.S.I.s[10]. with General Ryder, U.S. Army (in command of the assault on Algiers) and Major-General V. Evelegh, O.B.E. (in command of the British 78th Division), and spoke briefly to the ships' companies, landing craft crews, beach parties, and military and R.A.F. personnel embarked.

4. Whilst in the Clyde every endeavour was made to exercise both naval and military personnel and to prepare them for the parts they would be required to

play in the operation. In this connection great difficulty was experienced by the Senior Naval Officers of Landing in making contact with the M.T. ships of the slow convoy; this was due partly to delay in preparing ships and concentrating them and partly to the fact that berths were many miles apart. In the event, it proved impossible for the M.T. ships and their landing craft to be exercised at all.

5. H.M.S. BERMUDA and all Hunt class destroyers taking part in the operation carried out practice bombardments on the Arran range. All destroyers who were available were also given bombardment communication exercises with their own military F.O.O.s[11] ashore.

6. On 17th October, the Fleet minesweepers ACUTE (Commander M/S), CADMUS, ROTHER, SPEY, ALARM, ALBACORE, ALGERINE, HUSSAR and SPEEDWELL were exercised in special night sweeping operations which included the laying of lit dans.[12] These exercises were designed as far as possible to reproduce the actual requirements of the operation and proved most valuable.

7. On the night of 20th/21st October, Exercise "Flaxman", which had been prepared by the staff of Rear-Admiral Combined Operations, was carried out in the Loch Fyne area. Owing to many ships not being available, "Flaxman", which was designed to exercise fully all ships, military and R.A.F. personnel and units in combined operations, was on a very reduced scale. Moreover, as it was urgently necessary to conserve landing craft, which could not be replaced if damaged, only a minimum of troops, vehicles and equipment could be landed. In consequence, communication with the beaches was bad and little information of what was going on was received in the H.Q. Ship. Discussions on return to Greenock proved that while the exercise had been of value to the S.N.O.L.s,[13] military, landing craft crews and beach parties, etc., it was quite inadequate owing to the restrictions which had to be imposed.

8. On 22nd October, Convoy Conference for K.M.S.1 was held on board H.M.S. AVENGER; and on 25th October, the Convoy Conference for K.M.F. 1 was held on board the REINA DEL PACIFICO. At both these conferences the orders for the operation were gone through in detail with the Commanding Officers of naval forces and the Masters and S.N.O. (T)s[14] of Red Ensign ships.

From U.K. to passage of Straits.
9. Convoy K.M.S.1 sailed from the Clyde on 22nd October, 1942. At 2100 B.S.T. on 26th October, I sailed in H.M.S. BULOLO with Convoy K.M.F. 1 from the Clyde in single line ahead at 9 knots.

10. In view of the danger of moored mines, the Fleet minesweepers and twin-screw corvettes escorting K.M.S.1 and K.M.F.1 carried out Oropesa search ahead of both convoys from longitude 06° W. to the 100 fathom line. The search was made with double Oropesa in "H" formation and covered a 3 mile front 5 miles ahead of leading ships of the convoys.

11. At 0900 on 27th October, H.M.S. SHEFFIELD, wearing the Flag of Rear-Admiral C.H.J. Harcourt, C.B.E., Rear-Admiral Commanding, 10th Cruiser Squadron, joined K.M.F. 1 with the escort from Belfast, where she had embarked some 600 U.S. troops under the command of Lieutenant-Colonel Swenson, U.S. Army, and 50 naval ratings commanded by Captain H. St. J. Fancourt. R.N., who were to take part in the direct assault on Algiers (Operation "Terminal").

12. The passage of the convoy from the United Kingdom to the rendezvous with the additional escort off Cape St. Vincent, and the division of the convoy into K.M.F.A. l and K.M.F.O. l on 4th November, was wholly successful, and there is reason to believe that the convoy was never sighted or reported by U-Boats.

13. From 30th October to 3rd November, A/S[15] patrols were flown from H.M.S. BITER, and at 1700 on 30th October a Swordfish sighted a U-Boat on the surface 25 miles, 270° from the convoy. The U-Boat dived before the aircraft could attack, but the aircraft kept him down for sufficient time to enable the convoy to pass unreported. BITER's last Swordfish became unserviceable landing on in a swell after the dusk patrol on 3rd November. No A/S air patrol was provided on 4th November as the weather at Gibraltar was unsuitable. Shore-based A/S aircraft took over protection from 0700 5th November.

14. During the passage the convoy was frequently exercised in emergency turns and in changing from one cruising disposition to another. Outstanding in these exercises was the Polish BATORY leading the fifth column, who was consistently handled with the precision and skill of a well trained naval unit. All ships carried out functioning trials of their A.A. weapons in preparation for the air attacks we expected in the Mediterranean.

15. The convoy should have rendezvoused with the destroyers ESCAPADE, ISAAC SWEERS and MARNE in position 45° 50′ N., 26° 08′ W. at 0800 G.M.T. on 31st October. These destroyers had sailed from Ponta Delgada on 29th October and were joining as additional escort. Owing to the incorrect receipt of a cypher message, the rendezvous was, however, missed, and ROTHER was detached a.m. 31st to look for them but was unsuccessful. At 1815 on 1st November, H.M. Ships CLEVELAND, ALBRIGHTON and ESKDALE were sighted northbound to join K.M.S. 2 and they reported having seen ESCAPADE earlier in the day steering south-east. ISAAC SWEERS and ESCAPADE eventually joined the screen at 1200 on 2nd November, and MARNE at 0800 on 3rd November.

16. At 1830 3rd November, H.M.S. SHEFFIELD was detached and proceeded ahead independently to Gibraltar. Her fuelling of escorts had throughout been conducted most energetically under difficult conditions due to the following swell. On the passage out, escorts were fuelled from SHEFFIELD and ORBITA.

17. From 0930 4th November, the convoy was re-disposed preparatory to the Oran section parting company. At 1150 on 4th November in position 36° 13′ N., 13° 07′ W., H.M. Ships JAMAICA, VERITY, WISHART, VELOX, WEST-

COTT, ACHATES and ANTELOPE joined as additional escorts for K.M.F.O. 1 and K.M.F.A. 1; and at 1400 K.M.F.O. 1 proceeded independently under Commodore T.H. Troubridge, R.N., flying his Flag in H.M.S. LARGS. After re-disposing the screen K.M.F.A. 1's course was set for 093°, speed 12 knots.

18. At 0730 5th November, the A.A. ships PALOMARES and POZARICA and the destroyer AMAZON joined from Gibraltar. Dutch Ship ISAAC SWEERS was detached at 0745 to join Force "H" which had been sighted 10 miles to the northward at 0720. The 0800 position of convoy K.M.F.A. 1 was 36° 07' N, 09° 09' W.

19. A merchant ship bearing 110°, 7 miles sighted at 0925 5th November proved to be the Vichien CAUDEBEC bound for Casablanca with a cargo of wood. WIVERN was ordered to close her and to place an armed guard on board to take her to Gibraltar. Our first prize.

20. From 1600 to 1630 5th November, the convoy was formed into Cruising Order No. 24 for passage of the Straits. This was in three columns led by KEREN, BULOLO and KARANJA in that order from port to starboard column.

21. At 1830 on 5th November, ROYAL ULSTERMAN, ROYAL SCOTSMAN, ULSTER MONARCH and LEINSTER left the convoy for Gibraltar. They were escorted by SPIREA and JONQUIL who had joined from Gibraltar at 1700 for this purpose.

22. The passage of the Straits was uneventful. Several unidentified vessels, on a westerly course were passed when the convoy was abeam Cape Spartel at 2245, but no action was taken.

23. At 0230 6th November, BROKE, MALCOLM, VANOC and WRESTLER joined the screen as reliefs for AMAZON, ACHATES, ANTELOPE and WIVERN, who proceeded into Gibraltar.

From passage of Straits to Assault.

24. At 0925 on 6th November, the convoy, being ahead of time, was turned back on its course to 275° by emergency turns. This course was continued until 1010 when course was altered back to 080°.

25. At this time Force "H" and K.M.S.A. 1 were in sight against the Spanish coast to the westward. SHEFFIELD and supporting force had been sighted at 0900 to the eastward.

26. At 1045 6th November, the screen was augmented by the arrival of ACUTE, ALGERINE, ALARM, ALBACORE, CADMUS, SPEEDWELL, HUSSAR, BLYSKAWICA, WILTON, LAMERTON and WHEATLAND, whilst IBIS, ENCHANTRESS, CLARE, BROKE, MALCOLM, WRESTLER and VANOC were detached to join K.M.S.A. 1.

27. At 1230 6th November, the Spanish fishing vessel JESUS DEI GRAN was sighted to the south-east. I ordered LAMERTON to board her and to send her under armed guard to Gibraltar. The crew were apparently very friendly and in no way resented this interruption of their peaceful occupation.

28. At 1415 6th November, the first enemy aircraft to be seen passed over the convoy from south to north. It was identified as a German reconnaissance Ju.88. One salvo was fired by POZARICA but with no apparent effect.

29. Additional and most welcome escorts joined K.M.F.A. 1 at 1430 from K.M.S.A. 1. They were BRAMHAM, BICESTER, COWDRAY and ZET-LAND, all of whom were to play an important part in the later operations.

30. At 1500, the convoy was again turned back on its course to 277° and this course was held until 1600 when it was altered back to 086°.

31. At 1630, another German Ju.88 reconnaissance plane was to the south of the convoy steering east. Information was received at this time that a large naval formation had been reported by German aircraft off Cape Gata.

32. The night of the 6th November passed quietly until at 0520 (received 0535), H.M.S. TYNWALD reported low-flying aircraft bearing 010°, closing. At 0535, two guns or explosions were heard from the port side of the convoy and several H.A. bursts were also observed. Two emergency turns of 45° were made at 0553, making the final course for the convoy 016°.

33. At 0630, Captain C.D. Edgar, U.S.N., S.N.O.L.(C)[16], in U.S.S. SAMUEL CHASE, reported that an underwater explosion had damaged the stem of THOMAS STONE, a Combat Loaded Transport of his sector, and had caused her to stop. H.M.S. SPEY was detached to stand by her and V.A.C.N.A.[17] was asked to send tugs. At first it was thought that a T/B[18] aircraft had done the damage, but the weight of evidence now indicates that a submarine was responsible. At 0706, convoy resumed course of 086°.

34. At 0954 7th November, a submarine contact was reported on the port bow. The convoy made an emergency turn of 45° to starboard. BICESTER attacked with depth charges. Course of 086° was resumed at 1000.

35. At 1130 7th November, Force "H" was manoeuvring about 8 miles ahead of the convoy. Shortly afterwards SHEFFIELD and Force "R" were bearing 030°, 8 miles steering west. At 1400, H.M. Trawlers JULIET, RYSA, CAVA, HOY, OTHELLO, INCHOLM and MULL and the M.L.s 238, 273, 283, 295, 336, 338, 444, joined K.M.F.A. 1 from Force "R". M.L. 307 had joined at 1055 from eastward, and H.M. Trawler STROMA at 1545 also from eastward.

36. Hostile shadowing aircraft were in evidence at intervals during the afternoon of 7th November. From 1700–1745 considerable A.A. fire was observed from

Force "H" to the northward and many aircraft passed over and astern of the convoy in that direction. Several ships opened fire but no results were obtained.

37. At 1800, the convoy was wheeled to 180° and SAMUEL CHASE (Captain C.D. Edgar, U.S.N. – S.N.O.L.(C)), LEEDSTOWN,ALMAACK, EXCEL-LER and DEMPO escorted by TYNWALD, COWDRAY, ZETLAND, ALGERINE, HUSSAR, SPEEDWELL, CAVA, OTHELLO and ML.s 273 and 295, proceeded independently to C Sector.

38. At 1900, the convoy wheeled to 200° and at 1920 formation was changed to 2 columns. At 2130, the starboard column consisting of KARANJA, VICEROY OF INDIA and MARNIX escorted by POZARICA, BICESTER, BRAMHAM, ROTHER, CADMUS, RYSA, JULIET, STROMA and ML.s 283, 336 and 338, proceeded independently to A Sector, and the course of the remainder was altered to 110° by two 45° turns to port.

39. At 2140, radar from submarine P.48 was picked up. Speed was reduced to 6 knots at 2150, and at 2154, P.48 was sighted bearing 105°.

40. At 2230, BULOLO (H.Q. Ship) and the ships of B Sector, KEREN, WINCHESTER CASTLE, OTRANTO, SOBIESKI, AWATEA, STRATH-NAVER, CATHAY, escorted by PALOMARES, ACUTE, ALARM, ALBA-CORE, LAMERTON, WHEATLAND, WILTON, BLYSKAWICA, HOY, INCHOLM, MULL, and M.L.s 444, 238 and 307, were stopped in position 36° 52½' N., 02° 49' E.

41. At this tune there was a moderate N.E. breeze, slight sea, clear sky and good visibility. Cap Caxine and all coastal lights were burning, which was a re-assuring sign for the military.

The Assault on Algiers.
42. The ships of the fast assault convoy, with the exception of U.S.S. THOMAS STONE, were at their release positions as arranged by about 2230z[19] on 7th November. Submarines marking the release positions were in place in all three sectors and homing arrangements worked well.

43. From the time of arrival at the release positions until the move into Algiers harbour and Bay on D+1 escorts carried out an endless chain A/S patrol round the stopped transports.

44. Minesweeping was carried out entirely to plan, except at Sector B where it was decided that sweeping was unnecessary, and it was cancelled. No mines of any kind were swept or detonated throughout the operation. Fleet minesweepers did valuable work in the A/S patrol.

45. During the period that boats were being lowered, manned and assembled, a south-westerly set caused by the N.E. wind resulted in ships drifting as much as 5 miles from their proper release positions by the end of the first 1½ hours.

The Landings.

46. *A Sector.* The landing at A Sector was carried out most satisfactorily. S.N.O.L.(A) personally supervised the transfer of the pilots from the submarine to the motor launches, and at 2349, the assault flights moved off to the A GREEN and A WHITE Beaches. A GREEN flight beached at H hour (0100z) and A WHITE flight at H hour +8 minutes, both without incident.

47. *B Sector.* The landing at B Sector was marred by avoidable mistakes. The motor launch detailed to embark the pilot from submarine P.48 for B WHITE Beach first embarked the P.B.M.[20] from KEREN who assumed command of the M.L., and having failed to pick the pilot from the submarine, led a flight for B GREEN to A WHITE Beach, which was some six miles to the southward. In the meantime, as the submarine had to leave the release position for the inner beacon position, the pilot for B WHITE embarked in the nearest landing craft, which proved to be one of a flight bound for B GREEN Beach. He led in the first and second flights, and gave the order "Go" off B GREEN Beach at H hour +3 minutes. The first flight instead of following the approach directions went some way to the east before beaching; the second flight on the pilot's suggestion went straight in and touched down first.

The only craft to beach at B WHITE before dawn (0600) were 3 L.C.P.s[21] destined for B GREEN Beach. Other craft for B WHITE landed wrongly to the south-west of Sidi Ferruch and as far west as A Sector.

The mistakes at B Sector can largely be traced to lack of training and uncertainty whether the submarine and the M.L.s had received the latest orders. This caused the S.N.O.L. to delay the M.L. until the P.B.M. could be embarked and resulted in the M.L. failing to embark the pilot from the submarine.

It is of the utmost importance that similar uncertainty should be avoided in any future operation and that Flotilla Officers should be thoroughly trained.

48. *Scramble Landings.* Landing craft for RED 1, 2, 3 and 4 Beaches were very late in getting away from AWATEA, and one group had to be left behind. A number of craft lost touch with the escorting motor launch on the way inshore, in spite of reductions of speed. Troops were landed at Bains Romans and various beaches to the west. The two craft detailed for RED 1 Beach found their objective unaided, though 1¼ hours late. Six landing craft approached the Ilot de la Marine, some two miles south-east of their intended beach, and came under heavy fire. Four were sunk and the remaining two withdrew.

49. *C Sector.* Owing to the delay in the receipt of orders some confusion arose as to the beaches to be used. The pilotage party were only briefed for Ain Taya beach whereas the use of three beaches was contemplated.

A short conference was held in U.S.S. SAMUEL CHASE where it was decided that M.L. 273 should take a flight to C BLUE, the original beach; that M.L. 295 should lead a flight to C RED Beach, keeping station on the port quarter of M.L. 273 until reaching Bordelaise Rock, where they would break off; and that the pilot in Flotilla leader's craft should lead the Commando flight to C GREEN for the assault on Matifou.

Owing to delay in forming up, the assault flights for C BLUE and RED Beaches did not leave until H hour − 50 minutes. At Bordelaise Rock, M.L. 295 attempted to lead off the craft for C RED, but they all continued to follow M.L. 273 to C BLUE, where they touched down at H hour +25 minutes. Several craft for C GREEN were also mixed up in this flight, including those with ammunition for the Commando at C GREEN.

The flights for C GREEN were not finally loaded and assembled until H hour − 15 minutes, and as the convoy had by now drifted some 4 or 5 miles from its release position they did not touch down at C GREEN Beach until H hour +1 hour 50 minutes.

50. *General.* Generally speaking all landings were hampered by the unfortunate necessity of long delays in lowering craft and forming up into flotillas. The obvious solution to this is that all L.S.I.s carry sufficient landing craft to embark their own first flight and that these landing craft be lowered with their full load.

All landings, except that at Ilot de la Marine, were effected without opposition, which was fortunate, as, had there been any serious naval or military opposition, the confusion which arose at B and C Sectors might well have been disastrous.

51. At 0040, the ships of the slow convoy K.M.S.A. 1 began to arrive at B Sector, where H.M.S. BULOLO was lying, and they arrived at the correct times at the release positions of A and C Sectors.

52. At A Sector the L.S.I. of the fast convoy started to close the beach at 0100, the slow convoy following them in. Owing to the drift from proper release positions ships were not finally anchored until 0356. The ferry service then began to operate satisfactorily.

53. At 0130, as Cap Matifou battery showed no signs of activity, S.N.O.L. (C) moved his L.S.I. in to within 4,000 yards of the beach. At 0200, searchlights from the battery picked up and held H.M.S. ZETLAND, but neither side opened fire. H.M.S. ZETLAND turned away and made smoke and the transports were not illuminated. At 0340, ZETLAND was again picked up by this searchlight, and Cap Matifou battery opened fire on the westward transports. ZETLAND closed the battery and opened fire on the searchlight, which went out showing a glow as though it had been hit. At 0400, ZETLAND was picked up by another search-light and the battery again opened fire. ZETLAND closed the battery, dealing successfully with this searchlight too.

54. At 0131, I ordered H.M. Ships BROKE and MALCOLM to carry out Operation "Terminal".[22]

55. At 0237, information was received that Sidi Ferruch Fort had been captured without opposition, and I ordered KEREN and the ships at B Sector to close B WHITE Beach. Ships had by now drifted some 7 miles to the south-westward,

and it took them over 2 hours to reach the anchorage. Once anchored, the ferrying of personnel ashore proceeded rapidly.

56. By 0515 D day, the information received in H.Q. Ship was as follows:-

0131 From C.E.N.T.F.[23] – BROKE and MALCOLM proceed in execution of previous orders.

0159 Landing B WHITE successful.

0220 Signal station A GREEN open – nothing to report.

0220 From BROKE – MALCOLM in company and proceeding.

0223 Landing successful B GREEN.

0225 S.N.O.L.(C) – 1st and 2nd wave landed, am closing beach.

0237 Sidi Ferruch and infra-red installations captured.

0238 S.N.O.L.(B) – Loaded M.T. very slow due to conditions.

0246 C.E.N.T.F. to KEREN – Close beach as convenient; sweep B will not be carried out.

0246 S.N.O.L.(A) – L.S.I. anchored A WHITE. Landing delayed by swell. Assault flight landed 0147.

0257 S.N.O.L.(B) – B GREEN and WHITE landings successful. Sidi Ferruch captured. No RED Beach report.

0255 A Sector – No resistance reported so far.

0301 S.N.O.L.(C) – Am under way, all quiet here.

0315 Flares bearing 045° to seaward. Possibly BROKE and MALCOLM.

0327 S.N.O.L.(C) – Landing successful. Beach secure. No report from troops inland.

0332 B RED SCRAMBLES – Two forts captured.

0335 S.N.O.L.(B) – Ships are closing the beaches now.

0344 S.N.O.L.(B) – Division 1 close beaches. KEREN'S speed 8 knots. Division 2 and 3 follow.

0345 Gunfire between 075° and 085°.

0351 S.N.O.L.(A) to RYSA – Contact P.221 and escort her to sanctuary.

0415 Occasional flashes bearing 090°.

0421 From C.E.N.T.F. to BROKE – Report progress.

0430 BULOLO position – 260° 13 miles Caxine.

0435 From B WHITE flight to S.N.O.L.(B) – Have been landed on A WHITE Beach request instructions.

0435 From S.N.O.L.(C) – Matifou defences apparently not taken.

0435 From C.T. 168 to A.M.L.O. B WHITE – 260 men 2nd Battalion apparently landed A WHITE Beach.

0456 From Control B Sector – Serials 1 to 68 despatched. Serials 44 to 52 appear to have landed A WHITE. Difficulty with L.C.M.[24], only 5 L.C.M. disembarked from W.2. Shackles of lifting gear bent.

0500 BULOLO manoeuvring to close B Beaches.

0515 From BROKE to C.E.N.T.F. – MALCOLM damaged, two boilers out of action. Searchlights on Brise Lames Est very troublesome. Have made three attempts to find entrance. Am making another attempt with BROKE. Entrance would be easier if searchlights could be put out of action.

57. At 0600, BROKE reported that she had berthed alongside in Algiers harbour and was landing troops, and a few minutes later that she had little difficulty in entering.

58. At 0632, BROKE reported that a submarine was leaving harbour. This was attacked and forced to dive by aircraft from VICTORIOUS, and STORK and two A/S vessels were detached to search for it.

59. At this time news from shore was very scarce. The landing of the 11th Brigade at A Sector appeared to be going well; and General Mast, Commanding Algiers Division, was reported at Sidi Ferruch to be offering full co-operation and urging that our forces should push on to Algiers without delay. On the other hand it was known that Cap Matifou had not yet surrendered; and at 0625 WILTON, who was in support of landing craft at SCRAMBLE landings, reported that she was under fire from Fort Duperre. No hits were made and WILTON withdrew to the westward, joining patrol at B Beaches until the military situation clarified.

60. At 0827, the welcome news that Maison Blanche aerodrome had been captured was received. At 1000 the aerodrome was reported serviceable, and a few minutes later a squadron of Hurricanes flown from Gibraltar landed on. Although the R.A.F. did not formally take over the defence of Algiers until D + 2, R.A.F. fighters were operational on D day, making several sorties on D day and D + 1. This helped materially to supplement the extremely efficient air support given by the hard-pressed fighters and squadrons of R.A.A.[25]

61. At 0856, information was received that tanks were concentrating and moving along the road from Algiers in the direction of Maison Blanche. Three of these tanks subsequently returned to the harbour in an effort to dislodge BROKE; she had, however, made good her withdrawal before they came into action.

62. The unloading of M.T. was proceeding very slowly. B GREEN Beach had to be abandoned owing to the swell and general unsuitability. B WHITE had to be restricted to a width of 100 yards. C Beach was a lee shore, and felt the full effects of the slight swell, and many landing craft broached to.

63. At 0930, BROKE requested bombing of the battery on Jetée du Nord to cover her intended withdrawal at 1030, as her position was becoming untenable. Bomber support was also called for urgently on Fort Duperre at 1030. R.A.A. was asked to fulfil these commitments.

64. At 0934, a Martlet landed on Blida aerodrome and reported a friendly reception.

65. At about 1000, BROKE left harbour. The battery on Jetée du Nord was bombed most successfully at 1030. Twelve hits were obtained on this small target

and severe damage was done to the buildings and living quarters in the fort. BROKE was engaged by a number of batteries on her way out and was badly damaged. ZETLAND went to her aid, steering between her and Cap Matifou battery. This was successfully bombarded, hitting the control tower and putting the range-finder out of action. ZETLAND then stood by BROKE.

66. I consider that much credit is due to Captain H. St. J. Fancourt, R.N., Commanding Officer "Terminal" Force, for his courage and determination in pressing on with the attack after the initial repulse of his ships, and also to Lieutenant J.V. Wilkinson, Commanding Officer, H.M.S. ZETLAND, for the gallant and skilful manner in which he took his ship to the rescue of BROKE.

67. At 1130, Blida aerodrome was occupied by the military. One Ju.88 was sighted over B Sector at this time.

68. Shortly after 1300, Fort Duperre was bombed by naval Albacores. Subsequent reports say that the bombing broke the resistance of the defenders and the Commandos were able to take possession of the fort unopposed at 1515.

69. In response to urgent calls for support from F.O.O.7, Cap Matifou battery and Fort d'Estrées were bombarded by BERMUDA and bombed by naval aircraft almost simultaneously between 1400 and 1530. Both bombing and bombardment were most successful, and having driven the defenders underground, the Commandos occupied the forts without opposition.

70. At about 1600, the military situation did not appear to H.Q. Ship to be progressing favourably, 11th British Brigade in A Sector had reached all its objectives, but 168th U.S. R.C.T.[26] from B Sector was held up in high ground, to the west of Algiers, and Fort L'Empereur was reported as being strongly held. As a result, the 6 Royal West Kents were ordered to land to give additional weight to the attack. This order was subsequently cancelled. 39th U.S. R.C.T. from C Sector advancing on Algiers from the east were held up by shelling from Hussein Dey areas and reported heavy casualties. A concentration of tanks was also believed to be forming in this area. Unloading of M.T. at C Sector practically stopped, due to the rising wind and swell, and was proceeding very slowly at other sectors. It was therefore with considerable relief that the following signal was received from General Ryder at 1658: "Darlan wishes to negotiate immediately. He will not deal with any Frenchman. Recommend that arrangements for Algiers be presented. Resistance of Navy in isolated batteries has been severe. Resistance of Army has been token".

71. At dusk the first Axis air attack developed. Ships at C Sector were the objectives of dive and torpedo bombers. H.M.S. COWDRAY was hit and seriously damaged. U.S.S. LEEDSTOWN's steering gear was put out of action by a hit on the stern and U.S.S. EXCELLER suffered minor damage from a near miss. I had previously ordered screening ships to cover concentration of shipping

ld Marshal Viscount Alexander, whose
·trait, completed *c.*1943, is seen here,
npiled the first of the five despatches that
·m this volume. (*The National Archives*)

A portrait of Admiral Sir Andrew
Cunningham, who wrote the second and fifth
despatches in this volume, that was completed
*c.*1943. (*The National Archives*)

utenant General B.L. Montgomery, General Officer Commanding Eighth Army, watches the
·inning of the German retreat from El Alamein from the turret of his Grant tank, 5 November
·2. He is wearing his famous tank beret. (*US National Archives*)

As the fighting in North Africa progressed, the increasing strength of the Allied forces in that theatre would gradually overwhelm the Axis forces. Here, a large convoy of British vehicles is queued up during the Allied advance east. (*Historic Military Press*)

'Australians storm a strongpoint'. Taken on 3 November 1942, British Army photographer Sergeant Len Chetwyn's classic photograph of the Desert War was actually a fake, staged at rear headquarters using Australian troops. Nevertheless, it became one of the Second World War's most famous images. (*US National Archives*)

This stylised drawing which, depicting British gunners in action in North Africa, was commissioned by the Ministry of Information during the Second World War.
(The National Archives)

Troops of the US Army's 1st Infantry Division, known as 'the Big Red One', go ashore at Oran, Algeria, on 8 November 1942 during Operation *Torch*.
(US National Archives)

The severe damage to the stern of the anti-aircraft cruiser HMS *Delhi* seen here was caused during operations off North Africa in late 1942. On 20 November that year *Delhi* was attacked by Italian aircraft whilst she was making smoke to protect the fleet. (*Historic Military Press*)

Bombs fall away from a Boeing B-17 of the USAAF's Twelfth Air Force during an attack on the important Axis airfield at El Aouina near Tunis, on 14 February 1943. On the airfield below enemy aircraft can be seen burning. (*US National Archives*)

itish transport, in the background, passes a knocked-out Italian field gun in its emplacement. *istoric Military Press*)

vo German SC 1000 (1,000kg) bombs in front of a wrecked Heinkel He 111H bomber at Benghazi field in early 1943. Note the British biplane in the background. (*US Library of Congress*)

A few of the many. Three *Afrika Korps* prisoners of war are searched by Allied troops as the tide o
the fighting in North Africa turns against the Axis forces. (*US National Archives*)

he remains of a number of wrecked *Luftwaffe* Messerschmitt Bf 109 fighters pictured in late 1942.
'S National Archives)

n eighth Army officer inspects a German 88mm gun which had been put out of action by British
tillery during the fighting in North Africa. Note the victory rings around the gun's barrel.
'S National Archives)

Allied vehicles pictured travelling along a road heading in to Tripoli after the Allied victory in May 1943. In the foreground is an American Jeep alongside a sign which informs those passing by that the surrounding area still contains mines. (*US National Archives*)

Following the surrender of Axis forces in Tunisia in May 1943, Allied forces captured more than 275,000 enemy personnel. This photograph, taken by a USAAF aircraft on 11 June 1943, shows one batch of PoWs in a prisoner of war cage waiting to be processed. (*US National Archives*)

with smoke and this undoubtedly prevented more serious casualties. One enemy aircraft was shot down.

72. Unloading of M.T.s had to be stopped during the night due to the heavy swell and rising wind which caused large casualties to landing craft at all sectors.

73. At 2200, H.M.S. SPEY arrived with American soldiers from the damaged THOMAS C. STONE. They had left their ship 140 miles N.W. of Algiers in landing craft, escorted by H.M.S. SPEY, in a spirited attempt to take part in the assault. Weather and breakdowns necessitated abandoning the landing craft on passage.

74. I wish particularly to draw your attention to the courageous decision of Captain O.R. Bennehoff, Commanding U.S.S. THOMAS STONE, to send his landing craft and troops off on a journey of 140 miles to their beaches under the escort of the only A/S vessel then available to screen his ship, and also to the fine display of seamanship and determination given by Commander H.G. Scott, R.N., Commanding Officer, H.M.S. WISHART, in towing the helpless U.S.S. THOMAS STONE safely to Algiers in spite of bad weather and the perils of air and submarine attacks.

75. At 0500, I proceeded to Algiers harbour in BULOLO, berthing alongside at 0700. On the way round BULOLO was attacked twice by single Ju.88s; the first attack was unobserved, but in the second attack the enemy plane received a hot reception from the close-range weapons, and after complaining of his rough handling crashed into the sea.

76. An enthusiastic reception was given to us by the large crowd assembled on the dock side and on the road overlooking the harbour.

77. At 0800, all shipping was ordered into Algiers Bay. This concentration of shipping was attacked by about 30 Ju.88s at 1630. Twelve of these were shot down by Spitfires who were directed by visual control from BULOLO.

The Assault on Bougie and Djidjelli.
78. At 1700 10th November, the slow assault convoy sailed for Bougie, consisting of the M.T. ships GLENFINLAS (Commodore), STANHILL, URLANA, and OCEAN VOLGA, escorted by H.M. Ships ROBERTS, BLYSKAWICA, SAMPHIRE, PENSTEMON, HOY, INCHOLM and RYSA. The fast assault convoy consisting of L.S.I.s KARANJA, MARNIX and CATHAY escorted by H.M. Ships SHEFFIELD, TYNWALD, BRAMHAM, CADMUS, ALBA-CORE, ROTHER and SPEY, sailed at 2000.

79. The oiler DEWDALE left Algiers at 1800 10th November, having been delayed by oiling ships. H.M.S. MULL of the slow assault convoy escort remained behind to escort her to Bougie. DEWDALE and MULL arrived Bougie at 0600 11th November.

80. At 2310, L.S.I. AWATEA escorted by BICESTER and WILTON sailed for the assault on Djidjelli. STRATHNAVER had been detailed to carry out this task but had developed engine-room defects which restricted her speed; R.A.F. Commandos, stores and petrol had been transferred to AWATEA during the day.

It was then intended that STRATHNAVER should accompany the fast assault convoy to Bougie but she was not able to get away in time.

81. The Armistice at this time had not been signed, but I had been assured of a friendly reception. The Commandos for the assault of coast defence batteries were not despatched. Information was received after the assault shipping had sailed that the landing at Bougie might be opposed and in consequence I sent a signal to that effect to the Naval Commander, Captain N.V. Dickinson, R.N. On receipt of this signal at about midnight, Captain Dickinson ordered all landings to take place on D WHITE Beach, this beach being outside the range of shore batteries.

82. At 0345, H.M.S. SHEFFIELD (C.S. 10) left the fast assault convoy and acted independently to give surface cover to the assault.

83. H.M.S. ROBERTS escorted by PENSTEMON and SAMPHIRE parted company from the slow assault convoy when off Cap Carbon and stood off prepared to bombard.

84. At 0445, L.S.I.s stopped in the release position (105° Cap Carbon 7). Troops for the assault had been embarked in L.S.I.s MARNIX and CATHAY. KARANJA's boats were despatched to ferry CATHAY's assault troops ashore. The assault flight left for D WHITE Beach at 0530 from MARNIX and at 0600 from CATHAY. First troops landed at about 0615.

85. At 0609, KARANJA, MARNIX and CATHAY followed up astern of the assault flight, being swept in by ALBACORE, SPEY and CADMUS, and stopped one mile off D WHITE Beach.

86. At dawn, Force "O", consisting of H.M. Ships ARGUS, SCYLLA, CHARYBDIS, escorted by VANOC and WRESTLER, were off Bougie and provided a continuous fighter patrol off the beaches. The direction of fighters was carried out by TYNWALD. It was the intention that Fleet Air Arm fighters should provide fighter cover until the R.A.F. Spitfires could be established at Djidjelli aerodrome – the nearest suitable aerodrome to Bougie. H.M.S. ARGUS had been hit by a bomb at 1717/10 and had only 7 Seafires serviceable. At dawn, I ordered H.M.S. AVENGER, at the time in Algiers with engine defects, to put to sea and to fly off two sorties of four Hurricanes each to reinforce ARGUS. One of these sorties was unable to locate ARGUS and returned to AVENGER.

87. The slow assault convoy hove in sight at 0547 and closed the L.S.I.s. At 0614, AWATEA and escort were sighted. The S.N.O., Commander P. Stubbs, R.N., had decided to abandon the assault on Djidjelli because of the swell, which was

causing heavy surf on the beaches. AWATEA carried R.A.F. stores, maintenance personnel, and petrol, it having been the intention to operate R.A.F. fighters from Djidjelli aerodrome by noon at the latest to provide cover. This decision was to have far reaching effects.

88. In the meantime, friendly signals had been received from the coastguard station, and at 0540 ships were invited to enter. At 0702, BRAMHAM was ordered by the Naval Commander to enter the port and to find out the French intentions. At about the same time,

Rear-Admiral Commanding, 10th Cruiser Squadron ordered WILTON to carry out a similar mission.

89. At 0720, the Naval Commander decided to hoist all craft and close the harbour. Commander Thery and the Military Commander of Bougie boarded WILTON at 0800. As a result of the ensuing interview, KARANJA, CATHAY, MARNIX and AWATEA were anchored in Bougie Bay at 1000. The M.T. ships of the slow convoy anchored soon afterwards.

90. At 1140, Rear-Admiral Commanding, 10th C.S. received my order for Force "O" to withdraw to the westward. SHEFFIELD therefore closed ARGUS and her screen and withdrew as ordered. Fighter protection of shipping ceased at 1200. R.A.F. fighters were to have flown on to Djidjelli aerodrome during the forenoon of the 11th, but when the news of the failure to land petrol and stores at Djidjelli reached Algiers, their departure was delayed until the following day.

91. At 1345, the shipping in the bay was attacked by five S.M. 79 torpedo bombers. One was shot down, one probably destroyed, and two were damaged. There was no damage to ships.

92. During the afternoon the M.T. ships URLANA, GLENFINLAS and STANHILL entered harbour. Unloading of personnel from KARANJA, CATHAY, AWATEA and MARNIX continued from the bay.

93. At 1305, BLYSKAWICA and BRAMHAM sailed for Algiers, where they arrived at 1740. They were required to escort STRATHNAVER to Bougie.

94. At 1625, AWATEA had finished unloading R.A.F. personnel, stores and petrol, and sailed for Algiers with H.M.S. BICESTER and H.M.S. WILTON as escorts.

95. At 1640, a very heavy dusk air attack by about 30 Ju.88s developed. This was followed by a T/B attack by He.111 aircraft. One T/B was shot down.

96. S.S. AWATEA was hit by four bombs, one bomb causing a fire in No. 2 hold and others flooding the engine-room, causing a list of 40°. PENSTEMON, detached from A/S patrol by S.N.O., immediately proceeded alongside. Later BICESTER proceeded alongside too, but efforts to extinguish the fire were abortive and the ship was abandoned. About 300 survivors were taken off by

PENSTEMON, 26 others were rescued from 1 lifeboat by BICESTER, and 3 boat loads by MULL. The ship sank by 2300 in deep water.

97. H.M.S. ROBERTS was hit by two bombs. One of these exploded in the issue room and one on the sloping side armour. Boiler room fans were put out of action and the inner and outer bilges on the port side flooded, but otherwise the ship's fighting efficiency was not impaired.

98. CATHAY was hit by one bomb in the galley, which did not explode, and had some near misses. She still had 1,200 troops on board. All the available landing craft were sent over and the majority of the soldiers landed. The ship was abandoned by all. At 2315, a fire started. This took hold and the ship burned all night.

99. As CATHAY was known to have depth charges on board, KARANJA and MARNIX shifted berth. MARNIX anchored off Cap Aokas outside the A/S patrol.

100. The vital petrol for the fighters at Djidjelli had been landed from AWATEA before 1630, but as the AWATEA carried no M.T. (except a few Bren-gun carriers which were appropriated by the 5th Buffs) and as the M.T. ships had not yet been unloaded, the R.A.F. Servicing Commandos had no transport to take it to the aerodrome. It was not until 2030 that the S.N.O. ex AWATEA, Lieutenant R.H.H. Webber, R.N., who had taken over Beach Master in control of landing craft at the Eastern Boat Slip was asked by the M.L.O.,[27] Major Jordan, if the Navy would undertake the transportation of petrol to the aerodrome as there was no army transport available, priority one having been allocated to the 5th Buffs. Lieutenant Webber then volunteered to take the petrol, stores and R.A.F. Commandos by landing craft at dawn the next day.

101. At 0445 12th November, H.M.S. TYNWALD weighed anchor in readiness for the expected dawn air attack. Thirty minutes later, two violent explosions occurred and the ship settled down in seven fathoms of water. The ship was abandoned and survivors were picked up by boats from ROBERTS and SAMPHIRE. The cause of the explosion is not known, but it is thought to be mines laid by aircraft as flares were dropped over the harbour at 0205.

102. At dawn (0540), a small sharp air attack was delivered by a number of Ju.88s from low cloud. KARANJA was hit by at least two bombs. An oil fuel fire immediately broke out and the amidships portion burst into flames.

103. The fire spread very rapidly. Survivors from CATHAY and some military personnel lowered the lifeboats without orders. The ship's company of KARANJA behaved in an exemplary fashion, salvaging some Oerlikon guns and ammunition, and eventually abandoning ship at 0830 when nothing further could be done. The ship was empty except for some petrol.

104. At 0630, STRATHNAVER arrived, escorted by BRAMHAM and BLYSKAWICA, and secured alongside in the outer harbour.

105. Between 1000 and 1100, a heavy attack by about 30 Ju.88s developed. The principal targets of this attack were MARNIX and DEWDALE, but individual vessels on patrol were also attacked. Most of the planes were kept high by A.A. fire. The gunnery efficiency of DEWDALE and MARNIX undoubtedly saved these ships. The only damage was a near miss on BLYSKAWICA. Two Ju.88s were shot down by DEWDALE.

106. At 1100, MARNIX escorted by BICESTER sailed for Algiers. Unloading had not been fully completed.

107. Landing craft were delayed by all these attacks but left for Djidjelli with petrol and R.A.F. stores between 1100 and 1200, arriving late that night.

108. At 1240, the harbour was attacked by six torpedo bombers. At least two of these were shot down, one, the first, by a Spitfire patrol from Algiers; the other is claimed by DEWDALE. The attack was broken up and turned away, torpedoes being dropped at long range.

109. Two high level bombing attacks were carried out between 1330 and 1430. One attack was by ten planes, the other by four planes. One aircraft was shot down by A.A. fire. BLYSKAWICA sustained further casualties and damage from a near miss and was sailed for Algiers at 1600.

110. At 1655, Ju.88s carried out dive attacks from scattered low clouds. When the light was failing two waves of torpedo bombers attacked. The attack was directed against DEWDALE, who again came through unscathed. Two planes were shot down. WILTON was hit by a bomb which fortunately passed through the ship without exploding and only caused superficial damage. WILTON then sailed for Algiers, being practically out of ammunition.

111. At 2115, STRATHNAVER sailed for Algiers escorted by BRAMHAM.

112. Fighters had been providing cover intermittently throughout the day, but were only once present during an air attack. They had to be flown to and from Maison Blanche aerodrome at Algiers, which only permitted 20 minutes of patrol over Bougie. R.A.F. fighters at Algiers also had other commitments and the cover provided at Bougie was consequently thin and inadequate.

113. R.A.F. fighters were flown to Djidjelli aerodrome in the early morning of the 12th, but were not able to operate continuously until the 13th, because the attempts to land petrol and ammunition by landing craft did not succeed until midnight 12th/13th. By using up all the petrol in the tanks of its aircraft, the squadron was able to carry out one sortie in defence of Bougie, destroying a number of enemy bombers, before being grounded through lack of petrol.

114. At 1210, a bombing attack was carried out by fourteen Ju.88s, the attack being well pressed home. The M.T. GLENFINLAS was hit alongside whilst

unloading and subsequently sank. The French ship ALCINA was also hit and set on fire. Fighters drove off the raiders. ROBERTS shot down two of the attackers.

115. It was decided as a result of this raid that two French ships, unable to raise steam, should be scuttled to prevent them catching fire. Both ships rolled over and lay on their beam ends.

116. During the night the M.T. ships OCEAN VOLGA and STANHILL and the oiler DEWDALE sailed for Algiers, together with five French merchant ships.

117. The M.T. URLANA, the last ship of the assault convoy to be unloaded, was sailed during the night of the 17th.

118. On Sunday, 15th November, the A.A. ship POZARICA arrived at Bougie. I had sent her there on relief by DELHI from her duty as A.A. guardship, Algiers. Enemy air activity since then has been on a very reduced scale.

119. Before concluding my report, I would like to refer to the very happy relations which existed in H.M.S. BULOLO between the Navy, the Army, the Air Force and the American Army. In my quarters I was privileged to have Major-General C.W. Ryder, U.S. Army, Major-General V. Evelegh, O.B.E., 78th Division, and Air Commodore G.M. Lawson, C.B.E., M.C., R.A.F., and throughout the whole period there was complete understanding and co-operation between us and our services.

120. The operation was in many ways far more difficult than a straightforward Combined Operation in that the political factors were very strong and denied us the initiative in offensive action. The quick success of the operation was undoubtedly due mainly to surprise, good weather, and the number of places at which landings took place which gave the impression of overwhelming force. Had the operation taken place in bad weather and with strong opposition it might well have failed due to lack of training and rehearsal, and this fact should not be overlooked when planning further operations.

(Signed) H.M. BURROUGH,
Vice-Admiral.

ENCLOSURE II.

*Office of Naval Commander Centre
Task Force,
c/o Admiralty, S.W.1.
27th December, 1942.*

I have the honour to forward herewith the report of proceedings of the Centre Naval Task Force in Operation "Torch".

2. An operation of such magnitude and scope must of necessity produce many lasting impressions and of these the zeal and enthusiasm of every man, British and American, were the most outstanding.

3. With Major-General L.R. Fredendall, the Commanding General, and his staff, co-operation was easy, and from first to last we worked as one.

4. The altogether admirable discipline of the American troops evoked much favourable comment. Once they understood what was expected of them, they were untiring until the job was properly performed.

5. The value of preliminary practice in combined operations needs no emphasis and great value was gained from the exercise in Loch Linnhe and elsewhere prior to sailing.

6. Finally, it should never be forgotten by those who seek to draw conclusions from what follows, that the operation was to all intents and purposes unopposed, and it is important to bear constantly in mind this essential fact when planning combined operations in the future.

(Signed) T. TROUBRIDGE,
Commodore.

REPORT OF PROCEEDINGS – OPERATION "TORCH."
NAVAL COMMANDER CENTRE TASK FORCE.
Narrative of Events.

Monday, 26th October.

Under the orders of Rear-Admiral Sir Harold Burrough, K.B.E., C.B., D.S.O. in H.M.S. BULOLO, the combined fast convoy (K.M.F. 1), of which I acted as Vice-Commodore in H.M.S. LARGS, sailed from the Clyde after dusk and proceeded, without incident and in favourable weather, towards Gibraltar on the route ordered.

Wednesday, 4th November.

2. The Oran section, K.M.F.O. 1, parted company from the remainder of the convoy at 1315. The three "Ulstermen" (L.S.I. small) continued with the Algiers section, K.M.F.A. 1, until proceeding into Gibraltar to fuel. Course was altered to the westward and subsequently adjusted so as to lose 21½ hours on K.M.F.A. 1 in order to pass through the Straits after dark on 6th November.

Thursday, 5th November.

3. Rendezvous was made with AURORA at 1700 as previously arranged.

4. Several A/S contacts were obtained during the day by the screen and attacked but without visible results.

Friday, 6th November.

5. BITER flew off A/S patrol at daylight. Catalinas from Gibraltar carried out A/S patrol in the vicinity of the convoy. JAMAICA flew off Walrus to Gibraltar which returned before dark.

6. At 1600, the convoy formed into three columns for passage of the Straits. Cape Trafalgar was sighted shortly after dark. The passage of the Straits was unevent-

ful. Off Gibraltar, WIVERN, ANTELOPE, BRILLIANT and BOADICEA relieved WESTCOTT, VERITY, WISHART and VELOX on the screen, the latter proceeding to Gibraltar to refuel. Many small fishing craft were passed at the eastern end of the Straits.

Saturday, 7th November.

7. At daylight the M.L. Flotilla was in sight ahead, the "Ulstermen" in sight to the southward, and DASHER, escorted by AMAZON and ACHATES, astern.

The "Ulstermen" reported they had been sighted at some distance on the previous night by a French destroyer and two submarines proceeding eastwards. K.M.S.O. 1[28] was sighted ahead at 0700.

8. From daylight, A/S patrols were carried out over the convoy by (*a*) Swordfish from BITER, (*b*) Walrus from JAMAICA, and (*c*) Catalinas from Gibraltar.

9. K.M.S.O. 1 was ordered to form Cruising Order No. 40 by 1330 in preparation for joining company with K.M.F.O. 1, up to which time the fast convoy was manoeuvred in broad sweeps astern of the slow convoy.

10. Commencing at 1330, the two convoys and their escorts were joined together and divided into groups as previously arranged.

At this time there was a total of 97 vessels of all types in company, all of which had their allocated position to take up.

The manoeuvre was completed by 1630 and was well carried out.

11. At 1815, the two southernmost columns of the convoy parted company and, led by AURORA, proceeded towards the western marking submarine off X and Y Beaches. They made a successful rendezvous and then divided, 5 ships with their escorts for Y Beach and 7 ships with escorts for X Beach. The latter sighted a French convoy of four ships and an armed trawler straggled out across their line of advance and were obliged to slow down to avoid it. This made them late on the schedule, but the assault craft were eventually lowered and beached successfully half an hour after H hour (zero hour).

The assault craft for Y Beach were lowered and beached according to plan, their landing, in common with the remainder of the assault, being unopposed and undetected.

12. The column (of 7 ships) for Z Beach led by JAMAICA parted company at 1825, making for the eastern marking submarine, H.M.S. URSULA. TEGEL-BERG, the fifth in the line, lost touch with her next ahead and the column straggled badly in consequence. LARGS, which accompanied this column, acted as whipper in and by 2000 all ships were in station. The submarine's signal was sighted right ahead at 2100, and at 2205, Arzeu Island light and the glare over the town of Mostaganem were in sight.

By that time the wind was nil, the sea smooth, and even the stars obscured by cloud. Conditions were perfect.

13. The ships were stopped by orders from JAMAICA at 2315 and anchors lowered[29] on to the bottom in fifty fathoms. At the same time the assault craft were lowered and manned, and after assembling proceeded inshore. From LARGS, five cables on the beam of the anchored column, no sound was heard and not even the flash of a torch was observed.

Sunday, 8th November.

14. *H hour* (0100). – At Z Beach the assault craft touched down undetected within a few minutes on either side of zero hour and the troops and beach parties proceeded on their several missions unopposed. A company of U.S. Rangers whose mission was to capture the fort above Arzeu landed on a small beach near Cape Carbon. They did not even get their feet wet. The remainder of the Rangers landed in Arzeu harbour and quickly secured the dock area.

15. At 0100, seven M.T. ships from the convoy led by DEPTFORD and under the orders of Commodore Elliott in S.S. ALPHARD arrived at Arzeu Bay and anchored close to seaward of the assault ships. They began at once to unload.

16. An hour and a half after the landing there was still no sign of fighting ashore and although all along we had been sceptical, the Commanding General and myself were beginning to wonder whether the persistent claim of Mr. Rounds, the U.S. Vice-Consul at Oran (a passenger in LARGS), that there would be no resistance was justified. It seemed unbelievable that the French lookouts could be so indifferent. Shortly after 0230 tracer bullets were seen inshore by Arzeu.

17. At 0300, searchlights and gun flashes from the direction of Oran were seen in the sky over the hills above Cape Carbon. This, as it later transpired and was at the time suspected, was the French reception of H.M. Ships WALNEY and HART-LAND, which were due to enter Oran harbour at that hour. Their mission,[30] though gallantly undertaken, failed, and both ships were sunk in the harbour.

18. It being now evident that the French were resisting, orders were sent to the carriers to attack the enemy aerodromes, with the main weight on Tafaraoui, the naval aerodrome, at dawn. The reception of this signal was much delayed and the aircraft were airborne before it arrived. The Senior Officer of the Carriers, Captain T.O. Bulteel, R.N. in H.M.S. FURIOUS, having received no orders by 0430, had correctly used his judgment to carry out tasks laid down in the operation orders and concentrated the main weight of the attack on La Senia aerodrome where the bulk of the enemy fighters were located.

The attack was devastating in its thoroughness, eighty per cent. of the enemy aircraft being put out of action. The fact that most of the French fighters were destroyed either in the air or in the hangars at La Senia in all probability deterred such few bombers as remained serviceable from later taking off and interfering with the landings.

Later inspection of the aerodromes revealed the preparedness of the French; bombers were bombed up and fuelled, fighters were complete with ammunition and petrol, and at the seaplane station at Arzeu the aircraft had their torpedoes in place complete with pistols and ready in every respect for immediate action.

19. At 0456, the success signal indicating that the batteries covering Arzeu were in our hands was observed, and there being at the time no further use for the two destroyers detailed to support the landing with gunfire, they were sent to reinforce the Oran Bay patrol under AURORA.

The latter ship was soon busy in intercepting French destroyers which started to come out of Oran as soon as the alarm was raised. Aided by the destroyers she either sank or seriously damaged three of them soon after daylight but was obliged to keep her distance from the shore batteries, whose accurate fire at long ranges was one of the noticeable features of the operation. The French ships fought well against odds, their gallantry being worthy of a better cause.

20. Although unobserved by the patrols which were well inshore during the darkness, the submarines in Oran also came out and both AURORA and later RODNEY were attacked, happily without result.

21. At first light (0600), orders were given by the Senior Naval Officer Landing for ships to proceed to the inshore anchorage. REINA DEL PACIFICO was the first to anchor off Arzeu and shortly afterwards was fired at by a field gun battery behind the town. It scored three hits which luckily caused neither material damage nor casualties.

Landing craft in the vicinity put up an effective smoke screen round the ship, whereupon the battery shifted fire on to the two Maracaibos[31] which were in process of unloading their M.T. on the beach. No hits were scored and on the arrival shortly afterwards of VANSITTART the battery prudently ceased fire and withdrew.

22. The Maracaibos had beached themselves in accordance with plan at 0400. Owing to the gradual slope of the beach it was necessary to make use of a floating roadway to get the vehicles ashore. This had been brought in the ships and proved an outstanding success, the ships being cleared by 0800. The Maracaibos then backed off and later, when the weather became bad, were used for unloading the M.T. ships, the Maracaibos discharging on to the seaplane ramp in Arzeu harbour.

23. The remainder of the convoy consisting of low priority store and personnel ships arrived at daylight and all ships were anchored inshore by 0640. Unloading then proceeded in earnest.

24. The minesweepers which had swept a channel into Arzeu Bay ahead of the ships, and later swept the anchorage, now formed together with available sloops and destroyers an endless chain patrol off the anchorage. This was maintained day and night for the remainder of the week.

25. At X and Y Beaches the landing of troops and unloading of stores proceeded well, though at Y Beach a sandbar off the beach, a common feature in the Mediterranean, made things very difficult for the big L.C.M.s conveying heavy vehicles. At all beaches there was much grief among the propellers, rudders and "A" brackets of these craft and the need for a large number of spares was apparent.

26. At 0900, the Du Santon battery above Mers el Kebir opened fire on the ships off Y Beach and scored hits on MONARCH OF BERMUDA and LLANGIBBY CASTLE. The former was ordered out of range and would have been followed by LLANGIBBY CASTLE but for a call for fire on the battery from RODNEY being promptly and accurately answered; it ceased fire. Thereafter RODNEY was frequently engaged with Du Santon from extreme ranges and her fire, though it did not knock out the battery, was always sufficiently accurate to cause it to cease firing.

27. Y Beach was also visited by the French chasseur LA SURPRISE which, according to statements made later by prisoners, had orders to attack the ships there. She was engaged and finally sunk by BRILLIANT, the supporting destroyer off the beach.

28. At noon, information was received that the U.S. armoured force, for the most part landed from the Maracaibos, had taken Tafaraoui aerodrome and an immediate request was sent to Gibraltar for the U.S. Army Spitfires.

29. The naval aircraft, after the attack on the aerodromes, maintained standing fighter patrols over the area of operations and these aircraft directed by LARGS were used extensively for tactical reconnaissance. The latter was one of the features of the operation and was all the more important owing to the very scanty and uncertain nature of the army communications.

30. Twenty-four U.S. Spitfires arrived at Tafaraoui by 1600 and whilst airborne were in touch with LARGS by W/T.

Monday, 9th November.
31. During the night a considerable swell came in at all beaches and landing operations were delayed in consequence.

32. GARDENIA and FLUELLEN on patrol off X Beach were in collision, the former unfortunately sinking with the loss of three men.

33. During the forenoon JAMAICA and AURORA engaged two destroyers which came out of Oran, both destroyers being seriously damaged and beached under the batteries.

34. A French Zouave battalion from Mostaganem gave some trouble to the American battalion guarding the eastern flank of the beaches, and owing to the lack of good communications, which made the situation obscure in LARGS,

together with a panicky message from the British F.O.O. in that area, caused for a short time some anxiety. The situation was, however, quickly restored when JAMAICA arrived off the beach to give supporting fire and some accurate high level bombing by FURIOUS's three remaining Albacores caused the enemy to withdraw.

35. More U.S. Spitfires from Gibraltar arrived in the course of the afternoon together with a half squadron of Swordfish for A/S patrols. I therefore ordered the carriers to return to Gibraltar on completion of their last fighter patrol of the day. Their co-operation had been invaluable and was carried out with all the dash and efficiency that characterises the operations of naval aircraft.

36. By the evening, the situation ashore, both from the positions gained by the advancing troops and the quantity of the ammunition and stores that had been got up to them, determined the Commanding General to carry out a general assault on Oran at 0800 on the following day.

RODNEY, AURORA and JAMAICA were detailed to assist by bombardment of the two big forts at Du Santon and Cape Canastel, and FARNDALE and CALPE, under the orders of Captain J.S. Bethell, R.N., my Chief of Staff, were ordered to be ready to seize the earliest practicable opportunity of entering harbour to endeavour to stop any blocking operations, which all along I was convinced the French would undertake.

37. Early morning reconnaissance of the harbour from the air, however, revealed that this had already been carried out; consequently I decided to keep our ships clear. There was nothing they could have done and their presence at that stage would only have caused additional aggravation.

Tuesday, 10th November.
38. The assault went off as planned and by noon General Fredendall who had gone ashore early was taking the surrender of Oran.

39. News was received shortly afterwards that much of the French shipping in the port had been sunk, but that like most blocking operations hurriedly conceived and undertaken, the results were not so bad as they at first appeared.

40. The first follow-up convoys were due the following day and I ordered the five personnel ships of the fast portion into Mers el Kebir and the slow portion into Arzeu Bay.

Wednesday, 11th November.
41. RODNEY was sent to join Force "H" cruising between Algiers and Oran.

42. I embarked in AURORA during the forenoon and visited X and Y Beaches. As at Z Beach they had been much impeded by bad weather but with perseverance and resourcefulness were getting on very well. The big L.S.I.s, BATORY, MONARCH OF BERMUDA and LLANGIBBY CASTLE, had already been sailed empty for Gibraltar.

43. The NIEUW ZEELAND, which had been sailed independently from Arzeu, was unhappily sunk by a submarine when almost within sight of Gibraltar. I therefore arranged for all further returning ships to be escorted, and thereafter none were sunk in the Mediterranean.

Thursday, 12th November.

44. Unloading proceeded with great rapidity at all the beaches. At Z the unloading was confined to the harbour at Arzeu and it was found possible to get no less than seven ships inside, four of them alongside.

The congestion in the docks was bad and the stores, mostly petrol and ammunition, mountains high. It was as well that there were no air raids.

45. I visited the airfields of Tafaraoui and La Senia during the day, and to avoid disturbing the minds of those it was our policy to propitiate, covered my uniform with an American overcoat and tin hat. The local population appeared for the most part indifferent to the coming and going of the American troops.

The efficiency of the naval air attack on La Senia was impressive and I counted over forty wrecked aircraft on the aerodrome. The two hangars containing the fighters were completely wrecked, but the other hangars were virtually undamaged save for fragmentary perforation.

46. I went into Oran for an unofficial look at the port, which was now in charge of Rear-Admiral Bennett, U.S. Navy. The Americans had already cleared a passage through the blocked entrance sufficient to admit a freighter of average size, and a part of the follow-up convoy, which had been sent round under escort from Arzeu, was already in harbour or waiting off the entrance to berth.

47. A number of personnel ships and supply ships of the original convoy which had completed unloading at Arzeu were sailed escorted for Gibraltar in the evening. AURORA also sailed.

Friday, 13th November.

48. Further ships of the follow-up convoy went round to Oran and JAMAICA sailed for Gibraltar. S.S. BROWNING was sunk on her way to Oran, presumably by torpedo, though no track was seen and the escorts gained no contact. The ship was laden with T.N.T. and motor transport and it is not impossible that the explosion was internal. Witnesses saw no column of water usually associated with an external explosion. The ship was sunk well outside the 100 fathom line.

Saturday, 14th November.

49. All ships, save one which had a broken derrick, having now completed unloading at Arzeu, I collected them into three convoys and picking up the ships off X and Y Beaches and escorted by all available craft, sailed for Gibraltar, where they arrived safely the next and following days.

The ZEBULON B. VANCE with the broken derrick was sent round with the four last remaining ships of the follow-up convoy to Oran to unload.

50. Thus the forty-seven ships which had taken the resources of a number of British ports and three weeks to load were unloaded for the most part over beaches inside a week. Under the weather conditions prevailing, I much doubt whether the work could have been greatly bettered.

51. On Monday, the Centre Naval Task Force ceased to exist. At sunset I struck my broad pendant in LARGS.

Notes
1. The Naval Commander Western Task Force was Vice-Admiral H.K. Hewitt, U.S.N. The publication of the report of this Task Force is a matter for the United States Navy Department, and it is therefore not included with these reports.
2. Force "H" – a surface force covering the landings and providing fighter support.
3. Folbot – a collapsible rubber boat.
4. The British Naval Task Force Commanders were:- Eastern Task Force, Vice-Admiral Sir Harold M. Burrough, K.B.E., C.B., D.S.O.; Centre Task Force, Commodore T.H. Troubridge, D.S.O., R.N.
5. Lieutenant-Commander Willmott's report is not being reproduced here.
6. These H.Q. ships for the conduct of combined operations, accommodating combined service staffs, were the first to be converted for this purpose, and this was the first occasion on which they were used.
7. Norfolk House – in St. James's Square, London; the pre-operational H.Q. of the Allied Commander-in-Chief.
8. Flag Officer, Inshore Squadron – Vice-Admiral Sir Harold M. Burrough, K.B.E., C.B., D.S.O.
9. Deputy Naval Commander Expeditionary Force.
10. L.S.I. – Landing Ship, Infantry,
11. F.O.O. – Forward Observation Officer.
12. Dan – a marking buoy.
13. S.N.O.L. – Senior Naval Officer Landing.
14. S.N.O.(T) – Senior Naval Officer (Transport).
15. A/S – anti-submarine.
16. S.N.O.L.(C). – Senior Naval Officer Landing (C Sector).
17. V.A.C.N A. – Vice-Admiral Commanding, North Atlantic, whose H.Q. were at Gibraltar.
18. T/B – torpedo bomber.
19. The suffix "z" indicates G.M.T.
20. P.B.M. – Principal Beach Master.
21. L.C.P. – Landing Craft, Personnel.
22. See paragraph 11.
23. C.E.N.T.F. – Commander Eastern Naval Task Force.
24. L.C.M. – Landing Craft, Mechanised Vehicles.
25. R.A.A. – Rear-Admiral Air.
26. R.C.T. – Regimental Combat Team.
27. M.L.O. – Military Landing Officer.
28. K.M.S.O. 1 – the slow convoy for Oran, which had sailed from the Clyde on Thursday, 22nd October.
29. To avoid noise.
30. Their mission was to capture the port by a *coup de main* before harbour works could be put out of action or ships scuttled.
31. Maracaibos – the earliest and at that time the only existing "Landing Ships, Tank."

3

LIEUTENANT GENERAL K.A.N. ANDERSON'S DESPATCH ON OPERATIONS IN NORTH WEST AFRICA, 8 NOVEMBER 1942 TO 13 MAY 1943

The War Office, November, 1946.
OPERATIONS IN NORTH WEST AFRICA
FROM 8th NOVEMBER 1942 TO 13th MAY 1943.

PREFACE BY THE WAR OFFICE.

The Anglo-American expedition to French North Africa, discussed from the time of the United States entry into the war and finally approved in July, 1942, had as its main objects the securing of French Morocco and Algeria with a view to the earliest possible occupation of Tunisia. It was also hoped to secure communications through the Mediterranean. For its success it depended partly on surprise and partly upon the degree of opposition or assistance which might be offered by the French forces in North Africa.

The forces available for this operation were partly British and it was advisable that these, with their more recent operational experience, should play a leading part in the early stages of the campaign. On the other hand, the United States had maintained relations with the Vichy Government, whereas the British Government had recognised the movement headed by General De Gaulle. It was thought that, for this and other reasons, a United States expedition would find more local support in North Africa than an expedition in which British troops were foremost. Accordingly, an American officer, Lieutenant-General Eisenhower, was appointed Commander-in-Chief, with a British officer, Lieutenant-General Anderson, as Commander of the Eastern Task Force on which the burden of the initial fighting was likely to fall. It was planned, furthermore, that American troops should participate largely in the assault phase including the eastern landing, and that Lieutenant-General Anderson should not assume command until after that phase should be ended. His despatch commences, therefore, some two days after the operation began.

The landings in North Africa extended over a wide front from Casablanca to Algiers. The Western and Central Task Forces met little sustained opposition, but the move of the Eastern Task Force into Tunisia was countered by the simultaneous, and practically unopposed, arrival of German troops, many of whom came by air. General Anderson's force, after initial failure to reach Tunis and Bizerta, was then reinforced, partly by sea and partly by troops moving overland from Casablanca and Oran. By this process First British Army was formed together with 2 U.S. Corps.

Eighth Army, meanwhile, was making progress in Tripolitania, and it was decided, at a Conference held in Casablanca in January, 1943, that this Army would come under General Eisenhower's command when it crossed the border into Tunisia. This actually occurred in February, the forces then uniting to form 18 Army Group, immediately under the control of General Alexander as Deputy Commander-in-Chief.

This despatch covers, therefore, the operations of First Army up to the conclusion of the campaign. It also covers the operations of 2 U.S. Corps and 19 French Corps during a period (ending 18th February, 1943), in which they were co-ordinated, and finally commanded, by General Anderson.

The following despatch was submitted to the Secretary of State for War on 7th June, 1943, by LIEUTENANT GENERAL K.A.N. ANDERSON, C.B., M.C., GENERAL OFFICER COMMANDING-IN-CHIEF, FIRST ARMY.

8th November, 1942–13th May, 1943.

INTRODUCTION.

The initial assault landings in North Africa on night 7th/8th November, 1942, were undertaken entirely by United States troops, except at Algiers. There, the British 11 Infantry Brigade Group and two Commandos (all on assault scale) landed simultaneously with the troops of United States 34 Infantry Division, while a second Brigade Group of 78 Division was in floating reserve. The whole operation was under command of Major-General Ryder, United States 34 Infantry Division.

Although nominal opposition was offered in some quarters the landing was on the whole unopposed, and by 1600 hours envoys were received to discuss terms: after that time only sporadic fighting continued. On 9th November Algiers harbour was opened and the unloading of ships began.

Once this landing had been completed under American auspices, the rôle allotted to First Army was to establish a base at Algiers and to occupy Eastern Algeria and Tunisia as speedily as possible.

So, on 9th November, I left Gibraltar by air, landed at Maison Blanche airfield with a very small skeleton staff and took over command, immediately directing Major-General Evelegh (Commander British 78 Division) to carry out the pre-arranged plan for the capture of Bougie port and Djidjelli airfield with 36 Infantry Brigade Group, assisted by naval forces under command of Captain N.V. Dickinson, D.S.C., R.N.

And, on the final cessation of French opposition on 10th November, it became possible to redispose the forces available for the advance east. Orders were therefore given for all troops of 78 Division and the two Commandos to revert to command of 78 Division, while all other British troops were placed temporarily under command of 34 United States Division, which was charged with the security of the port of Algiers and the vital airfields at Maison Blanche and Blida.

If I was to forestall the Axis in Tunis and Bizerta, speed was quite vital.

Previous to leaving the United Kingdom I had prepared three alternative plans to meet the case of:-

(*a*) French resistance on a considerable scale.

(*b*) Short-lived resistance followed by non-co-operation or at least a period of confusion, or

(*c*) Active collaboration.

The same governing principles held good in each case – namely, seizure of coastal airfields and immediate installation of fighters, as a preliminary to the successive capture of the ports of Bougie, Philippeville, Bone and La Calle; together with the most rapid advance of my land forces by motor transport, landing craft and troop-carrying aircraft.

I must state here that when in the planning stage it was decided that no assault landing should be made East of Algiers, then, in my opinion, my chance disappeared of reaching Tunis before the Germans, unless the French put up a stout resistance to Axis entry into Tunisia.[I] In actual fact, the French resisted us in Algiers (feeble though their resistance was, yet its consequent repercussions caused delay and doubt) and did not resist the Axis in Tunisia. The first German landings at El Aouana airport on 9th November were not opposed.

36 Brigade landed unopposed at Bougie on 11th November and took over the port. The battalion destined to seize the airfield at Djidjelli and stock it with petrol was, however, unable to land by sea owing to the swell and went on by road from Bougie, not reaching Djidjelli until 13th November. This delay unfortunately prevented our fighters operating from the airfield and, as a result, the enemy bombers sank several ships in Bougie harbour before air cover could be provided. Losses in personnel were not high but in equipment were considerable, and the infantry were, for some time to come, operating only with what they could carry and in the clothes they wore when they left their ships.

The distances covered and the feats achieved by the brigades of 78 Division (in particular 36 Brigade) operating with a very reduced scale of first and second line transport, and with no third line, were one of the features of the early stages of the campaign. Similarly, owing to convoy limitations, aggravated by losses at sea, it was not possible to provide adequate transport for port clearance and other line of communication duties. This had serious repercussion on maintenance; ships could not be cleared, congestion occurred on the quays, and depots could not be kept filled to meet demands. Furthermore, an immensely long line of communication was created by the rapid advance eastwards, with very meagre railway resources that could not be properly co-ordinated or developed owing to limitations of staff. All these factors contributed to a situation that gave rise to great anxiety for some time.

The campaign can henceforth be divided into three main phases:-

(*a*) A race for Tunis and Bizerta, undertaken by a small force on assault or light scales and consequently much understrength in men and equipment. We just failed to win this race, after some bitter fighting in bad weather which gave us our first experience of Tunisian mud. This phase ended soon after Christmas, 1942.

(*b*) The period 28th December, 1942, to 27th March, 1943, during which both sides were building up their forces and attempting to hold on to or seize ground important for the future, while we also struggled incessantly to improve our immensely long communications. We were mainly on the defensive, suffered from an acute shortage of infantry, and were often very hard pressed in the mountainous country. I was forced to use the infantry battalions of 6 Armoured Division on ordinary infantry tasks of holding a sector of the front, away from the armoured brigade; and this misuse of the armoured divisional infantry continued up to the end of February, 1943. It is some consolation to know that the Germans had to do exactly the same with the infantry of 10 Panzer Division. Our greatest asset was our preponderance in artillery, and the front seemed at times largely held by artillery fire alone. The term "front" is deceptive. We covered the main passes through the mountains with small forces of up to a brigade group; the gaps between these defended areas varied from 10–18 miles as the crow flies. These spaces were inadequately patrolled by both sides.

(*c*) An offensive period, starting with our counter-attack at Djebel Abiod on 28th March, and ending with the final destruction of the Axis forces in Africa on 13th May, 1943.

But before narrating the march of events, I must refer to certain factors which intimately affected my decisions and actions on many occasions. They form the background to the adventure on which First Army was embarked.

(*a*) First and foremost was the matter of *Command*.[2] In the early days, when my forces were weak, General Eisenhower gave me every atom of help in his power by ordering up units of the United States Forces from Oran and Casablanca to help my advanced troops in their forward rush. These United States units arrived piecemeal, as fast as the very limited road and rail facilities could carry them, and had perforce to be employed as part and parcel of the British forces under British brigade or divisional commanders, and not independently as all of us would have wished. That the resulting friction was so small speaks volumes for the real desire to pull together which animated all parties. As soon as possible, United States units were concentrated under United States formation commanders, and continued for many weeks to co-operate closely and happily with our officers and men under command of 78 Division and 5 Corps. But it was long before our total Allied strength reached a point at which each nation could be made entirely responsible for its own particular sector.

The advent of the French as our active allies produced fresh complications in command which grew as the front increased. In the north were six battalions under General Barre, operating with, but not at first under command of, 5 Corps; in the centre the main French forces were concentrating in the Le Kef – Teboursouk area; in the south another force of about eight battalions was in the area Gafsa – Tebessa working with the small mobile United States force operating there, who were nominally under command of the French.

British mobile units were also, later, in the south under United States command for reconnaissance duties, while for several months First Army had to coordinate, and in most cases provide, the entire movement and supply organisation and most of the signal communications for all three nationalities.

The more the campaign progressed the more obvious it became that unified command was quite essential to avoid a chaotic muddle. But General Giraud would not agree to placing French troops under British command, while his manifold other responsibilities prevented General Eisenhower personally exercising the command himself from a forward headquarters. So a series of compromises and makeshifts was adopted in the course of which I, gradually and as commander of the only formation equipped and able to undertake the task, became in turn adviser, co-ordinator and, finally, commander of the whole Tunisian front. None of these steps was satisfactory, and even as commander I lacked the physical means to control efficiently so large a front of well over 200 miles.

The situation was not righted until 18 Army Group was formed later under General Alexander, who then took 2 United States Corps directly under his own control, leaving me with the British and French forces only – covering at the time a front of 120 miles.

(*b*) Another constant hindrance, already referred to, was closely related to the problem of command – *the inter-mingling of units of the three Allied Armies.* Obviously it is hopelessly unsound both for tactical and administrative reasons to mix troops in this way, but the chain of events as the campaign unfolded forced it upon me. It was my constant preoccupation to tidy up the mess, and give each nation its own sector, but this was not finally accomplished until mid-March when the steadily increasing Allied strength at last enabled the final transfers to be arranged – always excepting the retention of a considerable amount of British artillery with French 19 Corps right up to the end of hostilities and the use anywhere on the front, in the mountains, of the specialised Goums from Morocco.[3]

(*c*) *The state of the French Army and feeling throughout the country.* – I have no intention of touching on politics except in so far as they influenced operations. But in the early days of this campaign, politics intruded everywhere. The loyalties of all French officers were sharply divided, and many, even of those who had taken the plunge and sided with the Allies, were still openly expressing loyalty to the Marshal. Even while I was pressing forward with all vigour General Barre was still negotiating with General von Arnim in Tunis. This may have been a clever move to gain time, and I am now inclined to this view; but at the moment it did not inspire me with confidence. Many mayors, station and post-masters and other key officials with whom we had dealings as we advanced (for instance, the civil telephone was, at first, my chief means of communicating with my forward units and with Allied Force Headquarters) were lukewarm in their sympathies and hesitant to commit themselves openly, while a few were hostile. I can safely generalise by saying that at first, in the Army, the senior officers were hesitant and afraid to commit themselves, the junior officers were mainly in favour of aiding the Allies, the men would obey orders; amongst the people, the Arabs were indifferent or inclined to be hostile, the French were in our favour but apathetic, the civil authorities were antagonistic as a whole. The resulting impression on my mind was not one of much confidence as to the safety of my small isolated force should I suffer a severe set-back.

But from the moment General Barre refused the final German ultimatum on 19th November, the situation began to change. We met henceforth with increasing assistance and courtesy and our relations with the Army and civilians have grown closer and better every day. A French Army, under General Juin, amounting to a nominal thirty-two battalions of infantry and some hundred and twenty guns (when all was assembled), was ordered to mobilise. Its mission in November 1942 was to cover the right flank of the Allied Forces while they deployed. Later, the main body gradually moved eastward, with only minor contact with Italian patrols, to the line of the Eastern Dorsale by early January 1943. While six battalions remained in the British area around Oued Zarga – Medjez and several battalions continued to work with the Americans in the south.

The French mobilisation plan was prepared only for a campaign of 6–8 weeks. The equipment of the Army was lamentable; no anti-aircraft or anti-tank weapons, rifles and guns dating back to the period 1880–1914, no signal equipment or motor transport, no boots or proper clothing, staffs inadequate and not up to date, et cetera. Only in spirit was the Army formidable, and this spirit was carefully fostered by Generals Juin and Koeltz and a fine body of junior commanders. Co-operation and mutual trust between British and French reached a high level by the end of the campaign, but, even to the end, French units were not capable of offensive action against German troops, and could only operate safely in the mountainous sectors of the front.

It must be remembered that the French Army in Africa is largely a native army.

(*d*) *The Line of Communication Administrative difficulties and the build-up of First Army.* – Administrative matters are dealt with separately, but to understand correctly the background of this campaign it is essential to bear the following major facts in mind:-

(i) The huge distances. From Algiers to Tunis by road is over 560 miles.

(ii) The extremely mountainous nature of the country, and that at first only two roads and an inefficient railway were available eastwards.

(iii) That the Army was entirely dependent on what it brought overseas with it, in the way of transport, fuel, supplies, &c. Nothing whatever was available locally; indeed, we had to supply the railway with coal, and our Allies, out of our none too plentiful stocks, with rations, petrol and other supplies. First Army did not spring from the sea full-formed like Aphrodite, but grew in stature painfully slowly as convoys arrived at fortnightly intervals. The initial rush on Tunis was made by a force, at its strongest, equivalent only to one infantry division and one tank regiment on light scales. The leading infantry division (78th) was not complete until 1st December; the next division (6 Armoured) was not complete until 15th December; 46 Division reached the front by the first week of February 1943, 1 Division by 22nd March and 4 Division was not fully assembled until the end of the second week of April 1943.

For me it was an exasperating period in which I saw chance after chance disappear for lack of sufficient strength to seize them, and when reinforcements did arrive the enemy in his turn had also increased his strength. Always the need was for more infantry.

(e) *Air Support.* – In the early stages this was bad for obvious and I think mainly unavoidable reasons. All aircraft had to be flown in from Gibraltar or the United Kingdom; all stores, services, bombs, &c., came by convoy; airfields were few and far between – the nearest serviceable airfield to the forward troops at Tebourba in December 1942 being at Bone, 114 miles away; the Air Officer Commanding had to meet naval demands for protection and had other calls, in addition to supporting the Army, which tied him to Algiers while I was going ever further eastwards. As the situation stabilised so did our co-operation grow closer; but it was a slow growth and did not reach maturity until the reorganisation carried out in March 1943.[4] Again, in the early days, the great distances, poor means of intercommunication, and the inevitable early troubles which arise when the forces of two nations are beginning to work together all contributed to the undoubted lack of efficient co-operation between Army and Air Forces.

Goodwill there was in plenty, and with increasing experience and, above all, improved means of inter-communication the situation improved. By mid-March 1943, liaison was excellent; we were working as one team and, under Air Commodore Cross, the air support given to First Army in the last stages was intimate, immediate and intensely powerful.

(f) *Weather and the country.* – Before arrival I had imagined North Africa was a dry country. Although I knew that the winter was the wet season in North Africa, none the less, the extent of the rains in the Coastal belt and their effect on the roads, on cross-country movement, and on the airfields, came as a very unpleasant surprise. In the northern zone, in which First Army operated, the rains began in early December and continued until early April. March was the wettest month. Rain, mist and a peculiarly glutinous mud formed the background to all our operations during this period.

Northern Tunisia is a country of high mountains, narrow plains between the ranges, and few roads, with very limited scope for armoured action. In the south it becomes much more open and desert-like, but rocky hills occur everywhere.

FIRST PHASE. – THE RACE FOR TUNIS.

As I have already stated, on 9th November the first Germans landed at El Aouana airport, Tunis. By 13th November I had occupied Bougie and Djidjelli.

Every effort was now directed towards getting troops east as fast as possible, and an earlier proposal (which was not put into effect) was repeated for a landing at Sousse by a force from Malta.

The first troops to occupy Bone were two companies of 3 Parachute Battalion dropped by air to hold the airfield and 6 Commando, landed by sea on 12th November to seize the port. On 11th November a small column of all arms from 11 Infantry Brigade Group (known as Hart Force and made mobile by pooling all the available Brigade transport) left Algiers by road for Bone, where it arrived on 15th November. By 13th November the move of 36 Brigade main body had started, and one battalion had arrived at Sétif by rail and another battalion by sea at Bone, where it was joined by some artillery and servicing units. The carriers and motor transport of this brigade, however, were at this stage still unable to land.

36 Brigade, still on assault scales, lost no time in getting forward. By 15th November their advance guard had occupied Tabarka, and on 18th November their leading battalion repulsed an enemy attack at Djebel Abiod, destroying 11 tanks and armoured cars. The other battalions of this Brigade were following up quickly, and Hart Force, which had led the advance all the way, was operating to the east of Djebel Abiod. 78 Division had established their Headquarters at Bone.

On 15th November 1 Parachute Battalion attempted to drop at Souk el Arba landing ground, but was unable to do so until the following day owing to weather conditions. The appearance of this battalion had a stimulating effect on the local French troops. The battalion lost no time in getting forward (on foot and using local transport), and, by 17th November, was operating north-east from Béja and in contact with German troops.

While this general move forward was in progress, the follow-up convoy arrived on 13th November bringing the 17/21 Lancers Regimental Group (later known as Blade Force), 1 Parachute Brigade (less one battalion) and the balance to light scales of the transport of 78 Division (less one brigade group). Units and sub-units of 78 Division and Blade Force were moved east as fast as transport was unloaded, 11 Brigade Group being finally concentrated in the Béja area by 22nd November and Blade Force in the Souk el Arba area by 20th November. Advance Headquarters, First Army, also arrived by the follow-up convoy and, on 13th November, opened up at Hotel Albert, Algiers.

Simultaneously with the advance in the north, steps were taken to secure the early occupation of important airfields further south. On 15th November

503 United States Parachute Battalion dropped at Youks-les-Bains without opposition, with a view to making the airfield available for our use. This battalion, under the command of Colonel Raff, operated most energetically from its base at Youks. On 17th November detachments occupied Gafsa airfield, and mobile patrols in requisitioned transport roamed widely over the whole of the southern area, meeting small Italian forces. Contact was also made and good relations established with the French garrison at Tebessa, who co-operated in many patrols.

On 16th November arrangements were made for my force to be supplemented by the addition of two American tank battalions (one medium, one light), some armoured infantry and supporting arms, and steps were taken to get these troops up to the forward areas as soon as possible.

By 17th November the enemy strength was estimated at 500–1,000 fighting personnel in the area of Tunis and 4,000 at Bizerta, with some tanks in each case; in addition, a considerable number of aircraft had been flown in. The enemy had occupied Mateur and had pushed out west and south-west, in contact with 36 Infantry Brigade's advanced troops west of Djebel Abiod and with the French at Sidi Nsir and Medjez.

On 17th November orders were issued for 78 Division (still less one brigade group), after completing its forward concentration in the area Tabarka – Souk el Arba – Ghardimaou, to advance on Tunis and destroy the Axis forces. The French Command had agreed that they would, to the best of their ability, cover the concentration of 78 Division and the right flank of their subsequent advance, and it seemed possible that French troops would also actively assist in the northern sector. Further south the attitude of the French forces was very uncertain.

Subsequent operations took place on three clearly defined axes. These were:-

(*a*) The main road Béja – Medjez – Tebourba – Tunis.

(*b*) The road Béja – Sidi Nsir.

(*c*) The road Tabarka – Djebel Abiod – Mateur.

OPERATIONS DURING PERIOD
17TH NOVEMBER–25TH DECEMBER, 1942.

Northern Sector

36 Brigade was in contact with the enemy positions at Djebel Abiod. The carriers and reconnaissance cars of Hart Force, which had been pushed far forward and were then cut off by the German advance, made their way back to 36 Brigade by 19th November, but the infantry transport was lost. The infantry company took to the hills and did not rejoin 36 Brigade until 21st November, having conducted a successful guerilla campaign against the enemy's rear. The brigade advanced slowly against slight opposition and many mines and booby traps to Jefna, where the enemy occupied a very strong position on commanding ground. Several attempts to dislodge him from these heights failed. Losses were heavy. 1 Commando landed 14 miles west of Bizerta and worked south in an endeavour to get

behind and dislodge the enemy at Jefna. They did considerable damage but failed in their object and rejoined 36 Brigade on 3rd December.

Southern Sector

On 19th November French troops under command General Barre rejected the German ultimatum, at Medjez. The two German attacks which followed were repulsed. Persistent demands for air and tank support were made by the French and it was evident that they would not long be able to resist. In fact they withdrew from Medjez during the following night, leaving forward elements of Blade Force holding Oued Zarga and 1 Parachute Battalion holding Béja. At this time 11 Brigade and the remainder of Blade Force were completing concentration at Béja and Souk el Arba respectively.

On 21st November the enemy withdrew to the east bank of the river at Medjez. It was, however, evident that 78 Division were not yet strong enough to press the advance and orders were issued for it to delay any move forward temporarily until the build-up of forces and supplies was sufficient to give it a reasonable chance in the assault on Tunis.

Time was also required to clarify the confused situation existing with the French. The intention was that all French troops in 78 Division area should be relieved as soon as possible so that, under the command of General Barre, all the French forces could concentrate on the protection of the right flank on the line Le Kef – Teboursouk – Testour.

By 23rd November a preliminary verbal agreement had been reached that all troops of whatever nationality north of the line Le Kef – Zaghouan should be under command First Army and that all troops south of this line should be under French command.

By 24th November the forward concentration of 78 Division and Blade Force, reinforced by light tanks from the United States 1 Armoured Division, was completed and orders were issued for the immediate resumption of the advance with, as a first objective, the line Tebourba – Mateur.

On 25th November the advance was resumed and 11 Brigade attacked the enemy at Medjez, seizing the village and establishing crossings over the river.

On 27th November 11 Brigade occupied Tebourba and repulsed enemy counter-attacks supported by tanks and dive-bombers, destroying several tanks. On 28th November 11 Brigade and 2/13 Armoured Regiment were on the outskirts of Djedeida.

We had attained the nearest point to Tunis that was reached until the final stage of the campaign.

At the same time that 11 Brigade was operating up the Medjerda Valley, Blade Force with 1 Parachute Battalion and the 1 Battalion of the 1 Armoured Regiment, United States 1 Armoured Division, moved into the plain south of Mateur, not without considerable supply difficulties enhanced by the beginning of the rains. Here Blade Force was involved in its first successful armoured engagement on 26th November, an action which continued on and off for several days.

A successful raid by the United States light tank battalion resulted in the destruction of approximately 40 Stukas on the ground at Djedeida airfield.

It was now evident that the enemy intended to stand and fight along the entire front and was present in considerable strength – see Appendix "C."

The following week saw hard fighting followed by the start of our withdrawal. This week was notable for the heavy scale of enemy air attack, particularly by dive-bombers, to which the leading troops were subjected, and which our own air forces were at this stage unable to prevent.[5] They were still operating from Bone aerodrome, with an unreliable (owing to the mud) advanced landing ground at Souk el Arba.

11 Brigade were never able to occupy Djedeida, but remained in contact with the enemy on 29th and 30th November, with Blade Force concentrated in the area of Chouigui.

By 30th November Combat Command "B," United States 1 Armoured Division, was concentrated forward, and an attack on Tunis, with Combat Command "B" and Blade Force working to the east of the Medjerda, was ordered for 2nd December, and in conjunction with this 1 Parachute Battalion was to drop at Depienne and threaten Tunis from the south. The drop was successfully made and the parachutists reached Oudna, but the main attack did not take place, for on 1st and 2nd December the enemy counter-attacked with tanks and infantry towards Tebourba from the north and Blade Force was heavily engaged, suffering considerable casualties in tanks.

By the evening of 2nd December Blade Force was withdrawn west and the defence of the forward areas was left to 11 Brigade and the armoured infantry of Combat Command "B" who had to be ordered forward in a defensive rôle. Our tank losses up to date amounted to approximately 40. Many enemy tanks were destroyed, but as he was left in possession of the battlefield most of these were no doubt recovered. The survivors of 1 Parachute Battalion rejoined 78 Division on 3rd December.

On this date the enemy again attacked 11 Brigade in strength at Tebourba and penetrated their positions at several places. The Brigade was cut off and had difficulty in withdrawing during the night: 2 Hampshires, who failed to get the order to withdraw, suffered heavily but fought magnificently. Losses of equipment were considerable and enemy dive-bombing all day was on a heavy scale.

On 3rd December a series of enemy attacks on our positions at El Guessa developed from the south-east and tank and infantry battles took place all day between Combat Command "B" and the enemy, while 11 Brigade withdrew to more favourable positions north of Medjez.

During the period of the actions described, the administrative situation was precarious in the extreme. Dispatches of stores from Bone, which was intended as the main supply base for the forward area, were seriously affected by enemy bombing. An acute shortage of locomotives and rolling-stock, coupled with demands arising from the French mobilisation and the transfer of United States formations from the west, made compensating stores lifts from Algiers by rail impossible. There was no reserve pool of motor transport to fall back on. All resources were strained to the utmost.

It was clear to me that the offensive against Tunis would have to be postponed to give time to build up resources and to refit the troops who had been engaged for the past month. Several battalions of 78 Division were under three hundred and fifty strong and the strain of persistent dive-bombing was beginning to tell. The heavy rain had also put all my airfields out of action and movement off the main roads was becoming impossible. I did not consider that a further offensive could in any case be undertaken until at least one week's reserves of supplies of all kinds had been accumulated at railhead.

Meanwhile my Tactical Headquarters had moved in succession to Jemmapes, Constantine and Ain Seynour, while Main Army Headquarters opened at Constantine on 29th November.

By 10th December the garrison at Medjez, which included four French battalions, has been reinforced by 1 Guards Brigade less a battalion, preparatory to the temporary withdrawal of 11 Brigade and Combat Command "B" for refit. Enemy attacks on Medjez with infantry and tanks on 10th and 11th December were repulsed.

Although the withdrawal of 11 Brigade was carried out according to plan, that of Combat Command "B" was only accomplished at the expense of the majority of their vehicles. Owing to a mistaken order by a battalion commander of Combat Command "B," the route which had been ordered was not followed, with the result that all units were bogged and forced to abandon in the mud a very large number of tanks and transport vehicles. It was indeed a crippling loss. Combat Command "B" reverted to command 5 Corps and later the personnel who could not be re-equipped were ordered back to Guelma.

6 Armoured Division who had been ordered to operate offensively from Teboursouk were in contact with light enemy forces east and south-east of Medjez. The components of Blade Force returned to their parent formations on 12th December.

On 13th December I issued to 5 Corps a warning order to prepare to resume the advance on Tunis. The plan adopted by 5 Corps was as follows:-

As a preliminary, to capture Djebel el Ahmera (afterwards known as Longstop), a hill which completely dominated the exits from Medjez. Thereafter, 78 Division with 18 Regimental Combat Team, United States 1 Infantry Division were to advance north-east to Tebourba – El Bathan either side of the river Medjerda, while 6 Armoured Division moved direct on to the high ground at Massicault. Thence, both 78 and 6 Armoured Divisions were to drive straight on to Tunis. Combat Command "B" to be in Corps reserve. Four-fifths of my strength was allotted to this concentrated attack, which I consider had a very good chance of success.

While this major operation was in progress 36 Brigade were to attempt to get behind the rear of the German position at Jefna and advance on Mateur. Four

French battalions and one Commando were to hold the enemy in the area northeast of Béja.

Apart from planning and the regrouping of forces for the attack, the period from 13th–22nd December was one of patrol activity only, contact with the enemy being made all along the front. Enemy reinforcements were arriving fast.

The rain and the state of the ground gave me much cause for anxiety, and repeated trials showed that cross-country movement for any type of vehicle was becoming more and more difficult.

However, I decided to take the risk and ordered 5 Corps to proceed with the opening attack on Longstop on night 22nd–23rd December. This was carried out successfully by 2 Coldstream Guards, after severe and confused fighting: the Battalion was, on 23rd December, relieved by 1 Battalion, 18 Regimental Combat Team, United States 1 Infantry Division. With the dawn on 23rd December came torrential rain which went on for three days: the ground became a quagmire.

The attack on Tunis had to be postponed. Meanwhile 18 Combat Team had been heavily counter-attacked on 23rd December on Longstop and, mistaking their orders, withdrew from the crest: it was cleared again by 1 Guards Brigade on 24th December, lost again on Christmas Day and, owing to the mud, was then left in enemy hands. The fighting was bitter. Our troops returned to their original positions around Medjez, and there decisively repelled an enemy attack on the 27th.

Owing to failure of communications, the order cancelling the operation did not reach 5 Northants of 11 Infantry Brigade, who had been detailed to work through the hills to seize the pass west of Tebourba. The battalion pushed through the very difficult country in dense fog right up to the Djebel Lanserine before the commander, realising what had happened, halted his battalion and brought it back after some minor clashes with the enemy. This exploit was accomplished with only mule transport on a limited scale borrowed from the French.

At a conference held at 5 Corps Headquarters on Christmas Eve between General Eisenhower, General Allfrey and myself, it was finally decided to abandon any hope of a major attack on Tunis until the rainy season had ended. The Commander-in-Chief decided, in its place, to stage an attack in the south against Sfax by United States 2 Corps (which was now forming in the Tebessa area). This entailed the immediate removal from 5 Corps front of Combat Command "B" as well as other United States elements, leaving temporarily only 18 Combat Team in the Medjez area.

Thus ended my hopes of capturing Tunis by storm, and it now was clear that when the time came later to launch a new attack it would have to be on a much heavier scale against greatly-increased opposition.

It was a sad decision, but inevitable owing to the weather. And so began the next phase of the campaign, in which the battle front extended right down to Gafsa.

At about this time General Eisenhower again attempted to get the French to agree to unified command under myself as General Officer Commanding-in-Chief, First Army. But although General Juin agreed to this, General Giraud refused – on the ground that the state of feeling amongst his troops was still too delicate to permit him placing them under a British General. So the United States troops in the southern sector as well as the French in the centre sector remained direct under Allied Force Headquarters.

The boundary between First Army and the French Sector was to be (all inclusive to First Army) Souk Ahras – thence road to Le Kef – thence railway to Pont du Fahs – Zaghouan.

All troops of any nationality north of this line were to be under my command.

At about this time certain officers of pro-Axis sympathies were removed from the Staff of General Barre, thus easing a delicate situation.

At frequent intervals during the whole of this period I met Air Marshal Sir William Welsh in constant and mutual endeavour to improve the air support. Work was pressed on new airfields at Souk El Arba and Souk El Khemis, that at Bone was improved. Air Commodore Lawson was appointed as commander of all aircraft available to support 5 Corps and he placed his Headquarters next to Corps headquarters.

SECOND PHASE –
PERIOD 26TH DECEMBER, 1942–27TH MARCH, 1943.

On 1st January, 1943, I outlined to 5 Corps its future policy as under:-

(*a*) To contain the enemy by constant pressure and, by limited attacks, to seize ground required to facilitate a later offensive; plans for which were to be prepared. All attacks to have maximum artillery support. To be ready to advance, even without armour, if the enemy moved troops away southwards.

(*b*) To help the French as far south as Pont du Fahs in every way possible.

(*c*) To push on with the construction of airfields.

Widespread enemy parachute activities against my lines of communication during December accomplished little damage. On 1st January, 1943, Allied Force Headquarters assumed control of the lines of communication up to inclusive Bone – exclusive Constantine, thereby affording much needed relief to my administrative staff.

In the early stages of preparation for the United States 2 Corps operation against Sfax I took no active part, though First Army had to assume full responsibility for all maintenance arrangements, dumping programmes, &c. The attack was, however, eventually cancelled by the Commander-in-Chief, about the middle of January.

Meanwhile, on 3rd January, an attack by 36 Infantry Brigade to capture the dominating enemy positions on Djebel Azzag and Djebel Ajred was not very successful and by 5th January after severe fighting in heavy rain, we withdrew to our original front. Losses on both sides were relatively heavy. Again on 3rd January

6 Armoured Division made a reconnaissance in force in the Goubellat plain; and on 11th January followed this by a successful local attack north of Bou Arada.

On 18th January a strong German attack was launched against 6 Armoured Division down the Bou Arada Valley by infantry and at least fifty tanks of 10 Panzer Division, followed the same afternoon by an attack against the French 19 Corps. This was made by newly landed mountain troops supported by 501 Panzer Abteilung, in which the new Mark VI "Tiger" tank made its début. The attack was directed against the mountain area at the northern hinge of the two Dorsale ranges.

The attack against 6 Armoured Division was stopped dead after heavy fighting, with considerable enemy tank losses. 38 (Irish) Brigade particularly distinguished itself. But French resistance was overwhelmed; the enemy reached Robaa and Ousseltia on the 20th and the equivalent of seven battalions of infantry were cut off in the mountains; also many field guns together with nearly all their few anti-tank guns were lost. I went to see General Juin and found him personally courageous, but tired and not hopeful. I had in the meantime ordered 5 Corps to send 36 Infantry Brigade Group to the Robaa Valley and requested 2 United States Corps to send a Combat Command of United States 1 Armoured Division to the Ousseltia area – both to come under General Juin's orders on arrival. These reinforcements stabilised the situation on the general line Bou Arada – Djebel Bargou – Djebel Bou Dabouss, after fighting lasting until 23rd January.

Meanwhile, as a result of the obvious lack of co-operation and control between the British, French and American commanders, I was appointed by General Eisenhower, at a meeting with him on 21st January at Constantine, to "co-ordinate" the whole front in future, with one executive air commander (General Kuter, United States Air Corps) for the whole front. This, especially the appoint-ment of General Kuter, was a big step forward but that it did not go far enough soon became evident, and at a further meeting at Thelergma airfield on 24th January, the Commander-in-Chief made me "responsible for the employ-ment of American troops," though not yet in control of the French Corps. After a long conference with me that night General Juin agreed to place his Corps under my command, and next day this decision was confirmed by General Giraud.

If chaos were to be avoided, some one person had to command the whole front. As an example of the difficulties experienced at this time, I had to motor over 1,000 miles in four days to visit the various corps commanders. Distances were too great for radio telephony, ordinary telephone was most unreliable, air travel was impossible owing to weather. "Co-ordination" demanded discussion and often compromise and this could only be done by personal visits.

At the end of this period the French were beginning to feel the strain. The campaign did not look too rosy to them, supplies and equipment were nearly exhausted, motor transport was worn out and scarce and the troops were unable to face the German tanks owing to entire lack of anti-tank weapons.

At the end of January the enemy attack on Robaa was renewed, "Tigers" again being used, this time against 36 Infantry Brigade. The 5 Buffs stood their ground, five tanks (including two "Tigers") being destroyed, and the enemy withdrew with heavy loss. This local but successful action had an electric effect on the Tirailleurs, who were also deeply impressed by the efficiency of the British artillery. From this time on to the end of the campaign I gave French 19 Corps strong artillery support under a Commander Army Group, Royal Artillery, loaned, and also gave them 6-pounders and other equipment, which, with other American help, greatly raised morale. Thereafter they withstood remarkably well the effects of the Kasserine battle and the consequent withdrawal to the Western Dorsale, under the energetic leadership of General Koeltz.

Having been made responsible for the employment of all Allied Forces in Tunisia on 25th January, I spent the next week visiting the French and American sectors, meeting commanders and generally getting into the wider picture.

Two things seemed obvious to me: first, the mixture of nationalities had again become worse as a result of the recent fighting and must urgently be straightened out; second, our dispositions were too widely stretched in the south. In the early days, when forces on both sides were weak, it had been right to seize all we could in the attempt to hem the enemy into a narrow corridor. But a new situation had arisen. Apart from the large enemy reinforcements brought overseas into Tunisia, a fresh flow was now arriving from Tripolitania. The approach of Rommel's Army was beginning to be felt; many uninvited guests from opposite Eighth Army were entering my southern parlour, and it was clear that several weeks would elapse before Eighth Army was in a position to help to entertain them or sufficient United States reinforcements could arrive.

In addition, the French had seriously overstrained themselves and were insistently demanding relief of their tired troops; though at the same time General Giraud strongly urged that it was essential to preserve under French command a definite sector of the front, even though this sector contained American and British troops. So in the centre I formed a French Corps (19 Corps) under a commander to be appointed by General Juin (General Koeltz was selected) to hold a firm central pivot in the mountain area on the flanks of which the American 2 Corps and British 5 Corps could operate.

Owing to the peculiar circumstances prevailing in the French Corps area, I arranged for it to be divided into two divisional sectors, that on the right under command of United States 1 Division and that on the left under command of a French divisional commander to be appointed. Under command of the French division were to be 1 Parachute Brigade in the area of Djebel Mansour and, until relieved by re-equipped French units, 36 Infantry Brigade in the Robaa area. Combat Command "B," United States 1 Armoured Division, were to remain in the Ousseltia Valley under the command of General Koeltz until the situation stabilised, as a reserve.

It was decided in principle to withdraw French units from the line for re-equipment, and that, as soon as possible, they would return to relieve the British and United States units in the French Corps area. And all French troops still in the American and British sectors were to be returned to French 19 Corps.

On 30th/31st January the enemy attacked Faid and destroyed the French garrison before help from United States 1 Armoured Division at Sbeitla reached them. This defeat again seriously upset the French and they repeated their requests for early relief of tired troops.

I ordered the following steps to be taken during the first ten days of February:-

United States 18 Regimental Combat Team to return from 5 Corps and rejoin United States 1 Division, to strengthen French 19 Corps and relieve the most tired French units in the Pichon area.

United States 2 Corps to complete the raid being planned against Sened; to postpone the attack to retake Faid until stronger forces were available; to hold on to the Sidi Bou Zid position and form a strong mobile reserve in the Sbeitla area; to continue to hold Gafsa unless strongly threatened, when the garrison would be withdrawn on my order; the general task given to United States 2 Corps still being to protect the right flank of the Allies.

In addition, I formed for the first time an Army Reserve in the Kesra area, consisting at first of a reinforced Combat Command of two tank battalions from United States 1 Armoured Division. This to be reduced to one battalion as soon as the leading Combat Team of United States 34 Division (now coming up from the lines of communication) had taken over the Pichon area from French 19 Corps.

I warned General Koeltz to be ready at short notice to evacuate the Eastern Dorsale, as there were signs that a German attack was pending in the Pichon – Faid area.

Early on 14th February the enemy attacked strongly at Sidi Bou Zid and, after three days of heavy fighting during which it was most difficult to get a clear picture of the situation, broke through and captured Sbeitla on night 17th/18th February. During this period I released the Army Reserve to revert under orders of United States 2 Corps.

As a result of the loss of Sbeitla, United States 2 Corps fell back to the line Dernaia – Kasserine Gap – Sbiba, French 19 Corps conforming on the North and withdrawing from the Eastern Dorsale without loss. I sent up 1 Guards Brigade from 5 Corps to reinforce United States 34 Division at Sbiba.

After a short pause the enemy renewed his attacks. He was held at Sbiba but broke through the Kasserine Pass on 20th February and sent his armoured forces (15, 21 and parts of 10 Panzer Divisions were all identified) northwards towards Thala and westwards towards Tebessa. I ordered U.S. 2 Corps to move their only remaining reserve (Combat Command "B") to meet the westward threat, and at the same time despatched a composite force from 6 Armoured Division in the Kesra area, consisting of 26 Armoured Brigade Group, 2/5 Leicesters and some extra field and anti-aircraft artillery, all under Brigadier C.G.G. Nicholson, D.S.O., M.C., and known as "Nickforce," to Thala. This force was augmented on 21st February by two field artillery battalions of United States 9 Division and by 2 Hampshires. Combat Command "B" and "Nickforce" both were placed under orders of U.S. 2 Corps. During 21st/22nd February "Nickforce'" only just managed to hold on, but the German attack was halted finally by 1400 hours 23rd February. It had been a close shave. I then ordered 1 Guards Brigade across from Sbiba to Thala, but by the time it arrived the enemy had begun to withdraw.

I think the enemy took advantage of his initial easy success and decided to exploit it by a raid to cut our lines of communication at Le Kef, where he could have done much damage. I do not believe he intended at the outset to do more than hit U.S. 2 Corps a severe blow, in order to gain time and space for Rommel, who was himself in command of this operation.

British and American units pressed the enemy and followed his withdrawal back through Kasserine slowly, owing to the huge quantity of mines.

This was the last enemy attack against U.S. 2 Corps in the south: henceforth he was on the defensive.

A decision to re-equip 6 Armoured Division was taken at the end of December, and the convoy arriving on 20th January brought two hundred and forty-one Shermans. Courses of instruction were organised and the first regiment was due to take over its new tanks on 15th February. Operations, in the Kasserine Gap, however, retarded the programme, and its was not until 25th February that re-equipment started. The whole Armoured Brigade was re-equipped by 20th March, and after two weeks training went into action for the first time with Sherman tanks in the Pichon – Kairouan area on 8th April, The Valentine tanks thus released were handed over to the French, who received them with much satisfaction.

18 Army Group shortly afterwards took over command of all forces in Tunisia, taking United States 2 Corps directly under their orders, and leaving me in command of the British and French corps. Once again the various nationalities had perforce become very badly mixed.

By the end of February, 5 Corps consisted of 78, 46 and 6 Armoured Divisions; Headquarters 9 Corps had come out, and 1 Division was beginning to arrive at the ports.

I had got the greater part of 6 Armoured Division at last into Army Reserve, but General Alexander ordered it, with 9 Corps Headquarters and the Corps Troops, into Army Group Reserve almost immediately, though events delayed the completion of this move as the infantry brigade of 6 Armoured Division could not be spared at once.

For on 26th February von Arnim started an attack against 5 Corps on a wide front at Goubellat, at Medjez, at Sidi Nsir and at Jefna.

At Medjez it was defeated with heavy loss within a few hours, although German infantry penetrated deep into our gun lines in places. Further south a strong party of infantry and tanks also penetrated several miles behind our front through the wide gap at Tally Ho Corner and was only smashed just north of El Aroussa by Churchill tanks, which arrived in the nick of time to save a divisional head-quarters. Meanwhile 38 Infantry Brigade had heavily defeated an attack north of Bou Arada, and stood firm despite the threat far to their rear.

At Sidi Nsir an isolated detachment, of 5 Hampshires with 155/170 Field Battery, Royal Artillery, placed out as a delaying force, was overwhelmed by a heavy attack supported by tanks; but its very gallant fight gained a precious 24 hours, and enabled 46 Division to occupy the Hunt's Gap position, covering Béja, with 128 Infantry Brigade Group. The enemy abandoned his attack in the south, but continued to press strongly at Hunt's Gap, where heavy fighting in terrible weather continued for a week. 46 Division fought splendidly, but suffered very heavy losses in infantry. However, over 30 enemy tanks, including five "Tigers," were blown up by our sappers, many more were damaged, and heavy casualties were inflicted. By 3rd March the situation was in hand, though spasmodic fighting continued for several days.

Despite his first failure, the enemy on 2nd March renewed his attack near Jefna and gained a considerable local success, forcing 139 Brigade to fall back to Sedjenane. To strengthen the front there, I moved up the Parachute Brigade from the Robaa area, replacing them temporarily by the 26 Regimental Combat Team, United States 1 Infantry Division, which Army Group sent up to me.

Between 2nd and 24th March, the enemy persistently pressed his attacks in the northern sector, slowly driving 46 Division back to Cap Negro – Djebel Abiod line, and dominating the essential lateral road Djebel Abiod – Béja. It was not a happy period; things went wrong too often and we lost some most important ground. But this was the limit of his gains.

Meanwhile, owing to the final withdrawal off our French battalions from the Medjez area to rejoin French 19 Corps, the enemy had with little opposition been able to move forward and occupy all the high ground overlooking the Oued Zarga – Medjez road, including the villages of Toukabeur and Chaouach. They thus completely dominated Medjez, which was left in a dangerous salient.

The rain fell unceasingly in the north throughout this period.

The German objectives were Medjez and Béja, both of which they failed to attain. During their attacks they lost 2,200 German prisoners between 26th February and 24th March. But they had put 5 Corps into a difficult position, which demanded early righting.

THIRD PHASE. – THE OFFENSIVE PERIOD.

With the enemy at Djebel Abiod, on 18th March I ordered 5 Corps that there must be no further withdrawal whatever: that immediate preparations must be made to use 46 Division to drive back the enemy at least to Sedjenane – Cap Serrat in the north, and if possible to restore in its entirety our former position there, east of El Aouana: thereafter that the road Beja – Medjez and Medjez area itself must be completely freed from enemy domination by the recapture of the hilly country up to the Djebel el Ang and Heidous: and that plans were to be prepared at once for the capture of the high ground west of the Sebkret el Kourzia north of Bou Arada. These were all essential preliminaries to the launching of a major assault towards Tunis and Bizerta. To help 5 Corps I placed 1 Parachute Brigade, the Corps Franc and one Tabor of French Goumiers under their orders.

The country in the region Djebel Abiod – Sedjenane – Cap Serrat is extremely difficult; mountains strewn with boulders and covered with a dense scrub up to eight feet high, limiting visibility often to a few feet and often requiring axes and knives to cut a path through country where tracks are few and bad.

The attack of 46 Division and attached troops under Major-General H. Freeman-Attwood was begun in the darkness early on 28th March, with heavy artillery support from the artillery of two divisions plus army resources. At the same time the rain began again with redoubled violence and continued almost without pause for a week. Despite this 36 Brigade, 138 Brigade, 1 Parachute Brigade, the Corps Franc and the Tabor all reached their first objectives, taking over 750 prisoners. By a double flanking movement directed towards the rear of the enemy positions Sedjenane was retaken on the 30th March; Cap Serrat, El Aouana and the hills to north and south on the 31st. Pack-mule transport had to be employed on a large scale. An advance of some eighteen miles was made in four days, with a total of over 850 prisoners, half German, half Italian.

The Germans had taken three weeks to capture the same area, and a captured order of the day, issued by Major-General Manteuffel after reaching Abiod, showed that he was highly pleased with that result.

46 Division had now been continuously in heavy fighting since 26th February, had suffered much, absorbed large replacement drafts while still in close contact with the enemy and had then made this successful and swift counter-attack.

As all objectives had been reached a halt was called, and 5 Corps at once began preparations for the attack to clear the Béja – Medjez road.

78 Division, under Major-General V. Evelegh, undertook the task, again supported by heavy artillery concentrations throughout the whole operation.

This mountain land is a vast tract of country, every hill in which is large enough to swallow up a brigade of infantry, where consolidation on the rocky slopes is very difficult, in which tanks can only operate in small numbers, where movement of guns and vehicles is very restricted, and where the division had to rely on pack mules for its supplies and to carry wireless telegraphy sets, tools and mortars.

The general impression is one of wide spaciousness – a kind of Dartmoor or Central Sutherlandshire, but with deeper valleys and steeper hills.

In the early darkness of 7th April 78 Division started its attack north of Oued Zarga, gaining all objectives and taking over 400 prisoners, all German. For the next nine days, until 16th April, 78 Division methodically advanced on a front of about 10 miles to an ultimate depth of 10 miles, taking in turn each key position – the Mahdi, Hills 512, 667, Djebel el Ang, Tanngoucha and. the mountain villages of Toukabeur, Chaouach and Heidous – with concentrated artillery fire and splendidly helped by the Royal Air Force with close support bombing. But it was chiefly an infantry battle, fought by units who had been in continuous contact with the enemy without a break since November, 1942. In all, during these nine days 1,080 German prisoners were captured in a series of extremely fierce hand to hand fights, including much night work.

The performance of the Churchill tanks of 25 Army Tank Brigade under Brigadier R.H. Maxwell was very good: mechanically they stood well up to very heavy strain, while the courage and initiative shown by the crews were admirable. Though the tactical handling in close co-operation with infantry was at times at fault.

I consider the 78 Division deserves high praise for as tough and prolonged a bit of fighting as has ever been undertaken by the British soldier.

In close conjunction with 78 Division, 4 Division pressed the enemy hard to the north of Hunt's Gap, and by 14th April had reached the hills just south-west of Sidi Nsir after much hard fighting and against many counter-attacks. This was the first appearance of 4 Division in action.

5 Corps had now secured positions which completely freed Medjez and enabled me to begin dumping and other preparations for a large-scale attack in that area, while in the north I had cleared the vital lateral road and had re-established my advanced troops in positions suitable as bases for a further advance, and in time to hand these positions over to United States 2 Corps, which now started arriving from the far south – being transferred from the Gafsa – Maknassy area by order of 18 Army Group.

On 18th April United States 2 Corps (under Lieutenant-General O.N. Bradley) relieved 4 and 46 Divisions of 5 Corps and assumed command of the area north of the line Oued Zarga – Djebel Lanserine – Tebourba, having under command United States 1 and 9 Infantry Divisions, with a few days later United Stares 34 Infantry Division and 1 Armoured Division. On 20th April I moved Main First Army Headquarters to near Thibar.

Meanwhile, further south, 9 Corps (consisting of 6 Armoured Division, 34 U.S. Division, 128 Infantry Brigade Group from 46 Division and Corps Artillery, &c., under Lieutenant-General J.T. Crocker, C.B.E., D.S.O., M.C.), had on 8th April started an attack under orders of 18 Army Group to break through the German flank defences at Pichon – Fondouk, capture Kairouan and strike the Axis forces retreating in front of Eighth Army.

I ordered French 19 Corps to aid this attack on the north by seizing the Djebel Ousselat and the ridge of the Eastern Dorsale. This they did with the greatest élan, taking several hundred prisoners. By 18th April the enemy had withdrawn northwards, and French 19 Corps was holding the line Karachoum – Djebel Edjehaf – west of Djebel Mansour, in touch with patrols of Eighth Army on the right. During this fighting General Welwert, commanding the French Constantine Division was killed.

THE FINAL OFFENSIVE, 22ND APRIL–13TH MAY.

On 12th April I was ordered by General Alexander to prepare a large-scale offensive to capture Tunis and also to co-operate with United States 2 Corps in the capture of Bizerta, the target date being 22nd April. For this attack 9 Corps was placed under my orders, together with 1 British Armoured Division from Eighth Army.

United States 2 Corps remained under 18 Army Group, but I was made responsible for co-ordinating its action in the attack with that of First Army, and for issuing all the necessary orders and instructions direct. Eighth Army was also to attack on 20th April at Enfidaville, in order to draw enemy forces off First Army.

Enemy resistance was still formidable and he held strong positions. These had to be overcome and his strength exhausted before a real break through could be effected.

Although I had a big total superiority in numbers and material, a limiting factor was the division of my army (including 2 U.S. Corps) into three national sectors; this naturally restricted the full freedom of movement of reserves which otherwise I would have enjoyed with a homogeneous army.

There are three entrances into the Tunis plain:-

In the south – the Bou Arada gap. This was blocked by the strongly held Pont du Fahs defile and the hills on the southern edge of the Bou Arada valley were in enemy hands.

In the centre – across the Goubellat plain. There is a belt of broken country from north-east of the Sebkret el Kourzia to Ksar Tyr which blocks the eastern exits from the plain and is easily defended against tanks. But this area was weakly held by the enemy.

An essential preliminary to the use of either of the above passages is to capture the high ground west of the Sebkret el Kourzia.

In the north – along the axis Medjez – Massicault. This is the most direct way and the best tank country. But it was protected by very strong enemy positions which barred the way and prevented deployment of large forces across the River Medjerda. I expected very heavy fighting here before I could break through.

None the less, I decided my plan as follows:-

5 Corps to make the main attack from Medjez and to break into the enemy's main defensive system between Peter's Corner and Longstop.

9 Corps to capture the high ground west of Sebkret and then to push its armoured divisions across the Goubellat plain, in the hope that by speed of movement they might get through the hills to the east, swing north towards Massicault and in that area engage and destroy the enemy's armoured reserves and act against the rear of the defenders opposite 5 Corps. If the armour did not progress quickly north of the Sebkret I was not prepared to press home this attack; but instead to keep the armour to break through on 5 Corps front, after the enemy there had been fought to exhaustion. 46 Division to revert, in any case, to Army Reserve after the initial attack.

United States 2 Corps to make its main effort eastwards, to seize the high ground east and west of Chouigui and cover the left flank of 5 Corps. United States 2 Corps also to advance on Bizerta via the Sedjenane – Jefna and the Oued Sedjenane Valleys.

French 19 Corps to advance on the axis Robaa – Pont du Fahs. But this was not to start until I considered the attacks by 9 Corps (and by Eighth Army near Enfidaville) had softened the resistance opposite French 19 Corps.

My attack to be supported by 242 Group Royal Air Force, 12 Air Support Command and the Tactical Bomber Force, all working under Air Commodore

K.B.B. Cross, D.S.O., D.F.C. Western Desert Air Force was also available by mutual arrangement.

The composition of the Army and United States 2 Corps is given in Appendix "A."

The attacks were timed to start as under:-

0400 hrs. 22nd April … 9 Corps.
2000 hrs. 22nd April … 5 Corps.
0400 hrs. 23rd April … 2 U.S. Corps.

Not surprisingly, the enemy apparently was aware that trouble was brewing and on night 20th–21st April he launched a strong spoiling attack between Medjez and Goubellat and also against 9 Corps, using his Hermann Goering Division with tanks of 10 Panzer Division. He lost heavily, including 33 tanks destroyed by us and over 450 prisoners. That he did not succeed in seriously disorganising our final deployment for the big attack was a tribute to all units concerned, as naturally the confusion at one time was considerable when enemy tanks appeared in the dark amid our batteries, being deployed ahead even of our Forward Defended Localities. But the fighting against 46 Division on 9 Corps front did delay the launching of the attack there for four hours and created some confusion and fatigue amongst the troops of 138 Infantry Brigade forming up for the assault.

Without going into details of the very fierce fighting which developed all along the front from 22nd to 30th April, I can summarise the story as follows:-

9 *Corps.*

46 Division attack north of Bou Arada failed on the right, but on the left succeeded sufficiently to allow 6 Armoured Division to pass through by nightfall, 22nd April. During 23rd–24th April, 6 Armoured Division was followed by 1 Armoured Division, and both moved eastwards, meeting opposition but destroying many enemy tanks. However, we were not quick enough, and a strong enemy anti-tank gun screen in the broken country north-east and north of the Sebkret el Kourzia and near Djebel Kournine prevented eventually all further advance, despite many attempts. The enemy withdrew from the Seba Argout position opposite the right of 46 Division. Seeing that no further progress was likely, on 26th April I ordered 9 Corps to stand fast and to return 6 Armoured Division and 46 Division (less one Infantry Brigade Group) to Army Reserve. This attack by 9 Corps only just failed to achieve its object. It did, however, inflict severe tank losses on the enemy, drew his armoured reserves to the south and (based on subsequent statements by captured senior officers) seriously frightened him. It also had the effect of leaving the enemy opposite 19 Corps in a pronounced salient, from which they hurriedly withdrew on 25th April. Our losses were not severe.

19 *Corps.*

The enemy withdrawal just forestalled an attack by 19 Corps, which therefore followed up rapidly, and by 28th April had again come up against stiff resistance and strong artillery fire on the general line Djebel Derhalfa – road Enfidaville to Pont du Fahs – Station de Thibica. An advance of 18 miles.

5 *Corps.*

In a series of grim hand-to-hand attacks and counter-attacks against the Hermann Goering, 334 and 15 Panzer Divisions, the British 1, 4 and 78 Divisions with Army tank support advanced between 22nd and 30th April to a depth of about six miles and captured most of the enemy's main defensive positions facing Medjez in a semi-circle from Peter's Corner to Longstop. Every attack was given very heavy and concentrated artillery support. Losses were heavy, especially in commanding officers, but by the end of April I felt the enemy was nearly ripe for the break through. Almost the fiercest fighting of all took place on 29th April. On 1st May, Hermann Goering Division asked for an armistice to bury its dead. This was refused.

For the break-through I had then in Army Reserve 6 Armoured Division and 46 Division (less one brigade group), while 5 Corps had still in hand one infantry brigade of 4 Division and the best part of an Army Tank Brigade. And at last I had room to deploy armoured forces east of the river Medjerda, over which two more bridges were built.

2 *U.S. Corps.*

As the result of constant pressure and proper use of the big numerical preponderance they enjoyed to outflank the enemy defences, 2 U.S. Corps by 2nd May had cleared the enemy from Hills 609 and 612 north and east of Sidi Nsir and from the strong Djebel Ajred and Azag positions: Goums and the Corps Franc had reached the hills north of Lake Garaet Achkel. The capture of Point 609 by United States 34 Division was a particularly fine piece of work, against fierce opposition from the formidable Barenthin Regiment.

On 3rd and 4th May the enemy withdrew all along the front under heavy pressure to the line of hills west of Bizerta – east of Mateur – east of Oued Tine valley. Mateur was occupied by United States 1 Armoured Division.

The very big movement of United States 2 Corps from Gafsa area to the north, right across the lines of supply of First Army, the provision of all the necessary American types of ammunition, supplies and rations, and the dumping of huge quantities of ammunition for the guns of 2, 5 and 9 Corps within such a short period were great feats which the Staffs concerned have every right to be proud.

Meanwhile, on 30th April, General Alexander told me that in view of the difficult country opposite Eighth Army he had decided to transfer formations across to strengthen First Army for the final blow.

My first task was still to capture Tunis; thereafter to exploit eastwards to prevent the enemy establishing himself in the Cap Bon area. Eighth Army to co-operate in this phase as best it could. 7 Armoured Division, 4 Indian Division, 201 Guards Brigade, with the necessary divisional and administrative troops, were to be transferred at once to my command, with Lieutenant-General B.G.

Horrocks, M.C., from 10 Corps (to succeed Lieutenant-General J.T. Crocker, C.B.E., D.S.O., M.C., 9 Corps, who had been wounded).

This, of course, was a big reinforcement to the forces I already had in hand for my breakthrough.

The transfer and regrouping of formations began immediately, as did also the dumping of 450 rounds a gun for over 400 guns. Again an enormous task was accomplished by my Staff without a hitch, and by nightfall of 5th May all was completed and the Army regrouped ready for the assault. The composition of the various Corps is given in Appendix "B."

My orders in outline were as under:-

5 Corps to hold a firm base on their present line and, as a preliminary operation, to capture the dominating Djebel Bou Aoukaz on afternoon 5th May, so as to cover the left flank of 9 Corps in its subsequent attack.

9 Corps during night 5th–6th May to break into the enemy's position on a very narrow front with 4 British and 4 Indian Divisions. This to be followed up immediately by breaking out through the breach with 6 and 7 Armoured Divisions, with the object of seizing and holding the high ground 6 miles due west of Tunis and so breaching the inner defences of Tunis, before the enemy had time to man these defences.

5 Corps thereafter to keep open the corridor and to be ready to use one or more infantry divisions to sustain the attack of 9 Corps.

I emphasised that speed was vital.

United States 2 Corps to continue their attacks on Chouigui (and then to exploit towards Djedeida) and Bizerta.

French 19 Corps to attack on 4th May to capture the Djebel Zaghouan – a most formidable mountain massif.

1 British Armoured Division to be in Army Reserve in area Sebkret el Kourzia.

In the hope of confusing the enemy, from whom I could scarcely hope to conceal the colossal traffic movement (reminiscent of Derby Day) and the dust around Medjez, I arranged for a large dummy concentration of tanks and transport (with the usual movement) to be installed near Bou Arada. While making no attempt to conceal 1 Armoured Division near the Sebkret I hoped to make the enemy think I had moved 6 Armoured Division to the Bou Arada area, and to conceal altogether the arrival of 7 Armoured Division west of Medjez.

Subsequent events proved that this stratagem had a considerable measure of success, as the enemy did not suspect the heavy concentration of armour at Medjez and kept his 21 Panzer Division near Zaghouan to cover the imagined threat to Pont du Fahs. Captured staff officers from German General Headquarters later stated that although they had, in fact, seen tanks in Iaager south-west of Medjez yet they thought they were only a portion of 1 Armoured Division, and they placed 6 Armoured Division at Bou Arada. Thus, thinking that I had split my armour, they were under no particular apprehension of an immediate attack. I rather stress this point, as it emphasises first, the ease with which one can deceive the air reconnaissance: second, perhaps it explains in some way the later complete surprise which otherwise is almost incomprehensible. But, of course, the primary reason for the enemy's failure to detect our concentration was our overwhelming air superiority which practically kept the enemy out of the air except for a few isolated sorties. In the same connection, it is interesting to recall that I had usually failed to find warning signs of German attacks against me throughout the campaign, despite most active air reconnaissance.

Of the final assault there is little to narrate.

5 Corps' attack on the Bou was successful and it was held against counter-attack.

The attack by 4 British and 4 Indian Divisions in the dark at 0330 hours on 6th May on a front of 3,000 yards went smoothly. Scorpions and four battalions of Churchill tanks came up at dawn on 6th May. The final objectives, to a depth of 5,000 yards, were all taken by 1100 hours with very small losses, under a terrific artillery concentration – deepened by an unprecedentedly intense air bombardment. In the later stages German infantrymen broke and ran, throwing away their rifles. The prolonged and heavy fighting from 22nd April had well prepared the way for this hammer blow.

The two armoured divisions passed through the gap at once and after 6 Armoured Division had engaged enemy tanks (including "Tigers") south of the Tunis road, Furna was cleared and by nightfall Massicault was in our hands, pockets of resistance being by passed.

On 7th May, at 1540 hours, the Derbyshire Yeomanry and 11 Hussars entered Tunis. On 8th May 7 Armoured Division moved northwards of Tunis and cleared the country towards Protville, while 6 Armoured Division moved south-east towards Hammam Lif – where it met fierce resistance in the strong and narrow pass. On 10th May 6 Armoured Division had broken through, captured Soliman and that night reached Hammamet and at once pushed south towards Bou Ficha.

Meanwhile I had moved up 4 British Division and placed it once more under orders of 9 Corps. This Division was moved rapidly up to Soliman and, in a lightning sweep, cleared the Cap Bon peninsula.

At the same time I also placed 1 British Armoured Division from Army Reserve under 9 Corps, ordering it to move northwards via Ain el Asker and Moham-media. On 9th and 10th May it advanced via Creteville on Grombalia.

I also ordered 5 Corps to move eastwards with 4 Indian Division and 1 Division, and, in co-operation with the left wing of French 19 Corps, to complete the encirclement of the enemy.

The final attack of 6 Armoured Division was made southwards from Bou Ficha covered by heavy artillery fire and an air bombardment by Western Desert Air Force on 12th May, while 56 Division, of Eighth Army shelled the trapped enemy from the south. The fire plan was mutually arranged by wireless. After the bombardment a sea of white flags marked the end of all organised resistance.

In all cases the pursuit was pressed ruthlessly and without pause by night or day by 6 Armoured Division and 4 British Division.

On the American front events moved with equal swiftness, Ferryville and Bizerta being entered on afternoon 7th May by United States 1 Armoured Division and at 1100 hours on 9th May the Commander United States 2 Corps accepted the unconditional surrender of his opponents.

French 19 Corps attacked on 6th May and entered Pont du Fahs on the 7th. During the 8th–11th, after an initial withdrawal, the enemy, on the whole, stood firm in the mountains and any attempt by the French to advance was very heavily shelled. But on the 11th, after a successful attack with tanks and infantry, German officers came in under a white flag and on the 12th resistance ceased, with many thousands of prisoners coming in. It must have been a moment of peculiar satisfaction for the French 19 Corps.

The scenes in the Cap Bon peninsula area and to the south-west during the last three days were amazing. The rout of the German army was complete; prisoners swamped their captors and drove in their own transport looking for the cages. Thousands surrendered without attempting to resist further, while others fired their remaining stocks of ammunition at any target before giving themselves up.

On 12th May Colonel-General J. von Arnim, General Officer Commanding-in-Chief Army Group Afrika, surrendered with his staff to 4 Indian Division and was brought to me at Headquarters First Army.

The disaster was complete.

The total of prisoners eventually reached over a quarter of a million, if the 4,000 odd captured since 1st March are included; of these over half were Germans.

The booty was immense.

Dunkirk was amply revenged.

It was an amazing finish to a fascinating and unique campaign, which highly tested the qualities of the British soldier and proved him still to be as tough, resolute and good humoured as ever before in our long history.

In the later stages the co-operation between Army and Air Forces was excellent and frictionless, despite the difficulties always inherent in operations conducted with forces of different nations.

In the final phase the weight of air support played a very great part in ensuring the overwhelming victory; Army and Air Forces worked as one.

And no man in First Army ever forgot that we owed our daily life and being to the vigilance of the Royal Navy.

Right throughout the campaign we were all of us, in varying degree, thrown into intimate touch with the armies of our American and French allies, usually under conditions of stress and danger demanding instant decision and the closest collaboration. I say without hesitation that the mutual goodwill, tolerance, understanding, and above all the confidence which each of us had in the other was quite remarkable. Not only senior officers but also all ranks of our three armies soon realised that despite differences of language, customs and processes of thought the other fellow was also giving his best without reservation and that he was to be trusted. Even between British and French the initial and very understandable doubts very soon disappeared in mutual open respect and admiration.

Herein lies much hope for the future.

It has been for me an exhilarating experience.

I count myself indeed fortunate to have had under my orders such loyal and gallant men as General Koeltz and his soldiers of the French 19 Corps: while always my relations with United States commanders and men have been entirely frank, cordial and understanding. I owe much to General Eisenhower for his valient wisdom and encouragement, and to those of his commanders who served under me or with me with such loyal friendship.

The total British losses of First Army throughout the whole campaign amounted to:-

	Killed.	*Wounded.*	*Missing.*	*Total.*
Officers...	382	833	307	1,522
Other Ranks ...	4,061	11,792	6,235	22,088
	4,443	12,625	6,542	23,610

Of the above, 13,240 occurred during the period 1st April to end of hostilities.

A feature of the campaign has been the highly successful results achieved by early forward surgery. Throughout, the work of the Medical Services, in the care and treatment of wounded and sick and in the prevention of disease, is deserving of the highest praise.

When all have done so much, it is perhaps invidious to select particular services for mention, but I must pay tribute to all ranks of the Royal Army Service Corps and the Royal Army Ordnance Corps, who, despite every difficulty of climate, terrain and enemy action, understaffed and overworked, nevertheless never failed to deliver the goods.

APPENDIX "A."
OUTLINE ORDER OF BATTLE ON 20TH APRIL, 1943,
OF FIRST ARMY AND 2 UNITED STATES CORPS.

5 Corps–
    1 (British) Infantry Division.
    4 (British) Division.
    78 Infantry Division.
    25 Tank Brigade (less 51 Royal Tank Regiment).
9 Corps–
    1 (British) Armoured Division.
    6 Armoured Division.
    46 Infantry Division.
    51 Royal Tank Regiment.
French 19 Corps–
    Division d'Alger (Conne).
    Division du Maroc (Mathenet).

Division d'Oran (Boisseau).
Tank Group (Le Coulteux).
1 Kings Dragoon Guards.
United States 2 Corps-
1 United States Armoured Division (less one Regiment).
1 United States Infantry Division.
9 United States Infantry Division.
34 United States Infantry Division.
Corps Franc d'Afrique (three battalions).
One Tabor.

APPENDIX "B."
OUTLINE ORDER OF BATTLE ON 4TH MAY, 1943, OF FIRST ARMY AND 2 UNITED STATES CORPS.

5 Corps-
1 (British) Infantry Division.
46 Infantry Division (less 139 Infantry Brigade Group).
78 Infantry Division,
1 North Irish Horse.
1 Army Group Royal Artillery.
7 Régiment Tirailleurs Algériens (less one battalion).
9 Corps-
6 Armoured Division.
7 Armoured Division.
4 (British) Division.
4 (Indian) Division.
25 Tank Brigade (less two battalions).
201 Guards Brigade.
2 Army Group Royal Artillery.
French 19 Corps-
Division du Maroc.
Division d'Alger.
Division d'Oran.
One Tank Battalion.
Army Reserve-
1 British Armoured Division.
139 Infantry Brigade Group.
1 Kings Dragoon Guards.
51 Royal Tank Regiment.
United States 2 Corps-
1 United States Armoured Division (less one Armoured Regiment).
1 United States Infantry Division.
9 United States Infantry Division.
34 United States Infantry Division.

13 United States Field Artillery Brigade.
2626 United States Coast Artillery Brigade (A.A.).
Corps Franc d'Afrique.
One Tabor.

APPENDIX "C."
BUILD-UP OF AXIS FORCES.

When the Allied forces landed in Algeria, there were no Axis troops in French North Africa; in Tripolitania there was one Italian division (Spezia) and a substantial number of L of C troops. The German and Italian Armistice Commissions, however, were spread throughout French North Africa, and maintained a considerable measure of control over economic affairs and were very ready to interfere in other matters. The immediate reaction to our landing was the formation of a mainly German force to secure Tunis and Bizerta. This force was formed of units most readily available at that moment, and its impromptu formation is clearly shown in its composition. It began to arrive on the 10th November, personnel and light equipment being brought by air and heavy equipment by sea. The landing of this force was not opposed by the French, who were subsequently disarmed and their coastal and A.A. batteries taken over. Having seized the ports, and the important aerodromes of El Aouina (Tunis) and Sidi Ahmed (Bizerta), this force moved out with the intention of securing the high and mountainous country on the Tunisian – Algerian frontier and preventing the Allies debouching into the Tunisian plains. It made contact with Allied forces to whom a proportion of the French troops in Tunisia had rallied, on the general line Djebel Abiod – Béja – Medjez on the 26th Novemer, 1942. By this date the Axis forces in Tunisia consisted of the following units:-

German-
    Storm Regiment Koch (Air Force troops).
    Barenthin Regiment (Air Force troops).
    Marsch Battalions 17, 18, 20 and 21.
    Parachute Engineer Battalion Witzig.
    190 Tank Battalion (69 tanks).
    Advance elements of 10 Armoured Division.
    Miscellaneous Artillery and Anti-tank units.
Italian-
    10 Bersaglieri Regiment.
    Elements of Superga Division, including four infantry battalions.

Some of these units had been intended for Rommel's army; 190 Tank Battalion, for example, had been formed for 90 Light Division; one company, of Witzig's Battalion had already joined the Ramcke Brigade, and the Marsch Battalions had been destined to be reinforcement drafts but were in fact sent to Tunisia and put into the line, where they fought as infantry battalions. Regiment Koch of the

German Air Force was brought from France by air for which move it was readily available and trained, having been formed originally as 5 Parachute Regiment.

Barenthin Regiment was also formed of Air Force personnel, being chiefly composed of the staff and pupils of the Parachute School at Witstock and the Glider School at Posen.

Thus by the end of November, 1942, the Axis forces which had arrived in Tunisia, exclusive of Services, amounted to approximately 15,500 fighting troops, 130 tanks, 60 field guns and 30 anti-tank guns.

During the first half of December, the remainder of 10 Armoured Division and the Italian Superga Division were brought over, but in transit each division lost a substantial proportion of its heavy equipment transported by sea. As a result, 10 Armoured Division never could muster its full establishment of tanks, and both divisions were short of artillery. In addition to these two formations, further German Marsch battalions were brought over at regular intervals, some of which continued to be employed as independent infantry battalions, and were not broken up as reinforcements. These independent battalions were used either to bring up the original impromptu force to the strength of a division, which was originally called Division Broich and latterly Division Manteuffel after its commanders, or were used to reinforce the Italian Superga Division which had been stationed on the enemy's left flank in mountainous country south of Zaghouan. In addition, the Bafile and Grado Battalions of the Italian San Marco Marine Regiment and a Bersaglieri Battalion were also brought over. The most significant arrival at this time was 501 Heavy Tank Battalion with 43 tanks, of which 20 were the new Mark VI, which first went into action against the French 19 Corps on the 18th January, 1943.

In the second half of December, 1942, the German 334 Infantry Division began to make its appearance. This was a newly created formation of rather low quality. The division remained in northern Tunisia, and was completed by the arrival of its artillery in the second week in January.

On the 1st January, 1943, the estimated total of Axis troops in Tunisia, excluding air crews and ground staffs, was 55,900. The enemy tank strength was about 160 German tanks with in addition some Italian Medium and Light tanks, and by mid-January there were 14 12-gun batteries of artillery.

Enemy losses at sea in transports and cargo ships were very heavy, and it is reported that Hitler himself gave orders that personnel should travel only by destroyer or by air. The daily intake of reinforcements varied greatly, as the regular service of transport aeroplanes carried supplies as well as troops; at this period the daily average was between 700 and 1,000 men, some of whom were destined for Rommel's army.

In the last week of January, the Hermann Goering Flak Regiment – the original Hermann Goering unit – sent two of its batteries, the third remaining in Germany in its usual role as bodyguard to the Reichsmarschall. This proved to be the forerunner of the Hermann Goering Armoured Division which was built up in Tunisia on a most lavish establishment, though it was never completed to strength. It absorbed Parachute Regiment Koch which became Jaeger Regiment Hermann Goering and two Grenadier Regiments were formed in Germany and commenced to make their appearance in Tunisia in February.

Elements only of the Tank Reconnaissance, Artillery and Engineer units reached Tunisia by the end of the campaign, and a battalion of 2 Hermann Goering Grenadier Regiment arrived as late as the 24th April: but the Division was never completed.

On the 1st February the estimated total of troops had risen to 84,000, of whom 55,000 were Germans and 29,000 Italians. The tank state was about 380 – 280 German and 100 Italian, 21 Armoured Division having moved west into Tunisia with approximately 80 tanks; and there were 26 to 28 12-gun batteries.

During February Rommel's army had withdrawn to the Mareth area and became a potential – and later an actual – opponent of First Army. The German troops consisted of 15 Armoured Division, 90 and 164 Light Divisions, Panzer Grenadier Regiment Afrika, and the remnants of the Ramcke Brigade, with four reconnaissance units, six mobile batteries of 88-mm. guns, and many supply and L. of C. troops.

The Italians were composed of Spezia, Pistoia and the Young Fascists Divisions, part of Centauro Division, and the remnants of Italian divisions from El Alamein grouped under Trieste Division, together with a considerable amount of corps and garrison artillery, and a large and miscellaneous collection of Carabinieri, Frontier Guards and L. of C. troops. The figure for the estimated total of enemy strength in Tunisia on the 1st March therefore includes this large addition from Tripolitania and is increased to 190,500, including 116,500 Germans and 74,000 Italians.

Only one more formation was sent to Africa. This was 999 Division, which began to arrive at the end of March. It consisted only of 961 and 962 Infantry Regiments each of two battalions with artillery support. Its morale was low, the rank and file being partly drawn from personnel serving sentences for political or military offences.

The flow of Marsch Battalions continued, the highest known number being 57, though some of the intervening numbers were never identified; but these battalions and all other reinforcements were absorbed into units already in the country. After reaching Mareth the original German Libyan Army began at last to receive its share, and it was a large one. After the New Year the intake of men apart from those belonging to the Hermann Goering and 999 Divisions, was in fact, mainly devoted to the replacement of battle casualties and the building up of the depleted formations from Libya.

The estimated enemy strength on the 1st April was 196,700 – 124,300 Germans and 72,400 Italians.

During the later stages of the campaign, efforts were made to raise volunteer battalions locally. Their fighting value was low, as the volunteer element was noticeably lacking, and many men with Allied sympathies only joined because of the opportunity thus offered of crossing to our lines. One such native Algerian unit was formed, and two Tunisian Italian Battalions, as well as the Phalange Française, a French unit into which only 150 men could be attracted.

Enemy reinforcements continued to arrive until the last week in April. The final estimate on the 1st May, 1943, showed 48,700 Axis infantry, 120 infantry guns, 402 field guns, 180 88 mm. guns and 443 anti-tank guns, with about 100 tank runners. The total strength, excluding the air component, was approximately 220,000.

Notes

1. General Anderson refers, in this passage, to plans which were discussed, but eventually abandoned, for landings at Bone and Philippeville in addition to that at Algiers. The principal arguments against landing so far to the eastwards were based upon-

    (*a*) The need to concentrate the relatively small forces which could be landed; and

    (*b*) The danger of venturing without air cover into ports which the German bombers could reach.

    The reality of the bombing danger was proved by the shipping losses incurred at Bougie. Further to the east still heavier losses might have been expected, with proportionately serious results.

2. The difficulties about command which General Anderson describes arose, in part, from political considerations, and especially from the need to conciliate the French Command. At this stage in the war, however, much had still to be learnt about the command of allied armies in the field. It was as a result of the lessons learnt in this campaign that later organisation was so greatly improved.

3. Goums are Moroccan troops trained in Mountain Warfare.

4. Additional factors which, reduced the efficiency of air support were:-

    (*a*) Lack of all-weather airfields, which could not be constructed during the first few months of the campaign; and

    (*b*) Lack of line communications during a period when headquarters were frequently moved.

5. By the standards of later campaigns this enemy air activity was not on a serious scale. Its moral effect at the time, however, was increased by the inexperience of the troops and by the scarcity of light A.A. weapons.

4

GENERAL WILSON'S DESPATCH ON OPERATIONS 16 FEBRUARY 1943 TO 8 JANUARY 1944

The War Office, November 1936
OPERATIONS IN THE MIDDLE EAST FROM
16TH FEBRUARY, 1943, TO 8TH JANUARY, 1944.
The following Despatch was submitted to the Secretary of State for War on 31*st August,*
1944, *by GENERAL SIR H. MAITLAND WILSON, G.C.B., G.B.E., D.S.O.,*
A.D.C., Commander-in-Chief, The Middle East Forces.

I. INTRODUCTORY.

1. When I was appointed to Middle East Command, on 16th February, 1943, the Command included Egypt, Libya, Malta, Palestine and Transjordan, Cyprus, Sudan, Eritrea, most of Syria and a small part of Iraq.

2. The situation within the Command, and in the Middle East generally, was then more satisfactory than at any time since the outbreak of the war. The Axis armies had been driven back from the outskirts of the Delta to the borders of Tunisia, the possibility of a German attack through Turkey had been diminished, the Balkans were proving a serious burden to Germany, Italian morale was obviously cracking, and British equipment was better and British morale higher than at any previous time.

3. My main tasks, in order of priority, were to maintain Eighth Army and support its present operations to the utmost, to plan for future operations in conformity with the requirements of General Eisenhower, to prepare to support Turkey, and to conduct amphibious operations. In addition I was to make plans, when required, for land operations in the Balkan States, Crete, and the islands in the Ægean; I was to plan possible operations in Arabia and to be ready to assume command of the land forces in Aden should major land operations develop in or beyond the borders of that Protectorate.

4. Under my command, to carry out this role, were about 31,000 officers and 494,000 men, divided between the major commands of Ninth Army, British Troops in Egypt, Sudan, Palestine, Cyrenaica District, Aden and Malta. The Order of Battle of these troops is given in Appendix 1.

5. This total did not include the 8,500 officers and 180,000 men of Eighth Army, which had reached the borders of Tunisia by February, and which passed under

command of 18 Army Group on 20th February. Maintenance of Eighth Army during the remainder of the Tunisian Campaign, until 12th May, 1943, when the campaign ended with the capture of Tunis and Bizerta, remained my responsibility and proved a heavy one. All other claims were subordinated to this task. Expenditure in materials, vehicles, and, at times, in personnel was high, but the Army was always well-found and this, together with the absence of food deficiency diseases in a campaign fought over a thousand miles from the Middle East base, speaks better than anything else for the adequacy of the maintenance system.

6. During the later stages of the Tunisian campaign the second of my tasks, planning for future operations, began to assume increasing importance. Plans for the invasion of Sicily had been laid at the Casablanca Conference, and detailed planning of these operations was continued throughout the campaign in Tunisia. So, even before the Tunisian campaign was over, Middle East had already begun to train and equip units for Sicily.

7. The invasion of Sicily was to be conducted by two forces, of which the bulk of the Eastern Task Force was to be trained, equipped, mounted, and maintained in the early stages, from Middle East Command. This meant that Eighth Army had to be withdrawn from Tunisia, re-formed, re-equipped, trained for a new kind of warfare; and supplied with ancillary units necessary for amphibious operations. The resources of the whole Command, from Syria to Malta, were co-ordinated in this preparation for knocking Italy out of the war – and once more, as in Tunisia, the operation was successful.

8. With the conquest of Sicily and the invasion of Italy, Eighth Army passed out of the sphere of Middle East Command, as a direct maintenance responsibility, when 15 Army Group took over its administration and maintenance on 12th August, 1943. The actual maintenance, however, could not be transferred immediately, and Middle East slowly transferred the commitment during the ensuing weeks, thereafter being responsible only for partial maintenance on demands made by 15 Army Group. Even then, reinforcements and supplies for Eighth Army were still required in considerable quantities, and the 10th Corps remained to be mounted from Tripoli for the landing at Salerno. Meanwhile, with the collapse of Italy, Middle East Command had become engaged in another role.

9. Plans for action in the islands of the Ægean had already been prepared by Middle East Command and by September a division was mounted ready to carry out the operation. But the diversion of the shipping, and other commitments, caused this operation to be cancelled at the last minute; before other plans could be made, the armistice with Italy was announced and the Germans succeeded in gaining control over the Italians on the two key islands of Rhodes and Scarpanto. The most which we could achieve by extemporised action with the forces

available was to slip small garrisons into Cos, Leros, and Samos, and to place patrols in outlying islands.

10. With Rhodes, Crete and the airfields on the Greek mainland at their disposal, the Germans had command of the air in the Ægean, and with the loss of our only landing grounds at Cos on 2nd October we were unable to ship adequate reinforcements and were in no position to defend the other two islands. Leros was captured by assault, after a prolonged bombing and dive-bombing attack, on 16th November, and Samos was evacuated in the next few days.

Nevertheless, the German local air superiority was not sufficient to prevent our air and naval forces continuing to make the enemy's reinforcing efforts hazardous and for a time ineffectual.

11. Our lack of success in the Aegean undoubtedly affected our rising prestige in Middle East countries. Despite this setback, Middle East Command was able to fulfil its tasks, largely because the year was marked by internal security and confidence in the Allied cause. This was achieved although Egypt, Palestine, Syria and the Lebanon all suffered from political troubles: Egypt owing to the failure of the Wafd Government to remedy social and economic difficulties, Palestine owing to the ambitions, suspicions and lawlessness of some elements in the Jewish population, and Syria and the Lebanon owing to the clash between their demands for independence and the views of the French Mandatory authorities.

12. These various political situations demanded constant watchfulness and careful handling. During the year they were not allowed to interfere with military requirements and considerations, and British prestige has on the whole been enhanced during the period, with consequent advantages and increased freedom of action in the military situation.

13. As in our dealings with Middle East countries, so in dealing with our allies (always excepting the United States), there has been a constant danger that political considerations might prejudice military problems. Much effective work has nevertheless been carried out in stimulating and maintaining patriot activities in the Balkans and in equipping and training allied forces in the Middle East. The policy of supplying Turkey with armaments has also been carried out by Middle East Command, and large commitments have been undertaken to prepare that country for entry into the war.

14. In general, it may be said that during the year of my command the war moved away from Middle East, leaving it a role which was no longer operational but which was of great importance as a base and training centre.

II. NARRATIVE – TUNISIA.

15. By 16th February, 1943, when I took over command of Middle East Forces, Eighth Army had taken Tripoli (on 23rd January) and was preparing to advance in Tunisia. The first responsibility of Middle East Command was to supply Eighth Army for this advance.

16. This responsibility involved Middle East Command in three major administrative commitments: to repair the port of Tripoli and establish it as an overseas advanced base; to build up reserves in Tripoli in preparation for the advance; to supply the needs of Eighth Army during the advance, and to clear backloads and casualties from Tripoli.

17. 18 Army Group was set up on 20th February, 1943, under the command of General Sir H. Alexander. General Alexander was to command First and Eighth Armies, and 18 Army Group was to co-ordinate the operational and administrative efforts of the two armies. This, however, did not affect the role of Middle East Command, and the task of maintaining Eighth Army remained my first responsibility.

18. Until 3rd March, 1943, all arrangements for maintenance were made direct with Eighth Army, which, during this period, was bringing up parts of the 10th Corps from the Benghazi area, forming the New Zealand Corps for the attack on the Mareth position, and re-equipping itself for a further advance. The distance at which Eighth Army was working from Middle East Base made it necessary to modify this arrangement; Tripoli is 980 miles by sea from the Delta and 650 miles by sea from Tobruk, the nearest railhead.

19. Headquarters, Tripolitania Base and Lines of Communication, was therefore established and took up its role, under the command of Major-General Sir B.N. Robertson, on 3rd March, 1943. This headquarters was under command of Eighth Army, for which it acted as a rear echelon; under the general direction of General Headquarters Middle East, Eighth Army was to be responsible for the lay-out and administration of the advanced base. This was in conformity with the principle that the army should retain control of its sea-head. On all matters save those of policy, Headquarters, Tripolitania Base and Lines of Communication, was to deal direct with Middle East and, in effect, it consolidated Eighth Army's demands on General Headquarters Middle East, and distributed supplies to Eighth Army, thereby simplifying many of the problems of supply.

20. This re-organisation, valuable though it was, left Middle East Command still faced with the problems inseparable from the length of the supply route, the need for maintenance and guards, the time-lag involved, and the large tonnages required to stock the advanced base and to keep the army in action.

21. In order to prepare the port of Tripoli and to put it into working order as rapidly as possible, heavy repair and maintenance projects had to be carried through, with consequent demands for cement, oxygen, acetylene and labour.

22. The most important installation to need repair was the bulk petrol storage. Captured storage tanks with a capacity of nearly 11,000 tons were rapidly repaired and put into service, and bulk tanker shipments of petrol were begun immediately. It proved quicker to repair existing installations than to erect new

ones, and further repairs were continued; although not completed by the end of the Tunisian campaign, a total of 26,000 tons of petrol storage was in use by the end of May. In addition, a tin factory was despatched to Tripoli and erected there, but was not in use until 16th May. By that date it was too late to be of use in the Tunisian campaign, but proved of great value for subsequent maintenance of the line of communication and for building up reserves in preparation for the invasion of Sicily.

23. Another problem was the repair and operation of the cold-storage plant at Tripoli. The difficulties of keeping the army supplied with fresh meat were never satisfactorily solved to the end of the Tunisian campaign, owing to the shortage of refrigerator ships, of which there were only two available for this run. Although the cold-storage capacity at Tripoli was increased from 200 tons in February to 700 tons in April this was still barely adequate for the needs of the Army.

24. As a result of the repair and maintenance work carried out at Tripoli, by 23rd February the port had reached an average daily capacity of almost 3,000 tons, excluding bulk petrol which then averaged 1,000 tons a day. During March the capacity was further increased and at times reached 5,000 tons of stores a day in addition to bulk petrol. By the end of the campaign, in May, nearly 290,000 tons of stores and 66,000 tons of bulk petrol had been discharged at this one port.

25. Whilst these heavy repairs were being carried out at Tripoli, Middle East was also providing many of the new installations necessary to enable the advanced base to be set up.

26. The development of Tripoli as a medical base was slow owing to the limited amount of shipping space available, and some anxiety was felt before the Battle of Mareth because of the number of hospital beds available. By 13th March only two general hospitals and two African sections, with accommodation for 1,600 beds, plus a further hospital with stretchers for 200 light cases, had been opened. By 21st March this had been increased to 4,400 beds, and by the middle of April Tripoli had 5,100 hospital beds and a convalescent depot with a capacity of 2,000.

   Owing to the distance from Cairo it was also necessary to establish a base transfusion unit at Tripoli. Blood was got from troops in the Tripoli area, which relieved the strain on the unit at Cairo. During March to April over 2,800 bottles of blood and almost 2,500 bottles of plasma were sent to Eighth Army. This efficient blood transfusion service, and the mobile casualty clearing stations and field surgical units, avoided much suffering and saved many lives.

27. Middle East was also still responsible for fourth echelon repair after Eighth Army passed to the command of 18 Army Group, and to carry out this duty it was necessary to establish an advanced base workshop at Tripoli. This was installed and at work by the end of February. Although difficulties were anticipated,

during the campaign the field workshops of Eighth Army were always kept amply supplied with major replacement assemblies to meet the army's requirements.

28. This development of Tripoli as the advanced base for Eighth Army did not mean that the Western Desert ports and the road line of communication could be neglected. Much work remained to be done at Tobruk and Benghazi; at both ports water supplies were developed and improved, electric supply and drainage systems were repaired and kept running, and large slipways were constructed for the Royal navy.

On the line of communication both up to and forward of Tripoli, engineering work was handicapped by a shortage of transporters for moving forward heavy equipment; but the road system was put into working order after the systematic demolitions which it had suffered, the telephone system had to be reorganised and re-established, and there was also a considerable amount of work to be undertaken in the construction of airfields urgently needed for both the offensive and defensive operations of the Royal Air Force. In all twenty-two all-weather runways were completed in Cyrenaica and Tripolitania, in addition to about fifty fair-weather landing grounds and the numerous fighter strips made for Eighth Army.

29. The result of the successful establishment of Tripoli as an advanced base was that the build-up of Eighth Army for its further advance was carried through. Both the 30th Corps and the 10th Corps were brought up to strength, and by 3rd March, 11,318 reinforcements had been despatched from the Delta as against demands for 8,900. Sixty-two per cent. of Middle East's intake of vehicles was sent up to Eighth Army during the period up to 15th March, including a special despatch of 520 vehicles which was sent up on 23rd February, and by the end of March 20,000 tons of ammunition had been sent through Tripoli for distribution to Eighth Army.

30. Once the advanced base at Tripoli had been established, and Eighth Army prepared for its further advance, the forwarding of supplies and reinforcements for the army during the advance became my most serious commitment. Reinforcements were a heavy drain; from February to the end of the campaign the total received by Eighth Army was over 33,000, and by the end of the campaign practically all units in the army were brought up to strength, some being even stronger than they were before the Battle of El Alamein.

31. The successful reinforcement of Eighth Army was accomplished despite three adverse factors: the length of the line of communication, the heavy demands as a result of the casualties sustained in the Battles of the Mareth Line and Wadi Akarit, and the conflict of the claims of preparations for the invasion of Sicily.

32. The transport difficulties inherent in the length of the line of communication were overcome by making the maximum use of all available sea, road, rail or air lifts. For example, between 14th February and 3rd March, 3,047 reinforcements were despatched from the Delta to Tripoli on road convoys carrying stores for

Eighth Army, and at the end of March a special draft of 1,500 infantry reinforcements was sent forward by air. In all, as many as 7,000 reinforcements were flown forward.

33. To meet some of the difficulties involved in the supply of reinforcements, a transit camp was established at Tripoli and reinforcements were despatched unposted from the Delta, to be distributed from the camp among units as demanded by Eighth Army. From the end of April it was decided to despatch reinforcements from the United Kingdom via North Africa instead of round the Cape; drafts would then travel overland from Algiers to Tripoli and thence by sea to the Delta, such reinforcements as were required for Eighth Army being retained at the transit camp. The first convoy to use this route did not, in fact, arrive in North Africa until after the end of the Tunisian campaign, but the system was used for the reinforcement of units in Tripolitania and Tunisia until the Mediterranean was opened to shipping in August.

34. In addition to reinforcements and normal stores and supplies, 245 tanks were supplied to Eighth Army between 20th February and 12th May, as well as 109 armoured cars and 131 scout cars, and by the end of April all anti-tank regiments within the army had been equipped with one troop of 17 pounders per battery. Time fuzes were in short supply, but otherwise artillery equipment and ammunition were able to keep pace with the demands.

35. The policy of using North African postal facilities for providing mail services to and from the United Kingdom for Eighth Army and troops in Tripolitania and Tunisia was pursued to the fullest possible extent. Early in March, a direct air-mail service was set up between the United Kingdom and Tripoli to carry air-mail letter-cards, while arrangements were completed for the carriage of sea/air mail between Tripoli and Algiers by air, the journey between Algiers and the United Kingdom in both directions being made by sea. Later, when First and Eighth Armies made contact, Algiers was used for the handling of surface mails passing between Eighth Army and the United Kingdom in both directions, mails being conveyed overland daily via Pichon through the First Army lines of communication, thus materially reducing their transit time.

36. As Eighth Army moved forward, the ports to the West of Tripoli were brought into as full use as was possible. Zarzis and Gabes proved to be of little value and Sousse was, in fact, not used for Eighth Army maintenance. But Sfax, which was occupied on 10th April, was of considerable value. Although the channel was partially blocked, it could be used by light-draught vessels and on 15th April, 1,300 tons were discharged at this port. Oceangoing ships were loaded in the Delta for Sfax and sailed for Tripoli where they were lightened to meet the draught restriction of Sfax and were then called forward, together with such local tonnage as was available. Although limited by a shortage of powered harbour-craft (which was a limiting factor at Tripoli also), this system enabled a total of over 40,000 tons to be discharged at Sfax by the end of the campaign, an

average of over 1,300 tons a day. This, together with the discharge at Tripoli, gave a daily average discharge of stores and supplies from Middle East of over 5,000 tons including bulk petrol.

37. In spite of the development of the port of Sfax, Eighth Army still had to forward a large proportion of its requirements from Tripoli by road. This entailed a heavy strain on vehicles, for by the time that the army was in the Enfidaville area the turn-round was 820 miles. A reserve of "B" vehicles has been built up in the Middle East in readiness for the demands of the long line of communication, and by the end of May, 2,000 "B" vehicles had been despatched to Eighth Army, in addition to which two 10-ton General Transport Companies had been lent to the army to help the supply system forward of Tripoli. Since all available tonnage was needed for stores, these replacement vehicles could not be sent by sea. As many as possible were sent by rail to Tobruk, but even then they had a road journey of over a thousand miles before arriving at army, so that many of them required considerable overhaul at Tripoli before they could be issued, and thus took about a month in the journey from Middle East Base. Economies in shipping were effected by sending up these replacement vehicles loaded, but this had the disadvantage that quantities of stores were locked up on the line of communication for a long period.

38. The heavy demand for replacement vehicles, and the fact that they had to be sent forward by road, at least from Tobruk, not only created a major problem of supply and maintenance, but also meant that the road had to be kept in repair.

39. In addition to the provision of replacement vehicles, Middle East also equipped two divisions, the 1st Fighting French and the 56th Division, before sending them up to Eighth Army in April.

40. In setting up Headquarters, Tripolitania Base and Lines of Communication, I ordered that the evacuation of material and personnel to Middle East Base should be kept to a minimum; casualties and salvage (especially petrol containers) were the chief back-loads.

41. Arrangements for evacuating casualties were made by sea, either direct or via Benghazi, by rail from Tobruk, or by air. Despite initial delays owing to shipping shortage, the arrangements worked well. Approximately 15,000 casualties were received in Middle East Base during the period from February to May. Of these 1,688 were flown direct to the base. The successful evacuation of casualties by air was due to excellent co-operation between the medical services and the Royal Air Force, and to the pilots of the seven ambulance aircraft, who flew their machines in all weathers and operated from the most forward landing grounds; the chief difficulty was the shortage of suitable aircraft.

42. That Eighth Army was successfully maintained over a line of communication stretching some 1,000 miles by sea from Middle East Base and a further 400 miles

forward of the advanced base at Tripoli, is in itself proof of the success of the planning, organisation and co-ordination which went into the task.

43. The result, however, was not achieved without severe strain. The demands made on engineering, signalling and movement services by the long line of communications were very heavy, and the drain on Middle East stocks was also a serious factor, aggravated as it was by the large quantities locked up in transit and in the advanced bases. For example, the demands rose at times to as much as 900 tons of supplies a day, and to meet this demand reserve stocks had to be back-loaded from Syria and the Sudan. Similar steps had to be taken to meet the demands for anti-aircraft ammunition, of which supplies had to be called in from outlying areas and obtained from Persia and Iraq Command to meet Eighth Army's requirements. Reinforcements, too, had at times to be diverted from other tasks, and a draft of 1,500 which had been allotted a special role in preparation for the invasion of Sicily was sent up to Eighth Army at the end of March. An indication of the difficulties involved can be gathered from the fact that, although towards the close of the campaign great care was taken to prevent too much ammunition being sent forward, yet when the campaign ended there were 35,000 tons of ammunition in, or en route to, the forward areas.

44. When Eighth Army began to move forward, the system of normal deliveries, demanded well in advance by Headquarters Tripolitania Base and Lines of Communication, had to be supplemented on occasions to meet urgent demands for operational requirements, particularly for specialised stores such as signals, medical and survey equipment.

45. Throughout the Tunisian campaign all of these problems were further complicated by the fact that I had been given the task of training and mounting the Eastern Task Force for the invasion of Sicily; planning and training for this task were taking place from February onwards.

Cyrenaica.
46. As the lines of communication extended, the army had to be relieved, as much as possible, of responsibility for rear administration so that it could concentrate entirely on the maintenance of actual Operations. This was successfully done by the establishment of administrative headquarters, under Middle East Command, to control the sectors of the lines of communication.

47. The organisation and administration of a large portion of the lines of communication was carried out by Headquarters Cyrenaica District, which had been formed in the Delta under the command, of Major-General A.L. Collier, and had moved up to take over Benghazi from the Eighth Army on 15th February, 1943, by which date maintenance of Eighth Army through Tripoli was assured. Cyrenaica District assumed direct responsibility, under General Headquarters Middle East, for the whole of Cyrenaica. In March, Headquarters Cyrenaica District, moved from Benghazi to Barce, and on 15th April the southern

boundary of the District was extended to include Kufra, which had formerly been under Headquarters, Sudan.

48. Within the District the first task was to assist the forwarding of supplies to Tripoli and Eighth Army. In order to shorten the shipping run, packed petrol, oil and lubricants were sent up by rail to Tobruk and thence by sea to Benghazi and Tripoli. Pumping sets, floating pipelines, and bulk petrol storage to a capacity of over 6,000 tons were kept in repair at Tobruk, and over 11,000 tons storage capacity was maintained at Benghazi. A tin factory was also put into operation at Benghazi by 11th March, whilst extra sidings were built to the railways and docks at both of these ports.

49. Traffic on the Western Desert Railway declined, with the development of Tripoli Port, from 65,000 tons in January to 22,000 tons in March, but the line still had to be maintained and worked. At the same time, not only had the road itself to be maintained, but petrol points and staging areas for road convoys had also to be organised.

50. In addition to forwarding supplies to Tripoli, Cyrenaica District had to re-organise and administer its own territory when the army had passed westwards. Much valuable salvage work was achieved, with special emphasis on petrol containers (of which almost a million and a half were salvaged from the District by the end of the year), whilst stores left behind as the army advanced were also put into circulation again. There were, for example, 11,000 tons of ammunition left in Benghazi when maintenance of Eighth Army through that port ceased.

51. These tasks entailed heavy demands for both skilled and unskilled labour, some of which was provided by Middle East Command, some from civilian sources. A signals headquarters and three companies were required there, with a further headquarters and three companies for Air Formation Signals. This undertaking was later reduced as these units had to be made available elsewhere, and much of the responsibility for maintaining signal communications was taken over by a South African unit, the Union Defence Force Lines of Communication Signals.

52. By the end of the campaign there were sixty-eight pioneer companies stretched from the Egyptian frontier to Eighth Army area; the companies came from India, the High Commission Territories, East Africa, Mauritius and the Seychelles, and were mainly employed as shore labour in the ports, in the advanced depots, and on airfield and road construction. In addition, there were some 10,000 civilians employed forward of the Egyptian frontier. As far as Cyrenaica District was concerned, the extent of the problem may be gauged from the fact that in March, 1943, forty pioneer companies (13,000 men) were employed in the District.

To meet the heavy demand for labour, the experiment of using Prisoners of War Working units was tried. Three such units were in use, mainly on roads, by the end of May, and the number was increased to seven by the end of the year. On the whole, the experiment worked well.

53. A further source of labour was the civilian population. Under International Law I was responsible for the military government of occupied enemy territories in my command, and from 5th March, 1943, I delegated this responsibility to the Civil Affairs Branch and the Chief Political Officer, Middle East Forces, Brigadier H.R. Hone. Under him, the administration of the civilian population of Cyrenaica District was organised by the British Military Administration of Cyrenaica (the use of the formula Occupied Enemy Territory Administration – O.E.T.A. – being abandoned); the Deputy Chief Civil Affairs Officer dealt with the civilian population under the direction of the Military Commander. The British Military Administration in Cyrenaica was faced with a friendly but hungry population, and its chief tasks were the provision of food and the organisation of labour. Supplies were despatched from the Middle East Base to supplement captured stocks and local produce, and the control of supplies made the organisation of labour easier, since it was possible to secure local labour in considerable numbers by paying partly in rations, particularly in sugar, tea and cigarettes.

54. The provision of garrisons for the District was not a serious problem. At Tobruk and Benghazi anti-aircraft protection and coastal defence batteries were needed, while anti-aircraft protection was also necessary on the Cyrenaica airfields; but for ordinary local defence purposes, during the Tunisian campaign, only a battalion of the Sudan Defence Force was needed to supplement the Libyan Arab Force (recruited originally from Cyrenaican refugees in Egypt and from Cyrenaican prisoners of war volunteers, and later converted into the Cyrenaican Gendarmerie).

55. Although the traffic for Eighth Army through the ports of Tobruk and Benghazi declined rapidly as Tripoli was developed, the responsibilities of Cyrenaica District remained. Once the Tunisian campaign was over, the decline in the volume of traffic through the District became still more marked; for example, whereas traffic on the Western Desert Railway reached 65,000 tons in January, 1943, it had fallen to 6,000 tons in December; imports at Benghazi dropped from 50,000 tons in January, 1943, to 17,000 tons in December, and from April onwards no stores were brought into Tobruk by sea.

56. Nevertheless, during the summer months the facilities of the District were of considerable value. The Royal Air Force and the local garrisons had to be maintained and supplied, and when Eighth Army was re-formed for the attack on Sicily those units and formations which were recalled to Egypt were staged on their journey. For the invasion of Sicily, 2,700 personnel and 846 vehicles were embarked at Benghazi.

57. To conform to the reduction in the importance of the District, the organisation was changed from time to time. When it was originally established, the

District included 83 Area at Benghazi and 99 Sub-Area at Tobruk. In March, when District Headquarters moved to Barce, 93 Sub-Area relieved 83 Area at Benghazi, and in November, when the traffic through Tobruk had considerably declined, Tobruk Zone Headquarters relieved 99 Sub-Area there. Ultimately, on 15th December, Headquarters Cyrenaica District was abolished and Headquarters, Cyrenaica Area, took over, relieving 93 Sub-Area at Benghazi.

Tripolitania.
58. Similar arrangements to those made in Cyrenaica District were also made in Tripolitania. Here, Headquarters Tripolitania Base and Lines of Communication, took over responsibility from Gabes to El Hamma with Advanced Headquarters at Sfax on 24th April, when part of Rear Headquarters of Eighth Army was withdrawn to prepare for the invasion of Sicily. The Advanced Headquarters at Sfax was closed on 1st June, when First Army took over responsibility for Tunisia.

59. On 16th July, 1943, Headquarters Tripolitania Base and Lines of Communication, was replaced by Headquarters Tripolitania District, under the command of Major-General N. Clowes. Tripolitania District Headquarters was under direct command of General Headquarters Middle East, and was given a heavy task to perform in re-equipping parts of Eighth Army for operations in Sicily and in preparing the 10th Corps for operations in Italy.

60. In preparation for Sicily, the advanced base at Tripoli had to maintain a force of over 200,000 men during May and June. For this operation, 32,000 men, 6,000 vehicles and 310 guns were embarked from the port of Tripoli. For the attack on Italy, the whole of the 10th Corps Headquarters, the 56th Division and the 7th Armoured Division embarked from this port. This involved the use of 342 vessels and the embarkation of 73,000 men, 14,000 vehicles, 686 guns and 447 tanks.

61. After Eighth Army had departed for Sicily and Italy, the port of Tripoli was still used for its partial maintenance. In particular, Tripolitania became a medical base for the evacuation of casualties from Sicily, receiving 10,321 casualties by sea and 3,708 by air during the campaign.

62. Within Tripolitania District the same problems of maintenance, local administration and food supplies were encountered as in Cyrenaica District. Here also the British Military Administration set up courts, recruited a police force, assisted the Italian agricultural population, provided and distributed food, and assisted greatly in the provision of labour for military purposes.

63. Owing to its role in preparing for the Sicilian and Italian operations, the commitments of Tripolitania District did not decline quite so rapidly as did those of Cyrenaica District. But imports, which reached their peak with 131,000 tons in April, were only 91,000 tons in June and had dropped to 40,000 tons in July; during December they were down to 16,000 tons. Similarly the ration strength

dropped from 200,000 in June to 91,000 in October and 45,000 in January, 1944. Therefore, on 14th December, 1943, Headquarters Tripolitania District, was reduced to the status of Headquarters Tripolitania Area.

Sicily.

64. The successes achieved in Tunisia, to which the satisfactory maintenance of Eighth Army and the administrative arrangements in Cyrenaica and Tripolitania had largely contributed, removed the enemy threat to Egypt and the Canal from the West. The defensive period for my command was over, and I was free to develop offensive operations within the scope of my resources. The first stage in carrying the war into Europe was to be an attack on Sicily, to be followed by an invasion of the Italian mainland. As the Tunisian campaign reached its conclusion, my command was steadily freed to make preparations for this overseas offensive.

65. In the North, also, I was no longer concerned with the problem of countering an Axis threat to Egypt and was able to concentrate on plans and training for future operations. When the Russians held Stalingrad, and subsequently counter-attacked, the threat of a German advance through Turkey into the Lebanon and so, possibly, towards Egypt was removed. As long as this threat to Egypt from the North had been a serious possibility, Ninth Army had had an important opera-tional role in Syria and the Lebanon, and troops had been concentrated and plans made with this in view. When the threat was removed I was able to revise the role of Ninth Army and to turn it very largely into a centre for training.

66. The same considerations which enabled me to develop Ninth Army largely as a training centre made it possible for the War Office to revise the role of Persia and Iraq Command (which had been separated from Middle East Command in September, 1942) and to draft troops thence to Ninth Army for training for the invasion of Sicily and for other operations.

67. Many of these troops were administrative units, without which it would have been impossible to mount the Eastern Task Force for Sicily from Middle East resources. The two major formations so received were the 5th and the 56th British Infantry Divisions. Of these, the 5th Division arrived in Middle East on 16th February, 1943, and was re-equipped, fully trained, and ready to take its part in the assault on Sicily by July. The 56th Division arrived in Middle East in March, to train and re-equip for Sicily: but early in April it became necessary to send the Division (except for 168th Brigade, which remained to complete its training for Sicily) to Eighth Army, to gain battle experience and to replace the casualties sustained by the army at Mareth.

68. In addition to troops transferred from Persia and Iraq Command for training for Sicily, the 3rd Corps Headquarters was also transferred to Ninth Army for training and re-equipping in April. They brought with them from Persia and Iraq the 8th Indian Division and 7th Army Group, Royal Artillery, and also took under command the 10th Indian Division, from Cyprus. In addition, the

2nd Polish Corps arrived in Ninth Army in August and September, with Corps Troops, the 3rd Carpathian Infantry Division, the 5th Kresowa Infantry Division, the 2nd Polish Army Tank Brigade, the 3rd Carpathian Lancers, Army Group Polish Artillery and the 7th Polish Anti-tank Regiment. Ninth Army also received the 31st Indian Armoured Division from Iraq in October, and the 4th Indian Division was given its mountain warfare training there on its return from Tunisia, whilst the 13th Corps Headquarters carried out its early training for the attack on Sicily under Ninth Army before being brought to Cairo to act as the first planning staff for the operation.

69. All of these formations required considerable equipment, especially in vehicles, artillery, and signals stores; some of them needed re-organisation to bring them on to the latest British war establishments, and all of them made serious demands on the training establishments in Syria and the Lebanon, which had to be greatly enlarged. The Mountain Warfare Training Establishment, in particular, had to be increased, so that training could be given both to the formations destined for Sicily and to those for which other roles were reserved.

70. As early as February, 1943, plans and preparations for the invasion of Sicily were put in hand. The attack was to be carried out by a Western (American) and an Eastern (British) Task Force, for which Middle East Command had a four-fold role. I had to carry out detailed administrative planning for the Eastern Task Force; to organise, train and equip two Corps; to mount these two Corps for the operation, and subsequently to maintain the whole of the British forces in Sicily for a period. This maintenance commitment was to last from the fourth week of the attack until a later date, on which Allied Force Headquarters (Algiers) would take over administrative control; for the first four weeks of the operation, during which the first four convoys were due to arrive, formations were to be maintained by the command which mounted them. After Allied Force Headquarters had taken over administrative control of all forces in Sicily, Middle East was to be given a role of partial maintenance.

71. The first step in carrying out my task was the organisation of a staff to carry out the detailed planning for Eastern Task Force. In February, 1943, a planning headquarters was formed round the 13th Corps Headquarters in Cairo. As it became possible to release elements of Eighth Army Headquarters from the operations in Tunisia, Rear Headquarters of Eighth Army took over the planning from the 13th Corps Headquarters, and planning became the responsibility of Eighth Army Headquarters, assisted by a planning increment and planning staffs of the Royal Navy and Royal Air Force. At this stage the planning staff was designated Twelfth Army. The elements of Eighth Army Headquarters which were not absorbed in planning remained in Tripoli, commanding units and formations of Eighth Army.

72. Difficulties in detailed planning were to some extent inevitable owing to the need to give priority to the claims of Tunisia while planning a future operation

which was to be carried out by the same commanders, staffs and units. Nor were matters made easier by the fact that planning for yet further operations was begun even before the Sicilian attack was launched. These difficulties were particularly felt by Survey, who found the shortage of photographic units a great handicap.

73. A further great difficulty was the distance which separated Allied Force Headquarters from Cairo. This necessarily made co-ordination and liaison difficult, and planning would have been much easier had the staffs of the forces involved been concentrated in one area instead of being over 1,500 miles apart. My chief administrative officers and those from the War Office could then have made co-ordinated visits and held combined administrative staff conferences, at which problems could have been considered and decided, instead of examining these problems by signal, with inevitable delay.

74. The role allotted to Middle East remained unchanged, but its implications varied considerably as planning went forward. The operational plan for Eastern Task Force, which controlled the detailed planning in Cairo, originally contemplated an assault landing on the South-east corner of Sicily, followed by an assault landing at Catania. Both assaults were to be prepared by Middle East and were to be commanded by Eighth Army, under Allied Force Headquarters. The initial assault in the South-east was to be undertaken by the 13th Corps, with the 5th and 56th Divisions, an army tank battalion, an armoured regiment and a commando, all mounted from Egypt; the subsequent assault landing at Catania was to be undertaken by the 3rd Division, a brigade group and two commandos, all mounted from the United Kingdom and later coming under the command of the 13th Corps. There was also to be a follow-up division (not assault trained) from North Africa.

75. This plan, however, was subjected to both major and minor modifications as preparations went forward. The assault-landing at Catania was abandoned; the 56th Division was diverted to Tunisia and later to the 10th Corps, its place in the 13th Corps being taken by the 50th Division, which was withdrawn from Tunisia for re-forming and training. The 30th Corps was nominated as the second corps of Eastern Task Force, to carry out an assault on the South coast of the island in the Modica area, whilst Western Task Force concentrated its initial assault just to the West, in the Gela area; the 3rd Division was transferred to the 30th Corps when the assault on Catania was abandoned. Later, the 3rd Division was withdrawn and its place was taken by the 1st Canadian Division, with the 1st Canadian Army Tank Brigade, to be mounted with a commando from the United Kingdom. The 51st Division was eventually nominated as the second division of the 30th Corps, which was to include the 231st Brigade. The 1st Airborne Division was also given a role in Eastern Task Force, and the 78th Division was to be the follow-up division. Both of these divisions were to be mounted from North Africa, and Middle East only had the responsibility of planning for them and of providing the 4th Parachute Brigade for the 1st Airborne Division.

76. These changes very considerably increased the difficulties of planning, and of training and equipping the force; but preparations were in fact completed to time although the date of the assault was advanced and the period for preparation was cut down as planning continued.

77. Experience showed that the planning of combined operations requires far more detail and consequently a larger and possibly more specialised staff than normal operations.

78. The most important subject of detailed planning, to which all other considerations were preliminary and subordinate, was the ultimate embarkation and shipment of the force.

79. By the end of February an outline plan had been prepared. The force to be mounted from Middle East required sixty M.T. ships and twenty-five troopships in addition to a large number of landing craft. To enable vehicles and stores to be discharged in the order of priority laid down by Twelfth Army Headquarters, plans were made for stores-ships to be tactically loaded. To implement this, in mid-April a pre-stowage planning staff was set up at Cairo: this included representatives of the War Office and of the Ministry of War Transport, who had had experience of planning stowage for the landing in Algeria.

80. Planning for anti-aircraft defence involved a two-fold problem. It was necessary to provide strong anti-aircraft cover for the Suez Canal and for the Middle East ports of concentration in addition to anti-aircraft protection for the assault. The Middle East Bases would be valuable targets at any time during the last five weeks of preparation, and strong anti-aircraft reinforcements had to be deployed for their defence. Units for this reinforcement programme were provided by bringing back a proportion of the Eighth Army anti-aircraft units and by reinforcements from the United Kingdom.

81. The planning for the anti-aircraft and coast defences of ports and airfields in Sicily, when they should be captured, with its complicated problems of distribution and co-ordination, was carried out by an inter-services committee.

82. Signals planning had to deal with problems for implementing the inter-communications plan, the provision of units and equipment, the provision of special equipment for combined operations for non-signals units, and the provision of communications in embarkation areas during the loading of formations.

83. One of the main difficulties anticipated was that of bridging the gap between the landing craft and the water's edge on the very shallow beaches. To assist in the solution of this problem considerable experimental work had to be carried out.

84. Originally it was intended that Malta should be used as a casualty clearing station area, but this was vetoed by the Royal Navy. Arrangements were accordingly made for the evacuation of casualties from the beaches direct to Tripoli,

Sousse and Sfax; Middle East was responsible only for Tripoli, where plans were made to provide 9,000 hospital beds and accommodation for 4,550 convalescents. To implement the evacuation plan, eight hospital ships and four carriers were required. Of these the latter were provided from the United Kingdom and the former from the Middle East, India and South Africa. They were to rendezvous at Tripoli fully equipped.

85. Large dumps of stretchers, blankets and hospital linen were also established at base ports, and extra medical supplies and equipment were provided for the medical units in the assault, in addition to lightweight stretchers and locally designed folding splints for assault battalions. No suitable drug could be provided for the elimination of sea-sickness, but boiled sweets were prepared for issue on the approach voyage and steps were taken to eliminate sea-sick prone personnel; these measures did not prove completely satisfactory.

86. Preparations were also made to combat malaria, which is prevalent in Sicily; suppressive mepacrine treatment was prepared and one hundred per cent. bush or mosquito nets and veils were provided. Malaria control units were also equipped, as well as a malaria field laboratory, of which a section was to be landed early, for survey purposes.

87. In addition to these problems of the movement, communications and casualty clearance of the force, detailed planning was required on all aspects of equipping, mounting and maintaining so large an overseas operation. In particular, special plans were made for the equipment of units in the assault; landing reserves and beach maintenance packs of ordnance stores, limited to essentials, were planned and prepared. Under the guidance of Royal Electrical and Mechanical Engineers specialists, local manufacture of waterproofing materials for vehicles and artillery equipment was undertaken. In addition special arrangements were made for the provision of vehicle batteries at ports of embarkation and to accompany landing-craft and vehicles during transit. Stocks of ammunition had been built up continuously throughout the early part of 1943, and by June a total of 310,000 tons was held in the Middle East. This proved ample to meet the demand.

88. The results proved that meticulous care in detailed planning, methods of packing and marking, planned loading and off-loading, and co-ordination of supply problems can save casualties and can make maintenance through a beach-head a secure basis for an expeditionary force.

89. Whilst planning for Sicily was going forward, Eastern Task Force was also being assembled, equipped and trained. The Force was, in effect, to be Eighth Army, but the programme for the withdrawal, concentration and re-equipment of formations of Eighth Army was considerably delayed owing to the Tunisian campaign. By the end of the campaign in May, the only major formation which had been withdrawn was the 50th Division, which moved to the Delta in early May, by road and rail via Tobruk.

90. After the conclusion of the campaign, Headquarters of the 30th Corps, the 51st (H) Division, 23rd Armoured Brigade and 5 Army Group, Royal Artillery, all of which had been engaged in Tunisia, were withdrawn into the area Tripoli – Sfax. During April, the 231st Brigade moved from Malta to Alexandria and the 168th Brigade from Persia and Iraq Command to Kabrit. Other units and formations destined to form part of Eighth Army were concentrated either in Syria or the Delta. These were headquarters of the 13th Corps, the 5th and 50th Divisions, the 4th Armoured Brigade, and 31, 32, 33 and 34 Bricks for beach maintenance. The Bricks, each of about 2,300 men, were new units, which had to be formed; the main components were a headquarters, headquarters company, beach maintenance centre, beach engineer unit, signal platoon, anti-aircraft unit (of one heavy and one light battery), a defence company and two Bren-carrier sections, and the equivalent of nine working rifle companies, formed from the nucleus of an infantry battalion. Ordnance brick detachments were formed from volunteers who received intensive training in the procedure for the handling of stores on the beaches, and brick medical sections were also provided. Four beach brick repair and recovery detachments were also formed. The personnel and equipment for three of these were found from the third-line workshops of the force, the remainder from Middle East Base.

91. From experience gained in Tunisia it was decided to provide a uniform third-line workshop for each division, instead of the combination of armoured troops workshops and infantry troops workshops previously used. The additional personnel required were found at the expense of Middle East Base.

92. In addition, Middle East had to provide nineteen pioneer companies. In view of their good record with Eighth Army, Indians and Africans from the High Commission Territories of South Africa were chosen. Although Indian pioneers were, technically, enrolled non-combatants and unarmed, they were among the best pioneer troops available in the Middle East. As it was considered undesirable to send large bodies of unarmed men into what might be actual contact with the enemy, urgent application was made to General Headquarters, India, for the grant of combatant status. This was not agreed, but authority was given to arm the Indian pioneers for self-defence. Accordingly they were issued with rifles and light machine guns and fully trained in the use of these weapons before embarkation. A further four pioneer companies from Mauritius and four Basuto companies were also sent (similarly armed and trained) to Malta in March, 1943.

93. Ultimately Middle East Command reformed, trained, equipped and mounted Headquarters of the 13th and 30th Corps, the 5th and 50th Divisions, the 4th Armoured Brigade, the 231st Independent Brigade Group, four Beach Bricks, and all ancillary units, in addition to numerous army, corps and line of communication troops. All units were brought up to full strength. The bulk of this equipping and training was carried out in the Delta and Palestine. Headquarters, the 30th Corps, remained in Tunisia during this period and was mounted from

Tripoli, whilst the 51st Division and the 23rd Armoured Brigade, although partly equipped from Middle East Base, completed their training in Algeria and were mounted from North Africa. This, however, did not detract from my responsibility, although it decreased the pressure on facilities in the Delta. The 1st Airborne Division, in Eastern Task Force, was also mounted from North Africa; for this Middle East had only to provide some early training for the 4th Parachute Brigade.

94. Whilst this force, which was called Force 545 from March onwards, was being prepared for operations in Sicily, the dual problem of providing stores and equipment whilst at the same time preparing for subsequent maintenance had to be faced. This involved, first the re-equipment of formations and units for operations, and secondly the release of large quantities of stores to form landing reserves and beach maintenance packs. It was only the provision of certain items such as mine detectors and light base plates for the mortars of assault flights that occasioned difficulty. The emergency calls for stores after the operation had started were, it is believed, largely due to the inability of the army to distribute the stores locked up in the landing reserve and maintenance packs rather than to the insufficiency of the reserves.

95. Very large quantities of ammunition were provided for the maintenance of the Eastern Task Force. Although some difficulty was experienced in providing smoke generators, the demands were eventually met.

96. The main factor which delayed the preparation of the formations and units was the provision of vehicles. In addition to the 5th Division, which was completed on arrival from Persia and Iraq Command in April, the 231st Brigade from Malta was fully equipped, and the 50th Division was given 1,500 vehicles and 400 motor cycles. No. 11 Mobile Naval Beach Defence Organisation was also completely equipped, as its own transport from the United Kingdom arrived too late. These, and numerous administrative units, were prepared in Egypt, whilst in Tunisia the 51st Division was equipped partly by stripping other formations, but largely by Allied Force Headquarters.

97. The issue of vehicles was in the main completed by early June, together with the provision of a small immediate reserve of four hundred vehicles in Tripoli. A request from Allied Force Headquarters for assistance was met by the despatch of 2,970 vehicles by road from Egypt in the six weeks after 21st July.

98. The requisite number of Royal Army Service Corps units was made up from all sources in the Middle East, including a certain number of recently arrived units from Persia and Iraq Command. The Royal Army Service Corps Mobilisation Centre at Tahag was required to re-equip approximately 80 per cent. of the units, which involved a total of about 4,500 vehicles. Since many of these vehicles had been operating in the desert for some considerable periods, the repair programme was extensive. It was found quite impossible for the Royal Electrical and

Mechanical Engineers to cope with the Royal Army Service Corps vehicles in addition to those of all other arms. Accordingly a grouped workshop, comprising the Royal Army Service Corps workshops platoons belonging to the units being re-equipped, was formed at the Royal Army Service Corps Mobilisation Centre. Six hundred and fifty new vehicles were issued to the Royal Army Service Corps, and with these and the repair facilities of the grouped workshop, all units were re-equipped completely.

99. In addition to being provided with transport by Middle East Command, Eighth Army was issued with about a hundred and sixty armoured and scout cars. After re-equipping, formations moved with the following vehicles and guns, most of which were issued from the Delta: 2,136 "A" vehicles, 29,800 "B" vehicles and 1,604 pieces of artillery.

100. Besides equipping the artillery in its component of Eastern Task Force, Middle East Command despatched twenty-two 105 mm. self-propelled equipments to the 11th Honourable Artillery Company Regiment, Royal Horse Artillery, at the request of Allied Force Headquarters. These were provided at the expense of units in my command which were not taking part in the attack on Sicily.

101. No difficulty was experienced in equipping the light anti-aircraft units, but heavy anti-aircraft presented a different problem. All the equipment held by Eighth Army units had travelled some 2,000 miles and was in various stages of disrepair. The stocks in the ordnance depots were barely sufficient to cover normal casualties. The majority of guns and Radar equipment in transit to Middle East would not arrive in time, and the defence required for the concentration areas in Egypt and the Levant, and for the Suez Canal, made it impossible to withdraw much equipment from the units remaining in the Middle East. The only remaining source of supply was Persia and Iraq. All available serviceable guns and Radar equipment were despatched by land and sea from there, arriving in time to complete the re-equipment of all heavy anti-aircraft regiments with new or practically new guns. However, owing to the scarcity of Radar equipment, all units had to sail with only one gunlayer, Mark II, per battery.

102. No difficulty was experienced in the equipping of units with signal stores except those specially designed for combined operations. In the Tripoli area, units and formations were supplied from three signal parks and an advanced ordnance depot, and in the Delta direct from base ordnance depots. Owing to the fact that the ship conveying certain of the special combined operations' signal stores from the United Kingdom broke down, many of them did not arrive until the expedition was due to sail. This involved a considerable amount of improvisation. As a consequence none of the special stores were issued until 24th May, one week before the last day on which units could accept delivery, which severely handicapped the training of operators in these new types of equipment. A certain

amount of difficulty was also caused by the arrival of battle batteries in unserviceable condition. Fortunately a second consignment arrived, which eased the situation.

103. The re-equipping of the force for Sicily involved a heavy programme of production, as well as of planning, manpower allocation, and distribution of equipment and stores. In particular, many stores required for the landing and assault, and a very large number of petrol and water containers, were manufactured locally, whilst, to equip the assault and follow up forces to the maximum possible extent with returnable containers, all base and line of communication troops were provided with bulk and non-returnable containers, and as many captured containers as possible were back-loaded from Tripolitania and Cyrenaica. As a result of these efforts the assault and first follow-up convoys were completely equipped with small returnable containers, although subsequent convoys were only equipped with fifty per cent. returnable and fifty per cent. non-returnable containers.

104. During the preparatory period Royal Electrical and Mechanical Engineers Base workshops were fully employed in turning out "A" and "B" vehicles and guns for the re-equipment of Eighth Army. During the same period they also manufactured a considerable quantity of special items such as Scorpions, mine detectors and beach carts. From February they carried out experiments at Kabrit in water-proofing "A" and "B" vehicles, guns, etc., as the information then available from the United Kingdom was very meagre. Experiments were also carried out with materials manufactured locally. Out of some 15,000 vehicles prepared in Middle East ports, United Kingdom materials were available for only 4,500; the rest were waterproofed with local materials.

105. Survey, also, had its share of production. From material provided by the War Office, augmented by air photography in so far as the very inadequate supply of the necessary specialist aircraft permitted, just under four million maps for Sicily were printed in the Middle East, including an urgently required set of charts for the Royal Navy.

106. Air-letter forms, copies of the "Soldier's Guide to Sicily", and pamphlets were other minor, but not unimportant, products of local manufacture.

107. Whilst Middle East Command was busy maintaining Eighth Army in Tunisia, planning for Sicily and re-forming and re-equipping formations for that campaign, it had also to provide and staff the training establishments necessary for the new type of warfare on which Eighth Army was about to embark.

108. Training involved the preparation of two brigade groups in each of the 5th and 50th Divisions, and the 231st Independent Infantry Brigade Group, for the assault role, and of one brigade group in each division for the follow-up role. In addition to these formations, certain army and corps troops, No. 1 Commando and some Royal Air Force personnel were to be trained in combined operations.

109. To implement this programme, five brigade groups, in addition to normal training, were assault-trained at the Combined Training Centre, while two brigade groups were trained at the Mountain Warfare Training Centre and in Dryshod training to act as follow-up brigades. Four beach bricks were also trained in their role.

110. The Combined Training Centre, Kabrit, had previously been on a care and maintenance basis. With the staff and facilities available, the utmost that could be done was to train one brigade group in four weeks. This was inadequate, as the programme envisaged not only the training of a brigade group in three weeks, but also the training of the four beach bricks. To cope with this, a new system of training had to be devised to accelerate the training of brigades, and the existing Combined Training Centre was enlarged and new establishments setup. To reduce the time spent by a brigade at the Combined Training Centre all training which did not require the use of craft was transferred to Dryshod training wings, which were set up as far as possible in the areas in which formations were concentrated. In these areas, mock landing craft and ships' sides were erected, and training consisted of lectures, Dryshod exercises, craft drill and precision driving. After fourteen days at a Dryshod wing, formations moved to Kabrit for fourteen days' Wetshod training, culminating in a full-scale brigade landing exercise. In all cases brigades intended for assault roles did their training with the beach brick with which it was intended they should operate.

111. Considerable work was involved in providing facilities for Dryshod training and suitable beaches for Wetshod training. The latter involved very heavy dredging operations. The almost completed deep water quays at Adabiya Bay were taken over by the Royal Navy for berthing and maintaining landing craft and training their crews.

112. The Combined Training Centre was substantially increased, the bulk of the additional instructors being drawn from the United Kingdom. A Formations Combined Training Staff was organised primarily with the object of setting and running rehearsal exercises. In addition there were two increments for attachment to formations for advice on combined operations, planning and training.

113. A major exercise called BROMYARD took place for the 13th Corps in the Gulf of Aqaba in June, 1943. The convoy sailed from Suez on 10th June, and on 13th June all assaulting troops of the 5th and 50th Divisions, with associated beach bricks and special service troops, were landed on the beaches. Troops re-embarked on the following day. This involved the embarkation into twelve personnel and four M.T./Stores ships of 23,000 men and 350 vehicles; the stores ships were tactically stowed with dummy stores and non-operational vehicles specially issued for the exercise.

114. Bad weather prevented the rehearsal exercise of the 231st Brigade and 31 Beach Brick taking place at Sofaga. Accordingly the convoy was sailed to

Aqaba, where a landing exercise was carried out after the conclusion of exercise BROMYARD.

115. The training of the anti-aircraft units was difficult because many of the units had only recently arrived from the United Kingdom or Persia and Iraq Command, and had not been in active employment for a long time. On the other hand, the Eighth Army units had been so continuously engaged in operations that they had not properly absorbed recent technical developments and drills. The sixty anti-aircraft batteries involved were concentrated in the Delta and during May and June a training programme was carried out by which every battery was put through a practice camp.

116. No Bailey bridges arrived in the Middle East until 24th May. From this date until the launching of the operation, cadres from as many units as possible were given one week's intensive training in the new equipment which they were to use to such an extent during the operation.

117. Courses for Royal Electrical and Mechanical Engineers personnel in waterproofing were held at Kabrit. These personnel were used as instructors for training cadres of unit personnel so that units could waterproof their own vehicles. This plan, however, was revised when it was shown by the exercises and the early loading of a ship that the state of training of unit personnel was not good enough to allow units to do their own waterproofing and that it would have to be carried out by Royal Electrical and Mechanical Engineers personnel at the ports.

118. Small veterinary detachments were attached to both the 13th and 30th Corps to train units in animal management, first aid and the use of improvised pack transport, so that the best use might be made of civilian and captured animals acquired during the operation.

119. The assault on Sicily, when it took place, inevitably produced a crop of new lessons, and caused some of the doctrines taught during this period of intensive training to be revised. But the training establishments had none the less proved invaluable in teaching many essentials and in getting formations physically fit for their task.

120. As the climax of these preparations, Middle East Command was responsible for embarking, in addition to army, corps and line of communication troops, that part of the 13th Corps which consisted of the 5th and 50th Divisions and the 4th Armoured Brigade, and the 231st Infantry Brigade, which was in the 30th Corps. This commitment brought to the proof all the planning and training, and stretched the movement facilities to the maximum.

121. Sixty M.T./Stores ships, tactically stowed, and twenty-five troopships, in addition to a large number of landing craft, were required for the first two convoys. The outline plan was that M.T./Stores ships were to begin loading at Beirut, Haifa and Alexandria early in June. Personnel ships were to load at Suez at

the beginning of July. Half of the L.S.Ts. (tank-landing ships, with a capacity of fifty vehicles, or twenty-two tanks and twenty vehicles) were to load half at Suez and half at Alexandria. L.C.Ts. (tank-landing craft, with a capacity of ten vehicles or six tanks) were to load at Benghazi. The M.T./Stores convoys were planned to arrive as follows: the assault convoy on 10th July, first follow-up convoy on 13th July, and second follow-up convoy on 24th July. Thereafter reinforcements and maintenance convoys would be sailed every fourteen days until 22nd August, when they would be sailed every ten days.

122. Excluding personnel ships, sixty British and Allied and thirty United States vessels were allocated to form the first three convoys. The necessary work of fitting these vessels was begun at Ismailia, Port Said and Port Sudan early in April.

123. To avoid heavy calls on transport, the stores for the first convoys were moved by the middle of May to depots adjacent to the ports, ready to be called forward for loading. Loading in accordance with pre-stowage plans began early in June and, apart from initial difficulties with vehicle weights and measurements, proceeded very well.

124. During this period the strain was increased by the fact that vehicles and signal equipment, once waterproofed, could not be used for ordinary purposes, and a duplicate service had to be provided. This was particularly heavy on signals, who were also carrying a heavy weight of traffic over the long line of communication to Tripoli.

125. Another problem which had to be overcome was that of checking, changing and charging vehicles' batteries to ensure that they would hold their charge for the five to seven weeks during which they might have to stand in ships' holds. This was done by special arrangements, including the provision of batteries at the ports of embarkation and to accompany landing craft and vehicles during transit.

126. When loading started it was found that many vehicles were mechanically unfit, and arrangements were made to inspect all vehicles before they were called forward. Light repairs were effected on the spot and special arrangements were made in the nearest base workshops to carry out heavier repairs. Out of 3,200 vehicles inspected at Alexandria, 932 required repair and 138 were condemned as unfit for operational use.

127. Embarkation of all personnel in M.T./Stores ships took place at Beirut, Haifa and Alexandria and was completed by 5th July. While the M.T./Stores ships for the 5th and 50th Divisions and the 231st Brigade were being loaded at Beirut, Haifa and Alexandria, other formations were being moved to Malta in readiness for the assault or follow-up. The assault troops of the 51st Division were moved in landing craft from Sousse and Sfax, and Main Army Headquarters and the 30th Corps Headquarters with air formations, also in landing craft, from Tripoli to Malta. The ferrying of these troops with their vehicles, equipment and

maintenance stores, involved the most careful planning in conjunction with the Royal Navy for the use of the landing craft available. Before the attack was launched the Tripoli – Malta ferry had convoyed 7,000 personnel and 1,400 vehicles. In all some 32,000 personnel and 6,000 vehicles, as well as guns and tanks, were embarked at Tripoli for Sicily. Other headquarters and units with equipment, stores and vehicles were moved from Egypt to Malta in personnel and M.T./Stores ships. From 3rd to 10th June, 7,000 personnel and 600 vehicles were despatched from Alexandria to Malta.

128. Embarkation of the assault personnel on the assault-day convoy into fifteen personnel ships and of the follow-up personnel on the third-day convoy into twelve personnel ships took place at Suez on 29th–30th June and 1st July. Although in these three days approximately 46,500 personnel were embarked the operation was carried through smoothly.

129. The programme for loading the vehicles of the assault convoy was also successfully carried out. Since the date of the arrival of the L.C.Ts. through the Mediterranean left little margin for loading in Egypt, Benghazi was to be used as the port of embarkation. Assault personnel and vehicles of four brigades (the 15th, 17th, 151st and 231st Brigades) were therefore moved by rail and road from the Delta to Benghazi, where they embarked between 24th June and 5th July; this involved a total of 2,700 personnel and 850 vehicles.

130. On 16th June the loading of 8 L.S.Ts. with vehicles and escorts only was begun at Suez. The L.S.Ts. then sailed to Alexandria, where they embarked the remaining personnel and joined up with 9 L.S.Ts. which had been loaded there. The embarkation of the L.S.Ts. was completed by 21st June. In all, for the first two convoys a total of 65,000 personnel, 9,400 vehicles and 60,000 tons of stores was loaded.

131. The equipping, training and mounting of Eastern Task Force had been an extensive commitment, but it was successfully accomplished largely because most of the force had been withdrawn to the Delta for the purpose. Although the undertaking involved great quantities of equipment and large formations, most of the difficulties came from changes in the operational plan and from the wide area from which the assault was mounted.

132. Having launched Eastern Task Force, Middle East Command then had to implement its maintenance plans. It had been decided as a general principle that the commands in which formations were mounted would be responsible for the maintenance of these formations for the first four convoys, that is to say, convoys arriving in the first four weeks after the landing. Then Middle East would be responsible for all British forces in Sicily for the first seven weeks. After that date, maintenance of the forces in Sicily, other than United States Army troops, was to be based on the principle that such items as were considered to be Eastern Group

Supply (of Eastern origin) were to be shipped from Middle East and items of Western Group Supply from the United Kingdom or United States.

133. This system of maintenance was carried out as planned. Middle East received detailed loading programmes from Eighth Army for the first four convoys. Then, until Allied Force Headquarters assumed administrative control, Middle East received demands direct from Eighth Army, provided Eastern Group supplies and certain items of Western Group Supply, and laid off to the War Office the remaining demands, mainly for Western Group supplies, which it had been agreed would be shipped from the West.

134. From 12th August, 15 Army Group, under Allied Force Headquarters, took over both operational and administrative control in Sicily and so Allied Force Headquarters assumed administrative control of all forces in Sicily; thereafter the total demands ceased to be placed direct on Middle East, who now received from Allied Force Headquarters demands for Eastern Group supplies and from the War Office instructions to provide those items of Western Group supply which could not be provided from the United Kingdom or from the United States. In addition, demands for urgent requirements of controlled stores were made direct on Middle East by Allied Force Headquarters.

135. In all, from June to October a total of 230,000 tons and 19,500 vehicles were loaded for despatch to Sicily. Stocks of ammunition had been built up throughout the early part of 1943 and, therefore, little difficulty was experienced in providing the 30,000 tons exported for this operation; a certain amount of ammunition was earmarked in Tripoli for calling forward if necessary.

136. The provision of supplies presented no serious problems. Forty-eight hour mess-tin rations, provided as landing rations, were loaded in bulk and issued to each man prior to disembarkation. The mess-tin and composite rations proved very successful for an operation of this nature. The force was maintained on composite rations for the first three weeks, after which the change-over to Middle East Field Service hard-scale ration was made possible by the gradual building up of rations in the first three convoys. By the end of six weeks, stock on the ground represented seven days for 235,000 men, whilst reserves had been established at Malta and Tripoli.

137. Planning for the requirements of petrol and oil was based to a great extent on previous operational consumption in the desert and proved to be an over-estimate, as the line of communication was much shorter and the losses en route and on loading were much less than had been anticipated. A reserve dump of 6,000 tons was built up at Tripoli; this was not required and was eventually used for normal maintenance. In addition, Middle East provided facilities for bulk oil supply for the Royal Navy at Benghazi and at Tripoli.

138. Ordnance stores, of which some 90,000 items were issued from 4 and 5 Base Ordnance Depots, needed special precautions for packing and shipping; special

packing cases were designed and manufactured in the Middle East, limited in weight to one-man lifts. Engineer base depots also were heavily employed in packing and shipping stores for the operation. In all, 20,000 tons of engineer stores and about 500 items of heavy plant were shipped to Sicily from Middle East stocks.

139. These maintenance tasks were effectively accomplished, both during the assault, the subsequent period of maintenance through beachheads, and later when the ports of Augusta and Syracuse were in operation. The success was due to two main factors – our low losses at sea (thanks to the Royal Navy and the Royal Air Force) and the care and forethought which had been put into the preparations during the previous five months.

140. In addition to maintaining its quota of the Eastern Task Force with supplies and equipment, Middle East had to provide reinforcements, to handle rear signals and postal traffic and to receive casualties.

141. Pools of reinforcements were, therefore, built up in the Delta, Tripoli and the Sousse and Sfax areas from Middle East resources, in addition to personnel provided by British North African Force. No. I Advanced Second Echelon was established at Malta to serve both Middle East Forces and British North African Force. Advanced Second Echelon reported battle casualties direct to the United Kingdom and maintained reinforcement officers at Tripoli, Sousse and Philippeville. In close contact with these reinforcement officers and with Advanced Second Echelon, Libya, it was responsible for the supply of reinforcements to Sicily. It also served as a clearing-house for the supply of the necessary information to Second Echelon, Middle East Forces, and Second Echelon, British North African Force.

142. Middle East also supplied a base headquarters for Sicily. This was supplied from Tripolitania Base and Lines of Communication Headquarters, which went to Sicily almost *en bloc*, the Base Headquarters' duties in Tripolitania being taken over by Headquarters, Tripolitania District, from 16th July.

143. Whilst these arrangements were made for reinforcements, the provision of cashier and postal services caused some difficulty. In addition to providing and equipping cashiers to proceed with the force, arrangements had to be made for the provision and distribution of adequate supplies of British Military Administration currency and for the exchange into this currency of the local money in the hands of the embarking troops. In view of the large numbers of troops and the large sums involved, this entailed a considerable organisation.

144. Postal services laboured under severe difficulties. The need for the strictest security was a great handicap, the facilities enjoyed by the Middle East and British North African components of the force required adjustment to make them similar, and the division of complete units into several parties distributed

over the Middle East in transit to Sicily and in Sicily itself made the re-direction and diversion of mail extremely difficult.

145. As maintenance of Eighth Army was a Middle East responsibility in the initial stages, there was a large volume of administrative signal traffic between Middle East and Eighth Army. On 14th August (with Eighth Army finally established in Sicily), submarine cable fullerphone was established between Sicily and Malta to meet signal traffic back to 15 Army Group and General Headquarters Middle East, by means other than wireless. Malta cleared traffic to and from Algiers and the Delta by submarine cable. This fullerphone circuit was replaced by high-speed morse on 9th September.

146. Whilst Middle East Base played this important part in the Sicilian operations, Malta, an outlying portion of my command, also fulfilled a role which necessitated most careful planning and administration. The 231st Brigade was taken from the garrison, trained and re-equipped in the Middle East, and took part in the assault and subsequent operations. In addition to providing this brigade, Malta was also called upon to use all of its facilities to the utmost in preparation for the attack on Sicily.

147. Owing to the lack of accommodation and other facilities, it was decided that Malta should not be developed as an advanced base. Its role, therefore, became that of a combined advanced headquarters and staging post. In preparation for the assault it had to accommodate the assault troops of the 51st Division, numerous army and corps troops and Royal Air Force personnel, the main headquarters of the 30th Corps and Twelfth (later Eighth) Army, Headquarters of the Desert Air Force, Naval Headquarters and Tactical Headquarters of the Army Group; in all an additional commitment of approximately 30,000 personnel and 2,700 vehicles.

148. Although a large proportion of the vehicles arrived at Malta in landing craft, the discharge of the cargo ships placed a great strain on the movement and transportation facilities. To deal with this extra commitment a number of additional staff was sent to the island as well as extra administrative units, including two general transport and eight pioneer companies.

149. Accommodation on Malta, which had never been large, had been substantially reduced by bombing. Twelve tented camp sites and eighteen bivouac areas, each to accommodate 1,000 men and 70 vehicles, were therefore prepared. A well-boring section was despatched to the island and sixteen bores were sunk for military and civilian needs in areas where the existing water supply was insufficient.

150. Twelve hards, selected by the Royal Navy, were prepared in the Grand Harbour and Marsh Muscetto Harbour; of these only four could be used for L.S.Ts. owing either to lack of draught or to the unsuitability of road approaches.

151. Even when the Royal Electrical and Mechanical Engineers personnel in Malta had been strengthened by a draft from Middle East, not more than 300 vehicles could be waterproofed a day. Three vehicle marshalling parks were therefore organised within two miles of the hards. There vehicles, after waterproofing, were assembled until they were called forward for loading. These three areas could accommodate only 900 vehicles. Another vehicle marshalling park capable of holding 600 vehicles was therefore organised about five miles from the hards. It was realised that, after stage two of the waterproofing, vehicles should not be driven more than two miles, but in view of the congestion in the harbour area and the necessity to hold sufficient vehicles in readiness for embarkation, this distance was accepted.

152. Royal Air Force units were the first to arrive, on 3rd June, 1943. From this date until 7th July, units arrived continuously either by landing craft or by troopships. Stores of all natures, both reserves for Eighth Army and for the maintenance of Malta, were also received during this period.

153. Advanced holdings were established of 3,200 tons of supplies, 5,000 tons of petrol and oil and 6,000 tons of ammunition. In addition, small reserves were held of vital Ordnance stores, including hospital requirements and waterproofing kits. Ultimately, a substantial proportion of the petrol and oil and ammunition was not required and was used for Malta maintenance. The ammunition proved of great value, especially for emergency demands to cover unforeseen expenditure.

154. Originally it had been intended that Malta should be used as a casualty clearing area for evacuation from the beaches, but as the Royal Navy objected to hospital ships and carriers calling at the ports the plan was abandoned and Malta was prepared as a medical reserve area only, for the reception of such casualties as might arrive in normal naval and military craft destined for the island. For this purpose, 7,760 beds (including 1,000 for convalescents) were held ready, but in actual fact these were not all used. The casualties which passed through Malta were mainly airborne personnel and other survivors picked up by naval vessels.

155. During the period 8th–16th July, a total of 20,400 personnel, 2,700 vehicles and 3,500 tons of stores was embarked and loaded at Malta. The call forward of personnel and vehicles after the initial assault presented some difficulty, and quick turn-round of craft was maintained only at the expense of a certain amount of discomfort to the troops and congestion at the quayside. This arose because the number of craft available for the next flight was seldom known sufficiently early, so that it was necessary in some cases to move down to the docks personnel and vehicles ordered by the ferry control and to keep them there until craft became available.

156. Once the operations had started and the troops which had been staged there had been ferried to Sicily, Malta's role diminished. The dumps of supplies,

petrol and oil, ammunition and Ordnance stores were partially despatched. Supplies of bread, approximately 18,000 lbs. daily, were shipped from 22nd July to 13th August. Apart from that, little was done by the island except to meet small urgent demands.

157. Undoubtedly Malta was used to full capacity. The hards in the Grand Harbour were of necessity extremely close together and difficult of access, but our air superiority discouraged the enemy from attempting any appreciable interference. Further, owing to lack of suitable sites, three of the vehicle marshalling parks were also in the middle of the harbour area. One vehicle marshalling park was camouflaged most successfully, but lack of labour and material did not permit of this being done for others.

158. The administrative arrangements at Malta worked smoothly, thanks to the co-operation of the Royal Navy and the hard work of the garrison, and the island proved invaluable in the mounting of our overseas offensive in the Mediterranean.

159. The success achieved in preparing and mounting the offensive against Sicily was demonstrated by the operations. Eighth Army and its lines of communication and administration were firmly established, and on 12th August, 1943, 15 Army Group, under Allied Force Headquarters, took over administrative responsibility for Eighth Army. The actual hand-over took some weeks, but with effect from that date Middle East Command was officially relieved of this responsibility.

Italy.

160. In anticipation of the successful conclusion of the Sicilian campaign, plans were next made for exploitation in Italy. The planning was carried out at Allied Force Headquarters, and I was not directly concerned at this stage, although, at the request of Allied Force Headquarters, Middle East Survey revised some two hundred maps for the operation, despite the continued lack of suitable aircraft.

161. The plan, finally, called on Middle East to mount the 10th Corps Headquarters, Corps troops, the 7th Armoured Division and the 56th Division. These formations were to be mounted from the Tripoli area and were to take part in the attack either on the toe of Italy or at Salerno. In the end, although they were mounted for operations in the toe of Italy, they were launched against Salerno. The remainder of the force was to be mounted in North Africa and was not a commitment of Middle East Command.

162. Accordingly, the 10th Corps Headquarters, the 7th Armoured Division and the 56th Division were concentrated in the Tripoli area and were trained and equipped for their task. Re-equipment in artillery and vehicles was carried through, without any great strain, mainly by stripping the 1st Armoured Division and the 4th Indian Division, who were at that time without an operational role, whilst signals, engineer and other equipment was also provided and the formations were brought up to their full scale of both armoured and other vehicles.

163. The task of equipping these formations, at a distance of over a thousand miles from the main base in Egypt, and with the planning staff still further removed (at Algiers) provided a sharp contrast to the advantages which had been gained by withdrawing most of Eighth Army to Egypt for re-equipment for the attack on Sicily. Much confusion was caused by the inevitable lack of close liaison, and to meet urgent demands considerable use had to be made of air transport, as a result of which the freight carried by air from Cairo to Tripolitania rose from 1,600 lbs. in July to 135,000 lbs. in August and 154,000 lbs. in September.

164. The arrangements for concentration and embarkation were delegated very largely to Headquarters Tripolitania District, owing to the great distance from the main base at which the operation had to be mounted, and in spite of the fact that a single port was used for the embarkation of so large a force, and of the distance from main base, the task was successfully accomplished. For the assault, nine personnel ships, eight stores ships and ten L.S.Ts. sailed from Tripoli on 7th September, whilst a further 170 L.S.Ts. completed the Corps by mid-November. In all, including follow-up shipping, some 73,000 men, 14,000 vehicles, 600 guns and 400 tanks were embarked from Tripoli, involving the use of 342 vessels.

165. Eighth Army crossed from Sicily into Italy on 3rd September, and the assault landing at Salerno was carried out on the 9th by which date preparations for launching the 10th Corps were complete. Although most of this embarkation was successfully delegated to Headquarters Tripolitania District, the Middle East base ports were also called on to ship 4,500 tons of stores direct.

166. Middle East Command was responsible for maintaining this force for the first three weeks of the operation, that is to say, from 9th September to 2nd October. For this period, convoys were loaded with 43,500 tons of stores.

167. From 2nd October onwards, maintenance of the force in Italy was on the basis of the Eastern and Western Group system, which was also being used for the other forces, including Eighth Army, in Sicily and Italy. Under this system the War Office made demands on Middle East, but in order to simplify the shipping problem Allied Force Headquarters also informed Middle East, every ten days, of the separate demands for Naples and the toe of Italy respectively.

168. From 13th September, the normal ten day convoys from Middle East were switched from Sicily to Italy, but normal maintenance and the building up of reserves were affected by the demands made on port and shipping capacities by the move to Italy of follow-up divisions. This demand was made heavier because, in view of the low holding of reserve stores in Italy, the first three follow-up divisions had to take with them sixty days' reserves of all items; this was particularly necessary since Indian troops were involved, and their maintenance demanded their own special supplies.

169. The principal difficulty has arisen with the supply of meat, both frozen and fresh. Owing to the shortage of refrigerator coasters it became necessary to turn Malta into a "feeder" at which ocean-going refrigerator vessels discharged, the meat being subsequently discharged by coasters at Italian ports; fresh meat (largely for the use of Indian troops) was ultimately provided by shipping live sheep from the Middle East.

170. In answer to periodic calls for assistance, Middle East has subsequently had to ship various stores and equipment to Italy. Replacement vehicles and ammunition have been in demand, and vehicles have also been shipped to Italy from Tripoli instead of driving them back to Egypt.

171. To the end of my period in command, direct supply from the United Kingdom and the United States to the advanced Ordnance depots in Italy had not yet become effective, and the Ordnance depots in the Delta were being used as the bulk breaking point for all Eastern Group stores, as well as for certain Western Group stores, for the Central Mediterranean Force as well as for Middle East Forces. In September the Provision Branches of Central Mediterranean Force, British North African Force and Middle East Forces were amalgamated under the title of Deputy Director of Ordnance Services (Provisions), Mediterranean, and the organisation was based on Cairo. Consequently the number of troops for whom provision had to be made rose from 730,000 in January, 1943, to 1,750,000 in September and the ensuing months.

172. The magnitude of the part played by Middle East Base during this period is shown by the fact that from August to December 284,000 tons of stores and 23,000 vehicles were loaded for shipment to Italy.

173. The provision of medical facilities and the evacuation of casualties for the forces in Italy placed a further commitment on Middle East. Casualties from Sicily had been less than was anticipated, and the arrangements had worked smoothly. Casualties from Italy continued to be received in Middle East, by sea an air, up to the end of October, and although at one time the shortage of hospital ships for further transportation to the United Kingdom caused some anxiety and a danger of accumulation, the facilities proved adequate. Between 10th July and 7th January, forty-four hospitals and expansions amounting to 13,800 British, Dominion, Indian and African beds and 5,500 beds for convalescents were despatched from the Middle East to Italy.

174. Although the 10th Corps was the only formation which Middle East contributed to the assault on Italy, the subsequent build-up drew heavily on my reserves of manpower (and precluded the undertaking of any other enterprise demanding the use of a major formation). Allied Force Headquarters wished the build-up to take place as quickly as possible; in this the limiting factor was not the availability of formations but the intake capacity in Italy. A programme was laid down for the Middle East which envisaged the despatch of one division, with

corps and ancillary troops and vehicles, each month. In pursuance of this programme, the 8th Indian Division was despatched from Haifa and Beirut in September, the 2nd New Zealand Division was despatched from Suez and Alexandria during October, the 4th Indian Division from Alexandria during December, and the 3rd Carpathian Division (Polish) during January. Three medium regiments, Royal Artillery, were also equipped and despatched, and arrangements were also made for the 5th Polish Division and Headquarters and Corps Troops of the 2nd Polish Corps to be despatched. All of these formations had to be trained, re-equipped and shipped by Middle East.

175. Meanwhile, the 1st British Armoured Division, the 2nd Fighting French Armoured Division and the 1st Fighting French Infantry Division had been despatched from Middle East to Allied Force Headquarters, the total of pioneer companies provided by Middle East for Sicily and Italy had been brought up to fifty, and the 8th Armoured Brigade and a number of administrative units had been shipped to the United Kingdom.

176. In addition to mounting build-up divisions for Italy, Middle East Command also had to provide reinforcements, particularly for Indian, African and Local Colonial troops (for which Allied Force Headquarters had no facilities). In all, from 1st September to 8th January, Middle East despatched over 11,000 reinforcements to Italy; of these 5,000 were British, almost 3,000 Indian and 3,600 New Zealanders. Reinforcements and new formations between them took a total of 110,000 men from Middle East to Italy and Sicily during the months from September to December, a monthly average of 30,000.

177. This very heavy drain in men and administrative effort for Italy, even after Eighth Army had nominally passed out of my sphere, meant that any other operation which I might contemplate would have to be largely of a diversionary nature and could be undertaken only at the risk of unduly weakening troops required for internal security and garrison duties within the Command. This proved to be the limiting factory in the operations in the Ægean, which the overthrow of the Italian Government precipitated.

Operations in the Ægean.
178. Plans for the seizure of small islands in the Ægean as bases for raiding operations against the enemy's lines of communication had been under consideration for some time before I took over command in the Middle East, and in February, 1943, the Joint Planning Staff began seriously to consider the possibilities of a major assault on the Dodecanese (which were Italian possessions), with Rhodes and Scarpanto, the two most strategically placed islands, as the principal objectives. Planning for such operations was complicated by the conflicting ambitions of the Greeks and the Turks for the ultimate possession of the islands and, after considering all the possibilities, it was decided that the actual operations should be carried out by British forces only, and that the future of the Dodecanese should not yet be discussed with either of the interested parties.

179. Operations in Tunisia, however, were our first commitment at this time. When the possible withdrawal of some British troops from North Africa to the Middle East for Ægean operations was raised, General Eisenhower replied that the ability of North Africa to furnish British troops after the completion of the Tunisian campaign depended upon the decisions of the Combined Chiefs of Staff on the course of operations in the Mediterranean, following the planned invasion of Sicily. He declared, therefore, that the movement of troops from North Africa to Middle East should follow, and not precede, these decisions.

180. Nevertheless, although the prospect of obtaining troops from North Africa was uncertain, a detailed plan for a full-scale attack on Rhodes and Scarpanto, and the subsequent occupation of other islands, was produced by 2nd May. The principal feature of the plan was the landing of forces two hundred and fifty miles from their nearest air bases in Cyprus, and still farther from Cyrenaica, and the crux of the operation was the provision of the necessary air cover and adequate air reinforcements. But to offset this difficulty, other large scale operations would probably be in progress in the Central Mediterranean to deter the enemy from reinforcing the Ægean.

181. The minimum troop requirements for the whole Ægean operation, including garrisons for Rhodes, Scarpanto and other islands, were three infantry divisions, one armoured brigade, two independent infantry battalions, two parachute battalions and corps troops.

182. This plan was produced by No. 2 Planning Staff, which had just been formed in Cairo, and which was composed mainly of officers of the 3rd Corps Headquarters. No. 2 Planning Staff was re-designated Force 292 in June, 1943, when it seemed likely that active operations in the Ægean were to be undertaken and a Force Headquarters would be required to conduct operations in the field. But the uncertainty of Turkey's attitude, the complexities of the political situation in the Balkans, and the needs of Sicily and Italy made detailed planning difficult, and during the nine months from May, 1943, no less than seven plans were produced for the capture of Rhodes, Crete and other islands in the Dodecanese and the Ægean.

183. The scope of each plan varied in relation to the object to be attained, the varying degrees of opposition likely to be encountered and the scale of co-operation of the Turkish Government. The early plans, which envisaged not only the capture of the Dodecanese and Ægean Islands but further operations on the mainland of Greece, had to provide for crushing both German and Italian resistance. Later plans, after the collapse of Italy, dealt only with the capture of Rhodes or Crete held by the German garrisons supported by Fascist elements of the Italian garrisons. In some cases the plans had to be made in the absence of a Naval Planning Section, and consequently were never fully completed.

184. On four occasions a force was assembled and partially prepared to undertake the capture of Rhodes. As the collapse of Italy appeared imminent, the 8th Indian Division was actually embarked and rehearsed in a landing operation at Suez. This rehearsal took place on 24th, 25th and 26th August and the force was to be ready to sail on 1st September. Unfortunately, however, on 26th August I was informed that the transports had received orders to proceed to India,[1] and the force was disembarked and returned to its stations; the 8th Indian Division was sent to Italy almost immediately. When, on 8th September, the Italian armistice was announced and an opportunity for seizing the island arose, the shipping and the force which had been specially prepared for a quick seizure of Rhodes had been dispersed.

185. Thus the Italian armistice took me at a complete disadvantage. Owing to the claims of other Commands, a carefully planned and rehearsed operation had just been jettisoned and no urgent action was contemplated in the immediate future, since I was not kept informed of what was afoot and first learned that Italy was discussing terms only a few days before the public announcement that the armistice had been concluded. I therefore had neither time, troops nor shipping to prepare to take advantage of the chances which were thus offered, whilst, even before the Italian capitulation was announced, the movements of German troops in the Aegean and Ionian islands indicated that they were preparing to be attacked there, and that they expected to find the Italians of little fighting value.

186. Events immediately following the armistice showed that German plans to cope with such an eventuality had been well laid, and the attitude of General Vechiarelli, commander of the Italian Eleventh Army, at Athens, who refused to co-operate with us, and whose troops were ultimately disarmed, undoubtedly assisted the Germans to consolidate their positions. The German take-over in Crete was accomplished quite smoothly, and at Scarpanto the newly arrived German Fortress Infantry Battalion had little difficulty in asserting itself.

187. In spite of this, the opportunity for seizing Rhodes before the German garrison there could re-organise and adjust itself to the changed circumstances (provided the Italian garrison could exert itself in our favour) still existed. I therefore decided to despatch the 234th Brigade, a regular brigade which had come from Malta in June, 1943, to the island, to assist the Italians in overpowering the Germans.

188. At this time the German air forces in Greece and the Aegean were not considered sufficiently strong to constitute a major threat to these operations, nor were their land forces on Rhodes of any great consequence, consisting as they did of one division, General Kleeman's "Sturm" Division, six thousand strong, which was outnumbered by the Italians by six to one.

189. The expedition of the 234th Brigade was to be preceded by a small mission whose task was to make contact with the Italian commander in Rhodes and

induce him to take over control of the island. The mission left Haifa by sea on 8th September (the day on which the armistice with Italy was announced) and went to Castelrosso, which capitulated to a small detachment of the Special Boat Squadron on 10th September. Meanwhile, the very scanty warning of the Italian collapse which I had received was cut still further by the weather. The first attempt to drop two officers by parachute on Rhodes, on 9th September, failed, so that the Germans got an extra day in which to organise their positions on the island and to undermine the morale of the Italians. It was not until the night of 9th–10th September that Major the Lord Jellicoe and another officer were dropped by parachute and established contact with Admiral Campione, the Italian Governor, whose spirit was clearly affected by the delay and by the fact that the Germans were already present whilst we were not.

190. At 1715 hours on 11th September, information reached me that Campione had lost heart, had refused permission for us to enter the island and did not wish to have any further dealings with us. The 234th Infantry Brigade was in the meantime being prepared for operations, but, owing to the limitations of shipping and the time taken to collect it, the brigade could not be ready to sail until 18th September. The urgency was such that this delay was unacceptable, and one battalion was ordered to embark in motor launches and Royal Air Force launches for transit to Rhodes, while preparations for the mounting of the remainder of the brigade went on as fast as possible. It was, however, imperative that we should have a guarantee of unopposed entry into the port of Rhodes and an unopposed occupation of an airfield either at Marizza or on Cos before the expedition could be launched, since a landing against opposition was out of the question. Before anything could be done, the German commander, Von Kleeman, had taken advantage of Campione's weakness and indecision, and the Germans assumed undisputed control of Rhodes.

191. The positive nature of the enemy's reaction in Rhodes, and our inability to restore the situation, made it necessary to revise completely our planning for the Aegean. Hitherto all the plans which had been made involved the employment of considerable forces, and had as their first objective the capture of Rhodes. Future plans would, of necessity, have to be made on a smaller scale and, since it was essential to act quickly, they would have to be improvised.

192. German resources in the Aegean had been stretched to the limit by their recent takeover in Rhodes and Crete, and there was a possibility that by a rapid move we could obtain control of other Aegean islands, notably Cos, and by so doing partially neutralise the recent enemy successes over the Italians, enhance our prestige throughout the Middle East, and act as a diversion for the operations in Italy.

193. General Eisenhower had already made it clear that little material support, especially in the air, could be given by North Africa to such an undertaking, and had emphasised that the campaign in Italy must not be prejudiced by any other

operation in the Mediterranean. There was, however, a good chance that, even with the limited resources at our disposal, the occupation of such islands as Cos, which had an airfield and landing grounds, Leros, where there was an Italian naval base, and Samos could be undertaken, since the garrisons seemed likely to welcome the prospect of a British occupation.

194. With the limited number of German aircraft based on Greece and Crete at this time, and with our own fighters based on Cos, the possibility of major sea-borne or airborne German operations was slight, and with the aid of the loyal garrisons of Cos and Leros, who were thought to be reasonably well equipped for ground and air defence, there was every prospect of maintaining ourselves in these islands until an attack could be launched on Rhodes from the Middle East.

195. I therefore decided on the despatch of small forces to Cos, Leros and Samos, to act as stiffening to the Italians. Cos and Samos were secured by the detachment of the Special Boat Squadron which had occupied Castelrosso, and troop movements began, both by sea and air, on 15th September. Sea transport was almost entirely limited to Royal Navy destroyers going direct to Leros, or to small coasting vessels going as far as Castelrosso; thence the journey to the islands had to be made in small sailing ships. Owing to the shipping difficulties, the limitations of port capacity and disembarkation equipment, and our inability to break down Bofors guns and heavy equipment into small loads, troops could take with them only their personal weapons, rifles, mortars and Bren guns. No anti-tank, field or anti-aircraft guns could be taken, nor could any transport other than jeeps be sent. Reliance for such equipment had to be placed on the Italian equipment already in the islands, which, in the case of Leros especially, was thought to be reasonably up-to-date and effective. This regrettably was not the case. The defences of Leros were not at all well developed, much of the anti-aircraft material was out of date, and the system of fire control was deplorable; certain natures of ammunition were in short supply, and motor transport was always inadequate. The defences of Cos were on an even lower scale.

196. For the first few days the transport of troops went on without opposition, and in addition to the occupation of Cos, Leros and Samos, the islands of Simi, Stampalia and Icaria were occupied on 18th September. Air transport was used to reinforce Cos by day, troops being landed at Antimachia airfield, while destroyers went direct to Leros, the reinforcements to Samos going thence in small local craft.

197. Cos was easily the most important of these islands to us, since it possessed an airfield from which single-engined fighter aircraft could operate over the Aegean and could cover an attack on Rhodes when the time arrived for that operation to be resumed. By comparison with the facilities at Rhodes, this airfield at Antimachia was a poor one, and it was not considered possible, even from the start, to hold Cos in strength without Rhodes, for which Cos was to be a preliminary step. The island, about thirty miles long and nowhere more than seven

miles wide, is the most fruitful in the Aegean; water and food are plentiful and adequate for the population of 20,000 and for any garrison which we were likely to put in. The only port is the town of Cos, on the north-east coast, opposite the Turkish mainland; facilities here were very poor, with little depth of water and only one berth alongside the quay for a small vessel. A main road runs the length of the island, connecting Cos town with Antimachia airfield, some eighteen miles away, at the broadest part of the island.

198. The small force of fighters which could be operated and maintained on Cos was not sufficient, in view of the strongly reinforced German Air Force, to ward off for long the determined attacks on the landing ground which began on the 18th September. This was the more so since an adequate early warning system could not be established and the ground anti-aircraft consisted of twenty-four Bofors guns only, a few poorly manned and out-of-date Italian anti-aircraft guns and the small arms weapons of the British troops. Air Transport by day had, therefore to be cancelled and all future reinforcement took place by night.

199. The need for British anti-aircraft defences at Antimachia, and for the defence of other landing strips which were being developed on Cos, soon became acute in the face of the increasing number of German air attacks. Bofors guns were sent forward in destroyers, L.C.Ts. and even in submarines, while stocks of aviation fuel and ammunition were despatched in every kind of craft. The ever-growing intensity of German air attack was, however, still preventing the shipping of heavy equipment such as heavy anti-aircraft guns, heavy Air Force equipment for warning systems, and motor transport, all of which were urgently required.

200. Although heavy equipment was lacking, by the end of September the garrisons of Cos, Leros and Samos, had been built up to approximately the strength of one battalion with ancillary troops on each island; on Cos twenty-four Bofors guns were in action and detachments of the Royal Air Force Regiment had arrived and partly taken over the defence of the airfield and landing strips in the island.

201. From air reconnaissance carried out on 1st and 2nd October, it was known that a considerable enemy convoy was at sea; on the 2nd it was sailing east in Naxos area, and the garrison commander on Cos assumed it was a reinforcement for Rhodes. The enemy's air superiority made it impossible for the Royal Navy to intercept the convoy by day, and a sweep carried out by destroyers on the night of 2nd October failed to locate it. At first light on the following day R.A.F. Beaufighters attacked the convoy, but without success. The garrison was therefore only conducting its ordinary routine precautions when, at 0500 hours on 3rd October, the enemy assault on Cos began. The seaborne invading forces, consisting of troops from the Greek mainland and from Crete, landed from merchant vessels, landing-craft and caiques, covered by aircraft and three destroyers, while a strong force of parachute troops, flown from the Greek mainland, was dropped on Antimachia airfield, which our aircraft were unable to use since it had been

badly cratered in the air-raids which preceded the attack. By 4th October all organised resistance on our part had been brought to an end.

202. The enemy's success on Cos was due chiefly to the rapid build-up of his air force in Greece and the Aegean (achieved at the expense of his Italian strength and in spite of the bombing of bases by available R.A.F. and U.S.A.A.F. aircraft), and the heavy and unceasing effort he was able to maintain in the air which disorganised the defences. Our small garrison was concentrated mainly in the area of Cos town, whilst at Antimachia, some eighteen miles away, there was one company and a detachment of the Royal Air Force Regiment with some light anti-aircraft guns. The main enemy landing, on the north coast, took place virtually without opposition; striking inland, he quickly cut the road Cos-Antimachia and forced our garrison to fight two independent actions with no weapons other than small arms and a few light mortars, which were no match for the heavy mortars and infantry guns which the invaders had brought with them. In spite of a gallant resistance, the garrison, which consisted mainly of the 1st Battalion, the Durham Light Infantry, was overwhelmed and the greater part was made prisoner.

203. The loss of Cos deprived us of our only airfield from which single-engined fighters could operate over the Aegean. As a result, no adequate daylight cover could be given to our shipping, which now became exposed to attack by a greatly strengthened German Air Force based in Greece and Crete, which had been rapidly expanded until it was at least equal to that in Italy; sea transport was henceforth confined to darkness. The disposition of our forces in the Aegean was readjusted on 5th October, when the small garrison which we had established in Calino, the neighbouring island to Cos, was withdrawn; but patrols were maintained there and on Gairos, Kythnos, Stampalia and Simi.

204. As a result of their success, the Germans were enabled rapidly to consolidate their position in the Cyclades, and with the exception of Andros, where some resistance was offered, all the islands garrisoned by Italians fell into German hands. The enemy did not use any great number of troops for these operations, rather he seemed to be gathering his strength for an assault against the islands still occupied by British garrisons, particularly Leros.

205. Constant naval and air patrols were maintained to meet this threat, and on 7th October, the Royal Navy struck a heavy blow at enemy shipping by intercepting a large enemy convoy off Stampalia and destroying four ammunition ships, six landing craft and some armed trawlers. The Royal Air Force, too, and the U.S.A.A.F. were very active and, in addition to carrying out anti-shipping reconnaissances, made repeated attacks upon the Greek mainland, Crete and Rhodes, and other strategical points occupied by the enemy, including Cos (which had now become an objective).

206. The enemy assault on Leros, which had been expected soon after the fall of Cos, hung fire and in the meantime we were able to strengthen our garrison

there. It is probable that the first setback to the enemy's invasion plan was the destruction of the convoy off Stampalia on 7th October. The continued delay was certainly due to our naval and air offensive against shipping and German key points. Heavy toll was taken by British and American air forces, who, although handicapped by the lack of airfields, and operating from very considerable distances, kept up a ceaseless offensive under trying conditions.

207. Nevertheless, in spite of all we could do, the enemy continued methodically to consolidate his position in the smaller islands. Naxos and Paros were occupied on 12th October, and on 15th October Simi, which we had evacuated two days before after heavy dive-bombing raids had made the position untenable, was occupied by the enemy. The German Air Force was well dispersed; its heavy bombers were concentrated at Eleusis, its fighters at Kalamaki and Argos, its dive-bombers at Megara and Marizza, and from these bases constant attacks were made on Leros. Delayed-action bombs put Portolago Bay, on Leros, temporarily out of action on 16th October, and on 17th and 18th October, Castelrosso was bombed for the first time since our occupation.

208. On 26th October, air activity against Leros and Samos increased in intensity, but there was still no movement from the enemy's invasion fleet. The enemy concentrations remained in the Cos and Calino areas, and further considerable concentrations were seen in the Piraeus and at Khios; but from the middle of October onwards the bad weather which set in probably contributed to the postponement of the attack.

209. Up to the end of October, operations in the Aegean had been controlled by Middle East Command through the 3rd Corps Headquarters (Force 292) and the 234th Brigade (Major-General Brittorous) on Leros, but recent developments obviously justified the establishment of a separate command to take over operations in that sphere. On 1st November, Major-General Hall was appointed G.O.C. Aegean, with the specific task of holding Leros and Samos in order to cause as much damage as possible to the enemy's lines of communication in the Aegean. In addition, he was given command of all British, Allied and Italian land forces in the Aegean, including and north of Rhodes, Scarpanto and Crete, as well as of naval personnel in shore establishments not under Commander-in-Chief, Levant, or Senior British Naval Officer, Aegean, in that area. General Hall and Brigadier Tilney, who was to take the post of Fortress Commander, Leros, arrived at Leros on 5th November, and from that date Headquarters, Aegean, started to control operations.

210. After discussion with Major-General Brittorous, who relinquished command of the 234th Brigade, General Hall decided to make Samos his headquarters. He remained on Leros long enough to see the defences of the island organised to his satisfaction and to clarify relations with the Italians there, and since the re-organisation of the island's defences was proceeding satisfactorily, he

was able to leave for Samos about midnight on 11th November, leaving Brigadier Tilney in command on Leros.

211. It was unfortunate that at this time a planned extensive air effort against enemy bases and shipping was limited by the weather and the temporary un-serviceability of our Cyrenaican landing grounds owing to rain. The enemy, on the other hand, taking full advantage of the proximity of his air bases, was able to make our reinforcements of Leros difficult. The dropping of flares at night hindered unloading operations on certain occasions, and the laying of minefields also added to our difficulties; in spite of all this enemy activity the strength of the Leros garrison was built up to the strength of a brigade. The original garrison, which had arrived between the 17th September and the 2nd October, was the 234th Brigade Headquarters, and the 2nd Royal Irish Fusiliers, with a company from the 2nd Royal West Kents, the remainder of the battalion being on Samos. This was reinforced by 4th November by the 4th Buffs, although their Head-quarters Company was lost at sea, and early in November the 1st King's Own completed the Brigade.

212. From the beginning of November, some increase in enemy preparations was observed. On 3rd and 4th November, landing craft and escorts were reported in Lavrion, and on the 5th aircraft reconnaissance showed them moving eastwards. Between then and the evening of 10th November when they arrived in the Cos/Calino area they moved only by day under heavy fighter protection, dispersing and lying up during the night, first in the Paros/Naxos area and later in Amorgos, Levitha and Stampalia. Every effort was made by the Royal Navy and R.A.F. to intercept the force, but our efforts met with small success due by day to the heavy scale of enemy fighter protection and by night to the difficulty of spotting the craft, which were probably beached and certainly camouflaged in the many bays available. During the afternoon of 9th November, our troops moved to their battle stations to await the enemy attack.

213. The island of Leros consists of three mountainous regions connected by two narrow necks of land, neither of which is much more than a thousand yards in breadth, and so indented is the coastline that no point on the island is more than a mile from the sea. The northern and southern mountain areas are both pene-trated by a valley which runs roughly from North to South, so that an easy natural course is afforded to the main road; the central mountains alone are continuous, and here the main road has to skirt the coast to avoid the hills. There are prac-tically no possibilities of movement across country; the mountains are steep, stony and scored with ravines. The lower and flatter areas, which are intensely cultivated, are cut up into small fields by low rubble walls, which are a constant barrier to movement.

214. The main problems of the defence were the same as on Cos. We were certain to suffer from inferiority in the air – in particular, single-engined fighter

cover was impracticable and the available bomber forces including some diverted from Italian operations, were obviously not sufficient for the task of neutralising all the German air bases simultaneously. Moreover, the topography of the island made it easy to split any defence and to isolate sectors. To meet the threat of invasion, the island was divided into three sectors, within each of which all troops, including the Italians, came under command of a battalion commander. The three battalions under the 234th Brigade, 4th Buffs, 2nd Royal Irish Fusiliers and 1st King's Own, were made responsible for the northern, central and southern sectors respectively.

215. The enemy attack, supported by dive-bombers and destroyers, began about six o'clock on the morning of 12th November, when German troops disembarked on the extreme North-east of the island and at Pandeli Bay, to the East of Leros town. In the Northeast, about five hundred troops were landed and gained the high ground running from Dellapalma Bay to Grifo, including Mt. Vedetta. The enemy were held on this line throughout the day, but by two o'clock on the morning of 13th November, they had overrun Mt. Clidi and extended their bridgehead from Mt. Clidi to Ste. Madonne.

216. The landing at Pandeli was made by a much smaller force, about one hundred and twenty men in all. Some progress was made at first, but the landing was successfully counter-attacked by a company of Royal Irish Fusiliers, and was pinned down on the lower slopes of Mt. Appetici. It was here and to the immediate North, on the narrow Gurna – Alinda neck of land, that the move to split the defence up into isolated sectors developed. The Pandeli landing was reinforced during the night of 12th–13th November and a further night landing was made on the northern shore of Gurna Bay.

217. Meanwhile, during the afternoon of 12th November, the equivalent of a battalion of enemy parachutists had been dropped in the North-east and on Gachi Ridge, and although at 1600 hours our troops were still holding the high ground overlooking the ridge, the enemy had gained control of the Gurna – Alinda neck, thus cutting land communications between the southern and central and the northern sectors of the island.

218. On 13th November there was no significant change in the North-east, although some enemy infiltration took place to the South-east of Quirico. High winds and heavy seas probably prevented any further enemy reinforcements being landed during the day. No activity of any kind was reported from the southern sector, but in the centre the enemy, having strongly reinforced his troops in the Appetici area the previous night, unexpectedly captured Appetici at midday and thus exposed our right flank and strengthened his hold on the Gurna – Alinda neck.

219. That night a counter-attack by the reserve company of the King's Own, supported by heavy bombardment from His Majesty's ships Echo and Belvoir, was

launched against the enemy at Appetici, but it failed to achieve its object, and the enemy, striking South in strength with mortar and machine-gun support towards Meraviglia, made considerable progress and had almost reached our main head-quarters on Meraviglia by seven o'clock on the morning of 14th November.

220. The situation in the northern and southern sectors was more encouraging; the Buffs recaptured Mt. Clidi during the night of 13th–14th November and continued to advance, whilst a general advance in the southern sector made, in conjunction with the advance from the North, a converging attack on the enemy in the Gurna – Alinda neck. Good progress was made, and shortly after midday it was reported that the enemy was almost entirely surrounded in the Quaranta area. The Buffs were to his North and North-west, one company of Royal West Kents, brought from Samos and operating under command of Fortress Head-quarters, was also to his North-west, and the Royal Irish Fusiliers and King's Own had gained a strong footing on Gachi Ridge, although they were not in complete control. Over two hundred prisoners were taken in this action and fairly heavy casualties were inflicted on the enemy.

221. Our attack continued throughout the 14th November in spite of heavy enemy air activity, and at eight o'clock the next morning a further strong attack was launched against the enemy still holding out on Gachi Ridge. Further per-sonnel of the Royal West Kents, who had been landed from Samos the previous night, were able to give added weight to the attack, but shortly after midday on the 15th, it was reported that little headway was being made in the face of intense and continuous bombing and aerial machine-gunning by the enemy.

222. Communications were by now disrupted, making control and movement difficult, and, what was worse, our troops were showing obvious signs of fatigue. By the end of the day the Gachi objective had not been reached, and there is little doubt that the failure of the attack was due to the enemy air onslaught, which the Royal Air Force, operating under a heavy handicap, was unable effectively to counter. Some four hundred sorties were made by the enemy against our troops during the day.

223. During that night the enemy reinforced his positions and at first light launched a heavy attack on Meraviglia. By 0815 hours on the 16th November, it was reported that the situation was serious and that the Meraviglia position was being neutralised by dive-bombing attacks and machine-gun fire. Nevertheless, in spite of their extreme fatigue, our troops fought back desperately, and were able to report an improvement in the situation by 1130 hours; Meraviglia was still in our hands, communications had been partially restored and reorganisation was in progress. A further message, originated at 1200 hours, confirmed this and added that the Fortress Reserve Company had been re-formed.

224. By this time, however, the enemy had succeeded in building up a substantial reserve and had extended his bridgehead at Pandeli Bay. Another message

received during the afternoon said that the position had deteriorated and was becoming desperate, but there was still a hope of bringing the battle to a successful conclusion if the valley running from Alinda Bay to Pandeli Bay could be bombarded, since a heavy attack from that area on the fortress position was certain during the night.

225. Shortly after 1830 hours, all communications with the island faded out, and, in view of this, further troops which had been embarked at Samos for Leros were disembarked. It was later learned that the garrison had surrendered at 2000 hours.

226. Meanwhile, on Samos, to which a small mission had been sent via Turkey on the night of 9th September, the Italian garrison, under General Soldarelli, had been persuaded to espouse the British cause and to disarm the 1,500 Blackshirts on the island. A temporary civil government had been set up under the Metropolitan Archbishop, the local guerillas had been kept in order, and an Allied force of one infantry battalion (2nd Royal West Kents, less one company) and the Greek Sacred Squadron had been built up.

227. On Major-General Hall's appointment as G.O.C. Aegean, he made a thorough inspection of the defences of Leros and arrived at Samos on 12th November, the morning of the enemy's attack on Leros. The battle of Leros lasted five days, and from the beginning the Samos garrison was standing by to provide reinforcements should they be needed. On 12th November, Leros asked for the despatch of the Royal West Kents; preparations were put in hand to move the battalion that night, but in the absence of suitable shipping the men were returned to their battle stations. The next night, 13th–14th, a suitable vessel was found and one company was sent to Portolago, where it arrived the following night; the remainder of the battalion arrived by destroyer on the night of the 15th–16th. The Greek Sacred Squadron, too, was ordered to move and was actually embarked, but since it was reported that Leros had fallen on the afternoon of 16th November, the squadron stood down.

228. That night I instructed Major-General Hall to leave Samos and return to Cairo, leaving the conduct of operations in the hands of Brigadier Baird, the Military Governor of Samos. I also ordered that if, at a later date, the enemy were to attack Samos, and Italian resistance proved to be of no value, Brigadier Baird was to evacuate himself and his staff, leaving the Greek troops and the guerrillas to operate on the island.

229. On 17th November, the enemy switched his air offensive to Samos. At about midday Vathi and Tiganion were heavily bombed and extensive damage was caused, including the disruption of communications with Middle East.

230. Next day I ordered the withdrawal, if possible, of all British troops and the Greek Sacred Squadron, on the night of 18th–19th November. Brigadier Baird was to remain in Samos until the last possible moment for reasons of prestige, and maintenance was to continue as long as possible under arrangements to be made

with the Military Attaché at Ankara. I also ordered that arrangements should be made for evacuating some Greek civilians.

231. During the evening of 19th November, a caique fleet left Turkey and the evacuation was carried out, although the rendezvous on the Turkish coast had to be changed owing to the unwillingness of the caique captains to face the Samos channel, where German "E" boats were thought to be operating. The fleet arrived at Kusadasi early on 20th November, bringing with it Brigadier Baird and his staff, Colonel Tzigantes, commander of the Greek Sacred Squadron, General Soldarelli, the Italian Commander, the Metropolitan Archbishop and all British and Greek forces, with a hundred Italian civilians. The British Attaché at Ankara gained the consent of the Turkish Government for the evacuees to pass through Turkey in the guise of civilians.

232. Since it appeared, on 20th November, that the Germans had not yet occupied the eastern end of Samos, a second fleet set out on the night of 20th–21st November, and returned next morning with all British and Greek stragglers, one thousand Greek civilians and four hundred Italian troops. Meanwhile, some two thousand Greek civilians had arrived in Turkey by their own means, and arrangements were put in hand for the evacuation by rail of all refugees and military personnel. This was accomplished by means of special refugee trains which began to leave on 23rd November.

233. During 21st November, news was received that the Germans had landed on Samos, and permission was given to the Greek Sacred Squadron to organise a final round-up of stragglers. This they did, and a further two hundred Greek civilians and two thousand eight hundred Italians were successfully evacuated.

234. The only outstanding British commitments, apart from Castelrosso, were now isolated patrols from the Long Range Desert Group (playing a new role) on the islands of Seriphos and Nikonos; these were successfully evacuated to Turkey by 29th November. Castelrosso was kept, with a small garrison, as a base for possible future operations.

235. The maintenance of the forces in the Aegean was exceedingly difficult, and, owing to the complex lines of communication, which were liable to interruption, and the dispersion of the forces, presented a problem out of all proportion to the number of troops involved, which amounted in all to the equivalent of two brigades.

236. It was intended that reserves for each garrison in the islands, plus the civilian population and such Italian troops as were not evacuated, would be established as soon as possible on the general basis of thirty days' reserve and fifteen days' working margin.

237. Maintenance was to be by sea from the Middle East bases, supplemented (primarily for the civilian population) as far as was practicable from Turkey. The

main islands to be supplied were Castelrosso, Cos, Leros and Samos. The original sea movement plan was that direct shipments should be made to Castelrosso, Leros and Cos, from Middle East ports, including those in Cyprus, whilst for Samos and the other islands transhipments were to be made in caiques or L.C.Ts. from Cos and Leros or from Kusadasi in Turkey.

238. In the initial stages, until Cos fell, this plan was carried out, and small stores-ships sailed direct from Egypt and Palestine to Castelrosso, Leros and Cos; there the cargo was transhipped for distribution throughout the islands by caique and other small craft. Arrangements were also made for maintaining Cos by air, but this method was only used to meet urgent demands which could not be satisfied in time by sea. Between 14th September and 3rd October, aircraft of 216 Group, R.A.F., landed or dropped on Cos, 458,100 lbs. of freight, 714 Army and 310 Royal Air Force personnel.

239. With the fall of Cos, on 3rd October, and the consequent lack of single engine fighter cover, it became impossible to despatch stores-ships to Leros except when favourable opportunity offered. In the middle of October the Royal Navy also stopped stores-ships sailing to Castelrosso. A number of ships was held loaded in Middle East ports ready to proceed if suitable opportunity offered, but in fact they never sailed.

240. During the most difficult period, after the fall of Cos, the system of maintenance to Leros and Samos was either by caique from Castelrosso, by caique from Kusadasi in Turkey, by submarine from Beirut and Haifa, by destroyer from Alexandria, or by air-dropping from Cairo.

241. At this time Castelrosso became, to a certain extent, the main transhipment point for the islands. Supplies were taken there either by caique from Cyprus and Haifa, by stores-ships from Middle East until the middle of October, by L.C.T. from Port Said, Haifa and Cyprus, by other naval vessels from Alexandria, or by air from Abuqir. After the use of stores-ships to supply Castelrosso had been vetoed by the Royal Navy, and caiques had to be relied upon for this service, care was taken to ensure that only those caiques were used for this run which refused to sail into the Aegean. Supply by naval vessels was used only as an emergency measure. In addition, a number of flying boats and Italian float planes was flown from Abuqir Bay to carry forward personnel and stores urgently required. Originally, two Sunderlands and four Cants were available, but this number was reduced by November, when the daily lift did not exceed 3,000 lbs., excluding personnel.

242. A limiting factor to the transhipment of stores from Castelrosso was that there was available on the island storage space for only 4,500 tons, of which only 800 tons could be petrol. However, towards the end of the operations, three caiques were used as a floating reserve of about 250 tons of petrol and oil. Further, owing to the extremely erratic operation of caiques and schooners, no reliable estimate of the carry-forward was available for maintenance planning. All

that could be done was to ensure that supplies and stores of the right kind were always available when opportunity for transhipment offered.

243. In view of the difficulties of supplying Leros and Samos via Castelrosso, and of the short distance from Samos to the Turkish coast, the supply route through Turkey was developed as fully as was possible. The primary object of this route was to ship supplies for the civil population. But there was also hope that certain military maintenance might be provided from this source and, in fact, the Turks allowed certain military stores to be supplied.

244. Up to 11th October, the Turkish supply route for Samos and Leros was rather improvised and piecemeal, but none the less substantial shipments continued until, on the 11th October, I formally placed the main responsibility for the island with Military Attaché, Ankara, working through Kusadasi, and drawing from the dumps which, with other objects in view, we had established in Turkey. As a result of this decision, and of the decision not to evacuate Samos and Leros as an immediate consequence of the loss of Cos, it became necessary to arrange for increased supplies, both for civil and for military consumption. Suitable arrangements were made with the Turkish Government, and until the evacuation of the islands a regular service was maintained.

245. Supplies and stores were moved by rail and road from the dumps and were shipped in caiques from Kusadasi. But since only certain items, such as rations and a limited range of ammunition and stores, were available from these dumps, they were, by agreement with the Turkish Government, supplemented by stores (mainly supplies, petrol and oil) railed from Syria through Turkey to Kusadasi. Despatch started on 21st October, the first wagons crossed the frontier on 29th, and stores crossed the frontier at a daily average of 70 tons, until flow was stopped on 17th November after the fall of Leros. By this time a total of 1,400 tons had been sent into Turkey.

246. Although it was possible to move stores to Kusadasi, and the short journey to Samos presented no difficulty, the main problem was the onward distribution to Leros, since, after the fall of Cos, great difficulty was found in persuading the crews of the caiques to make the voyage to Leros. However, from 28th September to 16th November, a total of 3,000 tons was shipped to Samos and of 480 tons to Leros, including civilian foodstuffs.

247. From 11th October onwards, these supplies from Turkey were intended to be the main source of maintenance for the garrisons of Samos and Leros, but they were supplemented to a very considerable extent from other sources.

248. During the period, 16th October to 7th November, two British and five Italian submarines operated to Leros from Beirut and Haifa. The turn-round was estimated to be fourteen days and it was expected that 150 tons a week could be supplied by this method. The main limitation was the Royal Navy's inability to

sail the submarines during the period of the full moon owing to the risks involved. Another limiting factor was the size and weight of the package that could be carried, the ideal being a 16-inch cube which could be lifted by one man. However, this limitation was overcome by close co-operation between the submarine commanders and the army personnel responsible for loading, and amongst other awkward loads twelve Bofors guns, six 2-pounder guns and one Jeep were sent, in addition to eighteen M.M.Gs. and 250 tons of more easily handled stores.

249. Stores and personnel were also carried in destroyers, mainly from Alexandria. The loads that could be carried by destroyer suffered from limitations similar to those carried by submarine, but much was accomplished by co-operation and improvisation. In order that no lift in destroyers or submarines should be missed through stores not being available, 300-ton dumps were established at Alexandria, Beirut and Haifa, and 100-ton dumps at Famagusta and Limassol. A priority which altered from time to time to meet the operational requirements was laid down for the despatch of these stores. By this means, 250 tons of stores and ten Jeeps were moved forward. This work, carried out by the Royal Navy under the most hazardous circumstances, was invaluable, and one of the main factors enabling the islands to be held as long as they were. Over the period of the operation H.M. Ships carried the following totals of men, stores and equipment.

By Surface Ships.

4,990 men.
950 tons of stores.
32 vehicles plus trailers.
27 guns.

By Submarines.

17 men.
325 tons of stores.
I vehicle.
12 guns.

250. The limited lifts which the Royal Navy could accept were supplementary to a caique service to Leros and Samos, both direct from the Levant and Cyprus, and from Castelrosso. Many difficulties arose, however; the chief of these was to find crews willing to go beyond Castelrosso. This was partially overcome by the finding of some crews by the Royal Navy and of others by the Army.

251. Arrangements were also made for dropping by air; this method was used mainly to meet urgent demands for ordnance stores and in the latter stages of the operation for various natures of ammunition, as there was no other reliable and fast method of meeting such demands. Initially, one aircraft was used each night, but ultimately as many as eighteen were used. During the period, 5th October to 19th November, 334,000 lbs. and 200 personnel were dropped by 216 Group, Royal Air Force. A greater effort was attempted but thwarted by adverse weather.

252. The evacuation of casualties from the Aegean was carried out by destroyer, caique, and transport aircraft. From the end of October, the evacuation of casualties from Leros to the Middle East by sea or air was most difficult; accordingly arrangements were made with the Turkish Government whereby they agreed to accept up to forty seriously wounded men in hospital at Bodrum without internment. Cases requiring operation were to be sent to the Izmir French Hospital. Less seriously wounded men were evacuated by caique to Bodrum, whence they were sent on to Castelrosso.

253. Maintenance by all these methods, none of which was reliable, was necessarily somewhat erratic and very difficult to regulate. The maintenance of our forces could never be regarded as assured, but, in spite of this, the combination of the various methods employed proved successful in that, when the operations were finished, G.O.C. Aegean reported that there was no lack of any vital commodity during the final stages of the operations, which were never influenced by a shortage of ammunition or supplies.

254. In fact, throughout the Aegean operations, it had been accepted that our garrisons could be maintained in supplies and ammunition, but that the cost of such maintenance would be high and the difficulties, especially in shipping heavy equipment, serious and at times prohibitive. On the other hand, our presence there was certainly of great value in causing diversion to the Aegean of German material which was badly needed elsewhere. The enemy was forced to concentrate 350 aircraft in Greece, Crete and Rhodes (of which about 125 were reinforcements) and his aircraft casualties by 23rd October amounted to over a hundred destroyed, over fifty probably destroyed, and a large number damaged. He had also lost eight motor vessels totalling about 16,000 tons, seven lighters and seven escorts; these vessels, although only a small proportion of those available, were virtually irreplaceable from outside the Mediterranean.[2] Furthermore, as long as we held Leros the German position on Rhodes remained under threat, and in many ways the enemy's difficulties were at least as great as our own. The crux of the situation was that Leros could not be effectively built-up and the enemy's sea movement intercepted owing to the fact that our air bases were too distant to allow adequate cover to be given to the Royal Navy. If our position could be maintained long enough to effect the build-up on Leros and to take advantage of the German difficulties, the moral and political effect on the whole of South-East Europe would be so great that I decided to retain Leros as long as possible with the limited forces available, whilst making every effort to secure adequate air reinforcements. If these could be procured, not only would Leros be secured but the enemy's supplies by sea to the whole of the Dodecanese would be seriously threatened.

255. When the actual German attack came against the garrisons in the Aegean our failure to maintain our positions was due (as had been anticipated) to the impracticability of providing adequate air cover before and during the battles.

For this the underlying cause was that the Aegean operations had never been allowed to encroach on the prior demands of the Italian campaign. Major formations, aircraft and shipping alike, could not be diverted from Italy; for Italy, Middle East's available resources had been concentrated, and although an improvised operation in the Aegean was undertaken (on orders from London) in the hope of seizing the opportunity offered by the Italian capitulation, the risks, from the start, were great.

Middle East Base and Training
256. In fact, the Aegean operations were mounted by Middle East at a time when its role had largely been reduced from an operational command, with troops at its disposal, to that of a base and transit centre and, above all, a training centre for warfare in Europe.

257. As part of its function as a base and training centre, Middle East Command was given an important role in training and equipping allied contingents to take their place in field formations or to release British troops for operational roles. This duty involved a constant regard for the acute political problems which disturb all "refugee" governments, in addition to the difficulties of training the formations, equipping them on British war establishments, and instructing them in British methods, so that they could take their place in a British field force.

258. The 2nd Polish Corps, under command of General Anders, was the largest allied force to be trained and equipped in this manner. In August, 1943, a Polish Corps of two infantry divisions and one tank brigade began to move to Middle East from Persia and Iraq Command.

By the middle of October the first part of the move was complete, and most of the corps was concentrated for training in Southern Palestine. At the end of November the corps moved to Egypt, preparatory to moving overseas to Italy. Here re-organisation took place on the latest British war establishments, to bring the corps into line with British formations and units, and on 10th December the move to Italy began. The corps was landed in Italy fully equipped with the exception of a small number of technical vehicles, of which there were none available in the Middle East.

259. The Fighting French have also been trained and equipped by Middle East. In February, 1943, General de Larminat requested that a Fighting French Division should be formed from the two independent Fighting French Brigades then concentrated at Gambut. This was agreed, and the division was completely equipped by the end of March and moved from Tobruk to Tripoli on 18th April. There it came under command of the 10th Corps and moved up to relieve the 51st Division in the line at Enfidaville on 6th and 7th May. A Fighting French Flying Column was also placed under command of Eighth Army during the advance to Tunisia. It came under command of the 30th Corps at Ben Gardane, and after a short attachment to the 4th Light Armoured Brigade it passed, on

31st March, under command of General Leclerc as part of "L" Force, which had come up from Chad.

260. After the defeat of the enemy in Tunisia, the French forces were withdrawn to Tripolitania for re-organisation; the 1st Fighting French Division was organised as a normal British Division and the 2nd Fighting French Armoured Division was formed from "L" Force, the Flying Column, two Tank Squadrons which had arrived from the Delta by sea at the end of June, and from recruits from Tunisia. The 1st Fighting French Division remained on British war establishments and with British equipment, and its battle losses were made up from the 2nd Fighting French Armoured Division, who were to be equipped from American sources. Both divisions and the 4th Fighting French Brigade passed under French command at the end of August. French forces in Syria have acquitted themselves creditably in the static role to which they have been assigned.

261. The Poles and the French brought considerable numbers to be trained and equipped; the Greeks have been fewer in numbers, but have none the less presented a difficult problem. In February, 1943, two Greek Brigades were training under command of Ninth Army. At this time the formation of the 1st Greek Division, which was to be a training and administrative formation, was under consideration and the staff was being collected and trained in Cairo. Political unrest, which had been a considerable source of anxiety during the period under review, then broke out and at the beginning of March, 1943, led to a grave state of indiscipline in both brigades. The instigators of the disturbances were left-wing officers and men with violent anti-Metaxist sympathies. It became necessary to remove a number of officers, but for political reasons the ringleaders could not be removed. The formation of the 1st Greek Divisional Headquarters was discontinued and the command of both brigades was taken over temporarily by British Brigadiers. On 6th July further disturbances took place, this time mainly in the 2nd Greek Brigade, as a result of which two battalions of the 2nd Brigade were disbanded, and the 1st Brigade was completed to war establishment from the reliable elements of the 2nd Brigade. The 8th Greek Battalion, which was intended for guard duties only, was formed from the remnants of the 2nd Brigade, less the ringleaders, who were sent to the Sudan. There were no further disturbances throughout the period and in December, 1943, the 1st Greek Brigade was pronounced fit for an operational role.

262. The Greek Sacred Squadron, which represents the finest elements in the Greek Army, was part of General Leclerc's "L" Force from the middle of February to the end of March, 1943, and took part in active operations under command of the Fighting French Forces. On 1st April it came under command of the New Zealand Division, and on 17th April it left them at Enfidaville to return to the Delta. The Squadron was re-organised by the middle of May and came under command of of the Special Air Service Regiment. It was trained in combined operations as a parachute squadron, and on 29th October part of the

squadron went to Samos by sea, the remainder being dropped by air three days later. On the fall of Samos they were safely evacuated to Middle East through Turkey.

263. The Greek Armoured Car Regiment, of two squadrons, has been a first-class unit throughout my period of command. It has been stationed in Syria, under the command first of the 10th Armoured Division and then of the 9th Armoured Brigade.

264. At the beginning of February the Yugoslav Army in the Middle East consisted of a headquarters, one battalion and a depot. The battalion came under command of the 10th Indian Division (25th Indian Infantry Brigade) on 21st July 1943, and moved to Ar Rama; it has remained under command ever since. By October the battalion, fully equipped and up to strength, had reached a high standard of training and was included in the Order of Battle for operations in the Aegean.

265. At the end of December, Partisan propaganda leaflets were distributed in the battalion by the sympathisers of Marshal Tito. Shortly afterwards about one-third of the men and one officer from the battalion signed a declaration refusing to obey orders from the General Headquarters of the Yugoslav Forces, and placed themselves under British command until such time as they could join the Partisan Forces. They were segregated and put into a camp at Geneifa.

266. A Belgian Brigade Group arrived in the Middle East from the Belgian Congo between the middle of April and the middle of June, 1943. It was organised on Belgian war establishments and had been trained for jungle warfare.

267. The role for the brigade agreed between the War Office and the Belgian authorities in London was that they should carry out garrison duties only. It soon became clear, however, that this decision had not been communicated to the brigade, and on its arrival in the Middle East a demand was made for an operational role. This request was backed by Lieut.-General Ermens, C.-in-C. Belgian Congo, in his interview with me in July, 1943. I stated that, provided the Brigade Group was reorganised on British war establishment, it might be possible to contemplate an operational role after six months' guard duties. With this Lieut.-General Ermens agreed. The continued and extensive guard duties on which the brigade was employed throughout 1943 resulted in little training being carried out; the guard duties were partly responsible, too, for the general apathy to which the majority of the European personnel succumbed, but the promise of a relief from guard duties and of employment in a more active role gave a fillip to morale. At the beginning of 1944 the brigade was showing more aptitude for training.

268. Throughout the period, the Egyptian Army has never failed to meet any request of the British Forces to take over duties within Egypt, to free British troops for operations in field formations. They have taken over the duties of mine watching in the Suez Canal and much of the anti-aircraft and searchlight defence

of Egypt, in addition to the coast defence of Alexandria and Port Sudan. Frontier control has been carried out satisfactorily by the Egyptian Frontiers Control Administration, working in close co-operation with Headquarters, British Troops in Egypt.

269. Political problems have occurred in higher command, and the relations of high officers with the Egyptian Government have not always been smooth, but junior officers have been largely unaffected and the rank and file have been good. British Commanders with whom Egyptian units have co-operated have frequently expressed their appreciation of the degree of efficiency displayed, particularly in their anti-aircraft and searchlight duties. This state of affairs is the more praiseworthy since the Egyptian Army has been gravely handicapped throughout by shortages in transport and equipment of all types.

270. In addition to training and equipping Allied troops within the Command, Middle East has also played an active but difficult part in organising and equipping the guerilla movements in the Balkans. These guerilla operations have become, since the beginning of 1943, a serious commitment for the Germans. Movements for national liberation have gathered impetus and strength, and in Yugoslavia especially the Germans have been forced to tie up divisions which would most certainly have been of great use elsewhere: Unfortunately, the Partisans in Yugoslavia, Greece and Albania have not been able to agree on common action in their respective countries against the Germans. In fact their quarrels, which have been very bitter, have helped the enemy considerably and have undoubtedly postponed the realisation of their national liberation.

271. In Yugoslavia the Partisan movement has made the most effective military contribution to the Allied cause. Regular military formations have been organised, and a Partisan General Headquarters under Marshal Tito has been established. By August, 1943, Partisan troops numbered 100,000, and the collapse of Italy gave them increased morale and easier access to arms and supplies, both from Italian sources and because, with the opening of the Adriatic, it became possible for us to supplement air supplies by shipments. As a result, by the end of the year, Partisan forces in Yugoslavia numbered some 250,000 men. During the year they survived three major attacks and contained a force of sixteen German and six Bulgarian divisions, together with large numbers of Croat and Serbian troops under German command.

272. With Partisan General Headquarters, Middle East Command has maintained constant and cordial relations since the first British liaison officers were dropped by parachute in May, 1943. By the end of the year twenty liaison missions were being maintained with the Partisans, and over 6,000 tons of stores had been shipped to them in addition to 339 tons dropped by air.

273. As against the growing effect of Marshal Tito's Partisans must be set the fact that, by playing upon fear off Communism, German propaganda has succeeded

in nullifying the value of the other liberation movement in Yugoslavia, that of the Chetnicks, under General Mihailovic. Large numbers of Chetnicks have actively gone over to the Axis and have taken part in operations against Tito's forces, and by the end of the year the Chetnick movement was of no value to the Allies and was receiving no supplies from Middle East.

274. In Albania, British officers have been instrumental in training national forces, which amounted to four brigades at the end of the year. Here also there were political difficulties between the parties of the "National Front" and the more left wing "National Liberation" movement which, in fact, has carried out most of the operations.

275. In Greece, a British Mission had arrived during January, 1943, but for some time found it impossible to control the quarrels and unco-ordinated activities of the guerillas, among whom the rival bands of the left-wing E.L.A.S. and the Republican E.D.E.S. (commanded by Colonel Zervas) were engaged in constant fights. At last, in July, a National Band Agreement was drawn up to divide the whole country into area commands and control all guerrilla activities under a General Headquarters.

276. Under this co-ordinated command, a widespread and successful attack on communications was carried out before and during the attack on Sicily. But when Italy was invaded, the Greeks, realising that the liberation of Greece would not immediately be attempted, relapsed into a civil war in which the E.L.A.S. bands set to work to destroy all other bands, so that they might ultimately claim to be the sole liberators of Greece. During the civil war no more supplies were sent to E.L.A.S., but Zervas, our most loyal ally, was kept supplied. By 19th December, 1943, both parties were exhausted and ready to come to terms and, after an appeal by M. Tsouderos, the Greek Prime Minister, negotiations for a renewal of the National Band Agreement were begun.

277. In Crete, also, a small British mission was established, but the strength of the garrison has made large guerilla activities impossible. None the less, the Germans have been seriously disturbed, our mission has been maintained and increased, and Cretan morale stands high.

278. In Crete, and still more in Greece, the personal popularity of the British liaison officers has been of great value to them in their difficult task of organising (and at times restraining) the guerillas in their attacks on the Germans whilst at the same time seeking a settlement of the disputes between the bands.

279. Whilst these operations were being pursued to achieve the liberation of the Balkan countries, plans were also being made for their administration after their liberation. In February, 1943, the Allied Territories (Balkans) Committee was established, under the chairmanship of the Lieutenant-General in charge of Administration and including representatives of all interested organisations in

Cairo, to consider the steps necessary on military grounds to ensure efficiency of the civil administration in the Balkan territories after their liberation.

Planning was at first confined to Greece, but was part of a wider policy of planning relief for the civil population in the Balkans which was started, on War Office instructions, on 15th April, 1943. Middle East's responsibility was laid down as Greece, Yugoslavia, Albania and the Dodecanese only, and no planning was to be undertaken for Roumania or Bulgaria.

280. By October, 1943, it became apparent that owing to the speed of the Russian advance in South-east Europe the commitment might arise earlier than had at first been expected, and that planning to meet it would have to be accelerated.

On 12th October, 1943, therefore, British Military Liaison Headquarters (Greece) was set up, under command of Major-General Hughes, to maintain liaison with the Greek authorities and to plan for the relief of the country on evacuation by the Germans. The basis of the plan was that the Greeks themselves would be responsible for civil administration and for the execution of relief measures to the maximum extent compatible with their resources.

281. It was also accepted that only essential relief could be undertaken by the army and that the rehabilitation of liberated territories would be a matter for such civil relief authority, as might be later appointed. The period of military responsibility was arbitrarily fixed at six months from the date of occupation, during which time it was intended that the civil relief authority should have observers in the various territories to enable as smooth a transfer of responsibility as possible to take place.

282. A special Balkan planning section, attached to the staff of the Chief Civil Affairs Officer, was set up to prepare detailed estimates of requirements for the first six months' period. These estimates, which included, *inter alia*, requirements of foodstuffs, medical supplies, clothing, petrol and oil, chemicals, soap and coal, were based on intelligence received from the territories concerned and from information given by the War Office. The procedure adopted was that all estimates were passed to the "Q" Staff at General Headquarters, Middle East, for examination and, when finally agreed, forwarded through staff or service channels to the War Office for approval and action.

This planning section was later transferred to the staff of Major-General Hughes, leaving the Chief Civil Affairs Officer responsible for planning for the Dodecanese only.

283. The intention was to stockpile in Middle East sufficient quantities of the commodities required to tide over the period needed to organise supply direct from the United Kingdom or United States to Balkan ports. This period was estimated by the War Office as six to eight weeks, and by January, 1944, considerable shipments of grain had been received, but little progress had been made in the stockpiling of the remaining requirements, other than those available locally.

284. Another activity which came into greater prominence as the Balkans increased in importance was political warfare. The Political Warfare Executive, Middle East, had been active during the Tunisian, Sicilian and Italian campaigns, using leaflets and radio to soften enemy morale; officers trained by the Executive went with our forces to the Aegean islands, and now in preparation for activity in the Balkans much valuable work was done. For this theatre, a pool of trained officers was set up and a school was established for training field units.

285. Whilst training, organising, equipping and planning for those Balkan countries which were already involved in the war has been a difficult task, it has been even more difficult to perform the same functions for Turkey, since that country has been willing to enter the war only on its own terms and when it considers itself properly equipped to do so.

286. In the tortuous and interminable negotiations with the Turks, and in providing and forwarding the supplies which have been the main object of discussion, Middle East Command has been closely concerned.

287. Our programme of assistance, resulting from the Adana Conference on 30th and 31st January, 1943, was two-fold. First, we had to supply Turkey as soon as possible with sufficient equipment to provide her armed forces with one year's reserve for war. Secondly, we had to despatch to Turkey, if she were forced into war, a self-contained force under British command to provide fighter defence of vulnerable points and to support the Turkish Army in the field; in addition, certain British anti-tank and anti-aircraft units were to be placed under Turkish command. Later the Turks were given the choice of further strong Royal Air Force reinforcements or a corps of two armoured divisions; it was not considered practicable to provide both until at least the Aegean was opened to our shipping and the port of Izmir could be used.

288. The limiting factor to our programme of assistance, both in preparation for war and after Turkey should enter the war, was the capacity of the Turkish railway system, and it was agreed that the staff talks should be resumed at the earliest possible date to study this problem and to consider the means by which the capacity could be improved.

289. Accordingly, talks were resumed in Ankara on 26th February, 1943, under the chairmanship, on the British side, of the Military Attaché, Major-General A.C. Arnold. Progress was handicapped by Turkish inability or unwillingness to appreciate the limitations of the railway system or to give any reliable estimate of their own civil and military demands in war. In the absence of reliable information from the Turkish General Staff it was estimated that, without the use of Izmir port, 2,500 to 3,000 tons a day would be the maximum import figure and that, after meeting Turkish requirements, both military and civil, not more than 500 to 1,000 tons could be relied on for British requirements; it was realised that import capacity would be considerably increased by the use of Izmir. These

figures were inevitably guesswork, but were accepted as the basis of subsequent planning.

290. It was therefore decided in March that, to avoid concentrating in Turkey a larger force than could be subsequently maintained, the despatch of British forces would be phased. In the first phase twenty-five Royal Air Force squadrons would be sent, with an army component and two anti-tank regiments; in the second phase we would send twenty Royal Air Force squadrons, in the third phase three antitank regiments and five anti-aircraft regiments, and in the fourth phase, after Izmir port was opened, two armoured divisions. This plan was known as HARDIHOOD.

291. No. 3 Planning Staff was sent to Turkey in March to continue discussions on the operational employment of this force and to implement the programme of administrative planning required in Turkey for its reception and subsequent operation and maintenance. This was followed in March by a visit to Ankara by Air Marshal Sholto Douglas and in April by a visit by myself, in order to discuss the implications of the HARDIHOOD plan with Marshal Cakmak and the Turkish General Staff.

292. The maintenance requirements of the forces contained in the first three phases amounted to some 1,200 tons a day, or 200 tons a day in excess of the maximum capacity estimated to be available. We hoped, however, that the action we had taken and were continuing to take to improve the railways would enable the force to be maintained.

293. This action was mainly the provision of additional locomotives and wagons. We planned to earmark 100 locomotives and the equivalent of 2,500 15-ton wagons; of these 50 locomotives and 1,800 15-ton wagons were included in the Adana list and would be supplied when available; the remainder were to be held as a reserve in the Middle East. Action was also taken to build up a reserve supply of locomotive coal in the Middle East for use in Turkey should we have to maintain a force there. Holdings of Middle East railways were increased by 40,000 tons so that, in the event of Turkey coming into the war, it would be possible to divert incoming supplies direct to Turkish ports.

294. Further administrative preparations included pre-dumping of stores at certain selected places in Turkey and an extensive programme of airfield and base and lines of communication construction. Certain stores had already been pre-dumped in Turkey; for HARDIHOOD the number of dumps was increased from five to eleven, and dumping continued with a target of twenty-eight days for the first three phases of HARDIHOOD.

295. In the spring of 1943 there were sufficient airfields in Turkey to accommodate twenty-five Royal Air Force squadrons during the dry weather only; it was therefore necessary to undertake an extensive programme of development to

accommodate forty-five squadrons, including sixteen heavy-bomber squadrons, under all-weather conditions. This work was divided between the Turks and the British Royal Engineer construction parties already in Turkey. The target date for completion of runways and hard-standings was 31st October, 1943; later, certain minimum technical and domestic accommodation would be necessary. In addition to these airfields the Turks undertook to provide fair-weather landing grounds at Milas and Mugla in South-West Anatolia.

296. In July, 1942, an advanced base had been reconnoitred in the Ulukisla – Cakmak area, but by the spring of 1943 very little construction had been done, although certain covered accommodation was available and all the necessary material was on the site. It was agreed to continue with the project, and representatives of No. 3 Planning Staff were instructed to prepare a key plan for the HARDIHOOD forces. Later, after reconnaissance of both areas, it was decided to locate the advanced base at Afyon Karahinsar, which was more suited to the increased forces of Plan HARDIHOOD than Ulukisla. Further planned development of the lines of communication included port depots at Mersin and Iskenderun, a Royal Air Force base maintenance unit at Cakmak and a road-rail transhipment point at Ulukisla. These proposals were submitted to the Turkish General Staff in early June. Turkish consent to the construction of the advanced base was not given until August, and then only on conditions which made it quite impossible to complete the project by the end of the year. Work had to be carried out by the Turks, under the supervision of only those British personnel already in Turkey, and it had to be disguised as commercial construction. Permission to start constructions of the port depots was not given until December.

297. Plans were also produced to extend the existing petrol installations at Iskenderun, to provide tankage at airfields, to build hospitals and to improve communications by the construction of a network of trunk telephone routes.

298. Our plans in all cases were delayed by the Turks, with the result that little progress had been made by the end of the year, and if it had been necessary to implement HARDIHOOD, the administration and maintenance of the forces would have presented an almost insuperable problem.

299. In September, as a result of decisions taken at the Quebec Conference, a new directive defining the operational and administrative commitment of my command was received, in which no provision was made for HARDIHOOD other than the construction parties already in Turkey. Our various construction programmes, however, were to continue and No. 3 Planning Staff was to remain in Turkey to maintain continuity in planning.

300. In October, 1943, as a result of instructions to the Middle East Defence Committee by the Chiefs of Staff, an invitation was extended to Turkey to enter the war. The Chiefs of Staff pointed out that should Turkey enter the war Bulgaria might collapse, and the collapse of Roumania and Hungary would

probably follow. Under these conditions Germany would probably be unable to hold out very long owing to the cutting off of her Balkan sources of supply.

301. In the event of Turkey entering the war, three problems were outstanding: first, her two largest ports, Istanbul and Izmir were largely built of wood and were very vulnerable to air attack; secondly, her coal supply, which in the main, came from Zonguldak on the Black Sea, was also very vulnerable; and thirdly, her railways were not sufficiently developed to stand the strain of a modern war.

302. Obviously the main difficulty confronting a successful Allied plan was to provide sufficient fighter and anti-aircraft defences in time to forestall German air attacks. Owing to the great length of the Turkish lines of communication, it was essential that a major portion of our forces should be infiltrated into Turkey before she actually entered the war.

303. Accordingly, towards the end of November, plans for the establishment of eighteen Royal Air Force squadrons and five heavy and five light anti-aircraft regiments in Western Anatolia were considered. This plan was known as Plan 437 and No. 3 Planning Staff assembled in Cairo towards the end of November, becoming members of Headquarters, Force 686, which was responsible for its detailed planning.

304. Work was stopped on the heavy bomber airfields for HARDIHOOD, but construction was begun to make Milas and Kizilyaka all-weather airfields, as well as those at Dalaman, Gokova and Antalya, with a view to operations in the Aegean.

305. It was envisaged that Force 686, which was to carry out Plan 437, would be maintained from an advanced base at Izmir; pre-dumping had continued throughout the changes, with an initial target of thirty days for the whole force now contemplated, of approximately 33,000 personnel (13,000 Royal Air Force and 20,000 Army) and 5,000 vehicles: of these stores some were in fact used for the maintenance of the forces engaged in the Aegean operations. In mid-December the target was raised to forty-five days. In all, during the year, some 52,000 tons of stores were despatched to meet this commitment.

306. To carry out Plan 437 it was considered that 7,500 men must be infiltrated into Turkey, and the Prime Minister discussed this problem with President Ineunu immediately after the Cairo Conference. In December, however, the Turks agreed to the infiltration of only 250 specialists in plain clothes, of whom the majority was infiltrated. The Turkish Government later agreed to further infiltration of up to 1,750 specialists, subject to approval by the Turkish General Staff. None of these was sent forward, but action was taken to concentrate elements of Force 686 in Northern Syria.

307. The situation was by no means easy, and on 28th December a mission left the Middle East for Ankara to discuss the main problem of supplies and

infiltration. Although the mission was received most cordially when it arrived, it soon became apparent that there was a wide, divergence between the Turkish point of view and our own. The main differences were that the Turks expected thirty-six Royal Air Force squadrons as against our offer of eighteen, and they demanded an enormous amount of equipment, which they said they must have before operations could begin. It was estimated that the minimum time required to get this equipment into Turkey, even if it were available, would be about four months. Shortly after I relinquished my command, negotiations reached a dead-lock, the mission returned to Cairo and Force 686 was dissolved.

308. Although Turkey is still not at war, much valuable military construction has been carried out and considerable quantities of military stores have been dumped there for our own use in addition to those supplied to the Turkish Army. Turkish opinion of the correct state of equipment necessary to enable her to enter the war has varied considerably during my year of command in Middle East, and our supplies have never equalled her demands; but at least that country is now better equipped than she was a year ago.

309. For although by no means all that the Turks have demanded has been available, and supplies have at times had to be diverted to Italy, yet under the Adana Agreement, during the year 97,000 tons have been delivered to Turkey by sea, 11,000 tons have been delivered by rail and 1,300 vehicles, 300 tanks and 2,300 guns have been despatched by Middle East Command.

310. In addition to these freights to implement the Adana Agreement, much has been supplied both for Turkish military and civilian use and for our own dumps. During the year the total tonnage transported by Middle East to Turkey was 375,000 tons, including 48,000 tons for our own dumps. For this tonnage Middle East was either the supply centre or transit centre, or both, whilst 40,500 tons were supplied by Persia and Iraq Command but were routed by Middle East.

311. These considerable quantities have certainly not met Turkish demands, a fact which contributed to the breakdown of negotiations and the failure of our plans. But Turkish insistence on the supply of equipment is difficult to understand, for the land threat to Thrace has steadily diminished, their transport facilities could probably not have handled the quantities of goods which they demanded, and even after delivery the equipment could not be in use for many months. Moreover, it is extremely doubtful if the Turks could have put their materials to effective use at all, for despite urgent representations from our Military Attaché and the provision of personnel and courses by Middle East Command., they have not trained even adequate cadres for mechanised warfare.

312. Only in anti-aircraft training have the facilities offered been used to advantage. This fact is significant, for there can be little doubt that the German air superiority during the Aegean operations was as weighty an argument for

Turkish delay as was the non-delivery of stores, although it could not be used with as good a countenance.

313. This air inferiority over the Aegean might, however, have been avoided, and the course of the operations altered had Turkey been willing to take action. For in November, 1943, with the object of providing fighter cover for our forces in the Aegean and a small force to assist in the protection of Istanbul, two plans, called SUPERCHARGE and LITTLE HARDIHOOD, which envisaged Turkey as a co-belligerent, were produced. Our forces were to be maintained from depots in the Izmir and Istanbul areas and would require no advanced base. Executive action was taken to concentrate the forces for both these plans in the Aleppo area, but the fall of Leros on 16th November removed the need for the immediate establishment of these fighter squadrons in Turkey and the plans were abandoned.

314. Even after the fall of Leros and the evacuation of Samos, I thought it possible to drive the Germans out from the Aegean if air support could be provided from the airfields which, under Plan 437, were to be operated by the Royal Air Force on the Turkish mainland. Accordingly, in December, the 3rd Corps Headquarters began the preparation of Plan HERCULES, for the capture of the key island of Rhodes. On 2nd January, 1944, however, the landing-craft for this operation were diverted to the Anzio landing in Italy, and HERCULES was cancelled; nevertheless, in the hope that Plan 437 would ensure Turkish co-operation, planning was continued and all the possibilities of such an operation were investigated.

Politics and Internal Security.

315. However the precise weight of argument for the failure to bring Turkey into the war may be distributed between our failure to supply her demands and her fear of the Luftwaffe, the ultimate conclusion must be that Turkey doubted our power to save her from at least the initial stages of a German attack. Elsewhere in the Middle East, such political problems as affected the military situation during my year of command arose from precisely the opposite cause – a feeling that fear of German attack was removed and that political quarrels might be indulged more freely.

316. In Egypt this has caused no military problems, though there has been considerable political uneasiness. For although the Wafd Government, under Nahas Pasha as Prime Minister, has continued to support the United Nations war effort loyally, in its internal administration it has not proved so satisfactory.

317. The failure of the Government to take effective measures against those responsible for profiteering and hoarding has reduced its support in the country. From the British point of view the most serious factor in the internal security situation is the danger of an increase in anti-British feeling. There is a tendency to blame us for the state of affairs because we are supporting the Government

responsible; and there is evidence that the profiteers and other anti-social elements are endeavouring to lay the blame for their own acts on British shoulders.

318. Another result of the scandals and accusations in which the Wafd Government has been involved has been to widen the breach between the Prime Minister and the King, who pronounced the Government guilty of peculation and corruption and clearly expected their resignation. The King did not, however, dismiss the Government which, whatever its demerits, was affording the Allies full and valuable support; but the political crisis thus produced in May might well have caused serious interruption in the preparations for the attack on Sicily.

319. The Egyptian people generally are disillusioned by all the political parties, but although the political situation is clearly one which must cause much unrest for Egypt, it has not led to any diversion of the effort of Middle East Command from the prosecution of the war, and Egyptian policy has become increasingly pro-Allied.

320. In Palestine, on the other hand, the period under review has been noticeable for a gradual hardening in the attitude of the Jewish community towards His Majesty's Government, an attitude encouraged by the Jewish Agency and its associated bodies.

321. In February, 1943, four British deserters were arrested and charged with selling stolen arms and ammunition to an illegal organisation in Palestine. The ensuing major Military Court cases, in August, had widespread repercussions on the political and internal security situation in Palestine; for the defending officer, in mitigation, suggested that the real responsibility lay with the Jewish Agency. The case was heard in open court, and the defending officer's speech was given wide publicity and brought a protest from the Jewish Agency, which went so far as to say that the trials were a deliberate anti-Semitic frame-up and compared them with the Dreyfus case.

322. Hardly had this excitement died down when a search in the Jewish settlement of Hulda, for Polish deserters, uncovered a cache of weapons, and on 16th November another search with the same purpose in the village of Ramat Hakovesh resulted in a fracas. This was followed by a campaign of misrepresentation and threats on the part of the Jewish Agency, which left no doubt that any future searches would be met with strong resistance. The policy in regard to searches, reaffirmed in 1943, has been that only if reliable information is received should searches be made, and then with particular care to avoid any incidents. After this search, His Excellency the High Commissioner informed the General Officer Commanding in Palestine that for political reasons it was regarded as most important that action likely to lead to major incidents with the Jewish population should be avoided at the present time.

323. By January, 1944, the attitude of the Jewish Agency towards the Government had hardened to such an extent that any action conflicting with the policy of

the Biltmore Programme or for enforcing the White Paper met with opposition and obstruction. The Jewish Agency was in some respects arrogating to itself the powers and status of an independent Jewish Government. It no longer attempted to deny the existence of arms caches, but claimed the right not only to hold arms for self-defence but to resist any attempt on the part of lawful authority to locate them. It was, in fact, defying the Government, and to that extent rebellion could be said to exist.

324. There has also been some unrest among certain units of the Palestine Regiment. In August, 1943, a decision to send the 2nd Battalion of the Palestine Regiment out of Palestine for duty produced considerable unrest among the Jews, who argued that the decision arose from political rather than military reasons, and there is no doubt that this had a further adverse effect on the recruiting figures, which, throughout the period, have remained very low.

325. During November, 1943, the authorised badge for the Palestine Regiment became available for issue, and twenty soldiers of the 1st (Jewish) Battalion, the Palestine Regiment, and forty-nine from the 3rd Battalion refused to accept or to wear the badge. All these men were tried by Court Martial for disobeying a lawful command. In every case the defence took the line that it was against the men's religious principles and their conscience to wear the badge. They were all found guilty and given sentences varying from forty-five to sixty days' field punishment. It was obvious that this wholesale refusal was prompted by political considerations and on investigation it was ascertained that all the accused were members of the Revisionist Party. In an interview with the General Officer Commanding in Palestine, the head of the political branch of the Jewish Agency expressed the view that the incident was a stupid demonstration by a minor group and that their attitude was not supported by the Jewish Agency.

326. Some repercussions in the form of pamphlets and articles in the Hebrew Press were felt, but the official attitude that the men were soldiers who had refused to obey a proper order was unquestionable, and the incident soon lost any public significance.

327. The Arabs in Palestine have given no cause for anxiety from the security aspect. They have continued to acquire arms and have been carefully watching Zionist activities, but, unlike the Jews, they have remained unable to compose their differences sufficiently to allow of organisation in support of their aims.

328. Uneasy though the Palestinian situation remains, it did not assume such proportions as to warrant interference with military training or to cause major military decisions to be taken. The troubles were throughout caused by a minority. In Syria and the Lebanon, on the other hand, I was faced with a majority movement which at one time seemed likely to cause serious trouble.

329. Nineteen hundred and forty-three was the year of long-awaited constitutional changes in the Levant States. The proclamation of Syrian and Lebanese

independence in 1942 had left the population expectant, and delay in the holding of elections gave rise to some impatience in the early months of 1943. But a decline in the pro-Axis sympathies of certain political circles, encouraged by the rising tide of Allied success, boded well for our co-operation with whatever government might come into power.

330. In Syria the growth of the National Bloc Party outstripped that of the other political parties, but in the Lebanon the situation was less clear. Some slight political unrest, coupled with a food shortage, led to riots and strikes in Damascus in February and March, and minor disturbances over food were common in other parts of the country during the first six months of the year until a plentiful harvest restored confidence.

331. Appreciating the effect on military requirements of the transfer of powers to these States, whose administrations were ill-equipped to undertake the onus of government amidst the difficulties of wartime economy, the General Officer Commanding Ninth Army suggested an examination of the problems which might arise. Being anxious not to impede in any way the realisation of independence by the States, he approached His Majesty's Minister in Beirut in August with a view to reconciling the minimum requirements of the British authorities with the legitimate aspirations of the States. His Majesty's Minister did not agree with the suggestion; nevertheless, an examination of the military point of view was carried out and was completed in October, 1943.

332. The elections which had been held a few months previously in Syria and the Lebanon had passed off without any serious disorder, but the intensely nationalistic character of both of the governments caused some concern to the French authorities. Nothing of a serious nature occurred, however, until November. On 8th November, despite a request from the French Délégué Générale, the Lebanese Government exercised what it believed to be its rights under the constitution to eliminate all references to the Mandatory Power. The Délégué Générale reacted by arresting, on the morning of 11th November, the President of the Lebanese Republic, the Prime Minister, three other Cabinet Ministers and a leading Sunni Mohammedan Deputy.

333. Large crowds collected in Beirut, demonstrating violently against the French, and similar disturbances were reported from other parts of the country. The General Officer Commanding Ninth Army authorised the provision of British guards on internment camps and the replacement of French patrols, where necessary, by British military police, and he remained throughout the crisis in close touch with the French military commander.

334. The sympathy and moral support of the neighbouring Arab countries greatly encouraged the Lebanese people, who adopted a surprisingly united, calm, but firm, attitude while waiting to see what line His Majesty's Government would take. On 14th November it was reported that the Druze Emir Majed

Arslan, Minister of Defence in the Lebanese Government, had collected a small force of armed men in the hills to the south of Beirut; and tribes in South Lebanon were also reported to be gathered in armed bands.

335. In view of the gradual deterioration in the situation it became necessary to make preparations to take action to protect our communications in the Lebanon in the event of French failure to relieve the situation. Accordingly, I instructed Ninth Army to draw up the necessary plans for such an emergency, and a detachment of officers recently trained in civil administrative duties was despatched to the Lebanon. All arrangements were made for feeding the civil population, primarily of Beirut and subsequently of other centres and country districts. All necessary arrangements for the establishment of military control were completed, and arrangements were also made to extend it to Syria if necessary.

336. These plans, however, proved unnecessary, for on 22nd November General Catroux, who had been sent from Algiers with full powers to settle the matter, reinstated the President and released the other detainees. During the eleven days which the crisis lasted, feelings had run very high, and it was only the confidence that His Majesty's Government would see justice done that prevented a serious explosion. Once the detainees had been released and the Lebanese Government re-installed the situation rapidly returned to normal.

337. As a result of this political crisis, the General Officer Commanding Ninth Army anticipated a difficult period in regard to security, as there were indications that the Lebanese were no longer disposed to accept the limitations on their independence imposed by the necessities of the war. It was clear that both the Syrian and the Lebanese Governments would now demand a very considerable transfer of powers from the French, and that these demands would include a considerable share of the control of security arrangements and of the *Troupes Speciales* or native levies. After a preliminary examination of the problems involved, Ninth Army began discussions with His Majesty's Minister and the French military authorities, as a result of which it was hoped that full agreement would be reached as to the extent to which powers could be transferred to the local Governments, without damage to the interests of His Majesty's Government in the successful prosecution of the war.

Garrisons and L. of C.
338. The situation in the Lebanon was held in check until the arrival of General Catroux largely because the Lebanese had confidence in the British Government and in the local British military administration. These feelings have been general throughout the Middle East during my period of command and have been a condition without which the vast training and administrative commitments of the Command could not have been carried out.

339. Without such feelings, also, the burden of the garrison and line of communication troops would have been heavy. As things were, the garrison and line

of communication areas in my Command were able to provide troops to take part in active operations or to release others to meet the heavy demands which were made; Ninth Army and Palestine have been the only two areas in which problems of internal security have required serious consideration.

340. In Syria and the Lebanon the continued Russian successes created a new problem by removing the threat of German invasion; the demands of the Syrians and Lebanese for independence became more insistent and the task of maintaining an adequate standard of security more difficult. It therefore became of primary military importance to keep those populations quiet by maintaining a belief of operational urgency in spite of the continued progress of the Russian armies in the North.

341. The role of Ninth Army, in addition to the above, has been to prevent sabotage and spying by enemy agents, to assist in the operational training of formations located in the Ninth Army area, to supervise schools and training centres and to maintain law and order in Syria and the Lebanon.

342. Relations between the British and French military authorities in Syria have remained good. Feelings ran high for a few days during the November political riots, but on the resolution of the crisis the situation rapidly returned to normal.

343. In Palestine, apart from political agitation by the Jews, nothing of military importance happened throughout the year. The movement of troops from Persia and Iraq Command to Egypt and preparations for the mounting of the attack on Sicily entailed a good deal of work, but the organisation was able to cope with all that was demanded of it.

344. Although the political situation in Egypt has required constant watchfulness, and the rise in prices has led to increased pilfering and made additional train and other guards necessary, no serious problems have occurred. The decision of Admiral Godefroy to bring the French fleet at Alexandria over to the Allies, on 21st May, 1943, relieved a state of considerable tension and enabled me to release troops, detailed for action in case Admiral Godefroy should reach a different decision, to other duties.

345. In Cyrenaica and Tripolitania the administrative arrangements have worked smoothly; there has been no outbreak of serious trouble between Arabs and Italian settlers, the British Military Administration has won the confidence of the civilians, and it has been possible to use the facilities of these areas to the full and to reduce garrison troops to a minimum.

346. The defeat of the Axis in North Africa and Sicily removed the threat from Malta, and the island was used as an advanced headquarters and staging post for the attack on Sicily. The 1st Malta Brigade (later 231st) from the garrison was taken for this operation, and the 2nd Malta Brigade (later 234th) for the operation in the Aegean. Reconstruction and administration in the island have

proceeded without major incident since the completion of the programme for the invasion of Sicily.

347. The opening of the Mediterranean decreased the importance of the line of communication through West Africa from the Belgian Congo. In consequence, the movement of military stores on the Nile route declined to negligible proportions, and in Sudan and Eritrea dumps and installations left over from the Eritrean operations, as well as from Africa lines of communication and as reserves for Egypt (accumulated during the period before Alamein), have been disposed of. This has released many troops for other operations.

348. Throughout the period, the Sudan Defence Force troops have been employed in Cyrenaica and Tripolitania on line of communication and garrison duties. The 12th Division, which consisted of the 4th Motor Battalion, 7th and 8th Infantry Battalions and ancillary units, was established in the Tripoli area by mid-February, 1943. The 9th Motor Battalion moved to Benghazi in May and the 12th Infantry Battalion to Tobruk in August, 1943, and until the end of the year there were always considerable numbers of Sudan Defence Force troops in Libya. A regular system of reliefs was carried out.

349. No problems likely to provide a threat to internal security have arisen in Sudan or Eritrea, and the Sudan has continued to provide large quantities of supplies for Middle East. The principal items have been cattle and sheep (145,000 head in the year), cotton seed (60,000 tons) and beans (6,000 tons).

New Directive.
350. This very satisfactory internal security situation enabled the resources of Middle East Command to be used to the full for the base and training role, subordinate to the demands of the general operations in the Mediterranean theatre, to which the Command had been allotted under me. This role produced excellent results in Tunisia, Sicily and Italy, but it also resulted in the operations in the Aegean being denied the support necessary for success. Despite this setback, the security achieved in Middle East, and the need to place all available resources at the disposal of a unified Mediterranean Command for operations in Italy, and of 21 Army Group for a major planned attack on Western Europe, were such weighty considerations that towards the end of my period in command the role of Middle East was under consideration with a view to diverting from the Command the maximum possible support for these operations.

351. Early in September the Deputy Chief of the Imperial General Staff and the Quartermaster-General visited Cairo and held a number of conferences of which the object was to reduce the resources available in Middle East to the minimum compatible with security, and to make available the maximum contribution for the Mediterranean Command and 21 Army Group; a heavy contribution from Middle East was needed for these purposes.

352. My commitment, as laid down after these conferences in an Aide Memoire of 11th September, was, therefore, to maintain internal security, and to prepare for an unopposed occupation of Crete and Rhodes when the German garrisons should be withdrawn. For this, I was to have under my command at least two armoured divisions, one infantry division, and the equivalent of three further divisions of unbrigaded troops. I was to hold reserves and reinforcements for these six divisions and, in addition, for troops awaiting transfer to Italy, and I was to maintain permanent transit arrangements for New Zealand, Australian, Indian and African troops anywhere in the Mediterranean theatre. The maintenance of British troops in Italy was to be progressively undertaken by bases in Italy as they were developed during the ensuing six to nine months, and Middle East was to maintain its own "garrison", including services for the Royal Navy and the Royal Air Force, to provide Eastern Group Supplies for the Mediterranean theatre, to maintain any forces extra to the six divisions of "garrison" troops which might be in the Middle East, and to continue production for local consumption and to meet the requirements of the other Mediterranean theatres. No provision was made for sending troops to Turkey or to the Aegean.

353. With this new brief, I was to review the organisation of command in the Middle East, to achieve economy in staff and personnel, and was to prepare to transfer to Italy, or elsewhere, the base and line of communication units which would become redundant with the transfer of formations to Italy or with the achievement of more economic organisation.

354. The only serious novelty in this Aide Memoire was the plan to cut Middle East Base and administrative services so that Italy could build up an organisation capable of administering the forces there. This plan caused remonstrance from Admiral Lord Louis Mountbatten, Supreme Commander South-east Asia, when he attended a meeting of the Middle East Defence Committee on 4th October. The argument was advanced that the Middle East Base was a vast and complex organisation which could not be cut without loss of efficiency, and that the retention of the Middle East Base, in its existing form, was an integral necessity for the development of our strategy in South-east Asia.

355. The guidance of the Chiefs of Staff was sought on this clash of principles, and meantime Middle East continued to meet *ad hoc* demands for units in Italy, and lists and plans were prepared for reducing the establishment to the minimum scale to deal with the permanent commitment of maintaining internal security on the basis of six divisions. Pending a further directive from the Chiefs of Staff, a temporary embargo on the release of administrative units was imposed.

356. On 25th October, the Chiefs of Staff directed that my forces should not be reduced below the minimum required for the maintenance of internal security and for the fulfilment of the condition, which was now accepted, that Middle East Base would ultimately be required to support operations in South-east Asia. This decision was clarified on 17th November, when the Chiefs of Staff decided

that the primary function of Middle East Base was to support operations in the Mediterranean; units and personnel not required for that commitment must be released. We should eventually be required as a subsidiary base for South-east Asia Command, but this should not be allowed to influence the drafting away of units and personnel for Italy and 21 Army Group, since we should only be involved gradually in the commitment for Asia, and additional troops would be returned as the commitment became heavier. Nevertheless, no base installation or organisation was to be completely closed, but they were to be kept on a care and maintenance basis, and the army base was not to be reduced so as to prejudice present or future requirements of the Royal Navy, Royal Air Force, or Merchant Navy. On the basis of this directive, Middle East continued until the end of my period in command.

357. The operational counterpart of this subordination of Middle East to the Mediterranean Command and Italy came when, on 26th November, 1943, the Chiefs of Staff decided that there should, in future, be a unified command in the Mediterranean. To carry out this policy, the Commander-in-Chief, Allied Forces, North Africa, took over responsibility for operations in the Balkans, the Aegean and Turkey, but I remained directly responsible to the Chiefs of Staff for internal security within Middle East Command.

358. In fact, these directives had no effect on events in Middle East during the remainder of my tenure of command, for the programme for drafting troops to Italy and the United Kingdom had already been drawn up and was being acted on, and although no major operations took place in the Middle East during the latter months of the period of my command, administrative commitments continued on a large scale, and in some respects were greater than during the North African campaign. The administrative effort involved in the continued maintenance of our forces established in Sicily and Italy remained unaffected, and that the importance of the Middle East Base was enhanced and not diminished by the opening of the Mediterranean is shown by the fact that our military imports for August and September, 1943, reached the record figures of 305,000 and 297,000 tons respectively, whilst military exports throughout the year averaged over 200,000 tons per month.

359. The increased activity of the Middle East Base at this time is illustrated by the following statistics. During the period, February, 1943, to January, 1944, Royal Engineer workshops produced *inter alia* 2,660,000 forty gallon petrol drums and, including Jerricans, 5,400,000 four-gallon returnable petrol containers. The output of the Royal Electrical and Mechanical Engineers' base workshops was greater in December than in February, 1943, and included over 300 tanks, 600 armoured cars, scout cars or carriers, 3,500 "B" vehicles and 6,000 "B" vehicle engines. Similarly, the activity in ordnance installations during the quarter ending 31st December, 1943, was greater than during the quarter ending 31st March, 1943. Nearly 150,000 tons of ammunition were received

compared with 135,000 tons; 113,000 tons of ammunition were issued compared with 102,000 tons; while 173,000 tons of stores were received compared with 148,000 tons.

360. In the same way as the changed role of the Command has not affected the volume of administrative effort, it has left the number of men under command largely unaffected. Like the administrative commitment, they showed a slight increase, rather than a fall in numbers. When I took over command I had 520,000 officers and men under command; when I handed over, there were 635,000 troops in the Command, and of these the large proportion, of 113,000 were allies under training.

361. The change of role could not have taken place, and Middle East Command could not have maintained Eighth Army and mounted the forces for Sicily and Italy, without close co-operation with the Royal Navy and the Royal Air Force, an excellent administrative system, and confidence in internal security. For the last requisite, the uniformly good conduct of officers and men has been an invaluable contributory cause.

362. I wish to bring to notice the services of the undermentioned officers during my period of command: Lieut.-General Sir W. Lindsell, Lieut.-General in Charge of Administration, Middle East Forces. It was due to his outstanding capacity for administration and organisation that the Eighth Army in North Africa was maintained and the expeditions against Italy launched. In addition, as Chairman of the Middle East Supply Board and Civil Affairs Committee, he was responsible for the build-up and efficiency of these and other paramilitary organisations concerned with post-hostility problems. In his work he was assisted in a most hearty and able manner by:-

Major-General G. Surtees – D.Q.M.G., G.H.Q., M.E.F.
Major-General R.K. Hewer – D.Q.M.G. (Mov. & Tn.), G.H.Q., M.E.F.
Major-General C.M. Smith – D.Q.M.G. (A.E.), G.H.Q., M.E.F.
Major-General C. le B. Goldney – D.S.T., G.H.Q., M.E.F.
Major-General C.H. Geake – D.O.S., G.H.Q., M.E.F.
Major-General W.S. Tope – D.M.E., G.H.Q., M.E.F.
Major-General Sir P.S. Tomlinson, Director of Medical Services, by his foresight and initial planning produced successful results in the hospitalisation and evacuation of casualties in the Central Mediterranean campaign.

Lieut.-General R.W.G.H. Stone, Commanding British Troops in Egypt, was responsible for the local administration and movement of the various formations and units during the concentration period, which proved of invaluable assistance to the staffs concerned. He has paid particular attention to the welfare of the troops in the Command and is responsible for raising it to a high standard of efficiency and popularity. He was responsible, throughout the period, for the maintenance of good relations with the Egyptian Government, a difficult and exacting task which he executed with tact.

Lieut.-General W.G. Holmes, Commanding Ninth Army, established firm and good relations with the French authorities in Syria and the Lebanon, in spite of great difficulties and provocation. He maintained throughout an attitude which enhanced the prestige of the army and avoided friction. He was responsible for the training of British and Allied formations; he produced good results and also dealt with certain political troubles that arose with the Greek Force with acumen and tact.

Major-General D.F. McConnell, Commanding Palestine Area, carried out a difficult task with commendable firmness and tact. He is responsible for the excellent relations existing with the Civil Government for dealing with disturbances.

A list of recommendations and awards has been forwarded under separate cover.

APPENDIX 1.
ORDER OF BATTLE, MIDDLE EAST, 14TH FEBRUARY, 1943.
* Denotes under command G.H.Q.

1. British Troops in Egypt (Lt.-Gen. R.G.W.H. Stone):-
    *4 Airborne Division.
        10 Bn. Parachute Regt., Army Air Corps.
        156 Bn. Parachute Regt., Army Air Corps.
    *6 N.Z. Division.
        32 N.Z Field Regt.
        9 N.Z. Infantry Brigade.
            31 N.Z. Bn.
            32 N.Z. Bn.
            33 N.Z. Bn.
    *24 Armoured Brigade.
        45 Royal Tank Regt.
    *74 Armoured Brigade.
        101 Royal Tank Regt.
    *4 N.Z. Armoured Brigade.
        18 N.Z. Armoured Regt.
        19 N.Z. Armoured Regt.
        20 N.Z. Armoured Regt.
        22 N.Z. Motorised Bn.
    *17 Infantry Brigade.
        156 Field Regt.
        2 Royal Scots Fusiliers.
        2 Northamptons.
        6 Seaforth.
    Unbrigaded-
        *Yorks. Hussars.
        *3 County of London Yeomanry.
        *46 Royal Tank Regiment.
        *118 Royal Tank Regt.

> *124 Royal Tank Regt.
> *"K" Regt.
> 44 Recce. Regt.
> *2 Fighting French Armoured Car Squadron.
> *1 Greek Armoured Car Squadron.
> *4 Field Regt.
> *24 Field Regt.
> *98 Field Regt.
> *165 Field Regt.
> *2 Field Regt., Fighting French.
> *95 Anti-tank Regt.
> *105 Anti-tank Regt.
> 2 Highland Light Infantry.
> *14 Highland Light Infantry.
> *2 Royal Sussex.
> *4 Royal Sussex.
> 1 Argyll and Sutherland Highlanders.
> 1/2 Punjab.
> 1/9 Gurkha Rifles.
> 3 Baluch.
> 1 Rajputana Rifles.
> 3 Frontier Force Regt.
> Jaipur Guards.
> Jodhpur.
> 1 Rampur.
> *1 Battaillon de Marche, Fighting French Forces.
> *4 Battaillon de Marche, Fighting French Forces.
> 4 Greek Guard Bn.
> 2 Bn. Libyan Arab Force.
> Two Companies, 2/7 Gurkha Rifles.

2. Ninth Army (Lt.-Gen. W.G. Holmes):-
> Headquarters, 13 Corps (Lt.-Gen. M.C. Dempsey).
> 10 British Armoured Division,
>> 1 Royal Horse Artillery.
>> 104 Royal Horse Artillery.
>> 84 Anti-tank Regiment.
>> 9 Armoured Brigade.
>>> 3 Hussars.
>>> Royal Wiltshire Yeomanry.
>>> Warwickshire Yeomanry,
>>> 11 King's Royal Rifle Corps.
> Headquarters, 5 British Infantry Division.
>> 7 Cheshire (M.G.).

8 Division.
  Transjordan Frontier Force Mechanised Regt.
  3 Fighting French Infantry Brigade (forming).
  Recce. Group, Fighting French Forces.
  6 Battaillon de Marche.
  7 Battaillon de Marche.
1 Greek Independent Brigade,
  1 Greek Field Regt.
  1 Greek Bn.
  2 Greek Bn.
  3 Greek Bn.
2 Greek Independent Brigade.
  2 Greek Field Regt.
  5 Greek Bn.
  6 Greek Bn.
  7 Greek Bn.
Unbrigaded-
  Household Cavalry Regt.
  102 Royal Tank Regt.
  1 Jaipur.
  2/7 Gurkha Rifles.
  Transjordon Frontier Force Cavalry Regt.
  Druze Regt.
25 Corps (Lt.-Gen. I.T.P. Hughes), Cyprus, under command Ninth Army.
  10 Indian Infantry Division.
  97 Field Regt.
  10 Indian Infantry Brigade.
      4 Baluch,
      3 Royal Garhwal Rifles.
      2/4 Gurkha Rifles.
  20 Indian Infantry Brigade.
      4 Hussars.
      39 Royal Tank Regt.
      2/3 Gurkha Rifles.
  25 Indian Infantry Brigade.
      I King's Own.
      3 Mahrattas.
      2 Sikh.
  Unbrigaded-
      8 Hussars.
      4 Frontier Force Rifles.
      Nabha.
      Bhopal.

3. Palestine (Maj.-Gen. D.F. McConnell):-
    *1 Army Tank Brigade.
        8 Royal Tank Regt.
        11 Royal Tank Regt.
        42 Royal Tank Regt.
        44 Royal Tank Regt.
        One company Argyll and Sutherland Highlanders.
    Arab Legion.
        2 Mechanised Regt.
        3 Mechanised Regt.
        One Infantry company.
    Unbrigaded-
        4 Sikh.
        4 Gwalior Infantry.
        1 Bn. Royal Yugoslav Guards.
        One company I/2 Punjabs.
4. Cyrenaica District (Maj.-Gen. A.L. Collier):-
    *1 Fighting French Infantry Division.
        1 Field Regt., Fighting French.
        21 North Africa Anti-tank Company, Fighting French.
        22 North Africa Anti-tank Company, Fighting French.
        1 Fighting French Infantry Brigade.
        1 Bn. Foreign Legion.
        2 Bn. Foreign Legion.
        2 Fighting French Infantry Brigade.
        4 Battaillon de Marche.
        5 Battaillon de Marche.
        11 Battaillon de Marche.
    Unbrigaded-
        1 Bn. Libyan Arab Force.
        4 Bn. Libyan Arab Force.
5. Malta (Field Marshal The Viscount Gort, Governor and C.-in-C.;
Maj.-Gen. R. MacK. Scobie, G.O.C.):-
    1 Infantry Brigade.
        2 Devons.
        1 Hampshire.
        1 Dorsets.
        2 King's Own Malta Regt.
        3 King's Own Malta Regt.
    2 Infantry Brigade.
        8 King's Own.
        8 Manchesters.
        2 Royal Irish Fusiliers.
        1 King's Own Malta Regt.

3 Infantry Brigade.
>   11 Lancashire Fusiliers.
>   2 Royal West Kents.
>   10 King's Own Malta Regt.

4 Infantry Brigade.
>   4 Buffs.
>   1 Durham Light Infantry.
>   1 Cheshire (M.G.).

Unbrigaded-
>   "X" Squadron, Royal Tanks.
>   One independent troop, Royal Tanks.
>   12 Field regt.

6. Sudan (Maj.-Gen. B.O. Hutchison):-

Sudan Defence Force.
>   1 Motorised Bn.
>   9 Motorised Bn.
>   5 Equatorial Bn.
>   3 Infantry Bn.
>   12 Infantry Bn.
>   13 infantry Bn.
>   14 infantry Bn.

Unbrigaded-
>   Sudan Artillery Regt.
>   I Welch.
>   Alwar.
>   One company, 3 Frontier Force Regt.

7. Aden (R.A.F. Command):-
>   3/I Punjab.
>   3 Rajput.
>   Mewar.

Notes

1. It had been agreed at the Washington Anglo-American Conference in May, 1943, that in order to keep up the maximum pressure on the Japanese, a combined operation against the Arakan should be staged later in the year. This operation had been given priority for resources after the main operations against Italy. In view of the possible developments, part of the shipping destined for the Arakan operation was held for a time in the Mediterranean. In order to implement agreed strategy in the Far East, however, it was necessary to release those ships before the end of August. It was considered at the time that the Arakan operations would have been of greater benefit to the War as a whole than the capture of Rhodes. In the event, however, the Arakan operations were later cancelled.

2. Later information showed that the following losses, were, in fact, inflicted on the enemy:-

1. Merchant vessels sunk or destroyed in harbour (Approx. 18,000 tons)	9
2. F/Lighters and landing	14
3. Torpedo-boats, escort vessels and similar craft including small minelayer	13
4. Floating Dock	1
5. Armed caiques	5
6. Number of Germans put into sea	4,000

5

ADMIRAL SIR ANDREW CUNNINGHAM'S DESPATCH ON CONTROL OF THE SICILIAN STRAITS DURING THE FINAL STAGES OF THE NORTH AFRICA CAMPAIGN.

The following Despatch was submitted to the Lords Commissioners of the Admiralty on the 13th November, 1943, by Admiral of the Fleet Sir Andrew B. Cunningham, G.C.B., D.S.O., Commander-in-Chief, Mediterranean Station.

Mediterranean Station,
13th November, 1943.

OPERATION "RETRIBUTION."

Be pleased to lay before Their Lordships the enclosed reports[1] of proceedings of certain light forces which were engaged in the control of the Sicilian Straits during the final stages of the North African campaign.

2. The reports cover the period from the sinking of an enemy merchant ship and torpedo boat off Kelibia on 3rd May, 1943, by H.M. Ships NUBIAN, PALADIN and PETARD, which event marked the last serious effort by the enemy to supply his forces in Tunisia by sea, to the time[2] when all attempts by the enemy to evacuate Tunisia had ceased and when surface patrols had been reduced to that level necessary for the blockade of Pantellaria.

3. The possibility that the enemy might attempt a large-scale evacuation of Tunisia had been foreseen some months previously, and orders had been issued, under the code name "Retribution", for the concentration of naval forces to meet such a contingency. In the event, no such attempt was made, and the full written orders were never put into force. The orders, however, served a useful purpose in that all concerned were fully aware of the Commander-in-Chief's intentions, and the task of intercepting those of the enemy who were bold enough to take to the sea was made much easier in consequence. The codeword "Retribution", though never officially brought into force, was adopted for use by the naval forces taking part.

4. As the Armies began to close in on Bizerta and Tunis, night destroyer and motor torpedo boat patrols in the Sicilian Narrows were intensified, Mediterranean destroyers operating from Bone, and Levant destroyers from Malta. In daylight, the task of destroying any enemy shipping that escaped our submarine patrols and offensive minefields was at this time undertaken by the air forces,

since lack of fighter protection prevented our surface forces from operating against enemy supply routes by day.

5. With the rapid advance of the Armies in the first week in May, however, our fighters were able to operate from more forward aerodromes and so cover the south-western half of the Straits. By arrangement with the Air Commander-in-Chief, therefore, daylight patrols by destroyers were instituted on 9th May. It was arranged that the air forces should continue to attack enemy shipping and small craft within five miles of the Tunisian shore (*i.e.*, within range of enemy shore-based guns), and that surface forces should have complete freedom of action elsewhere. By night the inshore area was occupied by patrols of motor gunboats and motor torpedo boats of both the United States Navy and the Royal Navy.

6. This somewhat rigid dividing line between the responsibilities of the air and naval forces was necessitated by the fact that a large proportion of the pilots and air crews taking part had not hitherto been engaged in operations over the sea and were thus untrained in ship recognition.

7. The degree of air support given to our light forces from 9th May onwards may best be judged by the almost complete freedom from enemy interference enjoyed by them. Only one incident marred the co-operation between air and naval forces – the bombing of H.M. Ships BICESTER and ZETLAND on 9th May by our own fighter-bombers. This incident was immediately and fully investigated and was due to the fact that information as to the movements of the destroyers failed to reach some of the forward aerodromes before the aircraft took off early that day.

8. The whole sea area in which the destroyers were required to operate had been heavily mined, both by the enemy and ourselves. Most of our mines, however, had been set to flood by the beginning of May, and it was judged that our intelligence of enemy minefields was good enough to allow a sharp distinction to be drawn between areas where the risk of mines was great and those where the risk could be accepted. In the event, this judgment proved correct, and no casualties from mines were suffered by the destroyers.

9. The minefields had, however, a considerable effect on the operations, particularly the large field which extended north-eastward from Cape Blanc. The destroyers operating from Bone were forced to go a long way round the northern edge of this minefield when proceeding to and from patrol, and in doing so exposed themselves to air attack. This resulted in one casualty, when O.R.P. BLYSKAWICA was near missed and slightly damaged and was unable to take any further part in the operations.

10. Minesweepers had been concentrated at Bone as soon as the fall of Bizerta seemed imminent, and by 11th May they had swept a channel through to Bizerta. This early success on their part was a forerunner to the excellent work they performed in the succeeding weeks, and it contributed materially to the successful

work of the destroyer patrols by saving the destroyers a great deal of unnecessary steaming.

11. From 9th May onwards, ten to twelve destroyers were constantly on patrol off the Cape Bon peninsula, with a similar number of coastal craft in the inshore area by night, until all attempts by the enemy to evacuate had ceased. The patrols resulted in the capture of some 700 prisoners and in the complete denial to the enemy of any chance of evacuating by sea any important part of his forces.

12. To maintain the patrols at the strengths required meant a special effort on the part of the destroyers, coastal craft and maintenance staffs alike. That this effort would be forthcoming was only to be expected; all concerned met the demands that were made on them with the same cheerful spirit with which they faced the not inconsiderable risks that had to be run.

(Signed) A.B. CUNNINGHAM,
Admiral of the Fleet,
Commander-in-Chief.

Notes
1. These reports are not being published.
2. Approximately 15th May, 1943.

Index

(1) Index of Persons

(2) Index of Battles and Operations

(3) Index of Naval, Military and Air Force Units